D1248798

WHAT SHALL I READ NEXT?

F. SEYMOUR SMITH

———◆———

What shall I read next?

A PERSONAL SELECTION OF
TWENTIETH CENTURY
ENGLISH BOOKS

PUBLISHED FOR THE
NATIONAL BOOK LEAGUE
BY THE CAMBRIDGE UNIVERSITY PRESS
1953

PUBLISHED BY
THE SYNDICS OF THE CAMBRIDGE UNIVERSITY PRESS

London Office: Bentley House, N.W. 1
American Branch: New York

Agents for Canada, India, and Pakistan: Macmillan

Printed in Great Britain at the University Press, Cambridge
(Brooke Crutchley, University Printer)

INTRODUCTION

'As writers become more numerous it is natural for readers to become more indolent.' So said Goldsmith, with the tolerance and charm which has kept his name and work sweet. True in the middle of the eighteenth century, it must to-day have even greater application, for to the natural indolence of many readers we must add the bewilderment and confusion of us all as we contemplate a library of the great books of the past and the thousands of important books of the present century.

What then can any reader do, but select severely according to his known taste, his chance acquaintance with the books which are important for his own enjoyment and mental development, and to his memory of books read about or discussed. That is the excuse, if any be needed, for a complementary list to the present writer's *An English Library*, Cambridge University Press for the National Book League, 4th edition, 1950, 7s. 6d. There the selection was limited to the accepted classics of English literature and some standard and distinguished modern works by writers recently dead. No book by any living writer was included in *An English Library*, admittedly a convenient but a somewhat misleading limitation.

Between 1850 and 1903, that is to say between *The Scarlet Letter* and *The Way of All Flesh*, there are about 100 works of fiction which most adult readers would wish to have personal knowledge of, as distinct from the superficial acquaintance one picks up from text-books, essays, and book talk. For most readers in one form of literature alone here is sufficient reading for two or three years without drawing on contemporary literature at all.

Add to this selection something from each of the other eight main classes and forms of creative literature, and we have a considerable body of great books, which by common consent have become essential reading, to supplement the great classics of previous centuries and of other literatures of ancient and modern civilizations.

In the past, then, there is enough and more, to occupy the leisure of most of us. But the present has pressing claims, too. It is sometimes more important for us to read a current book with no claims to immortality or to life beyond its copyright, than to have read *Urn Burial*, or *Martin Chuzzlewit*. For most of us the matter must be one of balance and compromise.

Some years ago Sir Desmond MacCarthy, writing in *The Sunday Times*, asked if someone could devise a means of bringing noteworthy modern books in all classes of creative literature to the notice of successive generations of readers. This would be, it seems, the work of a sort of Society for the preservation of good twentieth-century books. Libraries and the great bookshops do indeed help in this matter. Many a worthy bookseller has tied up badly needed capital in the purchase of first-class books which wait for years before they find their destined places on the shelves of the kind of reader for whom they were written. But the problem is an important one, and will become increasingly difficult to solve as the production of good books becomes greater even than it is now. In some way we must prevent the book of quality from being submerged by the mediocre. In some way, the younger generations of readers must be made aware of the books that deserve a reading, because they are never superseded.

What Shall I Read Next? has been compiled to help solve this problem. Some will find it useful merely as a shopping list, reminding them of books they know something about already, and serving as a remembrancer. To others, and particularly to younger readers, it may introduce books which have so far escaped their notice. It is hoped, too, that for booksellers and librarians it will have a practical use as a desk book, for answering inquiries, for serving as a check-list for stock, and for use as a reference book when memory fails. The disadvantages of and drawbacks to a list of modern books limited to about 2000 titles are obvious, but not, it is asserted, too great to lessen its usefulness within its defined field.

The list should be judged by what it includes rather than by what is absent, for so great are the riches of contemporary English literature that it would have been an easy matter to have trebled the size of the catalogue.

The first half of the century having gone by, already literary historians are trying to assess its literature in text-books and in critical surveys. Of the many books of this sort, the present writer is indebted to the excellent series of illustrated pamphlets published by Longmans for The British Council, surveying the output in the various forms of literature in five-year leaps. For the period 1939–1945, Stephen Spender's *Poetry*, Henry Reed's *The Novel*, and John Hayward's *Prose Literature* are particularly useful and stimulating. For the succeeding five-year period, 1945–1950, we have had J. C. Trewin's *Drama*, P. H. Newby's *Novel*, Alan Pryce-Jones's *Prose Literature*, and Alan Ross's *Poetry*, all admirably charting a way through the work of new and established writers of good books. These handbooks are all published at 2*s*. 6*d*. each. For lengthier studies there are *Fifty Years of English Literature*, by R. A. Scott-James, Longmans, 1951, 15*s*. dealing with the years 1900–1950; and *A Hundred Years of English Literature* (1830–1930 and a little beyond) by Sherard Vines, Duckworth, 1950, 21*s*. We have been offered a masterly *Assessment of Twentieth Century Literature*, by J. Isaacs, Secker & Warburg, 1951, 8*s*. 6*d*., being the text of six lectures delivered on the Third Programme of the B.B.C. Professor B. Ifor Evans has dealt specifically with the period 1920–1940 in his *English Literature Between the Wars*, Methuen, 1951, 7*s*. 6*d*., and finally at the end of 1951, came *English Literature of the Twentieth Century*, by A. S. Collins, University Tutorial Press, 8*s*. 6*d*.

The compiler wishes to acknowledge with grateful thanks the help he has received from librarians, booksellers, and bookish friends who have put him on to many a good book he would otherwise have missed; and he should not omit thanks to the professional critics, who week by week throughout the year, keep both eyes open for talent, quality and genius.

A NOTE ON THE ARRANGEMENT

No work which is entered in *An English Library* has been included in this supplementary volume, but reference is made to the most important twentieth-century writers, excluded by reason of this limitation, at the end of each section.

The dates of authors no longer living have been given where known, and the nine main groups in which the books have been classified correspond to those used in *An English Library*. Within these groups the arrangement is alphabetical according to authors' and editors' surnames. Hyphened names are entered under the first part: that is, Sackville-West will be found under Sackville-West and not under West, Sackville-. The two exceptions to the arrangement by author are in the section of Biography, where the conventional arrangement of entries under the names of the subjects of the books has been followed, and in the History section where the main entry for the *Oxford History of England* will be found under the series heading.

Pseudonymity has been respected, and in general, authors' names are as given on the title-pages of their books. No attempt has been made to give Christian names pedantically in full, if the author's normal usage is to ignore them. Thus, Priestley, J. B., not John Boynton; Nicolson, Harold, not Harold George; Sackville-West, V., not Victoria.

Dates of first publication are given within parentheses. Dates of revised or later editions follow outside the parentheses, with the prices corrected to January 1952. If no prices are given this indicates that the books so entered were not in print or in stock at the publishers at the time of check.

These are years of abnormal difficulties and it is impossible for the information given about these matters to be accurate for more than a month or two. Booksellers and librarians usually have quick access to up-to-date information about prices and availability and will gladly help bookbuyers.

Finally, as in *An English Library*, English literature for the compiler's purpose has been understood to mean books written in English, whether first published in this country or abroad. Hence a number of first-class books by American writers have been included where they have been published in England, too, and have taken their place in the main stream of current English books. With one or two exceptions only, no translations have been included. For example, O'Crohan's *The Islandman*, a book of rare quality, and undoubtedly a modern classic, will be found amongst the autobiographies, although it was originally written in Irish, and was first introduced to English readers by way of translation.

CONTENTS

Autobiography (including Journals and Letters)   *page* 1

Biography (Individual)   11

Biography (Collective)   27

Essays, Belles Lettres (and Literary Criticism)   29

Prose Anthologies   50

Fiction in Short Stories   52

Fiction (Novels)   63

History (Social and Political)   113

Philosophy and Religion   143

Poetry and Poetic Drama   154

Poetry (Anthologies)   166

Prose Drama   170

Prose Drama (Collections)   179

Travel and Exploration   181

List of Publishers   198

Index of Authors and Editors   201

Index of Titles   211

AUTOBIOGRAPHY

(INCLUDING JOURNALS AND LETTERS)

Of the writers here selected, no fewer than fifteen have written distinguished books on their childhood and early youth. This significant concentration on the years of formation may be due to the lessons of modern psychology, but is more than likely to be the outcome of a yearning for the happy past. Perhaps the saddest comment the artist can make on life during most of the twentieth century as we have known it so far, is that with all its reforms and devices to make life worth living, these years have seen such degradation of the human spirit that recollections of a childhood and youth spent between 1875 and 1912 must necessarily gleam with the quiet beauty of an autumn morning.

Hence the charm of Julian Green's memories, the popularity of Vivian Hughes's successful re-creation of a Victorian life in London, the appeal of the poet's sensitive evocation of a happy past in Frank Kendon's little book, the exquisite happy-sadness of Mary MacCarthy's masterpiece.

But the full life is here too, in all its amplitude and dignity, ranging from the cultured ease of Mrs Belloc Lowndes to the grim, but successful, struggle of Sean O'Casey and the Palladian literary edifice of *Left Hand, Right Hand*.

AGATE, JAMES (1878–1947)

A Shorter Ego. *3 vols. Harrap (1946, 1949). 8s. 6d.; 8s. 6d.; 9s. 6d.*

These engaging rag-bags of anecdote, comment, wit, and prejudice, social and theatrical gossip, originally appeared in nine volumes starting in 1935 and finishing in 1948. Each of the selective volumes covers three of the larger.

BAX, CLIFFORD

Inland Far: a book of thoughts and impressions. *Heinemann (1925).*

Happy, peaceful days of cricket, talk, books and pleasant companions.

BERNERS, LORD (1883–1950)

First Childhood. *Constable (1934).*
A Distant Prospect. *Constable (1945), 1949. 8s. 6d.*

Two small volumes evoking with humour and in prose of distinction memories of the early years and schooldays of the musician who gave us the witty score of the ballet *The Triumph of Neptune*.

BROOKE, JOCELYN

The Military Orchid. *Lane (1948), 1951. 8s. 6d.*

Even during the war the author's passionate search for this rare orchid continued. A modern autobiography told with unusual grace of style and method. Continued in the semi-autobiographical *A Mine of Serpents*, Lane (1949), 10s. 6d. and *The Goose Cathedral*, Lane (1950), 9s. 6d.

CARDUS, NEVILLE
Autobiography. *Collins (1947). 12s. 6d.*

A best-seller of its year which will find new readers for many a decade. It has been said that Cardus is the only journalist who can criticize music in terms of cricket and cricket in terms of music. But apart from these two elements in his life story, Cardus has much to interest the reader who may (it is just possible) dislike both.

CARR, EMILY (1871–1945)
Growing Pains. *O.U.P. (1946). 21s.*

The story of the childhood and youth of a gifted artist who was born in Victoria, Canada, of English parents. In *Klee Wyck*, O.U.P. (1941), 12s. 6d., she writes of Indians and their lore, and the four plates in colour show her skill and style in painting.

CHAPMAN, CECIL MAURICE (1852–1938)
The Poor Man's Court of Justice. *Hodder (1925).*

Twenty-five years as a metropolitan magistrate.

CHURCHILL, WINSTON SPENCER
My Early Life: a roving commission. *(1930.)*

First published by Thornton Butterworth.

COWARD, NOEL
Present Indicative. *Heinemann (1937), 1950. 12s. 6d.*

From precocious youth to youthful maturity. Composer, singer, actor, librettist, producer, writer of the wittiest comedies since Wilde, Coward has a success story to tell and does it very well.

FARJEON, ELEANOR
A Nursery in the 'Nineties. *Gollancz (1935).*

The novelist grew up in a bohemian household and in the atmosphere of books and the theatre. As the granddaughter of Joseph Jefferson, the great American actor, she had the theatre in her blood.

FAUSSET, HUGH I'ANSON
A Modern Prelude. *Cape (1933).*

A poet's youth is often emotionally more highly strained and sharply felt than other men's. Here the distinguished literary critic and poet who has written notably of the growth of poetic mind in great writers of the past, tells the story of his own strict upbringing and gradual emergence as an artist. A sequel is offered in *Towards Fidelity*, Gollancz (1952), 15s.

GOGARTY, OLIVER ST JOHN
As I was Going Down Sackville Street. *Rich & Cowan (1937).*

A rich, gustily written 'phantasy in fact' by the Irish friend of Joyce, who is said to have had him in mind when writing of Buck Mulligan in *Ulysses*. Less autobiographical and more fictional, but still with a core of fact is the same writer's novel *Tumbling In the Hay*, Constable (1939).

GRAVES, ROBERT

Goodbye to all That. *Cape (1929).*

Continued scrappily in *But it Still Goes On*, Cape (1930), which, by the way, contains one of the best modern short stories *The Shout*. The autobiography was a best-seller in its day. The young man who was to become one of the best of modern poets and historical novelists had just recovered emotionally from the war of 1914–1918 and in writing the story of his life to date produced a personal account which ranks with Blunden's and Sassoon's. *See also under* Essays (p. 37) for particulars of a volume which reprints *The Shout* and other pieces.

GREEN, JULIAN

Memories of Happy Days. *Dent (1944), 1950. 6s.*

This was the novelist's first book to be written in his native English, for though an American by birth, France is his adopted country and French his first language as a writer. Delightful memories of a childhood rich with happiness and charm drawn from pleasant parents and friends and from the indefinable atmosphere of Paris and its countryside. Then he watched France recover superficially from 1914 to 1918; later had the agony of seeing her occupied by the New Order of 1940. This part is told in *Personal Record, 1928–1939*, published in 1940 by Hamish Hamilton.

HAMILTON, LORD FREDERIC

The Vanished World of Yesterday. *Hodder (1950). 15s.*

An omnibus of a popular trilogy published separately: *Days Before Yesterday*; *Vanished Pomps of Yesterday*; and *Here, There and Everywhere*. A record of a leisured life and of pleasant personalities at the turn of the century, and in the years of King Edward up to the time of the end of the old world in August 1914.

HARRISON, JANE ELLEN (1850–1928)

Reminiscences of a Student's Life. *Hogarth Press (1925). 5s.*

HUGHES, VIVIAN

A London Family, 1870–1900. *O.U.P. (1946). 21s.*

The three volumes grouped in this omnibus were published separately as *A London Child of the Seventies*; *A London Girl of the Eighties*; and *A London Home in the Nineties*. They re-create the Victorian domestic and social scene with such fidelity and charm that they have already taken their place as modern classics.

ISHERWOOD, CHRISTOPHER

Lions and Shadows. *Methuen (1938), 1953. 9s. 6d.*

'An education in the twenties', recreating for us that halcyon decade in prose worthy of George Moore. The young writer went from public school to Cambridge; thence to literary London, where he met many who are now famous authors themselves.

JEFFERSON, Joseph (1829–1905)

Rip Van Winkle. (*1890.*) *New edition, Reinhardt, 1950. 18s.*

Jefferson was the greatest American comedian of his time, and even the London audiences of 1865 took to him with delight when he played Rip Van Winkle for them. His great-grandfather had been in Garrick's Drury Lane Company. His granddaughter, Eleanor Farjeon, contributes a preface to the new edition. A book for all who like stage gossip, old plays, the old-time theatre, and half-forgotten actors.

JEPSON, Edgar (1863–1938)

Memories of a Victorian. *Gollancz* (*1933*).

Delightfully gay, racy memoirs of a writer whose stories of Lady Noggs were once popular. *Memories of an Edwardian and Neo-Georgian,* Richards (1937), although an entertaining sequel is not up to the standard of the first book.

JOAD, Cyril E. M. (1891–1953)

The Book of Joad. *Faber* (*1937*), *1950. 5s.*

First published 1933 under the title of *Under the Fifth Rib.* Then described by the author as 'a belligerent autobiography'.

KARSAVINA, Tamara

Theatre Street. *Constable* (*1930*). *Revised and enlarged, 1948. 10s. 6d.*

The great ballerina's life story is not only one of the best of its kind, but it also provides an indispensable historical record of the training and work of the Russian ballet in its days of supremacy.

KENDON, Frank

The Small Years. *C.U.P.* (*1930*), *1950. 12s. 6d.*

The childhood of a poet born in 1893. It is enough to say that Walter de la Mare thinks it 'extraordinarily vivid and abundant', and in his introduction says 'the immortal child in man lives on. He lives on in a chequered paradise. . . . Alas, how few of us can recapture it—and how very few indeed with Mr Kendon's lovely truth and clarity.' The new edition contains an additional chapter on Christmas Day.

LAWSON, Jack

A Man's Life. *Hodder* (*1932*). *Abridged edition, U.L.P., 1951. 5s.*

The story of a great career, told with modesty and simple charm. The author started life as a boy working in a coal mine. He rose to become a noted politician and to enter the House of Lords as Lord Lawson of Beamish.

LINKLATER, Eric

The Man on My Back. *Macmillan* (*1941*). *12s. 6d.*

Almost as lively a story as the writer's gay novels of picaresque adventure.

LOWNDES, ALICE BELLOC (1868–1947)
I, Too, Have Lived in Arcadia. *Macmillan (1941).*
Reprinted in Pan Books, 1952, 2s.

A record of love and of childhood which leaves little doubt that this popular writer meant her title to be read without the ambiguity of the original tag. Hers was a happy life, beginning in a charming French home with pleasant parents and a brother, who, as Hilaire Belloc, was later to share her literary Arcadia. The story is continued in *Where Love and Friendship Dwelt*, Macmillan (1943), 12s. 6d., notable for its record of literary Paris in the great days of Verlaine, Zola, Anatole France, the de Goncourts and Alphonse Daudet. *The Merry Wives of Westminster*, Macmillan (1946) and *A Passing World*, Macmillan (1948), 15s., were completed just in time.

LUBBOCK, PERCY
Earlham. *Cape (1922).*

Impressions and recollections of Earlham, Suffolk, which was the home of Lubbock's grandfather, and where he himself spent a happy youth.

LYNCH, PATRICIA
A Storyteller's Childhood. *Dent (1947). 10s. 6d.*

An Irish childhood and early youth, told by one of the best writers of children's books. Her *Turf-cutter's Donkey* (Dent), 8s. 6d., is a modern classic.

MacCARTHY, MARY
A Nineteenth Century Childhood. *Secker (1924).*
Reprinted, Hamish Hamilton, 1948. 6s.

She writes of an almost vanished world of scholarly leisure, quiet conversation and cultured ease. The society of Eton and the academic circle of her family nutured a fine, civilized intelligence.

MacGREGOR, ALASDAIR ALPIN
The Goat Wife. *Heinemann (1939).*
New and revised edition, Museum Press, 1951, 16s.

A description of life in a village in the Highlands before 1914. The author spent her youth in Edinburgh, but soon thrust the city away from her life, and went as a crofter with a flock of goats in the hills of the north.

MACHEN, ARTHUR (1863–1947)
Autobiography. *Richards Press (1951). 15s.*

Far Off Things (1922) and *Things Near and Far* (1923) are here offered in one volume, with an introduction by Morchard Bishop, as a modern classic. The veteran journalist and novelist of the fantastic and macabre, tells his life story in graceful prose and it may well survive as a memorable record of Victorian and Edwardian literary life.

MACKINNON, SIR FRANK DOUGLAS (1871–1946)
On Circuit, 1924–1937. *C.U.P.* (*1940*).

In 1937 the author became a Lord Justice of Appeal; previously he had been Judge of the King's Bench Division of the High Court. As President of the Johnson Society of Lichfield and editor of the best edition of Fanny Burney's *Evelina*, he was a perfect example of the happy marriage literature so often makes with law.

MARSH, SIR EDWARD (1872–1953)
A Number of People: a book of reminiscences.
Heinemann and Hamish Hamilton (*1939*).

A lifetime of friendships with literary and artistic people of genius and talent, a pleasant wit and urbane temperament, all go to make this volume one of the best literary autobiographies of our time.

MASEFIELD, JOHN
In the Mill. *Heinemann* (*1941*). *10s. 6d.*
New Chum. *Heinemann* (*1944*). *10s. 6d.*

The Poet Laureate is a born story-teller in both prose and verse. Here in two volumes is the tale of his own adventurous and hard-working youth. The first tells of his life up to the time of long days in an American factory; but the sequel is 'the yarn of a sailor' (albeit a young one on a famous training ship), 'an old yarn, learned at sea'.

MASSINGHAM, H. J. (1888–1952)
Remembrance: an autobiography. *Batsford* (*1942*).

This good countryman and fine writer, a kindly guide to the best that English rural life can offer a machine-dominated age, gives his reader a 'topographical life story'.

MAUGHAM, W. SOMERSET
The Summing Up. *Heinemann* (*1938*). *7s. 6d.*
Strictly Personal. *Heinemann* (*1942*).

Two studies in autobiography, with personal comment on the life of our times. The second concerns what happened to the author in the first fifteen months of the war of 1939–1945.

MUNTHE, AXEL (1857–1949)
The Story of San Michele. *Murray* (*1929*), *1948*.
9s. 6d. and cheaper editions from time to time. Illustrated gift edition, 42s.

An international best-seller which gained its immense popularity by recommendation, not by advertisement of the commercial type. It set the fashion for doctors' books and seems to appeal to each new generation of readers.

MURRY, J. MIDDLETON
Between Two Worlds. *Cape (1935).*
  One of the most interesting books of the first half century. The story of
the writer's youth and his Oxford years is of value as a record of the times
and of a creative writer's development; that of the later years, when he
was a literary figure of great distinction and a member of a circle of other
writers, all of whom had either genius or abundant talent, provides an
indispensable source book for the literary historian.

✓ O'CASEY, SEAN
I Knock at the Door. *Macmillan (1939). 18s.*
Pictures in the Hallway. *Macmillan (1942). 18s.*
Drums Under the Window. *Macmillan (1945).*
Inishfallen Fare Thee Well. *Macmillan (1949).*
Rose and Crown. *Macmillan (1952). 21s.*
  'Swift glances back at the things that made me.' A superb sequence,
inspiring in its vitality and variety.

O'CROHAN, TOMÁS (1856–1937)
The Islandman. Translated from the Irish by Robin Flower.
    O.U.P. (1929), 1951. 12s. 6d.
  This unique story of the life of a shrewd, hard-working God-fearing
Irishman who was born, worked all his life, and died on the Great
Blasket Island, found many readers in the first edition of the translation
(1934, Chatto) and in the Penguin Books edition of 1943. The 1951
edition is illustrated and in a format worthy of a lovable book which
may well take its place in the permanent gallery of the *World's Classics.*

OMMANNEY, F. D.
The House in the Park. *Longmans (1944).*
  Traveller and naturalist, author of *South Latitude*, Longmans (1938),
5s. and *North Cape*, Longmans (1939), he here returns in memory to the
lovely historic place that was his youth's home. With its round pond,
its gracious beauty, and haunting memories of a happy family, for him
it is now gone for ever, for it has 'returned to the Crown'. 'The Park' is
Richmond Park.

ORWELL, GEORGE (1903–1950)
Down and Out in Paris and London.
    Secker & Warburg (1933), 1949. 10s. 6d.
  An unusual record of the early years of a man of talent and character
down on his luck, but ready to take a turn at anything to earn a living
and gain experience of life. In parts a grim and realistic story.

O'SULLIVAN, MAURICE (1904–1950)
Twenty Years A-Growing. *Chatto (1933). New edition, World's Classics,*
    O.U.P. (1953), 5s.
  In the introduction, E. M. Forster points out that this is not only a good
book but also a unique one. It is a translation from the original Irish
and those who enjoyed O'Crohan's *The Islandman* will like this too.

7

READ, Sir Herbert

Annals of Innocence and Experience. *Faber (1940, 1946), 1949. 10s. 6d.*

The distinguished critic, poet and art teacher evokes memories of a Yorkshire childhood and ponders on his emotional and intellectual development. Part 1 (*The Innocent Eye*) was first published in 1933; *In Retreat* (1925), a fragment of experience taken from the 1914–1918 war in Europe, was added to the 1946 revision, in which the first and third parts remained unaltered.

ROBERTSON, W. Graham (1866–1948)

Time Was. (*1931.*) *Hamish Hamilton (1945).*

Wit, painter, playwright. A connoisseur of art and people. He seemed to know overyone of literary and artistic consequence at the turn of the century and during the Edwardian era. A light, gossipy diverting picture of an era of happiness and enjoyment.

ROWSE, A. L.

A Cornish Childhood. *Cape (1942), 1950. 12s. 6d.*

From the academic pinnacle of a Fellowship of All Souls, the historian and vigorous controversialist looks back on an early life nurtured with some hardness in the half industrial, half agricultural, maritime atmosphere of the wild west country.

SANTAYANA, George (1863–1952)

Persons and Places: the background of my life.
  Constable (1944), 1950. 10s.

Philosopher, poet, historian and novelist. With his Spanish-American background, his learning and loftiness of thought, he was a true internationalist. In *The Middle Span*, Constable (1948), 8s. 6d., he deals with his life in England and America from 1886 to 1905. The earlier work describes his youth in Spain and the New England of his mother. There is a notable gallery of witty portraits in both.

SASSOON, Siegfried

The Old Century and Seven More Years. *Faber (1938). 8s. 6d.*

Continued in *The Weald of Youth*, Faber (1942), 10s. 6d., the poet here retravels the years from 1907 to the year of the great break-up, 1914. In *Siegfried's Journey, 1916–1920*, Faber (1945), 10s. 6d., the writer emerges from the ordeal of war.

SHAW, George Bernard (1856–1950)

Sixteen Self Sketches. *Constable (1949). 7s. 6d.*

Fragments of autobiography lie scattered throughout his writings, in prefaces and in sociological essays. Here are gathered in one volume as near to a self-told life story as we shall now be offered.

SITWELL, Sir Osbert

Left Hand, Right Hand. *Macmillan (1945). 15s.*
The Scarlet Tree. *Macmillan (1946). 15s.*

Great Morning. *Macmillan (1948). 15s.*
Laughter in the Next Room. *Macmillan (1949). 18s.*
Noble Essences; or, Courteous Revelations. *Macmillan (1950). 21s.*

In five volumes of mannered prose we have what is perhaps the greatest autobiography of the first half of the twentieth century. In part the record of a vanished world of wealth, leisured culture and patrician eccentricity; in part a picture of a brilliant circle of writers, artists and important people. The final volume is a series of studies of writers: Firbank, Sir Edmund Gosse, Arnold Bennett and others.

SITWELL, SACHEVERELL

All Summer In a Day. *Duckworth (1926). New edition, Lehmann, 1949. 3s. 6d.*

Compared with his brother's canvas, this is an autobiography in miniature; a posy from a large garden, but as fragrant as its title.

SPRING, HOWARD

Heaven Lies About Us. *Constable (1939).*

'A fragment of infancy.' Continued in *In the Meantime*, Constable (1942), and *And Another Thing*, Constable (1946).

SQUIRE, SIR JOHN COLLINGS

The Honeysuckle and the Bee. *Heinemann (1937).*

Literature and life, cricket and good friends.

STARK, FREYA

Traveller's Prelude. *Murray (1950). 18s.*
Beyond Euphrates. *Murray (1951). 25s.*

The great traveller is recognized as one of the most remarkable women of the century and her autobiography must necessarily take its place as one of the most outstanding works. In the first volume she deals with childhood and youth, first ventures abroad, climbing adventures with W. P. Ker, and the personalities of her family circle. The period is 1893–1927. In the second the story is continued to 1935.

STEIN, GERTRUDE (1874–1946)

The Autobiography of Alice B. Toklas. *Lane (1933). 4s. 6d.*

Like so many other American writers who have made Paris their physical as well as their spiritual home the eccentric Miss Stein became more French than most Frenchwomen. As practitioner of the difficult art of infantilism in prose and verse she influenced the 'ad' writers of the 'twenties, who were almost alone in taking her work seriously. In this unusual story of life in France, of Picasso and other friends, of art and literature, she sometimes relapsed into the normal.

THIRKELL, ANGELA

Three Houses. *O.U.P. (1931). 7s. 6d.*

Fulham, Kensington, Rottingdean. All were houses lived in by men and women and children of grace and charm. To them came men of letters and artists. Those were days which may never return, for these memories of a happy childhood are of a period which seems to have gone for ever.

THOMPSON, FLORA (1877–1947)
Lark Rise to Candleford. *O.U.P. (1945). 16s.*

A trilogy with an introduction by H. J. Massingham. The separate volumes were *Lark Rise* (1939), *Over to Candleford* (1941), and *Candleford Green* (1943). The complete work is illustrated with wood engravings by Julie Nield. A singularly lovable personality with a rare literary gift, the author gives a picture of English village life in the latter half of the nineteenth century. She grew up in an Oxfordshire hamlet. Her book will probably live as a masterpiece of its kind.

TRENEER, ANNE
School House in the Wind. *Cape (1944). 4s. 6d.*
Cornish Years. *Cape (1950). 12s. 6d.*

Childhood and later life in remote, windy Cornwall.

UTTLEY, ALISON
Ambush of Young Days. *Faber (1937). 1951. 12s. 6d.*

The author grew up in the country, on a farm where father, grandfather, and many generations before them, had grown up also. The new edition is made even more delightful by the illustrations of C. F. Tunnicliffe.

WEBLING, A. F.
Something Beyond: a life story. *C.U.P. (1931). 10s. 6d. and 5s.*

A quiet story of spiritual struggle and development. The cheaper edition is in the *Cambridge Miscellany*.

WELCH, DENTON (1917–1948)
Maiden Voyage. *Routledge (1943). 10s. 6d.*

A rebellious youth who had little use for a Youth Movement with a membership of more than one. There was a touch of genius in him which he nurtured under terrible difficulties till it flowered in that most moving autobiographical novel *A Voice Through a Cloud*. We now have the posthumous *The Denton Welch Journals*, Hamish Hamilton (1952), 15s., edited by Jocelyn Brooke.

Other twentieth-century books will be found in *An English Library* under the following names: Henry Adams; Barbellion; Gertrude Bell; Arnold Bennett; John Buchan; G. K. Chesterton; R. G. Collingwood; G. G. Coulton; W. H. Davies; Havelock Ellis; Eric Gill; Edmund Gosse; Maurice Hewlett; W. H. Hudson; Rudyard Kipling; D. H. Lawrence; Katherine Mansfield; George Moore; Llewelyn Powys; Quiller-Couch; Forrest Reid; Logan Pearsall Smith; George Sturt; J. W. N. Sullivan; Beatrice Webb; and W. B. Yeats.

INDIVIDUAL BIOGRAPHY

In his brief but illuminating lectures, *The Development of English Biography*, Hogarth Press (1928), 5s., Harold Nicolson dates 'modern' biography from Froude's *Life of Carlyle, 1834–1881*, because of the startling introduction of 'the element of satire'. Froude's *Carlyle* was published in 1884, but as long ago as 1828 the beginning of a new style in biography can be discerned in J. T. Smith's famous *Nollekens and His Times*. It remained an isolated example of the critical and slightly malicious biography until Froude. This element in the biographer's art in some degree traverses the opinion held by many writers that an author must be in sympathy with his subject if he is to write a good biography. The matter resolves itself into a question of balance. Sympathy pointed with satire has certainly produced admirable, if not great, modern biographies.

From 1884 to Strachey's *succès de scandale* is a span of but thirty-four years. Strachey's influence was only a good one when it was felt by writers of talent, and it cannot be denied that it encouraged some mediocrities to try their hand at biographical essays in depreciation. After his death in 1932 Strachey suffered from depreciation himself, although his books maintained their popularity. Now there are few who would not agree that on the whole his influence was for the good.

As in historical writing, readers are fortunate in having many examples of the biographer's art written by scholars with academic scholarship and distinction but at the same time with a grace of style that gives them a wide popularity with the general reader. Harold Nicolson, Peter Quennell, C. V. Wedgwood, Lord David Cecil, Hesketh Pearson and many others not only charm the town but produce works of permanent value based on the hard work of original research. Some, like Evelyn Waugh, Aldous Huxley, Cecil Gray and Hugh Kingsmill, write only occasionally in this form, but have given us distinguished books which will always enrich the biography shelves.

Hand in hand with biography goes literary criticism. If the subject is a writer the two are usually mingled into a critical and biographical study. Hence it has been convenient to include in this section monographs such as Herbert Read's *Wordsworth*, Tillyard's *Milton*, Joad's *Shaw*, although they would be just as much at home in the next.

The time range is from Meynell's *Francis Thompson* of 1913 to Pope-Hennessy's delightful masterpiece on Monckton Milnes of 1950 to 1951. In scope the reader can sample from the list such brilliant miniatures as Brailsford's *Voltaire* in the *Home University Library* to Bryant's three-decker masterpiece on *Samuel Pepys* and the solid worth of J. M. Thompson's *Robespierre*.

Alberoni; or, The Spanish Conspiracy. By SIMON HARCOURT-SMITH.
Faber (1943).
Giulio Alberoni (1664–1752) was the son of a gardener. By 1714 he was Prime Minister of Spain; three years later he became a Cardinal. His is a story of intrigue, sharp personalities and statesmanship, almost as strange as the imagined material for a novel.

Ali the Lion. By WILLIAM PLOMER. *Cape (1936).*
Ali Pasha (1741–1822) was one of the most cruel and sensual tyrants mankind has so far produced. His utterly ruthless ability and diabolical cunning in playing off France against England, then England against France; his immense and largely stolen wealth; his concubines and sensual vices; his almost Napoleonic prowess in the field; all these qualities and attributes made him an object of fear and respect. Byron visited him; Hugo admired him. Although one of the most revolting life stories it is here told with admirable skill and power.

Matthew Arnold. By LIONEL TRILLING. *Allen & Unwin (1939). 25s.*
A major work of criticism by a young American critic and professor whose literary studies have all been accorded high praise.

Jane Austen: facts and problems. By R. W. CHAPMAN.
O.U.P. (1948). 12s. 6d.
Not biography; not entirely criticism: a mixture of both with some scholarly comment by the greatest authority on the novelist.

Jane Austen and her Art. By MARY LASCELLES. *O.U.P. (1939). 15s.*
The best modern critical study. For an informal book on Jane Austen see Sheila Kaye-Smith and G. B. Stern's *Talking of Jane Austen*, Cassell (1943), 6s., and a new edition may be noted of *Jane Austen*, by Elizabeth Jenkins, Gollancz (1938), 1950, 12s. 6d.

Maurice Baring: a postscript. By LAURA LOVAT.
Hollis & Carter (1948). 6s.
A moving personal tribute to a much-loved man, whose wit and courage responded to the call of his mind when his body was racked with a dreadful malady. Thus he lived a little longer, wrote a little more, and brought a few more smiles to the faces of his friends.

Beckford. By GUY CHAPMAN. *Cape (1937).*
New edition, Hart-Davis, 1952. 18s.
A well-fashioned life of the strange, rich man who built a costly folly, wrote a minor masterpiece still read to-day, but who died in squalor and left behind him scandals, half fiction, half truth. His biographer here sifts the evidence and re-creates the character of a great eccentric.

Bismarck. By C. GRANT ROBERTSON. *Constable (1918), 1947. 10s. 6d.*
The best short biography in English. Originally in the *Makers of the Nineteenth Century Series.*

William Blake. By MONA WILSON. (*1927.*)
  New edition, Hart-Davis, 1948. 21s.

The standard biography by Gilchrist (see *An English Library*) is to some extent superseded by this fine modern study. Well documented and sensitive, it is the best book on Blake for most readers. The first edition was limited, and the welcome new edition first made it generally available. The same publisher has issued the great *Blake Studies* (1949), 42s, written for the specialist by the authoritative scholar and bibliographer, Geoffrey Keynes. In *An Introduction to the Study of Blake*, the late Max Plowman wrote what is said to be a remarkable personal interpretation. First published in 1927, in the U.S.A., it was not issued in Great Britain until 1952, Gollancz, 12s. 6d. Geoffrey Keynes has said of it: 'much the best short exposition of Blake's philosophy that has ever been written'.

Brontës, The
  The Four Brontës. By LAWRENCE and E. M. HANSON.
  O.U.P. (*1949*). *25s.*

The latest study of the sisters and the brother Patrick, and the most substantial. An American writer who devoted many years to the study of the Brontës is Laura L. Hinkley, whose *The Brontës* (*Charlotte and Emily*), U.S.A. (1945); Great Britain, Hammond, Hammond (1948), 15s., is remarkable for its objectivity.

Brownings, The
  The Brownings. By OSBERT BURDETT. *Constable* (*1928*).

Chiefly concerned with the extraordinary courtship and marriage of the two poets. There are liberal quotations from the famous love letters. For a sympathetic and dramatic study see also *Andromeda in Wimpole Street* (1929), Eyre & Spottiswoode (1950), 18s., by Dormer Creston, where the story is told by a skilful selection from the letters, with a running commentary. An important new book has received superlative praise: *Robert Browning: a portrait*, by Betty Miller, John Murray (1952), 21s.

The Story of Fanny Burney. By MURIEL MASEFIELD. *C.U.P.* (*1927*). *10s. 6d.*

The Life of Robert Burns. By CATHERINE CARSWELL.
  Chatto (*1930*), *1951. 16s.*

The author died in 1946. This excellent biography, like her book on D. H. Lawrence, was highly praised by some, and the subject of considerable controversy with others. Her unfinished autobiography, *Lying Awake*, was published posthumously in 1950, Secker & Warburg, 15s.

Byron: the Last Journey (1823–1824). By HAROLD NICOLSON.
  Constable (*1924*), *1949. 10s.*

Every decade brings new studies of Byron's character. Numerous as they are, this one, written in the author's usual witty and lucid style, is by far the most readable short book on the subject we have had in this century.

Byron: the Years of Fame. By PETER QUENNELL. *Faber* (*1935*).
  Collins, 1950. 8s. 6d.

Byron in Italy. By PETER QUENNELL.
>Collins (*1941, 12s. 6d.*), *1951, 8s. 6d.*

Two major works good enough to take their place as standard books although so much has already been written on Byron. Pellucid prose and the art of narrative at its highest make them as readable as good novels.

Edmund Campion. By EVELYN WAUGH. *Longmans (1935).*
>*Reprinted, Hollis & Carter, 1947. 5s.*

One of the best biographies of the century. A moving study of the recusant priest who was put to death in 1581, the first of the English Jesuit martyrs. Awarded the Hawthornden Prize, 1936.

George Canning. By SIR CHARLES PETRIE.
>*Eyre & Spottiswoode, 1946. 12s. 6d.*

A major political biography by a scholarly historian.

Jane Welsh and Jane Carlyle. By ELIZABETH DREW. *Cape (1928).*

A delightful biography of Mrs Carlyle, which sends the reader to the shelves for her own diverting letters—amongst the best in the language. These have been collected and selected (see *An English Library*), but a recent selection must be noticed here: *Jane Welsh Carlyle*, edited by Trudy Bliss, Gollancz (1949), 21s. Much attention has been paid to the Carlyles in recent years, and Lawrence and E. Hanson's *Necessary Evil: a life of Jane Welsh Carlyle*, Constable (1952), 45s., was well praised on its appearance.

Thomas Carlyle: the life and times of a prophet. By JULIAN SYMONS.
>*Gollancz (1952). 21s.*

A timely reassessment, vividly written and fairly balanced in judgement.

Lord Carnock. By HAROLD NICOLSON. *Constable (1930). 10s.*

Subtitled 'A study in the old diplomacy', being the life of the author's father, Sir Arthur Nicolson, first Lord Carnock.

Chaucer's World. Edited by EDITH RICKERT. *O.U.P. (1948). 36s.*

A monumental work of scholarship, the last that this learned editor produced. It is a finely illustrated collection of material, one of a series of projects which grew out of the researches of Edith Rickert and J. M. Manly into the text of the *Canterbury Tales*. Apart from being a quite indispensable work of reference for the reader of Chaucer it is a fascinating miscellany of social life in the fourteenth century. Vivid extracts from records, manuscripts, day-books and other material light up the Chaucerian home, Chaucer's London, education, careers, entertainment, travel, war, the rich and the poor, death, burial, religion. There is a specification for a mason to make vaulted cellars in a tavern in Paternoster Row; a will of one Thomas de Walynton, citizen and clothier of London, dated 4 March 1402: 'I will that my library existing in two volumes be sold and the money given to poor scholars to pray for my soul....' A rich compendium.

The Poet Chaucer. By NEVILL COGHILL. *O.U.P. (1949). 6s.*

A volume in the Home University Library.

G. K. Chesterton. By MAISIE WARD. *Sheed & Ward* (*1943*). *20s.*
A full-length biography, with some correspondence, which does justice to the lovable personality and wit of one of the greatest writers of his time.

Samuel Taylor Coleridge. By HUGH I'ANSON FAUSSET. *Cape* (*1926*).
Of the many biographical and critical studies of the poet this is one of the most sympathetic and sensitive. Stephen Potter's *Coleridge and S.T.C.*, Cape (1935) and Herbert Read's *Coleridge as Critic*, Faber (1949), 6s., are two other distinguished contributions. The standard life is by Sir E. K. Chambers, O.U.P. (1938), 25s.

Benjamin Constant. By HAROLD NICOLSON. *Constable* (*1949*). *18s.*
The author of that remarkable short novel *Adolphe* here finds the perfect biographer, for the strange mixture of artist, statesman, changing loyalties, egotism and sensibility which make him something of an enigma have drawn from Harold Nicolson one of his best works. Readers may be reminded of Geoffrey Scott's *Portrait of Zélide* (see *English Library*) in which Constant's character in relation to a brilliant woman in his life is studied with irony and wit.

Coulton, George Gordon. Father: portrait of G. G. Coulton at Home.
By SARAH CAMPION. *Michael Joseph* (*1948*).
Seldom, perhaps never before, has a father been subjected to such frank treatment at the pen of his daughter; but then seldom have daughters had such a card as G. G. Coulton to put up with, love, manage, admire and get cross with. For 'Father's' story see *An English Library*.

William Cowper. The Stricken Deer; or, The Life of Cowper.
By LORD DAVID CECIL. *Constable* (*1929*), 1950. *7s. 6d.*
It is to be hoped that this sympathetic and finely written life will do something to bring back the poet to his rightful place in popular esteem.

Oliver Cromwell. By C. V. WEDGWOOD. *Duckworth* (*1939*), *1947. 4s. 6d.*
A short life by a scholar who has made a special study of the seventeenth century. It may be read against a less balanced, in fact a prejudiced, but most interesting and controversial study by G. R. Stirling Taylor, *Oliver Cromwell*, Cape (1928). This is the life of a bad man.

Curzon: the last phase, 1919–1925. By HAROLD NICOLSON.
Constable (*1934*), 1949. *10s.*
'A study in post-war diplomacy.' As much a piece of historical writing as a biography. Readers of the delightful *Some People* will remember with pleasure the chapter on Curzon and his unusual valet.

Thomas De Quincey. A Flame in Sunlight: the life of Thomas De Quincey.
By EDWARD SACKVILLE-WEST. *Cassell* (*1936*).
As readable as a novel, partly because of the intensely interesting subject, partly because of the author's sympathy and skill as a biographer. A smaller life is in Duckworth's series of *Great Lives*, by Malcolm Elwin (1935).

Charles Dickens. By UNA POPE-HENNESSY. *Chatto (1945). 21s.*

The author died in 1949. Of all her books this was the most substantial contribution to biography and literary criticism. It was the first to present Dickens with frankness yet fairness, as it was the first full-length study to be written after the publication of his letters in the fuller Nonesuch edition.

Blessington D'Orsay. By MICHAEL SADLEIR. *Constable (1933), 1947. 10s.*

A delightful book about the last of the dandies, who with Lady Blessington scandalized the town, spent money like water and gave the second quarter of the nineteenth century a chance to look at the spirit of the profligate wit of the preceding century having a last and dying fling.

George Eliot. By GERALD BULLETT. *Collins (1947).*

A welcome new life and reassessment, which may be read with profit alongside Joan Bennett's *George Eliot: her mind and art* (C.U.P., 1948, 10s. 6d.).

The Art of T. S. Eliot. By HELEN GARDNER. *Cresset Press (1949). 12s. 6d.*

A scholarly and helpful critical study, particularly of the later poems. Indispensable for many readers of the series *Four Quartets*, is Raymond Preston's *Four Quartets Rehearsed*, Sheed & Ward (1946), 5s., in which the allusions and sources which inspired the poet are made clear. The late F. O. Matthiessen's *The Achievement of T. S. Eliot* is an American work of permanent value. A new book which attracted great praise on its publication is *T. S. Eliot: the Design of His Poetry*, by Elizabeth Drew, Eyre & Spottiswoode (1950), 12s. 6d.

Ford Madox Ford. The Last Pre-Raphaelite. By DOUGLAS GOLDRING. *Macdonald (1948). 15s.*

The friend of the great novelist and man of letters (who has still to be accorded his rightful place in modern English literature) here gives an understanding sketch of Ford's character and life. See also the earlier book by the same author, *South Lodge*, Constable (1943). This is one of the best books of its kind and completes the portrait by its record of Violet Hunt, the novelist's relations with her, and the *English Review* circle.

E. M. Forster. By LIONEL TRILLING. *Hogarth Press (1944). 3rd edition, 1951. 7s. 6d.*

A penetrating study in appreciation by an American critic.

Edward Garnett. By H. E. BATES. *Max Parrish (1950). 6s.*

Garnett did so much for twentieth-century literature by his helpful and trenchant criticism, by way of encouragement, of work by unknown and new authors that this little portrait well deserves a place in any list of this kind. There is much here about the art of the short-story writer and of H. E. Bates in particular.

Edward Gibbon, 1737–1794. By D. M. LOW. *Chatto (1937). 15s.*

An authoritative centenary study and the best modern criticism and biography, which may be supplemented by G. M. Young's shorter work *Gibbon*, Peter Davies (1932).

Gladstone. By Francis Birrell. *Duckworth (1933), 1950. 4s. 6d.*
A brilliant little essay in the *Great Lives* series.

Sir Richard Grenville of the 'Revenge': an Elizabethan hero.
By A. L. Rowse. *Cape (1937), 1949. 18s.*

Lord Grey of the Reform Bill. By G. M. Trevelyan.
Longmans (1920), 1952. 30s.
One of the greatest biographies of the century. As a study of the life
and politics of Charles, second Earl Grey, it is as much a work of history
as biography, and is not likely to be superseded.

Handel. By Edward J. Dent. *Duckworth (1934), 1950. 4s. 6d.*
A notable volume in the *Great Lives* series by a learned musicologist.
The standard life in English is *George Frederic Handel*, by Newman Flower,
Cassell (1923), revised edition, 1947, 27s. 6d.

Hardy the Novelist. By Lord David Cecil. *Constable (1943). 7s. 6d.*
It is certain that Hardy will come to mean more and more to humanity
as time reveals the grandeur and permanence of his work. Edmund
Blunden's *Thomas Hardy*, Macmillan (1942), 1951, 5s., is another understanding book which deals with Hardy's poetry as well as his novels.

Frank Harris. By Hugh Kingsmill (1889–1949).
(1932.) New edition, Lehmann, 1949. 3s. 6d.
A damaging, diverting sketch of the career and dubious character of the
famous literary filibuster.

William Hazlitt. Born Under Saturn: the biography of William Hazlitt.
By Catherine Maclean. *Collins (1943).*
The standard life is by P. P. Howe (see *An English Library*); this later
work is a sympathetic portrait of a character of some complication.

Philip Heseltine. Peter Warlock: a memoir, 1894–1930. By Cecil Gray
(1895–1951). *Cape (1934).*
A rare piece of work and one of the most interesting biographies of our
time. 'Peter Warlock' was a good musician, a scholar and a delightful
character with a gaily-sad temperament and personality. Writing soon after
Heseltine's tragic death, Gray succeeded admirably in conveying some of
the charm and gaiety of his gifted friend.

Gerard Manley Hopkins, 1844–1889. By W. H. Gardner.
2 vols. Secker & Warburg (1947–1949). 25s.; 30s.
Of the many (perhaps too many) books on the poet this is one of the
best and most substantial.

Lord Houghton. Monckton Milnes. By James Pope-Hennessy.
2 vols. Constable (1950, 1952). 25s. each.
Vol. 1: *The Years of Promise, 1809–1851*; Vol. 2: *The Flight of Youth,
1851–1885*. A brilliant biography of Lord Houghton, author of the first
life of Keats.

David Hume. By J. Y. T. GREIG. *Cape (1931).*

The author, who has also edited the standard edition of Hume's *Letters,* was awarded the James Tait Black Prize for 1931 for this work of distinguished biography.

Henry James: the major phase. By F. O. MATTHIESSEN (1902–1950).
O.U.P. (1946). 9s. 6d.

An analysis of Henry James in his middle and later periods. Written for the ardent reader of James and for the scholarly literary student, it may not be wanted by many in its entirety. But it is such a fine piece of criticism that no 'Jacobean' can afford to overlook it. In *The Legend of the Master* Simon Nowell-Smith gathered together with great skill a fascinating collection of literary gossip, wit and anecdote about James. Published by Constable (1947), 12s. 6d., these selected letters, notes, critical remarks by others, etc., may be strongly recommended.

Joan of Arc. By V. SACKVILLE-WEST.
(1936.) New edition, Michael Joseph, 1948. 12s. 6d.

Samuel Johnson. By J. W. KRUTCH. *Cassell (1948). 21s.*

A successful attempt by an American critic to rescue Doctor Johnson from Boswell. Here Johnson is treated more as a man of letters than a 'Character'. A pleasant, gracefully written small study is *The Story of Dr Johnson,* by S. C. Roberts, C.U.P., second edition, 1919, 7s. 6d. and school edition, 3s. A controversial book notable for its entirely unsympathetic attitude to Mrs Thrale and for its frank and vigorous portrait of Boswell is *Ursa Major: a study of Dr Johnson and his friends,* by C. E. Vulliamy, Michael Joseph (1946). Admittedly an individualinterpretation it is so well done that it sends the reader to primary sources in search of his own opinion. And these primary sources have now increased enormously by the publication of the famous *Private Papers of James Boswell* which are in progress from Heinemann.

Father Joseph. Grey Eminence: a biography. By ALDOUS HUXLEY.
Chatto (1941). 8s. 6d.

The Capuchin friar behind Cardinal Richelieu provides the author with a subject which brings into play all his powers of keen analysis of character, with the interplay of motives and religious mysticism, traversed by a strange lust for worldly power.

John Keats: a life. By DOROTHY HEWLETT. *Hurst & Blackett (1937).*
Revised edition, 1949. 25s.

An excellent modern biography regarded by some critics as likely to become the standard work. Originally published under the title of *Adonais.*

Keats and Shakespeare. By J. MIDDLETON MURRY. *O.U.P. (1925). 15s.*

A study in the development of a poet's mind and art illustrated by an analysis of the influence of Shakespeare. Followed by *Studies in Keats,* O.U.P. (1930), which is a series of essays on the poetic life of Keats during the years 1816–1820.

Lady Caroline Lamb. By ELIZABETH JENKINS. *Gollancz (1932).*
A study in tempestuous character. See also Lord David Cecil's fine book on *The Young Melbourne* (p. 19), and *The Lambs*, by Katherine Anthony, Hammond, Hammond (1949), 15s., which is a study of Victorian England as seen in the life of Viscount Melbourne, his wife and their circle.

Savage Landor. By MALCOLM ELWIN. *Macmillan (1942).*
The best modern life of the poet and classicist, who knew Charles Lamb, yet outlived Thackeray.

D. H. Lawrence. Savage Pilgrimage. By CATHERINE CARSWELL.
(1932.) New edition, Secker & Warburg, 1951. 12s. 6d.
The best life, by one who knew Lawrence well, respected and liked him, but was able to take an objective view of his character and work. Withdrawn soon after its first publication it was reissued with slight emendations, and then went out of print for many years. A subjective, but extremely interesting book by J. Middleton Murry entitled *Son of Woman: a study of D. H. Lawrence*, Cape (1931), should not be overlooked. The most recent biography is *Portrait of a Genius, But...* by Richard Aldington, Heinemann (1950), 15s.

David Livingstone. Livingstone's Last Journey.
By SIR REGINALD COUPLAND. *Collins (1945). 12s. 6d.*
A name once on everybody's mouth, then a somewhat forgotten 'Eminent Victorian'. Here is a well-praised book on the missionary-traveller and explorer to adjust the balance.

Marlborough: his life and times. By WINSTON SPENCER CHURCHILL.
Original edition, 4 vols. Harrap (1933–1938).
New edition in 2 vols., 1947. 50s.

Melbourne. The Young Melbourne and the story of his marriage with Caroline Lamb. By LORD DAVID CECIL. *Constable (1939).*
The sub-title indicates the limits of this delightful narrative. The charm and wit of its telling make it a memorable piece of work. The strange, tempestuous creature whose name and fortunes were so oddly linked with those of the great statesman has a book to herself, mentioned above (*see under* LAMB). She appears again in the books on Byron dealing with the nine months in which she plagued him and nearly killed herself, 1812–1813.

Milton. By E. M. W. TILLYARD. *Chatto (1930), 1947. 18s.*
The best modern critical work, to be supplemented by the same author's *The Miltonic Setting: Past and Present*, first published by C.U.P., 1938, then Chatto, 8s. 6d. Another distinguished book, more biographical, and relating Milton to his contemporaries, by studying their influence on his thought, is *Milton: Man and Thinker*, by Denis Saurat, Dent (1925), revised and enlarged edition, 1944, 15s. A small book of worth is *Milton and the English Mind*, by Francis Ernest Hutchinson (1871–1947), English Univ. Press (1947), 6s.

William Morris, Prophet of England's New Order.
By LLOYD ERIC GREY. *Cassell (1949)*. *15s.*
Many biographies of William Morris have appeared of recent years, supplementing the standard life by W. J. Mackail (see *An English Library*). This one was praised by Bernard Shaw and by others who knew Morris well.

Napoleon Bonaparte: his rise and fall. By J. M. THOMPSON.
Blackwell (1951). *37s. 6d.*
Reviewed as an important, first-class piece of work, supplementing the standard books by the same author on the French Revolution, and on Robespierre.

Nelson. By CAROLA OMAN. 2 vols. *Hodder (1947)*. *42s.*
Southey's classic book will never be superseded, but this detailed, monumental work will undoubtedly be regarded as the standard life.

Florence Nightingale. By CECIL WOODHAM-SMITH. *Constable (1950)*. *21s.*
A great biography which was one of the non-fiction successes of its year and continues to attract a wide public.

Palmerston. By HERBERT C. F. BELL. 2 vols. *Longmans (1936)*.
Authoritative, scholarly, and to be enjoyed as a major historical and biographical work by the general reader.

Sir Robert Peel. By A. A. W. RAMSAY. *Constable (1928)*, 1948. *14s.*
Formerly one of the *Makers of the Nineteenth Century* series.

Samuel Pepys. By ARTHUR BRYANT. 3 vols. *C.U.P.* *(1933, 1935, 1938)*.
New editions, Collins, 1947, 1948, 1949. *15s. each.*
Vol. 1: *The Man in the Making*; Vol. 2: *The Years of Peril*; Vol. 3: *The Saviour of the Navy*. At once a work of scholarship and research and a vivid, popular study of a great public servant.

Edgar Allan Poe. Israfel. By HERVEY ALLEN (1889–1949). *Gollancz (1926)*.
A long study which attracted a large public when it first appeared, by the novelist whose *Anthony Adverse* was a best-seller of note. The title is taken from a poem by Poe.

Alexander Pope. By EDITH SITWELL. *Faber (1930)*. *15s.*
Penguin Books (1949). *1s. 6d.*

Richelieu and the French Monarchy. By C. V. WEDGWOOD.
Hodder (1949). *6s.*
One of the best volumes in the series known as *Teach Yourself History*, edited and planned by A. L. Rowse. Another study is *Richelieu*, by Hilaire Belloc. Cassell (1936), 5s.

Arthur Rimbaud. By ENID STARKIE. *Faber (1938)*.
Revised edition, Hamish Hamilton (1947). *15s.*

Robespierre. By J. M. THOMPSON. *2 vols. Blackwell (1935).*
A major work, considered to be the best life of the French revolutionary.
Reprinted in one volume in 1939, 10s. 6d. Both editions out of print in
1951.

John Ruskin. By PETER QUENNELL. *Collins (1949). 15s.*
Of the many books on Ruskin written in the last twenty-five years this
is probably the best objective study for the general reader. *Ruskin: the
Great Victorian*, by Derrick Leon, is another first-class book, published in
1949, Routledge, 30s. Sir William James's *Order of Release*, Murray (1948),
18s. was a best-seller owing to its exposure of Ruskin's private life with its
marital difficulties and the wellnigh tragic ending. An attempt, somewhat
unconvincing, to refute some of Sir William's charges will be found in
Vindication of Ruskin, by J. Howard Whitehouse, Allen & Unwin, 1950,
10s. There may the matter rest, so that lovers of literature, art and bright
thought, may think more of Ruskin the writer than Ruskin the adored son
and the unsatisfactory lover.

Lord Shaftesbury. By J. L. HAMMOND (1872–1949) and BARBARA HAMMOND.
Longmans (1923). Reprinted in Pelican Series, Penguin Books, 1939.

SHAKESPEARE STUDIES

*An extensive list will be found in each of the N.B.L. book-lists,
British Drama: History and Criticism (1950), and Shakespeare,
(1952), C.U.P. for the League, 1s. 6d. each*

A Life of William Shakespeare. By JOSEPH QUINCEY ADAMS.
Constable (1923). Student's edition, 1940. 21s.
A standard American work.

Shakespeare. By IVOR BROWN. *Collins (1949). 12s. 6d.*
A popular work, intended for the general reader.

William Shakespeare: a study of facts and problems.
By SIR EDMUND K. CHAMBERS. *2 vols. O.U.P. (1930). 63s.*
The great standard work to which all other writers on Shakespeare and
all students must always remain indebted. This principal authority for
reference and advanced study has been admirably abridged by Charles
Williams, as *A Short Life of Shakespeare*, O.U.P. (1933), 7s. 6d. Two other
books by Chambers, supplementing the major work, are: *Shakespearean
Gleanings*, O.U.P. (1944) and *Sources for a Biography of Shakespeare*,
O.U.P. (1946).

Shakespearian Comedy, and other studies. By GEORGE S. GORDON (1881–
1942). *O.U.P. (1944). 10s. 6d.*
This posthumous collection of essays is edited by Sir Edmund Chambers.

The Wheel of Fire. By G. WILSON KNIGHT. *O.U.P. (1930).*
4th revised and enlarged edition, Methuen, 1949. 21s.
Interpretations of Shakespeare's tragedies.

The Imperial Theme. By G. WILSON KNIGHT. *O.U.P.* (*1931*).
3rd edition, Methuen, 1951. 21s.
Further interpretations of Shakespeare's tragedies, including the Roman plays.

The Crown of Life. By G. WILSON KNIGHT. *O.U.P.* (*1947*).
2nd edition, Methuen, 1948. 18s.
Essays in the interpretation of Shakespeare's final plays.

Shakespeare. By JOHN MASEFIELD. *O.U.P.* (*1911*), *1912. 6s.*
A volume in the Home University Library; brief, stimulating, and notable for its sensitive insight into the poet's mind.

Shakespeare. By J. MIDDLETON MURRY. *Cape* (*1936*), *1948. 15s.*
See also under KEATS *for the same writer's* Keats and Shakespeare.

A Life of Shakespeare. By HESKETH PEARSON. (*1942*.)
Revised edition, Carroll & Nicholson, 1949. 9s. 6d.
The revised edition has a collection of quotations illustrating Shakespeare's development in style and his characteristic thought.

Shakespeare and the Nature of Man. By THEODORE SPENCER.
C.U.P. (*1942*).

Shakespeare's Imagery and What it Tells Us. By C. F. E. SPURGEON.
C.U.P. (*1935*).
The best work on this aspect of Shakespeare's poetry. It is a lengthy, detailed study which adds much to the reader's enjoyment of the plays.

Shakespeare's Last Plays. By E. M. TILLYARD. *Chatto* (*1938*). *6s.*
Cymbeline, The Winter's Tale, and *The Tempest* examined in an endeavour to discover the mood of the poet when he wrote them: was he serene or cynical; writing for the crowd or bored with life? Other books by the same author are *Shakespeare's History Plays,* Chatto (1944), 18s., and *Shakespeare's Problem Plays,* Chatto (1950), 8s. 6d.

What Happens in 'Hamlet'. By J. DOVER WILSON.
C.U.P. (*1937*), *1951. 25s.*
An indispensable study on an apparently inexhaustible theme.

———

Bernard Shaw. By ERIC BENTLEY. *Hale* (*1950*), *1952. 2s. 6d.*
A substantial study of Shaw's political thinking, his attitude towards religion and his contributions to contemporary philosophical ideas. The principal plays are analysed with the kind of illuminating comment which helps both reader and playgoer to pick up the points of the argument quickly.

The Real Bernard Shaw. By MAURICE COLBOURNE. *Dent* (*1930*).
Revised edition, 1949. 16s.

Shaw. By C. E. M. JOAD. *Gollancz (1949). 12s. 6d.*
In describing, amongst other things, the impact Shaw as teacher made on Joad, the author has written on behalf of a whole generation of students both inside and outside universities and schools.

Shaw. By DESMOND MACCARTHY. *Macgibbon & Kee (1951). 12s. 6d.*
The greatest dramatic critic of the century wrote on Shaw's plays from the days of the first performances of the earliest comedies up to notable revivals in the 'twenties and 'thirties. In this volume of collected criticism we have interpretative comment and discussion of the highest quality.

Thirty Years with Bernard Shaw. By BLANCHE PATCH.
Gollancz (1951). 12s. 6d.
Although the writer served Shaw faithfully as a secretary for so long, and during the years of his greatest influence as a world figure, she was never a Shavian. Hence the value of her book, which is almost completely matter-of-fact.

Bernard Shaw: his life and personality. By HESKETH PEARSON.
Collins (1942), 1950. 8s. 6d.
A gay book, greatly helped in the making by Shaw himself. In *G.B.S.: a postscript*, Collins (1951), 10s. 6d., the same author adds further biographical details obtained in conversations with Shaw, and brings the record up to the end in November 1950.

Bernard Shaw. By A. C. WARD. *Longmans (1950). 2s.*
Issued by the British Council as a Supplement to *British Book News*. A brief admirable summary of Shaw's life, work and influence, with a bibliography of all but his fugitive publications. The longer, full-length work by the same author *Bernard Shaw*, was published in 1951, Longmans, 10s. 6d., in the *Men and Books* series.

Shelley. By EDMUND BLUNDEN. *Collins (1946). 12s. 6d.*
'A life story', not a critical survey of the poet's work, seeking to unravel the complexities and to judge soberly on facts rather than by prejudice and hearsay evidence, or worse. Hence the importance of this last addition to an ever-growing library of books about the poet.

Sheridan. By LEWIS GIBBS. *Dent (1947). 15s.*

Sir Philip Sidney. By MONA WILSON. *Duckworth (1931).*
Revised edition, Hart-Davis, 1950. 18s.
The standard life of the great chivalrous man who died at Arnhem in 1586 at the age of 32.

Logan Pearsall Smith, Recollections of. By ROBERT GATHORNE-HARDY.
Constable (1949). 18s.
A sympathetic study in temperament by a friend of the scholarly critic, who born an American, found his literary and spiritual home in England.

23

Sydney Smith. The Smith of Smiths: the life, wit and wisdom of the Rev. Sydney Smith. By HESKETH PEARSON.
Hamish Hamilton (1934). 10s. 6d.

Also available in *Penguin Books*, 1948. One of the most enjoyable books of recent years, this tribute to the English Voltaire succeeds in conveying the kindly, tolerant and civilized character of the most brilliant wit of his time. It is a mine of good stories, gathered from correspondence and contemporary recollections, with liberal quotations from Sydney Smith's essays. The preface by G. K. Chesterton pays tribute to a great personality who once mounted the handsome stairway at Seven Albemarle Street on his way to the meetings of the famous club to which only wits were admitted, and where Sydney Smith shone as brightly as he did at all such gatherings. *Sydney Smith: a Biography and a Selection*, by Gerald Bullett, Michael Joseph (1951), 15s., is a new volume giving 93 pages of biography and 210 pages of Sydney Smith's best work.

Strafford, 1593–1641. By C. V. WEDGWOOD. *Cape (1935), 1949. 15s.*

A work of scholarship by an authority on English history in the seventeenth century, yet so well written that it may be read almost as a dramatic narrative and character study. Examination of the Wentworth-Woodhouse papers now going on may add further details to our knowledge of the tragic statesman whose character is here so firmly presented but this study will probably remain the best one-volume life for many decades.

Talleyrand. By SIR DUFF COOPER. *Cape (1932), 1950. 15s.*

Anton Chehov: a critical study. By WILLIAM GERHARDI.
Duckworth (1923). Reprinted in a collected edition, Macdonald, 1949. 7s. 6d.

Tchehov's famous short stories have been translated by Mrs Constance Garnett in a number of volumes published by Chatto and Windus. Twenty-five of the best stories were reprinted in *Select Tales*, Chatto (1927), 1949, 12s. 6d.

Tennyson: aspects of his life, character, and poetry. By HAROLD NICOLSON.
Constable (1923), 1949. 10s. 6d.

This biography and critical study did much to correct faulty judgements and to remove prejudices prevalent in the nineteen-twenties when Tennyson's position as a major poet was no longer taken for granted. A smaller study of value was *Tennyson*, by Hugh I'Anson Fausset (Cape, 1923). The latest life, *Alfred Tennyson*, by Charles Tennyson, Macmillan (1949), 30s., will probably supersede the earlier standard one by the second Lord Tennyson.

Thackeray. By J. Y. T. GREIG. *O.U.P. (1950). 12s. 6d.*

More critical than biographical; more controversial than academic. A vigorous, re-creative study.

Edward Thomas. As it Was; and, World Without End. By 'H.T.'
  Heinemann (1935), 1950. 2s. 6d.
A moving, poignant and personal study by the poet's wife, Helen Thomas.

The Life of Francis Thompson. By EVERARD MEYNELL.
  Burns Oates (1913, 1926), 10s.
Wilfrid Meynell (1852–1948) made it possible for the poet to live and work. Nineteen years of 'unbroken intimacy' helped to enrich the language with some of its greatest religious poetry. The sad life story is set down with understanding and devotion.

Leo Tolstoy. By E. J. SIMMONS. *Lehmann (1949). 25s.*
In spite of its many competitors, this new life was accorded superlative praise. 'By far the best that has been written, and one that for completeness should take a place among the great biographies' *T.L.S.*

Trollope: a commentary. By MICHAEL SADLEIR.
  Constable (1927; revised edition, 1945), 1951. 8s. 6d.
The best book on the man and his major work.

Voltaire. By H. N. BRAILSFORD. *O.U.P. (1935). 6s.*
Although compressed by the limitations of the *Home University Library* this brilliant little book is one of the best yet written on Voltaire.

Samuel White. Siamese White. By MAURICE COLLIS.
  Faber (1936). Revised edition, 1952. 15s.
During the reign of James II, Samuel White of Bath (1650–1689) was appointed by the King of Siam a mandarin of that country. He amassed a fortune by filibustering. The author's researches have unearthed an amazing story, almost fictional in its episodes.

Wilberforce: a biographical study. By SIR REGINALD COUPLAND.
  O.U.P. (1923). New edition, Collins, 1945. 12s. 6d.

Edward Wilson of the Antarctic. By GEORGE SEAVER.
  Murray (1933), 1950. 21s. and 10s. 6d.
The Introduction by Apsley Cherry Garrard is a noble tribute to his friend and companion. As the book is worthy of its subject it must necessarily be valued as one of the great biographies of the century.

Dorothy Wordsworth. By C. M. MACLEAN. *Chatto (1932).*
A sympathetic study which succeeds in rescuing Dorothy from her brother. The most substantial life is by Ernest de Selincourt, O.U.P. (1933), 30s.

Wordsworth. By HERBERT READ. *Cape (1930).*
  Revised edition, Faber, 1949. 15s.
A penetrating study almost indispensable for the reader of the poems who desires to go below the surface to deepen his knowledge of the best work and to read with interest the mediocre. *The Later Wordsworth*, by

E. C. Batho, C.U.P. (1933), 17*s.* 6*d.* is much used by students. H. W. Garrod's collection of lectures and essays, *Wordsworth*, O.U.P. (1923), 2nd edition, 1927, 7*s.* 6*d.*, is strongly recommended.

W. B. Yeats, 1865–1939. By JOSEPH HONE. *Macmillan* (*1943*).

The biographer of George Moore has in this first life of the last great poet to write in English set down all that he could collect and knew. It will be the source book for others and no doubt will remain the standard life for some time to come. An important new book is *The Lonely Tower:* studies in the poetry of W. B. Yeats, by T. R. Henn, Methuen (1950), 21*s.*

Reference may be made to *An English Library* for particulars of other twentieth-century books in this section by C. S. Terry, D. F. Tovey, W. J. Turner, Maurice Baring, G. K. Chesterton, Edward Thompson, G. T. Garratt, H. Festing Jones, J. L. Lowes, D. G. Hogarth, J. H. Rose, Edward Thomas and Philip Guedalla.

COLLECTIVE BIOGRAPHY

CECIL, LORD DAVID

Two Quiet Lives. *Constable (1948). 10s. 6d.*

Studies in kindred temperaments: Dorothy Osborne and Thomas Gray. The biographer draws their portaits sensitively and sympathetically, and finds in both a shyness, melancho¹y, introspection and reserve which unites them in spirit in his distinguished book.

DOUGLAS, DAVID

English Scholars, 1660–1730. *Eyre & Spottiswoode (1939).*
 Revised, enlarged and illustrated edition, 1951. 21s.

A biographical portrayal of the men who devoted themselves to investigating British history of the Middle Ages. Their work has permanent value. Dugdale, Hickes, Wanley, Kennett, Wake, Somner, Brady, Wharton, Thwaites and Rymer: these are the great names. The book was awarded the James Tait Black Memorial Prize in 1939.

FEILING, KEITH

Sketches in Nineteenth Century Biography. *Longmans (1930).*

The historian of the Tory Party was a university lecturer in history; these are brief studies arising from his specialized scholarship.

HOLMYARD, E. J.

Makers of Chemistry. *O.U.P. (1931). 10s. 6d.*

One of a series of illustrated introductions to the scientific discoverers and their work.

KINGSMILL, HUGH (1889–1949)

The Poisoned Crown.
 Eyre & Spottiswoode (1944).

A deeply interesting study in the characters of Cromwell, Napoleon, Lincoln, Queen Elizabeth, Hitler: an introductory essay establishes the connexion between this strange group of power holders; the title from Blake is the key; the theme, the effect of power on minds of quality and on evil minds. The author, a genial and witty critic of established reputation.

MACPHERSON, HECTOR

Makers of Astronomy. *O.U.P. (1933). 8s. 6d.*

A second volume in the series noted above. The others are out of print.

QUENNELL, PETER

Four Portraits: studies of the eighteenth century. *Collins (1945), 1951. 6s.*

Boswell, Gibbon, Sterne and John Wilkes sketched with delightful ease and mastery. All four essays will send the reader to the writings of the first three and to fuller studies of the last.

RAVEN, C. E.
English Naturalists from Neckam to Ray. *C.U.P.* (*1947*). *35s.*

Awarded the James Tait Black Prize for biography, 1947. The author of the standard biography of John Ray (1627–1705) develops a study in the making of the modern world by his presentment of the lives of the great naturalists and their work as pioneers of science.

SITWELL, EDITH
The English Eccentrics. *Faber* (*1930*). *Dobson* (*1951*). *9s. 6d.*

An engaging gallery of crack-brained, quixotic, men and women, whose quirks and oddities are once again made interesting by the author's sympathetic study.

SYKES, CHRISTOPHER
Four Studies in Loyalty. *Collins* (*1946*). *12s. 6d.*

The first is of the author's uncle, and his (at times somewhat sorely tried) loyalty to his monarch and friend, King Edward VII: the second of a Persian friend known to diplomatists; the third of that finely equipped intellectual traveller and art critic, Robert Byron, whose untimely death in 1942 was a grievous loss to art and literature; the fourth, of the country France and its heartening reawakening to greatness in a time of defeat and subjugation. All four studies are illumined by the author's richly endowed mind and creative experience.

THOMSON, GLADYS SCOTT
Family Background. *Cape* (*1949*). *10s. 6d.*

Four studies again; this time of the great Russell family from the fifteenth to the eighteenth century. A previous book, *The Russells in Bloomsbury*, Cape (1940), 15*s.*, deals with the same family from 1669 to 1771.

ESSAYS, BELLES LETTRES AND
LITERARY CRITICISM

From Sir Francis Bacon to Sir Max Beerbohm and Robert Lynd the English essayist has pursued his wayward course in literature, writing now of Gardens, now on A Piece of Chalk, and even on Nothing. Here more than in any other form of writing the way of saying is of greater importance than the thing said.

Formal histories of literature have been excluded from the section, but the reader may be reminded of the excellent series of *Introductions to English Literature*, edited by Bonamy Dobrée. Revised editions of all except one of the volumes have been recently published by the Cresset Press at 10*s. 6d.* each. It is a feature of these books to provide brief bibliographies as guides to reading. They deal not only with pure literature, but with the literature of sport, humour, science, and other subjects and forms. See below under Muir.

Guy Pocock's *Brush Up Your Reading*, Dent, 5*s.*, will be found helpful by many, while A. C. Ward's *Twentieth Century Literature, 1901–1940*, Methuen, 7*s. 6d.*, surveys the ground admirably.

ABBOTT, Edwin A. (1838–1928)
Flatland: a romance of many dimensions. *Blackwell (1884).*
   Facsimile edition, 1932. 7s. 6d.

Although written for the mathematically minded there are few who will not enjoy this ingenious presentation of a theory which underlies most twentieth-century physics and higher mathematical speculation connected with the idea of space-time. Originally published pseudonymously by 'A. Square'.

ALDINGTON, Richard
French Studies and Reviews. *Allen & Unwin (1925). 7s. 6d.*
Literary Studies and Reviews. *Allen & Unwin (1926). 7s. 6d.*

With a scholarly knowledge of French literature the critic unites an ability to interpret sensitively authors of the eighteenth century and onwards.

ALLEN, Beverley Sprague
Tides in English Taste, 1619–1800. *2 vols. O.U.P. (1937).*

A learned investigation in the interrelationship of the arts, and on changing fashions in architecture, design, literature and art. 'A background to the study of literature', with illustrations, placing the literary Englishman in his aesthetic setting.

ALLEN, WALTER
Reading a Novel. *Phoenix House (1949). 5s.*

A brief, stimulating book of seven chapters on the novelist's art, with an eighth on six famous novels selected to illustrate the critic's main arguments.

ALLEN, WALTER (Editor)
Writers on Writing: an anthology. *Phoenix House (1948). 15s.*

Of outstanding interest to those who wish to go behind the scenes to watch the creative artist at work. Although there are several books by poets on their art, this appears to be the first attempt to group together passages from French and English prose writers on the art of writing in the various forms of prose literature and on the making of masterpieces in fiction.

BARFIELD, OWEN
History in English Words. *Methuen (1926). Revised edition, 1933.*

On the evolution of the English language. The author strips off layer after layer of meaning from his chosen words, offering in the course of his investigation sidelights on social history and the development of ideas.

Poetic Diction. *Faber (1928), 1952. 18s.*

A study in the poetic art and in meaning. The new edition has a preface of 25 pages addressed to a new generation of readers.

BATESON, F. W.
English Poetry: a critical introduction. *Longmans (1950). 12s. 6d.*

'Romantic poetry died long ago': that is the critic's verdict; romantic criticism should die too: that his thesis, which he illustrates by reference to specific poems.

BEERBOHM, SIR MAX
And Even Now. *Heinemann (1920), 1950. 10s. 6d.*

In this volume by the greatest essayist of the century will be found some of his best work, including the immortal *A Clergyman*—'Fragmentary, pale, momentary; almost nothing; glimpsed and gone...'. Here, too, is the famous essay on Swinburne at *No. 2, The Pines.*

A Christmas Garland. *Heinemann (1895), 1950. 10s. 6d.*

Probably the best book of prose parodies in the language. Henry James, H. G. Wells, Arnold Bennett and other contemporaries are all delicately and lightly flicked with the whip of irony and satire, sometimes wielded with just the faintest touch of malice. In the new edition there is an additional parody 'On the Art of a Certain M. .r. .ce B. .r. .ng'.

Seven Men—and Two Others. *Heinemann (1919), 1950. 10s. 6d.*

The original edition has six unique studies in character. These alone would have given the author a permanent place in literature. The new edition has the 'two others'.

Works. More. *Lane (1896, 1899), 1951. 8s. 6d.*

The gaily impudent title of the writer's first small volume of essays, and its laconic successor, gave an early indication of his individual style and attitude to life and literature. The two were later issued in one volume, when the publisher entered into the spirit of the thing, by appending a learned and exhaustive 'bibliography'.

Yet Again. *Heinemann (1909), 1950. 10s. 6d.*

BELL, CLIVE

Art. *Chatto (1914), 1947. 7s. 6d.*

It was in 1907 that Roger Fry startled the public by arranging an exhibition in London of paintings by Cézanne, Matisse, Derain, Picasso and others, for whom he found the convenient and enduring label of Post-Impressionists. Clive Bell had already formed his own opinions about the principles of aesthetics, art and ethics and had been arguing, 'more or less amicably' with Roger Fry over a number of years. When this book of essays first appeared it did as much to educate a newly interested public in these themes as any book of its kind, and is still one of the best general discussions of fundamentals.

Since Cézanne. *Chatto (1922), 1929. 5s.*

A stimulating series of essays on modern artists, including Duncan Grant, Bonnard, Derain and Rousseau, with others on such topics as Art and Politics, Negro Sculpture, and Standards.

BELL, QUENTIN

On Human Finery. *Hogarth Press (1948). 12s. 6d.*

BELLOC, HILAIRE

An Anthology of his prose and verse. *Selected by* W. N. ROUGHEAD. *Hart-Davis (1951), 15s.*
Selected Essays. *Introduction by* J. B. MORTON. *Methuen (1948), 1950. 10s. 6d.*
Stories, Essays and Poems. *Dent (1938), 1950. 5s. (Everyman's Library.)*

BENEDICT, RUTH

Patterns of Culture. *Routledge (1935). Revised edition, 1949. 14s.*

A study in social anthropology: the general, specific and the conditioned impulses affecting behaviour in communities. The author refers specifically to the Pueblo of New Mexico, the North West coast of America, and the Dobu of New Guinea.

BIRKETT, SIR NORMAN

The Use and Abuse of Reading. *C.U.P. for N.B.L. (1951). 2s. 6d.*

BLUNDEN, EDMUND

Charles Lamb and His Contemporaries. *C.U.P.* (*1932*)
Cricket Country. *Collins* (*1944*). *8s. 6d.*

On a beloved subject that has already attracted much fine writing the poet produced a book of rare distinction, in which classic games, school cricket and village cricket are recalled with charm and relish, with a backward glance at other writers.

A Section of Poetry and Prose. *Made by* KENNETH HOPKINS.
Hart-Davis (*1950*). *15s.*
Nothing from recent books is included.

BODKIN, MAUD

Archetypal Patterns in Poetry. *O.U.P.* (*1934*). *12s. 6d.*

These psychological studies of imagination are of permanent value. They examine with penetration and subtlety tragic poetry generally, and then Coleridge, Milton, *Othello* and *Lear*, and a modern masterpiece, *The Waste Land*.

BOWEN, ELIZABETH

Collected Impressions. *Longmans* (*1950*). *18s.*

Delicate, yet sharply pointed essays and criticism contributed to magazines over a score of years, including the text of the pleasant war-time broadcast entitled *Anthony Trollope: a new judgement*.

BRADBROOK, M. C.

The School of Night. *C.U.P.* (*1936*). *8s. 6d.*

'A study in the literary relationships of Sir Walter Raleigh.' An important little book for all readers of Tudor and Jacobean literature.

BROOKS, VAN WYCK

The World of Washington Irving. *Dent* (*1946*). *15s.*
The Times of Melville and Whitman. *Dent* (*1948*). *15s.*
The Flowering of New England, 1815–1865. *Dent* (*1941*), *1950*. *12s. 6d.*
New England: Indian Summer, 1865–1915. *Dent* (*1941*), *1950*. *12s. 6d.*
The Confident Years, 1885–1915. *Dent* (*1952*). *21s.*

American life and the literature that grew out of it until the collapse of the Old World in 1914 are interpreted in this widely read series with singular grace and understanding. A reading of the last three is as essential for the proper appreciation of the American national character and customs as a formal history.

BROWN, IVOR

Book of Words. *Cape* (*1944*), *1951*. *3s. 6d.*

There are six word books altogether, this one being a reprint in one volume of the first two: *A Word in Your Ear*, and *Just Another Word*. The others are: *I Give You My Word* (1945), 3s. 6d.; *Say the Word* (1947), *No Idle Words* (1948), and the final *Having the Last Word* (1950), 6s. All published by Cape.

CARDUS, NEVILLE
The Essential Neville Cardus.
    Edited with an introduction by RUPERT HART-DAVIS.
    Cape (1949). 12s. 6d.
    A pleasant selection from the cricket writings and essays. Those who
must sit through the whole game have welcome reprints of the classic
trilogy: *Days in the Sun*; *Good Days*; *The Summer Game*, Hart-Davis
(1948), 7s. 6d. each.

CECIL, ALGERNON (1879–1953)
A House in Bryanston Square. *Eyre & Spottiswoode (1944), 1950. 18s.*
    An unclassifiable book, being part autobiography, with tender memories
of a loved one haunting house, writer and reader; part philosophical
reflexions, with many illuminating quotations from a wide range of
authors. A book for which the term 'belles lettres' would have had to be
invented if it had not already existed.

CECIL, LORD DAVID
Early Victorian Novelists. *Constable (1934), 1948. 10s.*
    'Essays in revaluation', being lectures on seven writers, with an intro-
duction.
Poets and Storytellers. *Constable (1949). 10s.*
    Contemporaries and classics of English and foreign literature.

CHASE, STUART
The Tyranny of Words. *Methuen (1938), 1950. 7s. 6d.*

CHILD, HAROLD H. (1869–1945)
Essays and Reflections. *C.U.P. (1948). 10s. 6d.*
    A collection of much prized contributions on music and plays, life and
letters, made to the *T.L.S.*, *The Times*, and *The Observer*. Edited with
a memoir by S. C. Roberts.

CHURCHILL, WINSTON SPENCER
Maxims and Reflections. *Eyre & Spottiswoode (1947), 1951. 2s. 6d.*
    Arranged and with an introduction by Colin Coote.

COLLIS, J. S.
Down to Earth. *Cape (1947). 9s. 6d.*
    A distinguished country and farming book.

COMFORT, ALEX
The Novel and Our Time. *Phoenix House (1948). 5s.*

CONNOLLY, CYRIL
The Condemned Playground: essays 1927–1944. *Routledge (1944). 10s. 6d.*
    Literary, satirical and other essays collected from the writings of the
Editor of *Horizon*.

Enemies of Promise. *Routledge (1938). Revised edition, 1949.*

The literary scene from 1918 to 1938. The author found a dearth of creative writing. Some of the best chapters are on his own development as a youth at Eton and later as a literary critic.

The Unquiet Grave. By 'Palinurus'. *Hamish Hamilton (1944).*
Revised edition with a new introduction and a frontispiece, 1951. 8s. 6d.

A *journal intime* which first appeared from the offices of the literary magazine *Horizon.* It may well take its place as one of the key books of our time, being a war-time year's journey through the mind of one of the most intelligent literary men of the century.

CURTIS, BRIAN

The Life Story of the Fish. *Cape (1949). 12s. 6d.*

His biography, manners and morals. A diverting and original work of general as well as scientific interest.

DARWIN, BERNARD

Every Idle Dream. *Collins (1948). 12s. 6d.*

Agreeable essays by the well-known golfer and journalist. His *Golf Between Two Wars*, Chatto (1944) is so well written that even non-golfers have been known to read it.

DE LA MARE, WALTER

Behold, this Dreamer. *Faber (1939). 1952. 42s.*
Love. *Faber (1943). 25s.*

Creative anthologies of an individual kind that only this poet can make. Quotation and selection, with commentary, interpret the theme and subtly illuminate the chosen passages. There is a pleasant selection of his *Stories, Essays and Poems* in *Everyman's Library*, Dent, 5s.

DENNIS, GEOFFREY

The End of the World. *Eyre & Spottiswoode (1930), 1949. 10s. 6d.*

In prose of imaginative splendour the author considers the final 'incident'. Distinguished by the award of the Hawthornden Prize.

DOBRÉE, BONAMY

The Lamp and the Lute. *O.U.P. (1929).*

Studies in six modern authors: Ibsen, Hardy, Kipling, E. M. Forster, D. H. Lawrence and T. S. Eliot.

Modern Prose Style. *O.U.P. (1934). 10s. 6d.*

Intended more for the reader than the critic or the writer. Why do we like one author better than another? We read for pleasure, but not only for one kind of pleasure.

Restoration Comedy, 1660–1720. *O.U.P. (1924). 10s.*

Restoration Tragedy, 1660–1720. *O.U.P. (1929). 12s. 6d.*

ELIOT, T. S.

Essays Ancient and Modern. *Faber (1936). 7s. 6d.*

The author's own collection of essays in criticism, being a revision of *For Lancelot Andrewes*, Faber (1928); some essays have been omitted; five have been added, including a long essay on Pascal's *Pensées* which does not appear elsewhere. Four essays from this volume are included in *Selected Essays* noted below.

Points of View. *Faber (1941), 1951. 6s.*

A general introduction to the prose works by means of a selection varying from short passages to complete essays, made with the author's approval by John Hayward.

The Sacred Wood: essays on poetry and criticism.
    Methuen (1920), 1951. 7s. 6d.

Selected Essays. *Faber (1932). 3rd revised and enlarged edition, 1951. 20s.*
The author's choice of his prose written since 1917.

The Use of Poetry and the Use of Criticism. *Faber (1933). 8s. 6d.*

Eight lectures delivered when the author held the Charles Eliot Norton Chair of Poetry, 1932–1933.

ELTON, LORD

The Two Villages. *Collins (1949). 8s. 6d.*

ELWIN, MALCOLM

Old Gods Falling. *Collins (1939).*

A survey of English literature from 1887 to 1914, revaluing some of the literary reputations of the period.

EMPSON, WILLIAM

Seven Types of Ambiguity. *Chatto (1930). Revised edition, 1947. 12s. 6d.*

An examination of the use of words in poetry, with particular attention to Shakespeare's work and his sustained imagery and puns.

EVANS, BERGEN

The Natural History of Nonsense. *Michael Joseph (1947). 12s. 6d.*

A witty record of some of the preposterous errors and legends that mankind insists on believing in spite of evidence to the contrary.

EVANS, JOAN

Pattern: a study of ornament in Western Europe from 1180 to 1900.
    O.U.P. (1931), 1949. 168s.

A major contribution to scholarship and art criticism with a range of interest far beyond the specialist. Profusely illustrated, it illuminates social history, art and literature.

Taste and Temperament. *Cape (1939), 1946. 10s. 6d.*

An illustrated study in aesthetics, and of psychological types in their relation to the visual arts.

FARLEIGH, JOHN

The Creative Craftsman. *Bell* (*1950*). *21s.*

Forty double-column pages of line drawings and notes trace the evolution of design from early man to Robert Adams. Then follow conversations with masters and craftsmen in their own workshops.

FORSTER, E. M.

Abinger Harvest. *Edward Arnold* (*1936*), *1940*. *6s.*

The 12*s.* 6*d.* edition contains the text of the *Abinger Pageant* which was omitted from the pocket edition. There are about 80 essays collected by the author from his occasional writings before 1939. Arranged in sections (a commentary on current events; books; the past; and the East) they form a distinguished volume of reflexions on life and literature.

Aspects of the Novel. *Edward Arnold* (*1927*), *1949*. *6s.*

Informal lectures delivered at Trinity College, Cambridge. One of the best books on the novel as a form written in this century. The subject is approached (after a long introduction) by way of the story and people created by the genius of the creative writer, and then proceeds to the plot, fantasy, prophecy, pattern and rhythm. 'The development of the novel' might become important, 'because it implied the development of humanity.'

FOTHERGILL, JOHN

My Three Inns. *Chatto* (*1949*). *10s. 6d.*

Selections from two earlier volumes: *Confessions of an Innkeeper* (1938) and *An Innkeeper's Diary* (1931), with a new section. The author is no ordinary innkeeper and the highly individual nature of his contribution to this ancient calling is engagingly revealed in his books.

GARROD, H. W.

Genius Loci, and other essays. *O.U.P.* (*1950*). *10s. 6d.*

Six essays with more salty comment and bookman's wisdom to the page than many academic studies have to the chapter.

GAUNT, WILLIAM

The Pre-Raphaelite Tragedy. *Cape* (*1942*), *1950*. *10s. 6d.*
The Aesthetic Adventure. *Cape* (*1945*), *1950*. *10s. 6d.*
The March of the Moderns. *Cape* (*1949*). *12s. 6d.*

A trilogy of gaily written surveys of the growth of modern art and literature, and the ideas which have been the mainspring of English culture since the last quarter of the nineteenth century. Personalities and pictures, eccentrics and rebels, genius and outmoded talent: all these form the background, with the witty chatter and scandal of the talkers and writers in the forefront.

GOWERS, SIR ERNEST

Plain Words: a guide to the use of English. *H.M.S.O.* (*1948*). *2s.*

The most useful official publication ever issued by H.M.S.O. Intended to teach the Civil Servant, it might well be made compulsory reading for all students; it will probably help everyone who has to write a business letter or draft a staff regulation.

A new edition entitled *A B C of Plain Words*, H.M.S.O. (1951), 3s. (paper covers); 4s. 6d. (bound) has been published for a wider public.

GRAVES, ROBERT

The Common Asphodel. *Hamish Hamilton (1949). 15s.*

The author's collection of his essays published in journals 1922 to 1949, on the nature of poetry and the work of some of his contemporaries. Vigorous, controversial writing, meant to provoke, as well as illuminate.

Occupation: Writer. *Cassell (1951). 12s. 6d.*

A gathering of scattered 'by-works', including the impudently amusing monograph on the art of swearing, *Lars Porsena* (it lives up to the wit of its title in every paragraph); an overlooked masterpiece of a short story, *The Shout*, two plays, and some miscellaneous essays.

GRAVES, ROBERT and HODGE, ALAN

The Reader Over Your Shoulder; a handbook for writers of English prose.
Cape (1943). Abridged edition, 1947. 10s. 6d.

Stern teachers both, analysing, dissecting, scolding and occasionally praising.

GRIERSON, SIR HERBERT J. C.

Cross-Currents in English Literature of the Seventeenth Century.
Chatto (1929). 15s.

Milton and Wordsworth: poets and prophets. *Chatto (1937). 12s. 6d.*

Five of the seven chapters are devoted to Milton. A study in the reactions of the poets to the politics of their own day.

Rhetoric and English Composition. *Oliver & Boyd (1944).*
Revised edition, 1945. 7s. 6d.

A severe title but by no means severe in treatment. Written for a wider audience than the classroom.

GRIERSON, SIR HERBERT J. C. and SMITH, J. C.

A Critical History of English Poetry. *Chatto (1944). 25s.*

Learned, and of considerable value to the reader, particularly in the seventeenth-century period, but lacking in perception and sympathy when it approaches twentieth-century work.

GROVE, VICTOR

The Language Bar. *Routledge (1950). 12s. 6d.*

A stimulating and important study in philology and the emergence of a bar between audience and writer in the sixteenth century which by now, it is asserted, has become a sociological issue between highbrow and lowbrow. A modification of teaching methods is suggested to overcome some of the bad results.

HARDY, G. H.

A Mathematician's Apology. *C.U.P.* (*1940*). *4s. 6d.*

A vindication of the mathematician as artist and philosophical thinker.

HARRISON, FREDERICK

A Book About Books. *Murray* (*1943*). *5s.*

A companionable book on the history of books and their making, on libraries and printing.

HARRISON, G. B.

The Story of Elizabethan Drama. *C.U.P.* (*1926*).

HAYNES, E. S. P. (1877–1949)

The Lawyer: a conversation piece. *Eyre & Spottiswoode* (*1950*). *16s.*

Selections from *A Lawyer's Notebook*, Secker (1932), and other books. The author was an eccentric in the best tradition.

HEALY, MAURICE (1887–1943)

Stay Me With Flagons. *Michael Joseph* (*1940*)
   Revised edition, 1949. 10s. 6d.

Of wine and the pleasure of drinking wisely. Rich with humour and judicial wit from the title-page to the last. Useful, even practical; mellow, and so delightful in style that even teetotallers may read it with pleasure and maybe with a touch of envy, too.

HEATH-STUBBS, JOHN

The Darkling Plain. *Eyre & Spottiswoode* (*1950*). *10s. 6d.*

A study of romanticism from Darley (1846) to Yeats, somewhat in opposition to F. W. Bateson's view (see p. 30). Patmore, G. Manley Hopkins, and Francis Thompson are each studied in separate chapters.

HEMINGWAY, ERNEST

Death in the Afternoon. *Cape* (*1932*), *1950. 25s.*

A study of bull-fighting, praising a sport which shocks even a fox-hunting man. But the novelist, who has done some bull-fighting himself, finds something spiritual in the strange ritual of the arena and the emotional bond between victim, fighter, and crowd. His book is the best yet written in English for those who want to understand the art, its terminology and prominent personalities. The many fine action photographs add greatly to the quality of the book.

HERBERT, SIR ALAN P.

What a Word! *Methuen* (*1935*), *1951. 10s. 6d.*

Salutary advice on the use of the King's English. With Gowers and Graves (see pp. 36, 37) it forms a trilogy for all writers and readers.

HINE, REGINALD L. (1883–1949)

The Confessions of an Uncommon Attorney. *Dent (1944). 18s.*

The author of one of the best local histories written in our time, this solicitor of Hitchin in Hertfordshire gave us in this finely produced volume, a miscellany of odds and ends, anecdotes, characters, and curious episodes, unique in modern literature.

HUXLEY, ALDOUS

Along the Road. *Chatto (1925). 7s. 6d.*

Notes and brief essays of a tourist on travel in general, on places, works of art and things seen 'by the way'. The writer is in his happiest mood.

Do What You Will: essays. *Chatto (1929). 7s. 6d.*
Ends and Means. *Chatto (1937). 7s. 6d.*
Music at Night, and other essays. *Chatto (1931). 7s. 6d.*
The Olive Tree, and other essays. *Chatto (1936). 7s. 6d.*
On the Margin: notes and essays. *Chatto (1923). 7s. 6d.*

Mainly on books and authors, with a tilt at the collector of first editions, and a glance at Tibetan ways and customs.

Proper Studies. *Chatto (1927). 7s. 6d.*

On dogma, education, equality, religion, and other serious subjects.

HUXLEY, JULIAN

Bird Watching and Bird Behaviour. *Chatto (1930).*
  New edition, Dobson, 1950. 6s.

A scientist's book addressed to general as well as scientific readers. The same writer's book on *Ants*, Chatto (1930), new edition, Dobson, 1950, 6s., in like manner imparts much scientific information, separating myth from fact, and asks for a scientific approach to natural history instead of a sentimental one.

On Living in a Revolution: fifteen essays. *Chatto (1944). 12s. 6d.*

JACKSON, HOLBROOK (1874–1948)

The Reading of Books. *Faber (1946). 15s.*

The theme: that the reading of books can be an art and the reader an artist. What goes on behind the screen of words? What interaction should there be between the writer and reader? Finally, on the cult of ambiguity and on books as intoxicants. The discussion, as always with this allusive writer, is illuminated by extensive quotation. In his *The Eighteen Nineties*, Cape (1927), will be found one of the best surveys of the literary scene during this important decade.

KELLETT, E. E.

Reconsiderations. *C.U.P. (1928). 10s. 6d.*
Suggestions. *C.U.P. (1923). 10s. 6d.*

Literary essays of distinction by the author of *Ex Libris*, Allen & Unwin (1940).

KINGSMILL, HUGH (1889–1949)

After Puritanism, *1850–1900. Duckworth (1929).*

Penetrating literary studies of Samuel Butler, Frank Harris, W. T. Stead and others of the period.

Progress of a Biographer. *Methuen (1949). 10s. 6d.*

Contains 'the best literary criticism in the language, at least if there is anything to compare with these essays for imaginative insight, unfailing commonsense, careful appraisement, spiritual illumination, and sustained humour, I should like to hear of it' (Hesketh Pearson), in *About Kingsmill*, by Hesketh Pearson and Malcolm Muggeridge, Methuen (1951), 10s. 6d.

KNIGHTS, L. C.

Explorations. *Chatto (1946), 1951. 12s. 6d.*

'Essays in criticism, mainly on the literature of the seventeenth century.' Contains the famous essay on *How Many Children Had Lady Macbeth?*

LACK, DAVID

Robin Redbreast. *O.U.P. (1950). 15s.*

A book in honour of 'Slant-legged Robin, with autumn on his chest.' Its object is entertainment, not the advancement of learning. Here is everything the author has been able to find out about the charming little bird in its relation to man. Robin in the wintry fields and on the cold-crisp lawn; Robin dead ('Who killed Cock Robin?'); Robin in poetry and drama and song; Robin hopping lightly through literature from old Skelton to old Hardy. Robin in politics, at home and in the nursery. The charming illustrations, learned notes, and easy, allusive style all go to make this a treasure of a book, worthy of its pretty, heart-warming subject.

LAMBORN, EDMUND ARNOLD GREENING (1877–1950)

The Rudiments of Criticism. *O.U.P. (1916), 1926. 7s. 6d.*

A simple but remarkably effective introduction to the enjoyment of poetry and the appreciation of poetic technique.

LANE, FRANK W.

The Elements Rage. *Country Life (1945). 10s. 6d.*

It is almost a relief to find from the graphic descriptions and the illustrations of storm and meteor that Nature can even now outdo the rocket and the flying bomb and the atomic explosion.

LEAVIS, F. R.

The Great Tradition. *Chatto (1948). 12s. 6d.*

Studies in the novel and its structure as exemplified by the work of George Eliot, Henry James and Joseph Conrad.

New Bearings in English Poetry. *Chatto (1932).*
Revised edition, 1950. 8s. 6d.

A revised edition of a controversial book which aroused much interest when it first appeared. The same author's *Revaluation: Tradition and Development in English Poetry*, Chatto (1936), 10s. 6d., started a storm about Milton and other poets which has not yet died down.

LEJEUNE, C. A.

Chestnuts in Her Lap: 1936–1947 in the cinema. *Phoenix House (1947).*
Revised and enlarged edition, 1948. 10s. 6d.

LEWIS, WYNDHAM

The Lion and the Fox. *Richards (1927). Methuen, 1951. 21s.*

A subtle analysis of the influence of Machiavelli and his thought on Elizabethan dramatists and particularly on the role of the Shakespeare hero.

LIDDELL, ROBERT

A Treatise on the Novel. *Cape (1947). 9s. 6d.*

LUBBOCK, PERCY

The Craft of Fiction. *Cape (1921).*

LUCAS, F. L.

Studies French and English. *Cassell (1934), 1950. 6s.*

On poets and essayists, with three chapters on 'the modern world': Flaubert, Proust and modern criticism.

LYND, ROBERT (1879–1949)

Essays on Life and Literature. *Dent (1951). 5s. (Everyman's Library.)*

A selection of Y.Y.'s best work with an introduction by Desmond MacCarthy. Drawn from 30 volumes, 1908–1945, and arranged in three groups: 'Irish and English'; 'Book and Authors'; and 'Miscellaneous'. A fuller selection from his major work will be found in a new volume, *Books and Writers*, Dent (1952). 16s.

MacCARTHY, SIR DESMOND (1878–1952)

Drama. *Putnam (1940).*

The doyen of English critics selects some of his best work in dramatic criticism from early days at the Court Theatre, London, to the nineteen-thirties.

Portraits. *Putnam (1931)*
New edition, Macgibbon & Kee, 1949. 10s. 6d.
Sketches in biography and character.

McCUTCHEON, ROGER P.

Eighteenth Century Literature. *O.U.P. (1950). 6s.*

A brief but valuable study in the Home University Library.

MAIR, G. H.

English Literature: modern, *1450–1939 (Home University Library).*
Revised by A. C. WARD, *O.U.P., 1944. 6s.*

MASEFIELD, JOHN
A Book of Prose Selections. *Heinemann (1950). 10s. 6d.*
'The best I have been able to do.'

MASSINGHAM, H. J. (1888–1952)
The Curious Traveller. *Collins (1950). 12s. 6d.*
A record in journal form of England and English Life away from the
towns; a comment on the folk and their landscape in village and on fell;
the lore and the lost crafts to be found in lonely cottages and isolated
hamlets. Here is a charming mixture of literature and rural wisdom.
The Wisdom of the Fields. *Collins (1945). 12s. 6d.*

MATHEW, THEOBALD (1866–1939)
Fifty Forensic Fables, by 'O'. *Butterworth (1949). 12s. 6d.*
Selected from three much liked books known to all legal students and
lovers of legal wit and wisdom.

MAUGHAM, W. SOMERSET
A Writer's Notebook. *Heinemann (1949). 12s. 6d.*

MILNE, A. A.
Those Were the Days. *Methuen (1929), 1948. 12s. 6d.*
An omnibus of 884 pages containing *The Day's Play*; *The Holiday
Round*; *Once A Week*; *The Sunny Side*. These lighthearted pieces, essays
and stories were contributed to *Punch* between 1900 to 1914.

MOORE, DORIS L.
The Vulgar Heart. *Cassell (1945). 15s.*
An analysis of public opinion as expressed in popular journalism and
some flashy writings. Salutary, witty, pungent, disturbing. A thinker and
critic over your shoulder.

MOORE, JOHN
Brensham Village. *Collins (1946). 12s. 6d.*
Portrait of Elmbury. *Collins (1945). 12s. 6d.*

MORGAN, CHARLES
Reflections in a Mirror. *2 series (1944, 1946). Macmillan. 8s. 6d. each.*
As 'Menander' the novelist-critic contributed some of the best critical
essays of the war years to the *Times Literary Supplement*. Here is his
selection of the most important, together with some lectures and other
essays.

MORTIMER, RAYMOND
Channel Packet. *Hogarth Press (1942).*
Critical articles contributed over a number of years to literary journals.
In many ways the best interpretation of the French literary scene of our
time.

MUIR, Edwin

Essays on Literature and Society. *Hogarth Press (1949). 8s. 6d.*
The Present Age, from 1914. *Cresset Press (1939).*
The Structure of the Novel. *Hogarth Press (1928). New edition, 1947. 5s.*

MURRAY, Gilbert

The Classical Tradition in Poetry. *O.U.P. (1927). 12s. 6d.*
Euripides and His Age. *O.U.P. (1913). 2nd edition, 1946. 6s.*
(Home University Library.)

MURRY, J. Middleton

Countries of the Mind. *2 series. O.U.P. (1922, 1931).*
Essays in literary criticism.

John Clare and other studies. *Nevill (1950). 12s. 6d.*
Some of the critic's best essays from his early books now out of print.
They were among the best critical essays of the period between the wars.
The Problem of Style. *O.U.P. (1922). 9s.*

NICOLL, Allardyce

British Drama. *Harrap (1925).*
Fourth revised and enlarged edition, 1947. 12s. 6d.
A history, less literary than dramatic, and a critical record from the
moralities and interludes to the present day. There is an exhaustive
bibliography, and illustrations.

NICOLSON, Sir Harold

The Development of English Biography. *Hogarth Press (1927), 1949. 5s.*
A brief but compelling essay: the author thinks that Froude's life of
Carlyle was the first biography to point the way to twentieth-century
method in that there, for the first time, a biographer adopted a critical
attitude to his subject.

Some People. *Constable (1927), 1949. 7s. 6d. Folio Society, 1951. 16s.*
One of the most delightful books of this century. On the surface a series
of nine character sketches of people the author has known: ranging from
Arketall, Lord Curzon's slightly tight butler to sweet Miss Plimsoll, the
governess: 'Don't you think, dear, that we must be *very* careful, not to
become a muff?' A book of charm, of wit, and of unusual delight:
something to recommend but never to borrow or to lend.

O'FAOLAIN, Sean

The Short Story. *Collins (1949).*
An analysis of this form of fiction, choosing Daudet, de Maupassant,
Tchehov for particular study. There are eight short stories by these three,
with R.L.S., Henry James, Frank O'Connor, 'Elizabeth' and Hemingway
chosen by the author as masterpieces to illustrate his thesis.

OLIVIER, EDITH (1879–1948)
Country Moods and Tenses: a non-grammarian's chapbook.
Batsford (1941).

An illustrated comment on English country life at its happiest: infinitive in its range; indicative in its allusions; imperative in its format.

ORWELL, GEORGE (1903–1949)
Critical Essays. *Secker & Warburg (1946), 1951. 10s. 6d.*
The Lion and the Unicorn: Socialism and the English genius.
Secker & Warburg (1941). 2s.

'One of the most moving and yet incisive portraits of the English character, and a minor classic in itself.' (Arthur Koestler.)

Shooting An Elephant. *Secker & Warburg (1950). 11s. 6d.*

A last collection of essays contributed to journals from 1931 to 1949. A third are from the series *I Write as I Please* which gave stimulating pleasure to readers of the *Tribune*; others are reminiscences of life and experiences in Burma before 1939.

POWYS, JOHN COWPER
The Pleasures of Literature. *Cassell (1938). 12s. 6d.*

PRIESTLEY, J. B.
Self-Selected Essays. *Heinemann (1937), 1950. 10s. 6d.*

PRITCHETT, V. S.
The Living Novel. *Chatto (1946). 8s. 6d.*

Chapters in criticism of the contemporary novel.

READ, HERBERT
Art Now. *Faber (1933). Revised edition, 1948. 25s.*

Probably the best introduction to the theory of modern painting and sculpture, both of which offer so much difficulty to many. From backgrounds the critic proceeds to science and symbolism (the break-up of academic tradition), to the subjective realism of the German Expressionists, the theory of abstract form, and the subjective idealism of Picasso. The volume is well illustrated.

Coat of Many Colours. *Routledge (1945). 8s. 6d.*

Brilliant critical articles culled from magazines the author has contributed to over a number of years. They have that quality which sends the reader to the works criticized.

Collected Essays in Literary Criticism. *Faber (1938), 1951. 18s.*

General theories and particular studies collected from *The Sense of Glory, Form in Modern Poetry* (1932), *In Defence of Shelley* (1936) and *Reason and Romanticism* (1926), with some new essays.

English Prose Style. *Bell (1928). Revised edition, 1952. 15s.*
Form in Modern Poetry: an essay in aesthetics. *Vision Press (1948). 6s.*
The Meaning of Art. *Faber (1931), 1951. 10s. 6d.*
Phases of English Poetry. *Hogarth (1928). Faber, 1950. 10s. 6d.*

Two new chapters have been added to the revised edition.

The Sense of Glory. *C.U.P. (1929). 6s.*

Evocative essays in criticism originally contributed to *The Times
Literary Supplement*, presented in a revised form. Froissart, Malory,
Descartes, Swift, Sterne, Hawthorne, Bagehot, Henry James and Vauven-
argues are selected to uphold the bright banner of romantic glory.

REEVES, DAVID

Furniture. *Faber (1947). 16s.*

Unlike any other book on furniture, this literary book on the subject
discusses the sense of form in the craftsman's mind and shows us how
a piece of cabinet work comes into being.

REID, FORREST (1876–1947)

The Milk of Paradise. *Faber (1946).*

These 'thoughts on poetry' were originally lectures to young people,
and printed, they are an introduction to the pleasures of poetry and
are worthy of a permanent place in English literature. The lyrical beauty
of English verse demands an immediate and personal response: this is the
theme so eloquently developed.

ROBERTS, MICHAEL (1902–1948)

Critique of Poetry. *Cape (1934).*
The Modern Mind. *Faber (1937).*

A gifted poet and critic who first edited a collection of poetry by his
young contemporaries (*New Signatures*, 1932).

RUSSELL, BERTRAND

Unpopular Essays. *Allen & Unwin (1950). 8s. 6d.*

Unpopular because the author has been told that much of his writing
annoys a number of people or is too difficult for them. A pleasant joke,
for all of the essays in this volume will be valued by the promisingly large
public who do not like to miss any non-mathematical word the great
philosopher writes. It contains an amusing and just 'self obituary'
contributed to a *Times* happily not yet published.

RUSSELL, LEONARD (Editor)

The English Wits. *Hutchinson (1940). 8s. 6d.*

Sparkling contributions by James Agate, Desmond MacCarthy, D. B.
Wyndham Lewis and others in which the glitter and gaiety of some famous
legal and literary wits is admirably conveyed by comment and anecdote.

RYLANDS, George W. H.

Words and Poetry. *Hogarth Press (1927).*

A remarkably interesting essay in the nature of poetry studying the almost magical effect of some words in the minds of the great poets. The principal examples are drawn from Shakespeare.

SANTAYANA, George

Little Essays Drawn from the Writings of George Santayana by Logan Pearsall Smith. *Constable (1920).*

SAVAGE, Derek S.

The Personal Principle. *Routledge (1944).*

Studies in modern poetry.

The Withered Branch. *Eyre & Spottiswoode (1950). 10s. 6d.*

New studies in the modern novel: Hemingway, E. M. Forster, Virginia Woolf, Aldous Huxley, James Joyce and Margiad Evans.

SCOTT-JAMES, R. A.

Fifty Years of English Literature: 1900–1950. *Longmans (1951). 15s.*
The Making of Literature. *Secker & Warburg (1928), 1948. 10s. 6d.*

SHAW, G. Bernard (1856–1950)

Doctor's Delusions. *Constable (1932), 1949. 7s. 6d.*

Contains something about doctor's delusions, crude criminology and sham education.

London Music in 1888–9. *Constable (1932), 1937. 7s. 6d.*

'As heard by Corno di Bassetto (later known as Bernard Shaw) with further autobiographical particulars and a portrait.'

Major Critical Essays. *Constable (1932). 7s. 6d.*

The Quintessence of Ibsenism (1891); *The Perfect Wagnerite* (1898); and *The Sanity of Art* (1895).

Music in London, 1890–94. *3 vols. Constable. Revised and reprinted for the standard edition (1932), 1949. 7s. 6d. each.*

Weekly contributions to *The World.*

Our Theatres in the 'Nineties. *3 vols. Constable (1932). 7s. 6d. each.*

For the standard edition the earlier American selection made by James Huneker entitled *Dramatic Opinions and Essays* (2 vols., 1907) was revised and enlarged. They were originally notices contributed to *The Saturday Review,* 1895–1898.

Pen Portraits and Reviews. *Constable (1932). 7s. 6d.*

SINCLAIR, Robert

Metropolitan Man: the future of the English. *Allen & Unwin (1937).*

SITWELL, Constance
Flowers and Elephants. *Cape (1930).*
Foreword by E. M. Forster.

SITWELL, Edith
Aspects of Modern Poetry. *Duckworth (1943).*

SITWELL, Sir Osbert and BARTON, Margaret (Editors)
Sober Truth. *Duckworth (1930). New edition, Macdonald (1944).*
'A collection of nineteenth-century episodes, fantastic, grotesque and mysterious.' The extracts are from contemporary sources. Introduction by Sir Osbert Sitwell.

SITWELL, Sacheverell
The Hunters and the Hunted. *Macmillan (1947). 15s.*
Sacred and Profane Love. *Faber (1940).*
Splendours and Miseries. *Faber (1943). 18s.*

SPENDER, Stephen
The Destructive Element; literary criticism. *Cape (1935).*

STEVENSON, J. A. R.
The Din of a Smithy. *Chapman & Hall (1932).*
School edition, C.U.P., 1936. 5s.

STEVENSON, R. A. M. (1847–1900)
The Art of Velasquez. *Bell (1895). 45s. Cheaper edition, 1898.*
The author was a cousin of R.L.S. His book was considered by D. S. MacColl to be 'the most substantial contribution to the theory and defence of modern painting since Ruskin.'

STRACHEY, John
Post D: experiences of an air-raid warden. *Gollancz (1941). 3s. 9d.*
Of all the books on what happened after any air raid during 1940–1945 this one lingers most in the mind as a work of permanent value.

STREET, A. G.
In His Own Country. *Eyre & Spottiswoode (1950). 15s.*
A comprehensive selection made by the author from 22 of his books published between 1934 and 1945. This illustrated collection is arranged under group headings covering aspects of farming and country life.
Wheat and Chaff. *Faber (1950). 12s. 6d.*
The author's chosen passages from three books of broadcast talks: *Hedge Trimmings* (1932); *Country Days* (1933); and *Thinking Aloud* (1934).

STRONG, L. A. G.
Shake Hands and Come Out Fighting. *Chapman & Hall (1938), 1953. 9s. 6d.*
Great days in the ring recalled in vigorous and enjoyable prose.

SWINNERTON, Frank

The Georgian Literary Scene, 1910–1935. *Hutchinson (1935). Revised edition, 1950. 15s. Earlier edition, reprinted 1938 in Everyman's Library. Dent, 5s.*

Tokefield Papers Old and New. *Hamish Hamilton (1949). 10s. 6d.*

Pleasant essays in appreciation originally published by Secker (*Tokefield Papers*, 1927) and for the new edition revised and enlarged.

THOMAS, Sir William Beach

A Countryman's Creed. *Michael Joseph (1946).*
A Year in the Country. *Wingate (1950). 12s. 6d.*

The naturalist's colleague on the *Observer*, J. C. Trewin, has selected here some of the best contributions, and arranged them as a narrative following the course of a year. There are pleasant illustrations by Philip Gough.

THURBER, James

My Life and Hard Times; and, The Owl in the Attic.
Hamish Hamilton (1950). 7s. 6d.

Modern classics of American satire and humour, with the author's devastating drawings showing man (and his woman) frequently at their worst, and dogs at their best. The two were published separately in 1933 and 1931 respectively. See also *The Cream of Thurber*, Hamish Hamilton (1939) for a delightful volume skimming the best from four books.

TILLYARD, E. M. W.

Poetry Direct and Oblique. *Chatto (1934). Revised edition, 1945. 7s. 6d.*

'Direct' poetry is that written closely to a subject; 'oblique' poetry that which is remote from its subject, and may be regarded as a crystallization of the poet's thoughts.

TODD, Ruthven

Tracks in the Snow. *Grey Walls Press (1946). 12s. 6d.*

Studies in Blake, Fuseli, Martin and others.

TREVELYAN, G. M.

Clio, a Muse; and other essays. *Longmans (1930). 10s. 6d.*

The essay on *The Present Position of History* is the title essay written again in maturity.

TURNER, E. S.

Boys Will be Boys. *Michael Joseph (1948).*

An amusing survey of magazines produced for boys from the days of the early 'blood and thunder' weeklies of about 1850 to the present time. Sexton Blake, Billy Bunter in Frank Richards's seemingly immortal *Magnet* stories, and the *B.O.P.*; these are all described with lively comment and quotation, and sometimes with reproductions of the original illustrations.

VINES, SHERARD

100 Years of English Literature. *Duckworth (1950). 21s.*

A record and critical commentary on books first published between about 1830 and 1940.

WEEKLEY, ERNEST

The English Language.
> *Benn (1928). New edition, Andre Deutsch, 1952. 9s. 6d.*

Jack and Jill. *Murray (1948). 7s. 6d.*
A study in Christian names.

The Romance of Words. *Murray (1912).*
> *Reprinted in Guild Books, 1949. 1s. 6d.*

Words Ancient and Modern. *Murray (1947). 7s. 6d.*

WEST, REBECCA

The Strange Necessity: essays. *Cape (1928).*

WILSON, EDMUND

Axel's Castle. *Scribner (1931). 18s.*

One of the most influential volumes of critical essays of the century by America's foremost literary critic.

The Triple Thinkers. *O.U.P. (1938). New edition, Lehmann, 1952. 15s.*

These twelve (originally ten) essays on literary subjects may now be supplemented by a recent collection of the writer's best work on the literary output of the twenties and thirties: *The Shores of Light*, W. H. Allen (1952). 25s.

WILSON, RICHARD ALBERT

The Miraculous Birth of Language. *Dent (1937). 10s. 6d.*

A theory of the growth of language much admired by Bernard Shaw who commends it, with his own theories added in a 50,000 word preface.

WITHERS, PERCY

Friends in Solitude. *Cape (1923).*
In a Cumberland Dale. *Cape (1933).*

Both volumes have introductions by Lascelles Abercrombie. The latter volume was first published in 1914 by Grant Richards.

YOUNG, ANDREW

A Prospect of Flowers. *Cape (1945). 10s. 6d.*
A Retrospect of Flowers. *Cape (1950). 10s. 6d.*

A poet's flower books in which botany is enticingly mingled with the English poets' tribute to floral beauty. The first has a fine frontispiece by John Nash.

ANTHOLOGIES OF PROSE
(ARRANGED UNDER EDITORS)

ALDINGTON, RICHARD
The Religion of Beauty. *Heinemann (1950). 12s. 6d.*
Extracts from the writings of over one hundred authors most of whom flourished at the end of the nineteenth century. The selections are in prose and verse.

ARMSTRONG, MARTIN
The Major Pleasures of Life. *Gollancz (1934).*

BELL, ADRIAN
The Open Air: an anthology of English country life.
Faber (1936), 1949. 10s. 6d.
The later edition has wood engraving illustrations by Reynolds Stone. Most of the authors are nineteenth and twentieth century.

THE ENGLISH ASSOCIATION
English Essays of To-day. *O.U.P. (1936). 6s.*

GOLLANCZ, VICTOR
A Year of Grace: chosen to express a mood about God and man.
Gollancz (1950). 12s. 6d.
Man in contemplation of God. There is more prose than poetry, but the latter includes some contemporaries.

INWARDS, RICHARD (1840–1937)
Weather Lore. *(1869.) 4th revised edition by* E. L. HAWKE.
Rider (for the Royal Meteorological Society). (1950.) 15s.
The third edition (1898) was the last Inward edited for although he lived nearly forty years after, his other interests were too strong to allow him to give the time to add to this fascinating collection of sayings, writings, and odds and ends about weather.

JACKSON, HOLBROOK (1874–1948)
A Bookman's Holiday. *Faber (1945). 10s. 6d.*
A bibliomaniac's beano. A delectable little scrapbook. Books and authors on authors and books. You can read here what so-and-so thought of Macaulay, and next to this what Macaulay thought of so-and-so. 'A recreation for book lovers.'

KINGSMILL, HUGH (1889–1949)
Invective and Abuse. *Eyre & Spottiswoode (1945).*

LOCKITT, C. H.
The Art of the Essayist. *Longmans (1949). 3s. 6d.*
An introduction and forty essays showing the development of the form from Bacon to the twentieth century.

MACAULAY, Rose
The Minor Pleasures of Life. *Gollancz (1934).*
There are some poems and prose extracts from English and foreign literature in translation. No contemporary authors are included.

Personal Pleasures. *Gollancz (1935).*

READ, Herbert and DOBRÉE, Bonamy
The London Book of English Prose.
Eyre & Spottiswoode (1932), 1949. 12s. 6d.
An introduction, followed by extracts from English writers from Malory to Peter Quennell, arranged in groups: autobiography and Journals; Letters; Scientific; Philosophy; Law; Strategy and Tactics; Sport; Narrative; etc.

For details of books by other twentieth century writers see also in *An English Library* under J. C. Bailey; Maurice Baring; Arnold Bennett; J. B. Beresford; A. C. Bradley; A. H. Bullen; R. W. Chambers; G. K. Chesterton; Arthur Clutton-Brock; H. C. Colles; Ernest de Selincourt; W. Macneile Dixon; J. H. Driberg; Havelock Ellis; Oliver Elton; Lord Ernle; Ford Madox Ford; Roger Fry; Edward Garnett; Eric Gill; G. S. Gordon; Sir Edmund Gosse; Harley Granville-Barker; Sir William H. Hadow; Maurice Hewlett; J. W. Hills; W. H. Hudson; W. P. Ker; John Maynard Keynes; Stephen Leacock; Vernon Lee; J. W. Mackail; G. H. Mair; Alice Meynell; C. E. Montague; H. W. Nevinson; J. S. Phillimore; Sir Arthur Quiller-Couch; Sir Walter Raleigh; Forrest Reid; George Saintsbury; Geoffrey Scott; Logan Pearsall Smith; Lytton Strachey; George Sturt; Arthur Symons; T. E. Welby; Charles Whibley; Virginia Woolf; H. C. K. Wyld. Details of thirty other anthologies of English prose will also be found in the relevant section of that work.

FICTION IN SHORT STORIES

In the 'twenties there used to be published every year a masterly selection of the best English and American short stories written or published in periodicals during the twelve months preceding. Edited by E. H. O'Brien (1890–1941) they did much to attract the attention of readers to a form of fiction which at one time had relatively few admirers. With volumes of poetry, short stories collected in volume format were expected barely to pay their way.

The cessation of O'Brien's volumes left a gap which has been filled in part by Woodrow Wyatt's annual selections entitled *English Story*. Volume x was published in 1950, Collins, 8*s.* 6*d.* The former prejudice of the great fiction reading public against short stories has disappeared now and contemporary English and American literature has many brilliant practitioners of the art. Many daily newspapers 'feature' a short story; many have been adapted into excellent films; some few expanded into full-length plays.

The greatest living English short story writer after Somerset Maugham, has also written one of the few modern books on his craft, and readers will find in *The Modern Short Story*, by H. E. Bates, Nelson (1945), 6*s.*, a brief, but most interesting discussion of current technique and influences.

The most notable series of short stories drawn from many authors, and not confined by a time limit beyond that imposed by the fact that most of those selected have been written in the last quarter of a century, is the Faber & Faber collection of volumes. Some of these excellent volumes are the authors' own selections of their best stories in a particular category: there are, for example, volumes entitled *My Funniest Story*; *My Best Mystery Story*; *My Best Detective Story*; *My Naughtiest Story*, and so on. Other volumes have a compiler's choice of notable stories drawn from various authors writing on a particular theme, such as Norman Macmillan's selection of *Best Flying Stories*; Ann Ridler's selection of *Best Ghost Stories*; the late Peter Cheyney's *Best Stories of the Underworld*, etc. There are at present thirty-four of these volumes, published at prices ranging from 8*s.* 6*d.* to 12*s.* 6*d.* Attention should be called to a promising new series in John Pudney's *Pick of To-Day's Short Stories*, two volumes of which have been published, 1949 and 1950, Odhams Press, 8*s.* 6*d.* each. A pleasant 'County' group came under the editorship of Denys Val Baker, in *One and All: a Selection of Cornish Short Stories*, Museum Press (1951), 9*s.* 6*d.* The authors drawn upon were Charles Lee of the old school; with earlier examples from R. S. Hawker, S. Baring Gould; living writers such as A. L. Rowse, and stories about Cornwall written by 'foreigners'.

Some other collections are noted below, under their editors, including a distinguished newcomer under the editorship of the publisher John Lehmann.

ARMSTRONG, MARTIN
Selected Stories. *Cape (1951). 10s. 6d.*

BARKER, A. L.
Innocents. *Hogarth Press (1947). 7s. 6d.*
'Variations on a Theme' which won for this young author the Somerset Maugham Award.

BATES, H. E.
The Bride Comes to Evensford, and other tales. *Cape (1949). 9s.*
Cut and Come Again. *Cape (1935), 1951. 10s. 6d.*
Day's End. *Cape (1928), 1950. 8s. 6d.*
My Uncle Silas. *Cape (1939), 1950. 8s. 6d.*
In this character Bates has created as likeable an old rogue as there is in modern literature.

Thirty-One Selected Tales. *Cape (1947). 10s. 6d.*
Twenty Tales. *Cape (1951). 10s. 6d.*
The Woman Who Had Imagination. *Cape (1934). 10s. 6d.*
The above is a representative selection of short stories by the greatest master of the short story in English of the generations of writers who followed Kipling and the earlier Somerset Maugham. Some of his best work, among which the compiler would place *The Bridge* and *The Kimono*, is with the best in the language. The last volume contains two other great stories in *A German Idyll*, and *The Death of Uncle Silas*.

BEACHCROFT, T. O.
Collected Stories. *Lane (1946). 5s.*
Being thirty-one stories from three volumes: *A Young Man in a Hurry* (1934); *You Must Break Out Sometimes* (1936); and *The Parents Left Alone* (1940). Another volume was *Asking For Trouble*, Lane (1946), 7s. 6d.

BELLOC, HILAIRE
Stories, Essays and Poems.
Dent (1938), 1950. 5s. (Everyman's Library.)

BENSON, THEODORA
Best Stories. *Faber (1940).*

BIBESCO, ELIZABETH (–1945)
Haven. *James Barrie (1951). 12s. 6d.*
Short stories, poems and aphorisms. Preface by Elizabeth Bowen. '*Red Hair* is substantial: it ranks with the La Perronière Letters (which has a grimness worthy of Maupassant. . .) as Elizabeth Bibesco's most acute, finished work.' (Elizabeth Bowen.)

BLACKWOOD, ALGERNON (1869–1952)
The Empty House. *Richards Press (1948). 7s. 6d.*
One of the many volumes by a master of the supernatural and macabre who has entertained thousands of listeners as well as readers with his own readings on the air.

BLIXEN, KAREN
Seven Gothic Tales. *Putnam (1934), 1951. 10s. 6d.*

BONE, DAVID W.
The Brassbounder. *Duckworth (1910). Revised edition, 1949. 7s. 6d.*
In the old days an apprentice on a sailing ship was known ironically as a 'Brassbounder', because he usually came aboard for his first voyage in a smart brassbound uniform. This was soon discarded for workaday clothes. There is probably more fact than fiction in this almost autobiographical volume.

BOTTOME, PHYLLIS
Innocence and Experience. *Faber (1947). 8s. 6d.*

BOWEN, ELIZABETH
The Cat Jumps. *(1934.) Cape, 1949. 7s. 6d.*
The Demon Lover. *Cape (1945), 1950. 7s. 6d.*
Encounters. *Sidgwick & Jackson (1923), 1949. 8s. 6d.*
Look At All Those Roses. *Cape (1941), 1951. 8s. 6d.*

BROWN, HILTON (Editor)
Best Broadcast Stories. *Faber (1944). 9s. 6d.*

BULLETT, GERALD
Twenty-Four-Tales. *Dent (1938).*
The author's choice from his four earlier books then out of print, together with five new tales.

BURKE, THOMAS (1886–1946)
Best Stories. *Selected with an introduction by John Gawsworth.*
Phoenix House (1950), 1952. 5s.
The best writer of stories of London's East End and Chinatown. His most famous book was *Limehouse Nights* published by Cassell (1916).

CHAPLIN, SID
The Leaping Lad, and other stories. *Phoenix House (1947), 1949. 5s.*
The author is a miner and this, his first collection of short stories, attracted praise from the discriminating and brought him recognition in the shape of an *Atlantic Award*.

CONNOLLY, CYRIL (Editor)

Horizon Stories. *Faber (1943). 8s. 6d.*

The gifted editor of the monthly magazine *Horizon* which had such a heartening success during the dark days of the war, has selected from the pages of his publication the cream of the many excellent stories contributed to it by authors known and new.

COPPARD, A. E.

The Black Dog, and other short stories. *Cape (1923), 1949. 9s. 6d.*

Eighteen fine examples, of which one, *Tamil*, is as good as anything in *The Arabian Nights Entertainments*.

Selected Tales. *Cape (1946). 9s. 6d.*

In 1931 there was an omnibus volume called *Fares Please*. This was three separate volumes in one: *The Black Dog*; *Silver Circus* (1928); and *The Field of Mustard* (1926). A new collection of twenty-one of his stories of the supernatural is *Fearful Pleasures*, Peter Nevill (1952), 11s. 6d.

COWARD, NOEL

Star Quality. *Heinemann (1950). 10s. 6d.*
To Step Aside; seven short stories. *Heinemann (1939).*

DE LA MARE, WALTER

Best Stories. *Faber (1942). 8s. 6d.*

The author's own selection of his greatest stories from many volumes, of which *On the Edge* (1930) and *The Connoisseur* (1926) are the most notable.

Stories, Essays and Poems. *Dent (1938), 1950. 5s. (Everyman's Library.)*

DOYLE, LYNN

Ballygullion. *Duckworth (1908). 1924. 6s.*
Green Oranges. *Duckworth (1947), 1950. 8s. 6d.*
The Shake of the Bag. *Duckworth (1939).*

THE ENGLISH ASSOCIATION

Short Stories of Today. *O.U.P. (1939). 6s.*

FORSTER, E. M.

Collected Short Stories. *Sidgwick & Jackson (1948). 12s. 6d.*

The separate volumes entitled *The Celestial Omnibus* and *The Eternal Moment* form the greater part of the collection, and contain some modern masterpieces, of which one, *The Machine Stops*, is surely the most frightening story written in the century that needs its lesson most. Others exhibit that individual quality characteristic of this author to a high degree, in which fantasy is delicately mingled with parable and comedy.

FREEMAN, R. AUSTIN (1862–1943)

Dr. Thorndike Intervenes. *Hodder & Stoughton (1933), 1951. 6s.*
The Famous Cases of Doctor Thorndike. *Hodder & Stoughton (1929), 1952.*
18s.
An omnibus volume of 1088 pages.

GREENE, GRAHAM

Nineteen Stories. *Heinemann (1947).*

One of these, *The Basement Room*, good as it is, was transmuted into an
even better film, the notable *The Fallen Idol*. The other great film made
from a Graham Greene scenario, *The Third Man*, was written specially
for production, and has been published only in the original version
written for film treatment together with the film version of *The Fallen
Idol*, Heinemann (1950), 6s.

GUNN, NEIL M.

The White Hour and other stories. *Faber (1950). 9s. 6d.*

A selection made by the author; there are twenty-six stories contributed
over twenty years to magazines, and some from a volume entitled *Hidden
Doors*, published in 1929.

HANLEY, JAMES

Half an Eye: an omnibus of sea stories. *Lane (1937).*
A Walk in the Wilderness. *Phoenix House (1950). 8s. 6d.*

Five short stories, all of which, like the title story, have sad themes; the
loneliness of the aged; the sailor returning 'home' to no home; the terribly
scarred warrior's ghastly first walk in the wilderness of everyday life
among luckier people. All have a quality springing from the author's
humanity, which makes them memorable.

HEMINGWAY, ERNEST

The Essential Hemingway. *Cape (1947). 15s.*

The whole of the novel *Fiesta* is included, together with extracts from
A Farewell to Arms, To Have and Have Not, and *For Whom the Bell Tolls*;
twenty-six of the best short stories; and the epilogue from *Death in the
Afternoon.*

The First Forty-Nine Stories. *Cape (1939), 1950. 10s. 6d.*
Selected Stories. *Cape (1939), 1951. 4s. 6d. (New Traveller's Library.)*
Nineteen stories and a preface.

HOLME, CONSTANCE

The Wisdom of the Simple, and other short stories.
O.U.P. (1937). 5s. (World's Classics.)

HUXLEY, ALDOUS

Brief Candles. *Chatto (1930). 7s. 6d.*
Little Mexican. *Chatto (1924). 7s. 6d.*

Limbo. *Chatto (1920). 7s. 6d.*
Mortal Coils. *Chatto (1922). 7s. 6d.*
Two or Three Graces. *Chatto (1926). 7s. 6d.*

The title story, which is a 'long-short', is one of the best things Huxley has written; it exhibits his genius in an unexpectedly tender mood.

KAVAN, ANNA

Asylum Piece, and other stories. *Cape (1940).*

LARDNER, RING (1885–1933)

Round Up. *Williams & Norgate (1929).*

Stories with a strictly national American flavour. Some are severely satirical about American life and character.

LAVIN, MARY

The Long Ago, and other stories. *Michael Joseph (1944).*
Tales from Bective Bridge. *Michael Joseph (1943). 8s. 6d.*

LEHMANN, JOHN (Editor)

English Stories from New Writing. *Lehmann (1951). 10s. 6d.*

Twenty-four distinguished stories contributed to the literary magazine *New Writing*, between 1936 and 1948.

LEWIS, ALUN (1915–1944)

The Last Inspection, and other stories. *Allen & Unwin (1942). 7s. 6d.*

Twenty-three stories by a young soldier-poet; eighteen of them concern army life in the 1940's.

MACHEN, ARTHUR (1863–1947)

Tales of Horror and the Supernatural. *Richards Press (1948). 12s. 6d.*

Stories gathered from famous books of a previous generation's first delight: *The Great God Pan* (1894); and *The Terror* (1917). The collection has a long critical and biographical introduction by Philip Van Doren Stern.

McLAVERTY, MICHAEL

The Game Cock, and other short stories. *Cape (1949). 9s.*

MACLAREN-ROSS, J.

The Stuff to Give the Troops. *Cape (1944).*

When they first appeared, these brief, skilful sketches of army life appeared so authentic and were so humorously told that they seemed worthy of more than a brief existence.

MANHOOD, H. A.

Selected Stories. *Cape (1947). 5s.*

A distinguished volume, selected from the author's published work from 1928 to 1944. *Nightseed* (1928) and *Fierce and Gentle* (1935) from the same publisher were among the best of their years.

MAUGHAM, W. Somerset
Complete Short Stories. *3 vols. Heinemann (1951). 15s. each.*
A new edition of all the work in this form of the greatest short story writer of the century, with a preface by the author. He has grouped his stories so as to bring the Malayan scenes together. The collection supersedes *Altogether* (1934), a one-volume omnibus.

Ashenden; or, The British Agent. *Heinemann (1928). 8s. 6d.*
Creatures of Circumstance. *Heinemann (1947). 8s. 6d.*
The Mixture as Before. *Heinemann (1940).*

MEYNELL, Viola
Follow Thy Fair Sun. *Cape (1935).*
Kissing the Rod, and other short stories. *Cape (1937).*

MITCHISON, Naomi
Black Sparta. *Cape (1928). 5s.*
When the Bough Breaks. *Cape (1924). 5s.*

MORDAUNT, Elinor
Traveller's Pack. *Dent-Secker (1934).*

O'CONNOR, Frank
Crab Apple Jelly. *Macmillan (1944).*

O'DONNELL, Peadar
Islanders. *Cape (1927).*

O'FAOLAIN, Sean
A Midsummer Night Madness. *Cape (1932).*
A Nest of Simple Folk. *Cape (1933).*
A Purse of Coppers. *Cape (1937).*
Teresa, and other stories. *Cape (1947). 7s. 6d.*
Introduced in the first volume by Edward Garnett.

O'FLAHERTY, Liam
Short Stories. *Cape (1949). 10s. 6d.*
The best of many fine volumes of Irish stories gathered together.

ONIONS, Oliver
Collected Ghost Stories. *Nicholson & Watson (1935).*
The best of the separate volumes was *Widdershins* (Secker, 1911) which contained the famous *The Beckoning Fair One.* This is one of the best ghost stories in twentieth-century literature.

PARKER, Dorothy
The Best of Dorothy Parker. *Methuen (1952). 10s. 6d.*
'The wittiest woman in America' of the thirties has some neat, sharp studies in satire in her three separate volumes from which this new selection has been made.

PHILLPOTTS, EDEN
The Human Boy. *Methuen (1899).*

One would expect stories of this type to have lost their savour after fifty years; not so: here are smiling exploits of an earlier and more amusing 'William'. *The Human Boy and the War* (1916) and *The Human Boy's Diary* (1924) were once available with the first volume in an omnibus which may still be obtained secondhand.

PLOMER, WILLIAM
The Case is Altered. *Hogarth Press (1935), 1949. 8s. 6d.*
Four Countries. *Cape (1949). 10s. 6d.*

A selection of short stories from *I Speak of Africa* (1927); *Paper Houses* (1929); and *The Child of Queen Victoria* (1933).

PORTER, KATHERINE ANNE
Flowering Judas. *Cape (1936).*
The Leaning Tower. *Cape (1945), 1950. 7s. 6d.*

POWYS, T. F.
Bottle's Path and other stories. *Chatto (1946).*
The Left Leg. *Chatto (1923).*

Two volumes of the many written by an author with an individual style, half parable, half anecdote, in which primitive peasants are the chief characters.

PRITCHETT, V. S.
It May Never Happen. *Chatto (1945). 5s.*

The conversational brevity of tap-room gossip is used skilfully enough in many of these stories, some of which are noteworthy, but none of which quite reaches the high level of that masterpiece of grim amusement *A Sense of Humour* to be found in *Nothing Like Leather*, Chatto (1935).

QUEEN, ELLERY
Case Book. *Gollancz (1950). 8s. 6d.*

637 pages of excellent detection and crime, being an omnibus of *The Adventures of Ellery Queen* (1935); *The New Adventures of E.Q.* (1940); *Problems in Deduction*; fifteen short stories, a short novel (*The Lamp of God*) and a group of four sports mysteries.

QUEEN, ELLERY (Editor)
Rogues Gallery: the great criminals of modern fiction.
    Faber (1947). 10s. 6d.

The ideal bedside book, being a selection by the expert in fictional crime of some of the finest examples to be found in the files of magazines and in famous or half-forgotten books. Every tale reaches a very high level of excitement, ingenuity and suspense.

RUNYON, DAMON (1880–1949)

All This and That. *Constable (1950). 12s. 6d.*

Thirty-nine of these unusual anecdotes in the patois and present tense of Broadway spivs, with a memoir by Clark Kinnaird. None of the stories had appeared in Great Britain before this collection.

Runyon on Broadway. *Constable (1950). 12s. 6d.*

An omnibus of 720 pages containing all the stories from *More Than Somewhat* (1937); *Furthermore*; and *Take It Away*, with an introduction by E. C. Bentley, and portrait and pictures drawn by Nicolas Bentley.

SAROYAN, WILLIAM

Best Stories. *Faber (1942). 8s. 6d.*

These are unlike any other living American's work. Separately, the two volumes which gave him a public in this country were *The Daring Young Man on the Flying Trapeze*, Faber (1934), 1944, 5s.; and *My Name is Aram*, Faber (1941), 7s. 6d. A selection, *The Insurance Salesman*, and other stories is available in the prose section of *Sesame Books*, Faber (1941), 3s. 6d.

SAYERS, DOROTHY L.

Hangman's Holiday and other stories. *Gollancz (1933). 3s. 6d.*

Only one of a very large output of detective stories which have a distinctive place of their own.

SAYERS, DOROTHY L. (Editor)

Great Short Stories of Detection, Mystery and Horror.
Formerly 3 series (1931–1939). Now reissued in 6 parts.
Gollancz (1952). 6s. 6d. each.

A standard and popular collection.

SHAW, G. BERNARD (1856–1950)

The Black Girl, and some lesser tales.
Woodcuts by John Farleigh, with a preface by the author.
Constable (1950). 7s. 6d.

SITWELL, SIR OSBERT

Collected Stories. *Macmillan (1953). 25s.*
Open the Door. *Macmillan (1941). 7s. 6d.*

Strange hauntings and happenings in stories of unusual quality and style.

Triple Fugue, and other stories. *Duckworth (1924). Penguin Books. 1940. 1s. 6d.*

SPENDER, STEPHEN

The Burning Cactus. *Faber (1936).*

STRONG, L. A. G.
The Travellers. *Methuen (1945). 8s. 6d.*
A gathering of thirty of the best stories from many volumes, including the Rabelaisian tale of the drunken inn-keeper who went to live with the gypsies for a bit. The volume was awarded the James Tait Black Memorial Prize. It has now been followed by *Darling Tom, and other Stories,* Methuen, 1952. 10s. 6d.

SWINTON, SIR ERNEST D.
The Green Curve Omnibus. *Faber (1942).*
The original *Green Curve* volume, by 'Ole-Luk-Oie', was published in 1909.

VERNÈDE, ROBERT ERNEST (1875–1917)
The Port Allington Stories, and others. *Heinemann (1921).*
Edward Arnold (1932), 1950. 4s. 6d.
The reprint is in *The Kingfisher Library* pocket series.

VICKERS, ROY
The Department of Dead Ends: short stories of crime.
Faber (1949). 9s. 6d.
These have a quality of their own, being stories of misdeeds and murder in which the clues left are so slender or complicated that the author's detectives almost give up the cases in despair, but not quite.

WARNER, SYLVIA TOWNSEND
The Museum of Cheats, and other stories. *Chatto (1947). 5s.*
Wit, grace and gentle satire.

WATTS, STEPHEN
The Pale Horse, and other stories. *Macmillan (1943).*

WELCH, DENTON (1917–1948)
Brave and Cruel. *Hamish Hamilton (1949). 8s. 6d.*
An exciting display of a very remarkable talent by a brave young man indeed, whom life treated cruelly. *A Last Sheaf*, Lehmann (1951), 12s. 6d., contains nearly all his other work in this form, together with his poems and reproductions of some of his pictures.

WELTY, EUDORA
A Curtain of Green. *Lane (1943).*
Recommended in an introduction by Katherine Anne Porter.

WEST, REBECCA
The Harsh Voice. *Cape (1935), 1950. 6s.*
Four short novels.

WHITAKER, MALACHI

Selected Stories. *Cape (1949). 9s. 6d.*

Frost in April, Cape (1929) was the early collection which attracted much attention and praise.

WILSON, ANGUS

The Wrong Set, and other stories. *Secker & Warburg (1949). 9s. 6d.*

This volume by a newcomer to the art of the short story achieved immediate success. It was followed by *Such Darling Dodos*, Secker & Warburg (1950), 9s. 6d. The dominant note in both collections is satirical.

NOVELS

Writing for publication in book form having now become an industry it is inevitable that the novel should suffer more than other forms of literature from over-production, repetition and mediocre imitation of successful types of the immediate past. The characteristics of all modern industry include the production in large numbers of an article for which there is either a known market to be exploited or a market which can be created by skilful advertisement. Hence it is not surprising to find the task of selecting a few hundred from many thousands of novels depending more on chance acquaintance and recommendation than it should. The late George Saintsbury, who had probably read more novels than any other man of letters of his time, wrote in a letter to Norman Douglas, that in forty years of reading and reviewing he had 'come across just two new novelists who have given me something that I can recommend to a friend'. The author of *South Wind*, he concluded, 'is the second in order of time, not rank'.

Such austerity can find no place here; one can only hope that the astringent critic's first choice, unknown, alas, does find itself in the pages that follow. These give details of the novels which the compiler remembers with pleasure; some, unread as yet by him, which have been offered by other readers whose judgement he has learned to respect; others which have been skimmed with sufficient attention to enable their qualities to be savoured with relish; yet others which have attracted in their time the praise of critics who do their best day by day to ensure that merit is noticed and the worthy recommended to readers of taste and discrimination.

The competence of the commercial novelist and the sometimes enormous financial rewards reaped by his skill in his art, must not be allowed to prejudice a selector in his judgement if his list is to be truly representative of the output in fiction during the last fifty years. Best-sellers of the past have become established as classics; many best-sellers of contemporary fiction are far superior to older novels which are kept alive for antiquarian interests more than for their literary qualities.

The interesting task of assessment will go on generation by generation. Already we find in critical monographs such as *The English Novelists Series*, and in the British Council's supplements to *British Book News*, critics of the younger generations assessing the qualities of novelists still at work or only recently dead. The former series, published by Arthur Barker at 7s. 6d. each, includes a first-rate study of J. M. Barrie, a brilliant little book on Ronald Firbank, and an interesting attempt to place the work of that strange genius D. H. Lawrence in its proper perspective.

Some studies of the novel and of contemporary fiction will be found listed in the preceding section of Essays and Belles Lettres, notably those by E. M. Forster, Robert Liddell, Sean O'Faolain, Edwin Muir, V. S. Pritchett, and Percy Lubbock; the 1951 Annual Lecture of the National

Book League was devoted to a personal, subjective discussion of the art of fiction by its most distinguished living practitioner, W. Somerset Maugham; and in 1948 the poet and sociologist, Alex Comfort, gave us a brief but penetrating essay in his *The Novel and Our Time*, published by Phoenix House, 5s.

A strangely puritanical mistrust of fiction is more widespread among readers than many suppose. A recent discussion by members of a youth club taking part in a radio programme, gave one the impression that even among teen-agers of the present day there are some who assuage their thirst for 'facts' and 'knowledge' by avoiding fiction and devoting their whole reading time to biographies and travellers' tales. A writer may produce a documentary play or a sociological essay, and the reading of his books will be recorded by librarians as worthy efforts on the part of their public to take home 'non-fiction'; let the same writer put the same arguments and reasoning into fictional form, and the issue of his book to public library readers will often almost be a matter of apology by the librarian to his committee, who will debate whether it is a proper use of public money to provide 'mere fiction' for their fellow-citizens.

But the novel is undoubtedly the characteristic form of literature of our time. In spite of the pressure of commercialism great novels are still being written, and in the brief list below there are at least five masterpieces.

ALDINGTON, RICHARD

All Men Are Enemies. *Heinemann (1932). Barker, 1952. 6s.*
The Colonel's Daughter. *Heinemann (1931).*
  Penguin Books. 1939. 1s. 6d.
Death of a Hero. *Heinemann (1929).*
  Penguin Books. 1936. 1s. 6d.

One of the most noteworthy novels to come from the bitterness and frustration engendered in the minds of writers through the 1914–1918 war.

ALLINGHAM, MARGERY

Flowers for the Judge. *Heinemann (1936).*
  Penguin Books. 1944. 1s. 6d.

One of many much admired detective novels by this author.

ASHFORD, DAISY

The Young Visiters; or, Mr. Salteena's Plan. *Chatto (1919), 1951. 4s.*

Artless juvenilia written when the author was a child of nine. The humour and fun was so unforced and charming that in its day it became a best-seller. Indeed many thought it was the work of a clever adult guying 'Ouida'. It still retains its charm and will probably continue to attract many readers. Sir James Barrie introduced it in 1919.

ASHTON, HELEN

William and Dorothy. *Collins (1938). 7s. 6d.*

A sensitive study in fiction on the emotional and artistic relationship between Wordsworth and his sister Dorothy.

AUSTIN, F. BRITTEN

Forty Centuries Look Down. *Eyre & Spottiswoode (1936), 1941.*
The Road to Glory. *Eyre & Spottiswoode (1935), 1942.*

Two military novels strongly recommended by Field-Marshal Viscount Wavell. The first is on Napoleon's campaign in Egypt, the second on his Italian campaign.

BAGNOLD, ENID

National Velvet. *Heinemann (1935), 1950. 7s. 6d.*

A popular book with older children as well as adults; the classic story of a race-horse which may become the modern *Black Beauty*.

BAILEY, H. C.

The Lonely Queen. *Methuen (1911).*

An historical novel portraying with skill and care the first years of girlhood of the Princess Elizabeth, and the first years of her reign as Queen Elizabeth I.

BALCHIN, NIGEL

Mine Own Executioner. *Collins (1945), 1950. 6s.*

A study in psychoanalysis, and the tragedy of a man whose actions after his release from the war are at variance with his surface character.

The Small Back Room. *Collins (1943), 1950. 5s.*

Amongst the best of the novels produced by the war and written during it. The thrilling suspense of the research war-work of those behind the scenes is never allowed to overshadow the authenticity and seriousness of the characters and the subsidiary theme of self-conquest.

BARKER, GEORGE

The Dead Seagull. *Lehmann (1950). 7s. 6d.*

The torment of love and lust is portrayed with a flood of emotion and sexual imagery which repelled some critics. It is the work of a poet.

BARNES, DJUNA

Nightwood. *Faber (1936), 1950. 12s. 6d.*

The reprint contains a preface by T. S. Eliot which he wrote for the first New York edition. He comments on its 'brilliance of wit and characterisation, a quality of horror and doom, very nearly related to Elizabethan tragedy'.

BARON, ALEXANDER

From the City, From the Plough. *Cape (1948). 8s. 6d.*

Probably the best war novel to describe with striking realism the citizen army once more called from useful work and happy lives to service for the nation in uniform.

BATES, H. E.

Charlotte's Row. *Cape (1931), 1950. 9s. 6d.*
The Fallow Land. *Cape (1932), 1950. 8s. 6d.*
House of Women. *Cape (1936), 1951. 8s. 6d.*
The Poacher. *Cape (1935), 1951. 10s. 6d.*
The Purple Plain. *Michael Joseph (1947). 6s.*
Spella Ho. *Cape (1938), 1950. 10s. 6d.*
The Two Sisters. *Cape (1926), 1950. 8s. 6d.*

From *The Two Sisters* till the war made him 'Flying-Officer X' this gifted writer produced a remarkable number of distinguished novels and stories in which characters and scenes are nearly always drawn from English country towns and lonely farms. The experiences of war changed the scenes to Burma, to France and elsewhere, but the tenderness of his approach to men and women is a quality common to all his books.

BATES, RALPH

The Olive Field. *Cape (1936). 7s. 6d.*

BEERBOHM, SIR MAX

The Dreadful Dragon of Hay Hill. *Heinemann (1931).*
The Happy Hypocrite. *Lane (1897), 1946. 4s. 6d.*

Described as 'a fantastical allegory'.

Zuleika Dobson. *Heinemann (1911). New edition, 1947. 10s. 6d.*

Unique satire; delightful wit. The fable of another Helen, this time of Oxford, is told with complete realism. An Edwardian masterpiece which will never grow old, but may eventually be accepted as the kind of invention founded on truth. It will then be as immortal as Robin Hood and Dick Turpin.

BELL, ADRIAN

Corduroy *(1930).* **Silver Ley** *(1931).* **The Cherry Tree** *(1932).*
Lane. 6s. each.

A country-farmer's trilogy, once issued together in an omnibus. There are five other novels of a similar character and quality.

BENTLEY, E. C.

Trent's Last Case. *(1913.) Dent, 1950. 6s.*

Once described as an 'epochal' detective story, and likely to remain a permanent classic of this form. Its successors have their admirers too: *Trent's Own Case* (with H. W. Allen), (Constable, 1936); and *Trent Intervenes*, Nelson (1938).

BENTLEY, PHYLLIS

A Modern Tragedy. *Gollancz (1934).*

BERKELEY, Anthony

Trial and Error. *Hodder (1937). Penguin Books. 1947. 1s. 6d.*

One of many brilliant detective novels, by an author of famous books under another name. His output is all on a high level: many readers think *The Poisoned Chocolates Case* (Collins, 1929) is his best.

BILLANY, Dan (1913–1945)

The Trap. *Faber (1950). 10s. 6d.*

A novel of the war, written on active service and whilst in a prison camp. The author was killed in Italy but the MS. of his novel was forwarded to England by an Italian farmer. It is a remarkable piece of work, and shows the author to have been a born novelist. Air-raid scenes in England; a brief, tender love episode; army life at home and abroad: all these sections are written with unusual power and realism.

BIRMINGHAM, George (1865–1950)

Spanish Gold. *Methuen (1908). 7s.*

Of the many comedies written by this popular author during his long life as clergyman (the Rev. Canon J. O. Hannay) and novelist ('George Birmingham') this is the book that continues to find a public in each generation of readers. *Bindon Parva*, Mills & Boon (1925), and *The Major's Candlesticks*, Methuen (1929) were others of note.

BLACKWOOD, Algernon (1864–1952)

The Education of Uncle Paul. *Macmillan (1909).*
Jimbo. *Macmillan (1909). 3s. 6d.*
A Prisoner in Fairyland. *Macmillan (1913). 3s. 6d.*

BLAKE, George

Down to the Sea. *Collins (1937).*
The Shipbuilders. *Faber (1935).*

BLAKE, Nicholas

The Beast Must Die. *Collins (1938). Lehmann, 1949. 3s. 6d.*
The Smiler With the Knife. *Collins (1939), 1950. 4s. 6d.*
Thou Shell of Death. *Collins (1936), 1950. 4s. 6d.*

Crime and detection stories of ingenuity and style, told by a poet and writer of academic distinction, whose scholarly reputation has been made under his real name of Cecil Day Lewis.

BODEN, F. C.

Miner. *Dent (1932). 4s. 6d.*

BOTTOME, Phyllis

London Pride. *Faber (1941). 6s.*
The Mortal Storm. *Faber (1937). 5s.*
Private Worlds. *Lane (1934). 5s.*

A novel of mental analysis by the biographer of Adler, the famous psychoanalyst.

BOWEN, ELIZABETH

The Death of the Heart. *Gollancz (1938). Cape, 1948. 9s. 6d.*

This poignant study in the emotional life of a young girl, written with great beauty of style and feeling, and having chapters of distinguished high comedy as well as pathos, has surely claims to be placed amongst the best dozen novels of the century.

Friends and Relations. *Constable (1931). Cape, 1951. 8s. 6d.*
The Hotel. *Constable (1927). Cape, 1950. 7s. 6d.*
To the North. *Gollancz (1932). Cape, 1950. 7s. 6d.*

These are now all in the uniform edition in progress from Cape. *The Hotel* is already a period piece, being a story of prosperous English visitors on the Italian Riviera; *To the North* is a delicately told story of a love affair, written mainly from the woman's point of view. Others in the new edition are *The Last September* (1929), Cape, 1948, 7s. 6d.; and *The House in Paris* (1935), Cape, 1949, 9s. 6d., all embellished by Joan Hassall.

BOWEN, MARJORIE (1886–1952)

Dickon. *Hodder (1929).*

A fine novel presenting the character of Richard III in a much more favourable light than is usual in historical fiction.

I Will Maintain. *Methuen (1910). Penguin Books. 1944. 1s. 6d.*
Defender of the Faith. *Methuen (1911).*
God and the King. *Methuen (1911).*

A trilogy on the life and times of William of Orange.

Prince and Heretic. *Methuen (1914).*
'William By the Grace of God.' *Methuen (1916).*

A serious study in two novels on William the Silent.

The Viper of Milan. *Lane (1906). 6s.*

A full-blooded romance of Lombardy in the fourteenth century, and of its Duke, Visconti. The introduction to a reprint of this perennial historical novel rightly gives it a high place in Edwardian literature. For other good novels by this prolific writer see under her pseudonym of 'George Preedy' and under 'Joseph Shearing', although it should be stated that she has never acknowledged the latter, and other guesses have been made.

BOYD, MARTIN

The Lemon Farm. *Dent (1935).*
The Night of the Party. *Dent (1938), 1950. 5s.*

BRIDGE, ANN

Four Part Setting. *Chatto (1939). 6s.*

A good example of the work of this writer, most of whose novels, as in this one, have settings in modern China, of which she has first-hand knowledge.

BRIER, ROYCE
Boy in Blue. *Lane (1937).*
A novel of the American Civil War.

BROMFIELD, LOUIS
The Strange Case of Miss Annie Spragg.
    Cape (1928). Penguin Books. 1935. 1s. 6d.
An early novel by a writer who became a best-seller in his native America and in England with *The Rains Came*, Cassell (1937), 1951, 12s. 6d.

BROPHY, JOHN
Gentleman of Stratford. *Collins (1939), 1946. 8s. 6d.*
Perhaps the best novel ever written in which the chief character is Shakespeare.

Immortal Sergeant. *Collins (1942).*
Portrait of an Unknown Lady. *Collins (1945).*
The story of a young man who is impelled to meet the girl whose portrait he sees has interesting and unusually realistic scenes in which the world of art-dealers and the commercial side of art is portrayed.

Waterfront. *Cape (1934). Pan Books. 1950. 1s. 6d.*

BROSTER, D. K. (1878–1950)
The Flight of the Heron *(1925).* **The Gleam in the North** *(1927).* **The Dark Mile** *(1929). Heinemann, 1950. 7s. 6d. each.*
An excellent trilogy on the Jacobite Rebellion of 1745, with the escape of Prince Charles, the wanderings and sometime betrayal of his companions and supporters, and their subsequent adventures.

BROWN, IVOR
Master Sanguine. *Hamish Hamilton (1934).*
A witty satire owing something to *Candide.*

BUCK, PEARL S.
Good Earth. *Methuen (1931), 1950. 6s.*
Won the Pulitzer Prize for its year and has been a popular novel ever since.

Sons. *Methuen (1932), 1951. 6s.*

BULLETT, GERALD
Judgement in Suspense. *Dent (1946), 1950. 5s.*
The Jury. *Dent (1935), 1950. 5s.*
The Pandervils. *Dent (1943).*
A revised edition of two novels *Egg Pandervil* (1928) and *Nicky, Son of Egg* (1929). A family story with a background of English farming life in the first half of the nineteenth century. Egg subsequently becomes a grocer. The novels established the reputation of the author.

BURNETT, W. R.
Little Caesar. *Cape (1929).*
One of the better written tales of crime and gangsters.

CABELL, JAMES BRANCH
Jurgen. *Lane (1921). 6s.*
A 'comedy of disenchantment' which swept the world of readers off its feet in the early 'twenties. Saucy, naughty, arch, allusive and graceful; an amusing pastiche in the manner of Anatole France at his average.

CAIN, JAMES M.
The Postman Always Rings Twice. *Cape (1934), 5s.*
This was the novel of a crime which really started the flood of imitations, from passable trivialities to the lowest type of terse savagery in fiction. Yet the prototype has considerable qualities and may remain the best of its kind.

CALDER-MARSHALL, ARTHUR
About Levy. *Cape (1933).*
At Sea. *Cape (1934).*
Pie in the Sky. *Cape (1937).*

CAMBRIDGE, ELIZABETH
Hostages to Fortune. *Cape (1933).*

CANFIELD, DOROTHY
The Bent Twig. *Constable (1915).*

CANNAN, GILBERT
Mendel: a story of youth. *Fisher Unwin. Benn (1916).*
The realistic story of the development of a young Jew. It was the best of three good novels by an author who promised much. The others were *Round the Corner* (Nash, 1913), and *Young Earnest* (the romance of a bad start in life), Fisher Unwin, (1915).

CARR, JOHN DICKSON
Death-Watch. *Hamish Hamilton (1935), 1949. 6s.*
An ingenious thriller: Dr Fell on the prowl in Lincoln's Inn Fields; a skull watch (genuine); a murder.

CARTER, REGINALD
He and His. *Cape (1940).*
Told in the old-fashioned leisurely style of the Victorians.

CARY, JOYCE
Herself Surprised. To Be A Pilgrim. The Horse's Mouth.
Michael Joseph (1941, 1942, 1944). Uniform 'Carfax' edition, 1951. 10s. 6d. each.

A trilogy of high comedy and satire, with scenes of great drollery. The period covers about 60 years of British life. 'Designed to show three characters, not only in themselves but as seen by each other.'

The Moonlight. *Michael Joseph (1948). 10s. 6d.*

A cleverly told drama of love, family troubles and complications.

CHANDLER, RAYMOND

The Big Sleep. *Hamish Hamilton (1939). 6s.*
The Lady in the Lake. *Hamish Hamilton (1944), 1949. 6s.*

Swift, American crime, written in the terse, 'essentials only' style which is now the fashion. Enjoyable pastime reading, quickly forgotten, but written with considerable skill.

CHAPLIN, SID

The Thin Seam. *Phoenix House (1950), 1952. 4s. 6d.*

One of the best novels of the year; a moving tale of life as experienced by a typical miner, by an author who has himself worked at the coal face.

CHRISTIE, AGATHA

The Murder of Roger Ackroyd. *Collins (1926), 1951. 5s.*
Murder on the Orient Express. *Collins (1934). Penguin Books. 1948. 1s.6d.*
Why Didn't They Ask Evans? *Collins (1938), 1950. 4s. 6d.*

No other writer of detective stories has been able to keep up the high level of excellence attained in these three, year after year in novel after novel. To date this author has written fifty books of this kind.

CHURCH, RICHARD

The Porch and **The Stronghold.** *Dent (1944), 1950. 6s.*

Originally published separately in 1937 and 1939 respectively. The first novel was awarded the Femina Vie Heureuse Prize.

CLEWES, HOWARD

Dead Ground. *Lane (1944). 7s. 6d.*

CLOETE, STUART

Turning Wheels. *Collins (1937), 8s. 6d. 1950, 7s. 6d.*

The first of a projected series of South African novels, based on records of the Great Trek.

COLLIER, JOHN

His Monkey Wife; or, Married to a Chimp. *Macmillan (1930).*

Amusing fantasy in the manner of *Lady into Fox.*

COLLINS, NORMAN

Love In Our Time. *Collins (1939), 1950. 7s. 6d.*

A simple, unaffected but affecting little story of a young couple who start married life in the usual little house in the usual little suburb of London. 'Shall we have a car or a baby?' is the first of many little problems. Authentic down to the 'bus number from Archway station.

71

COMFORT, ALEX

The Power House. *Routledge (1944). 10s. 6d.*

COMPTON-BURNETT, IVY

Brothers and Sisters. *(1929.) Gollancz, 1950. 10s. 6d.*
Daughters and Sons. *Gollancz (1937), 1950. 10s. 6d.*
A Family and a Fortune. *Eyre & Spottiswoode, 1949. 10s. 6d.*
Men and Wives. *(1931.) Eyre & Spottiswoode (1949). 10s. 6d.*
More Women Than Men. *(1933.) Eyre & Spottiswoode, 1949. 10s. 6d.*

These remarkable novels of dialogue delight some readers and bore others. With plots of family dispute and individual antagonisms, sometimes with quite startling implications, and with mannered dialogue slightly reminiscent of Henry James, yet with a bite all its own; dateless (but probably the turn of the century will do); upper-middle class characters who all obey the law of the jungle in conversation, even at the breakfast table. Others are *Parents and Children*, Gollancz (1941), 1947, 10s. 6d. and *Manservant and Maidservant*, Gollancz (1947), 7s. 6d.

CONNOLLY, CYRIL

The Rock Pool. *(1935.) Hamish Hamilton, 1947. 8s. 6d.*

Lucid and pellucid in style; sharply analytical in characterization. Sad, unhappy, brightly intelligent people, moving from one southern café-bar to another. Immoral, amoral, amative, talkative and always slightly tight. A period piece, unaccountably banned from England when it first appeared.

CONVERSE, FLORENCE

'Long Will.' *(1903.) Dent. (Everyman's Library.) 5s.*

A story of William Langland and *Pierce the Plowman*.

COOPER, WILLIAM

Scenes from Provincial Life. *Cape (1950). 9s. 6d.*

Told in the first person. The narrator is a science master. The time just before 1939. A story of love in our time of a different sort. Beautifully told, with an ease of style that makes it a delight to read and lifts it well above most other novels of its year.

CROFTS, FREEMAN WILLS

The Cask. *Collins (1920). Penguin Books. 1952. 2s. 6d.*

A classic of the detective story type which must surely be included in any list of the fifty best of this century.

CRONIN, A. J.

The Citadel. *Gollancz (1937). 4s. 9d.*

A prodigious best-seller and a successful film story. By many it is rated higher than *Hatter's Castle*, Gollancz (1931), 5s. The first is a powerful story of medical life and modern social conditions; the second owes something to the Victorian Kailyard School novel *The House With the Green Shutters*.

CURTIS, JAMES

They Drive By Night. *(1938.)* *New edition, Lehmann, 1948. 3s. 6d.*

Lorry drivers; road house cafés; casual pick-ups; roadside amours; crime. A crisp realistic melodrama of the new night life which grew up in the 'twenties and the 'thirties on the main roads from London to the North.

DANE, CLEMENCE

Broome Stages. *Heinemann (1931).*
Regiment of Women. *Heinemann (1917).*

DAVIES, RHYS

The Black Venus. *Heinemann (1944). Pan Books. 1950. 2s.*

A sly Welsh comedy, told with a master's command of character and language. The old Welsh custom of trial wooing and the almost ritualistic ceremony of courting in bed provide the author with a plot after his own heart and the reader with a diverting tale. Perhaps the best of all this writer's fiction.

DE LA MARE, WALTER

Memoirs of a Midget. *(1921.) Faber, 1945. 10s. 6d.*

A unique piece of work. The author's delicate understanding of a minified world as seen by an abnormally small person living in a world of normal sized humans, lifts the novel from fantasy to reality.

DE SELINCOURT, HUGH (1878–1951)

The Cricket Match. *Cape (1924). Hart-Davis, 1949. 7s. 6d.*
The Saturday Match. *Dent (1936).*

DEEPING, WARWICK (1877–1950)

The Red Saint. *Cassell (1909).*

A notable example of the early work of a popular novelist. It is an historical novel set in the reign of Henry III and Simon de Montfort.

DENNIS, GEOFFREY

Harvest in Poland. *Heinemann (1925).*
Mary Lee. *Heinemann (1922).*

DOS PASSOS, JOHN

U.S.A.: a trilogy. *(1937.) New edition, Lehmann, 1950. 15s.*

An omnibus of 1163 pages comprising *The Forty-Second Parallel* (1930); *Nineteen-Nineteen* (1932); and *The Big Money* (1936). Considered to be one of the major works of fiction to come from America. The contemporary scene is mirrored with the technique of the cinema newsreel and the newspaper headline.

DOUGLAS, NORMAN (1868–1952)

South Wind. *Secker & Warburg (1917), 1950. 7s. 6d.*

 The new edition corrects a number of misprints in other editions, and is divided into the fifty chapters as originally planned by the author. It is a novel of a vanished world of light, learned wit, leisure, conversation and gay diversions on the island of 'Nepenthe' near Sicily, told in the manner that Peacock would have admired. For the aged Saintsbury, who had read thousands of novels, it was one of the two novels of 'this so-called age' which he felt he could recommend to a friend.

DU MAURIER, DAPHNE

Jamaica Inn. *Gollancz (1936). 4s. 6d.*
Rebecca. *Gollancz (1938). 4s. 6d.*

DUGUID, JULIAN

A Cloak of Monkey Fur. *Cape (1936).*
 A romance of the days of Cabot.

EDWARDS, HUGH

All Night at Mr. Stanyhurst's. *Cape (1933).*

 An extraordinarily intense novel of quite outstanding quality. Eighteenth-century amorous comedy with strong, simple characterisation; swift, violent action as sharp as a duel; over all, the finely evoked atmosphere of passion, wine and foreboding.

ERTZ, SUSAN

Julian Probert. *(1931.) New edition, Lehmann, 1948. 3s. 6d.*
Now East, Now West. *(1927.) New edition, Lehmann, 1950. 3s. 6d.*

FARJEON, ELEANOR

Martin Pippin in the Apple Orchard. *Collins (1922). 5s.*
  New illustrated edition, O.U.P., 1952. 12s. 6d.

 Followed by *Martin Pippin in the Daisy Field*, Michael Joseph (1938). These charming fairy fantasies are more suitable for older readers than for children.

FARJEON, J. J.

Detective Ben. *Collins (1938), 1950. 4s. 6d.*
The Disappearances of Uncle David. *Collins (1949). 8s. 6d.*
The Sinister Inn. *Collins (1926).*

 Three characteristic mystery novels by a writer whose prolific output, and ability to weave ingenious plots conveying the atmosphere of the sinister have been much admired by his fellow craftsmen.

FARNOL, Jeffrey (1878–1952)

The Amateur Gentleman. *Low (1913), 1951. 7s. 6d.*
The Broad Highway. *Low (1910), 1951. 7s. 6d.*

Perennial favourites for those who like romance in the days of flowered waistcoats and knee-breeches; old inns; gallant young heroes; lovely women in distress; fights with pistol, sword and fist; and everything right at the end.

FARRELL, James

Studs Lonigan. *Constable (1936).*

Being *Young Lonigan* (1932); *Young Manhood of Studs Lonigan* (1934); and *Judgement Day* (1935). A realistic study of development of a young American, which has attracted as much abuse as it has praise.

FAULKNER, William

The Intruder in the Dust. *Chatto (1949). 9s. 6d.*
Pylon. *(1933.) Lehmann, 1950. 3s. 6d.*
Sanctuary. *Chatto (1931). 8s. 6d.*
Soldiers' Pay. *Chatto (1930). 5s.*

The 1950 Nobel Prize Winner for Literature. These are grim, realistic novels of America which, like *Studs Lonigan* by James Farrell, have been both praised extravagantly and abused violently. In *Pylon*, the author's personal experiences of flying enable him to convey the atmosphere of the flying ground and hangars with considerable power.

FERGUSON, Rachel

The Brontës Went to Woolworth's. *Benn (1931), 1953. 6s.*

FORESTER, C. S.

Brown on Resolution. *Lane (1929). 6s.*
Captain Hornblower, R.N. *Michael Joseph (1939), 1950. 12s. 6d.*

Comprising the three books narrating the exploits of the famous Hornblower: *The Happy Return* (1937); *A Ship of the Line* (1939); and *Flying Colours* (1938). All published separately at 5s. Others in the series are: *The Commodore*, Michael Joseph (1944), 6s.; *Lord Hornblower*, Michael Joseph (1946), 6s.; and *Mr Midshipman Hornblower*, Michael Joseph (1950). 10s. 6d. The uniform *Greenwich* edition is in progress at 9s. 6d. each volume.

Death to the French. *Lane (1932). 6s.*
The Gun. *Lane (1933). 6s.*
Payment Deferred. *Lane (1926). 6s.*

Must be accorded a place amongst the best dozen crime novels of the century. A study in murder, followed by moral decay and punishment for an uncommitted crime. It made a fine play and an excellent film, with Charles Laughton as the homely man who succumbed to temptation.

The Ship. *Michael Joseph* (*1943*), *1950. 6s.*

A popular novel of action on the perils of convoy work, reprinted six times to date.

FORSTER, E. M.

Howard's End. *Edward Arnold* (*1910*), *1950. 6s. and 4s. 6d.*
The Longest Journey. *Edward Arnold* (*1907*), *1950. 6s.*
A Passage to India. *Edward Arnold* (*1924*), *1950. 6s. and 4s. 6d.*
A Room with a View. *Edward Arnold* (*1908*), *1950. 6s.*
Where Angels Fear to Tread. *Edward Arnold* (*1905*), *1950. 6s.*

FRASER, RONALD

The Flying Draper. *Cape* (*1931*).

An ingenious and diverting fantasy.

FREEMAN, H. W.

Hester and Her Family. *Chatto* (*1935*).
Joseph and His Brethren. *Chatto* (*1928*).

Pleasant romances of men and women of farms in East Anglia.

GARNETT, DAVID

Beany-Eye. *Chatto* (*1935*).

A long-short story of a simpleton, witless and pathetic; told with the quiet realism characteristic of this author.

The Grasshoppers Come. *Chatto* (*1931*).

Reprinted in a new edition with *A Rabbit in the Air* (1932), which was a record of the author's experiences when being taught to fly solo. Chatto, (1934), 7s. 6d.

Lady into Fox. *Chatto* (*1922*).

Reprinted with that other delightful fantasy, *A Man in the Zoo* (1924), Chatto, 7s. 6d. The first story gained both the Hawthornden and the James Tait Black Memorial Prizes, and swept the public off its feet. Both are unique little stories.

No Love. *Chatto* (*1929*). *7s. 6d.*
Pocahontas; or, The Nonpareil of Virginia. *Chatto* (*1933*). *8s. 6d.*

One of the best historical novels of the century. It is the strange, pathetic story of the native Indian girl, known when she came to London as La Belle Sauvage. The Virginian scenes, Jamestown in 1612, her marriage to the Englishman John Rolfe, and her untimely death off Gravesend, are all told with complete verisimilitude.

The Sailor's Return. *Chatto* (*1925*). *6s.*

A sad little story of Tulip, a charming coloured girl who marries an English sailor, only to meet with tragic hostility from his narrow, uncivilized neighbours who come to the little inn for their evening drinks.

GARSTIN, CROSBIE (1887–1930)

The Penhales. *Heinemann (1933).*

A trilogy of Cornish passion, smugglers, adventures with gipsies, voyaging: originally published separately as *The Owl's House* (1923); *High Noon* (1925); *The West Wind* (1926).

GERHARDI, WILLIAM

Futility. *(1922.) Macdonald, 1947. 6s.*

A novel on Russian themes; witty; charming; amorous; high comedy; autumnal sadness. In *The Polyglots* (1925), also reprinted in the uniform edition, Macdonald, 1947, 6s., there is a similar background with characters probably drawn from the life.

GIBBON, LEWIS GRASSIC (1901–1935)

A Scots Quair: a trilogy. *Jarrolds (1946), 1950. 12s. 6d.*

A first-class series of novels: *Sunset Song* (1932); *Cloud Howe* (1933); and *Grey Granite* (1934). The author's real name was James Leslie Mitchell; he wrote at his best from his own individual view of life and his own experience. The very stuff of Scotland both of farm and city is here. The reprint in one volume has a biographical introduction by Ivor Brown, who knew him.

GIBBONS, STELLA

Cold Comfort Farm. *Longmans (1932). 6s.*

A warmly-welcomed satire on the *Desire Under the Elms* type of novel and play, written with feminine wit and lightness of heart and touch. It won the Femina Vie Heureuse Prize and was later followed by sequels in *Christmas at Cold Comfort Farm*, Longmans (1940) and *Conference at Cold Comfort Farm*, Longmans (1949), 5s.

GIBBS, SIR PHILIP

The Street of Adventure. *Hutchinson (1900), 1949. 4s. 6d.*

An early novel of a prolific writer who has put the contemporary scene in his novels as the century has unfolded itself. This excellent early book is a story of Fleet Street.

GLOVER, HALCOTT (1877–1949)

Both Sides of the Blanket. *Constable (1945).*
Louise and Mr Tudor. *Constable (1946).*
Louise in London. *Constable (1948).*

An interesting trilogy, being *romans á clef*. The theme is the Lewes-George Eliot story.

GODDEN, RUMER

Black Narcissus. *Peter Davies (1937). 5s.*
Breakfast with the Nikolides. *Peter Davies (1942). 8s. 6d.*

GRAVES, ROBERT

I, Claudius. *Methuen* (*1934*). *8s. 6d.*
Claudius the God and His Wife Messalina. *Methuen* (*1934*). *8s. 6d.*

The first of the pair won both the Hawthornden and the James Tait Black Prizes for the year of publication. They are amongst the best historical novels in the language, and perhaps the best of all English novels of ancient Rome.

Count Belisarius. *Cassell* (*1938*). *12s. 6d.*
The Golden Fleece. *Cassell* (*1944*).
    Pocket edition 1950. 6s.

Published in America as *My Shipmate Hercules*.

King Jesus. *Cassell* (*1946*). *12s. 6d.*
Sergeant Lamb of the Ninth. *Methuen* (*1940*).
Proceed Sergeant Lamb. *Methuen* (*1941*). *8s. 6d.*

The writer's intuitive gifts of historical reconstruction and the research which is behind these novels have attracted the praise of scholars; his skill as a novelist has brought him considerable popularity both in Great Britain and America.

Seven Days in New Crete. *Cassell* (*1949*). *9s. 6d.*

A departure in style, being a comedy, half satire, half pure fun.

GREEN, F. L. (1902–1953)

Odd Man Out. *Michael Joseph* (*1945*). *6s.*

A tale of crime and pursuit which stands high in its class, and provided the story for one of the best English films.

On the Night of the Fire. *Michael Joseph* (*1939*). *8s. 6d.*

GREEN, HENRY

Living. *Hogarth Press* (*1929*), *1949. 8s. 6d.*
Loving. *Hogarth Press* (*1945*). *8s. 6d.*
Nothing. *Hogarth Press* (*1950*). *8s. 6d.*

Examples of the work of a gifted writer with a Gallic touch and individuality. The last named is a beautifully written and proportioned comedy of middle-age and youth in 1948. Owing nothing to easily aroused excitement, but everything to craftsmanship and talent, it yet achieved a considerable popularity amongst discerning readers who appreciated the enjoyment of a difficult piece of work finely done.

GREENE, GRAHAM

Brighton Rock. *Heinemann* (*1938*), *1950. 8s. 6d.*

Horrifying tension and violence presented with the skill of a modern master.

Gun for Sale. *Heinemann* (*1936*), *1950. 8s. 6d.*

Its only rival is the French film (French version, now, alas, destroyed by an act of selfishness) *Le Jour Se Lève.*

The Heart of the Matter. *Heinemann (1948), 1951. 8s. 6d.*
The Man Within. *Heinemann (1929), 1952. 8s. 6d.*

An early novel. A 'costume' piece, but displaying already the characteristic gifts and style of its writer.

Stamboul Train. *Heinemann (1932), 1950. 8s. 6d.*

GREENWOOD, WALTER

Love on the Dole. *Cape (1933), 1950. 5s.*

Of some social importance. This simple, realistic story of the wretched days of unemployment amongst skilled workers in Northern manufacturing towns, and the 'means test' devised to mete out just, if niggardly treatment, hitting both worthy and unworthy alike, may well survive as a social document.

GUNN, NEIL M.

Highland River. *Faber (1937). 8s. 6d.*
Awarded the James Tait Black Prize.

Morning Tide. *Faber (1931). 5s.*
Another prize-winning novel.

The Silver Darlings. *Faber (1941). 12s. 6d.*

HAMILTON, PATRICK

Hangover Square. *Constable (1941), 1949. 8s. 6d.*

A grim study in crime and the type of man with what is popularly described as a 'split personality'. Sub-titled: *The Man With two Minds*, a story of darkest Earl's Court in the year 1939.

Twenty Thousand Streets Under the Sky. *Constable (1949). 10s.*

A 'London' trilogy comprising: *The Midnight Bell* (1929); *The Siege of Pleasure* (1932); and *The Plains of Cement* (1934). The omnibus has an introduction by J. B. Priestley.

HAMMETT, DASHIELL

Omnibus. *Cassell (1950). 21s.*

Containing *The Thin Man* (1932); *The Maltese Falcon* (1930); *The Glass Key* (1931); and some others, making in all 955 pages of crisp, swift, crime, with not a word wasted. The three main novels mark an epoch in this type of American crime fiction.

HAMPSON, JOHN

Saturday Night at the Greyhound. *(1931.)*
New edition, Eyre & Spottiswoode, 1950. 6s.

William Plomer introduces with praise the new edition in The Century Library of this best of Hampson's novels. First thought of as a play, it is a strongly characterized novel with a first-class plot. The perfect book for a train journey.

NOVELS

HANLEY, James
The Furys. *Chatto (1935). 10s. 6d.*
The Secret Journey. *Chatto (1936).*
Our Time is Gone. *Lane (1940).*
   New edition, Phoenix House, 1949. 1951, 6s.

A great trilogy of Dublin working-class life, with an end-piece in

Winter Song. *Phoenix House (1950). 12s. 6d.*

in which Dennis and Fanny Fury, as two old people, come to the end
of their journey through life in an atmosphere of peace. Some good
critics think Hanley is the best novelist now living and consider

Hollow Sea. *Lane (1938). New edition, Nicholson & Watson, 1950. 6s.*

to be his masterpiece. Its theme is the voyage of a troopship in time of
war.

HARE, Cyril
Tragedy at Law. *Faber (1942), 1951. 6s. 6d.*

A detective story written with great skill by a barrister.

HARLAND, Henry (1861–1905)
The Cardinal's Snuff-box. *Lane (1900).*
   Reprinted, Penguin Books, 1948. 1s. 6d.

The only novel to survive by an American writer who, as a voluntary
exile in London, was the founder-editor of the celebrated *Yellow Book*
of the 'nineties. Delicate Edwardian wit; charming period piece.

HARTLEY, L. P.
The Shrimp and the Anemone. *Putnam (1944), 1951. 9s. 6d.*
The Sixth Heaven. *Putnam (1946), 1950. 9s. 6d.*
Eustace and Hilda. *Putnam (1947), 1950. 9s. 6d.*

One of the most distinguished contributions to the twentieth-century
English novel. A trilogy. The last part was awarded the 1947 James Tait
Black Prize.

HATHAWAY, Katherine Butler
The Little Locksmith. *Faber (1944), 1951. 3s. 6d.*

HEMINGWAY, Ernest
A Farewell to Arms. *Cape (1929), 1950. 4s. 6d.*
   In 'The New Travellers' Library', 1950. 4s. 6d.

One of the finest novels to come from the 1914–1918 war. A simple
story of love and affection ending in tragedy. Here are some of the
most poignant pages in twentieth-century fiction.

For Whom the Bell Tolls. *Cape (1941), 1950. 12s. 6d.*

A story of the Spanish Civil War.

To Have and Have Not. *Cape (1937), 1950. 4s. 6d.*

The story of one-armed Harry Morgan, his wife, and a boat. Tough, terse, frank and realistic. Its style has been imitated by many, but not successfully enough to submerge its outstanding excellence.

For the contents of *The Essential Hemingway*, see under Short Stories, p. 56.

HENRIQUES, ROBERT

No Arms, No Armour. *Collins (1939). Revised edition, 1951. 10s. 6d.*

A novel of Army life between the wars.

HERBERT, SIR ALAN

Holy Deadlock. *Methuen (1934), 1950. 6s.*

A humorous and vigorous attack on the absurdities of the English divorce laws. A novel with a purpose which it helped, with its author's persistent Parliamentary advocacy, to achieve in some measure, and which can be enjoyed in its own right as an excellent story.

Secret Battle. *Methuen (1920), 1950. 6s.*

The first novel of this famous writer. Not a comedy, but a serious story arising from the 1914–1918 war.

The Water Gypsies. *Methuen (1930), 1950. 6s.*

Perhaps the most popular of all his books. A piece of English fiction in the best tradition.

HICHENS, ROBERT (1864–1950)

The Green Carnation. *(1894.) Unicorn Press, 1949. 8s. 6d.*

An epigrammatic novel satirizing Oscar Wilde and the aesthetes of the 'nineties in a brilliant style worthy at times of the victim. A prolific novelist, Hichens is remembered by the enormous successes of *Bella Donna*, Heinemann (1909), *The Garden of Allah*, Methuen (1904), and later *The Paradine Case* (1933), Benn, 1947, 8s. 6d.

HODSON, JAMES LANSDALE

Harvest in the North. *Gollancz (1934). 5s.*

In his early novel *Grey Dawn—Red Night*, Gollancz (1930) this writer produced one of the best novels of the first World War. It tells of the progress of a Manchester man from the city to the trenches—and beyond.

HOLME, CONSTANCE

The Splendid Fairing. *O.U.P. (1919). 5s.*

Awarded the Femina Vie Heureuse Prize, and honoured by an edition in the World's Classics Series. A number of her other novels of Cumberland and Westmorland life have also been reprinted in this series.

HOME, MICHAEL

City of the Soul. *Methuen (1943). 6s.*
The House of Shade. *Methuen (1942). 6s.*
The Place of Little Birds. *Methuen (1941). 6s.*
Grain of the Wood. *Methuen (1950). 10s. 6d.*

Like most of this novelist's stories this is set in Norfolk, where we are introduced to Fred Burling, antique furniture dealer. The realism and the confident manner in which this delightful character is built up from his beginnings in the auction room to success, made this one of the best novels of its year.

HORNIMAN, ROY (1872–1930)

Israel Rank. *(1907.) Eyre & Spottiswoode, 1948. 6s.*

The new edition in the Century Library has an introduction by Hugh Kingsmill calling attention to the qualities of a neglected little masterpiece.

HOUGHTON, CLAUDE

Christina. *Collins (1926), 1950. 7s. 6d.*

A powerful study in disintegration in which the chief character discovers after his wife's death that she had been unfaithful to him.

A Hair Divides. *Eyre & Spottiswoode (1931).*
I Am Jonathan Scrivener. *Eyre & Spottiswoode (1934). 6s.*

HOULT, NORAH

Time, Gentlemen, Time. *Heinemann (1930). 5s.*

The title, with its association with the English pub, gives the clue to this study in the downfall of a solicitor. A book of first-class short stories, *Poor Women* (1928), new edition, Cape (1931) deserves rescuing from the 'long out of print' class.

HOUSMAN, LAURENCE

King John of Jingalo. *Cape (1937).*
Royal Runaway. *Cape (1937).*

A sequel to the above. Both satires of life and manners in modern England.

Trimblerigg. *Cape (1924).*

HUGHES, RICHARD

A High Wind in Jamaica. *Chatto (1929). 7s. 6d.*

Notable for the descriptive prose and the vividly realistic children who are the principal characters.

HULL, RICHARD

The Murder of My Aunt. *Faber (1934).*

A little classic of its kind; told with wit and excitement, with a denoue-ment of a most delightful and surprising nature.

HURST, FANNIE

Lummox. *Cape (1924).*

A sympathetic study of an inarticulate, illiterate servant. It is probably the best of this American novelist's fiction.

HUTCHINSON, R. C.

Shining Scabbard. *Cassell (1936), 1949. 7s. 6d.*
Testament. *Cassell (1938), 1950. 15s.*

A long novel, highly praised for its engrossing plot and finely-drawn characters. It was awarded the *Sunday Times* Gold Medal for Fiction.

The Unforgotten Prisoner. *Cassell (1933), 1950. 10s. 6d.*

HUXLEY, ALDOUS

After Many a Summer. *Chatto (1939). 6s. and 7s. 6d.*

Gruesome but compelling fantasy commenting wittily on life.

Antic Hay. *Chatto (1923). 7s. 6d.*

The first novel to exhibit to the full the characteristic powers of this gifted writer: scarifying satire of certain types of intellectuals; urbane wit; an immense range of artistic and literary knowledge; limpid, lucid style.

Ape and Essence. *Chatto (1949). 7s. 6d.*

A horrifying fable of the shape of things which might come if humanity survives an atomic war.

Brave New World. *Chatto (1932). 7s. 6d.*

Ironic prophecy; some of it has nearly come true.

Crome Yellow. *Chatto (1921). 7s. 6d.*

A young man's book. By contrast with the above, sunny, Peacockian, delightfully witty from the first page to the famous last with its apt quotation from Landor.

Eyeless in Gaza. *Chatto (1936). 8s. 6d.*

For many readers the most substantial and lasting of all his novels.

Point Counter Point. *Chatto (1928). 8s. 6d.*

Others think this is his masterpiece. In its somewhat intricate technique it recalls Gide's famous novel, *Les Faux-Monnayeurs.*

Time Must Have a Stop. *Chatto (1945). 9s. 6d.*

Characters that differ little from the earlier *Antic Hay*; a little lechery; some wit. The scene soon shifts from Hampstead Public Library to the author's beloved Italy, bringing with it a strange mysticism as a new element.

ILES, FRANCIS

Malice Aforethought. *Gollancz (1931), 1952. 8s. 6d.*

Described as 'the story of a commonplace crime', this best of all modern murder stories will probably live to delight many generations of readers.

The pseudonym masks an author of other well-known books but authorship has never been acknowledged. In *Before the Fact* (Gollancz, 1932) the same skilful pen nearly brought it off again.

INNES, MICHAEL

Death at the President's Lodging. *Gollancz (1936). 6s.*
A collector's item in modern detection.

Hamlet, Revenge! *Gollancz (1937). 8s. 6d.*
Some readers place this as high as the first. Others assert that

Lament For a Maker. *Gollancz (1938)*
is the best of the three.

IRWIN, MARGARET

The Bride. *Chatto (1939), 1941. 8s. 6d.*
The story of Louise and Montrose.

The Gay Galliard. *Chatto (1941). 10s. 6d.*
The love story of Mary, Queen of Scots.

The Proud Servant. *Chatto (1934), 1937. 8s. 6d.*
The story of Montrose.

Royal Flush. *Chatto (1932). 8s. 6d.*
The story of Minette.

The Stranger Prince. *Chatto (1936). 8s. 6d.*
The story of Rupert of the Rhine.
All five novels form a notable sequence of the Stuart period.

ISHERWOOD, CHRISTOPHER

Goodbye to Berlin. *Hogarth (1939). Chatto, 1952. 6s.*
A beautifully pellucid style, charming wit and tender characterization make this one of the best novels of our time, leaving the reader regretful that so little has come from the same pen.

Mr Norris Changes Trains. *Hogarth (1935), 1950. 7s. 6d.*
A skilful, slightly repellent, study in the type of character that made the Berlin of the 'twenties a byword in Europe.

JAMESON, STORM

Cousin Honoré. *Cassell (1940), 1950. 4s.*
Her story is continued in

Cloudless May. *Macmillan (1943).*
Both deal sympathetically with some of the causes for the downfall of France in 1940.

The Lovely Ship. *Cassell (1927), 1950. 4s.*
The Voyage Home. *Cassell (1930).*
A Richer Dust. *Cassell (1931).*

A well-conceived trilogy concerning the fortunes of a family of ship-builders.

Then We Shall Hear Singing. *Cassell (1942).*

JENKINS, ELIZABETH

Harriet. *Gollancz (1934). 2s. 6d.*

A reconstruction of a suburban crime.

JENNINGS, JOHN

Next to Valour. *Hamish Hamilton (1939).*

A long, historical novel dealing with the aftermath of the '45 rebellion and Wolfe's campaign up to the fall of Quebec.

JEPSON, SELWYN

Man Running. *Macdonald (1948). 9s. 6d.*

One of a series of 'Man' books. All are first-class thrillers.

JESSE, F. TENNYSON

The Lacquer Lady. *Heinemann (1929).*
  New edition, Evans, 1951. 10s. 6d.

The story of Fanny and of the tragi-comedy which brought Upper Burma under British rule. The new edition has a preface by the author.

JOHNSTON, MARY

Audrey. *(1902.)*
By Order of the Company. *(1900.)*
  Reprinted, Eyre & Spottiswoode, 1951. 7s. 6d.

The Old Dominion. *(1899.)*
  Reprinted, Eyre & Spottiswoode, 1951. 8s. 6d.

A popular trilogy of historical novels of Old Virginia from the beginning of the seventeenth century to the middle of the eighteenth.

JONES, JACK

Rhondda Roundabout. *Faber (1934).*
  Reprinted, Hamish Hamilton, 1949. 9s. 6d.

A novel of the miner's life, with its hardships, loyalties and conditions in decades of pre-war neglect and depression. With Greenwood's *Love on the Dole*, see above, p. 79, it may take a high place in realistic fiction of value to social historians.

KAYE-SMITH, Sheila

Green-Apple Harvest. *Cassell (1920). Pan Books, 1950. 2s.*
Joanna Godden. *Cassell (1921), 1952. 8s. 6d.*
Sussex Gorse. *Cassell (1916). 6s.*

Three of the best of her many novels, most of which, like these, are romantic stories set in the Sussex farming countryside.

KENNEDY, Margaret

The Constant Nymph. *Heinemann (1924). 5s.*

A poignant story of a young girl's love and the clash and sympathy with the temperament of the artist. It was the great fictional success of its time and has remained popular ever since.

KERSH, Gerald

The Night and the City. *Michael Joseph (1938).*
   Uniform edition, Heinemann, 1951. 6s.

KEVERNE, Richard

William Cook, Antique Dealer.
   Constable (1928). Penguin Books. 1942. 1s. 6d.
An excellent mystery story, well-told, and popular.

KING, Francis

An Air That Kills. *Home & Van Thal (1948).*

KINGSMILL, Hugh (1889–1949)

The Dawn's Delay *(1924).* **The Return of William Shakespeare** *(1929).*
   The End of the World. The Disintegration of a Politician, 'W.J.'.
All reprinted in one volume, Eyre & Spottiswoode, 1948, 10s. 6d.
The Fall. *Methuen (1930).*

KITCHIN, C. H. B.

Death of His Uncle. *Constable (1939).*
Death of My Aunt. *(1929.) Lehmann, 1949. 3s. 6d.*

KNOX, Ronald A.

The Footsteps at the Lock. *Methuen (1928), 1950. 6s.*
A novel of detection with an ingenious plot.

LANGLEY, Noel

Cage Me a Peacock. *Barker (1935). New edition, Methuen, 1949. 6s.*
A sly, cheeky and amusing treatment in modern style, of some well-known personalities of Ancient Rome.

LAVER, James

Nymph Errant. *Heinemann (1932).*
A gay, high-spirited and entirely indecorous comedy.

LEHMANN, ROSAMUND

The Ballad and the Source. *Collins (1944), 1950. 5s.*
Dusty Answer. *Chatto (1927). 6s.*
A Note in Music. *(1930.) New edition, Lehmann, 1948. 3s. 6d.*
The Weather in the Streets. *Collins (1936), 1951. 6s.*

LEVERSON, ADA (18?–19?)

The Limit. *(1911.) Chapman & Hall, 1950. 7s. 6d.*
Love's Shadow. *(1908.) Chapman & Hall, 1950. 7s. 6d.*

Light Edwardian social comedies, written in a style which would have delighted Oscar Wilde, whom the author befriended at a time when social London offered him little but hostility and unkindness.

LEWIS, EILUNED

The Captain's Wife. *Macmillan (1943). 1951. 6s.*

A simple, quiet story of Lettice, her daily round of work and pleasure in a Welsh sea village, and of her ever-present anxiety for her sailor husband.

Dew on the Grass. *Peter Davies (1934), 7s. 6d.*

Delicate evocation of childhood: the scene, a remote country house on the Welsh border.

LEWIS, SINCLAIR (1885–1951)

Ann Vickers. *Cape (1933).*
Babbitt. *Cape (1923), 1950. 6s.*
Elmer Gantry. *Cape (1927). 5s.*
Main Street. *Cape (1923). 5s.*
Martin Arrowsmith. *Cape (1925), 1951. 10s. 6d.*

Five celebrated studies in American life and character, all of which illuminate their respective themes with powerful satire. Babbitt: the American business man; Elmer Gantry: the hypocritical evangelist and smooth voiced sensualist; Main Street: the typical American provincial town; Martin Arrowsmith: the man of ideals and integrity in a society which pretends to admire both—at a safe distance.

LEWIS, WYNDHAM

Tarr. *Chatto (1918.) Revised edition, 1928. Methuen, 1951. 9s. 6d.*

A notable satiric novel of that halcyon period 1918–1930, when conversations could be serious, even gloomy, but when life was hopeful and gay. The scene is Paris after the war, with a young student, the eponymous hero, as the focal point, and a German artist who is the subject of profound analysis.

LINKLATER, ERIC

Juan in America. *Cape (1931), 1953. 12s. 6d.*
Juan in China. *Cape (1937), 1950. 8s. 6d.*

Two high-spirited, impudent satires, investing a young man of our times with something of the temperament and a good deal of the wit of Byron's hero.

Magnus Merriman. *Cape (1934), 1950. 10s. 6d.*
Poet's Pub. *Cape (1929), 1952. 10s. 6d.*

A witty, exuberant, conversational comedy.

Ripeness Is All. *Cape (1935), 1950. 9s. 6d.*

The new editions are in a uniform set known as *The Orkney* edition.

LISTER, STEPHEN

Marise. *Peter Davies (1950). 8s. 6d.*
Mistral Hotel. *Peter Davies (1940). 8s. 6d.*
Savoy Grill at One. *Peter Davies (1939). 9s. 6d.*
Sun and Heir. *Peter Davies (1949). 8s. 6d.*

Autobiography or fiction? Who cares. A gay series.

LOWNDES, ALICE BELLOC (1868–1947)

The Chink in the Armour. *(1912.) Eyre & Spottiswoode.*

'Society is conducted on the assumption that murder will not be committed.'

The Lodger. *Methuen (1913), 1950. 6s.*

A remarkable study of a special type of murderer; the Victorian boarding house atmosphere is most skilfully conveyed.

The Story of Ivy. *Heinemann (1928).*

MACAULAY, ROSE

Orphan Island. *Collins (1924). New edition, Lehmann, 1951. 3s. 6d.*
Going Abroad. *Collins (1934). New edition, Lehmann, 1948. 3s. 6d.*
Potterism. *Collins (1920), 1950. 6s.*

A penetrating satirical piece, with Mr Potter of Potter's Bar and family as not unlikeable targets.

Staying with Relations. *Collins (1930).*
Told by an Idiot. *Collins (1923).*

MacCARTHY, MARY

A Pier and a Band. *Secker (1918).*
New edition, Hamish Hamilton, 1950. 9s. 6d.

The new edition has an appreciation by David Garnett which he originally contributed to the revised edition formerly issued in Secker's New Adelphi Library. A charming comedy, which has been likened to *Cherry Orchard* in an English setting.

MACDONALD, ISOBEL

The Buried Self. *Peter Davies (1949). 12s. 6d.*

The background in fictional form to the poems of Matthew Arnold, 1848–1851.

MACHEN, Arthur (1863–1947)

The Great God Pan. (*1894.*)
The Hill of Dreams. (*1907.*)
The Three Imposters. (*1895.*)

Three old-fashioned but compelling stories of the macabre, formerly published by Secker.

MACKENZIE, Compton

The Adventures of Sylvia Scarlett. *Macdonald (1950). 10s. 6d.*

Two picaresque novels, formerly published separately: *Sylvia Scarlett* (1918); and *Sylvia and Michael* (1919).

Carnival. *Secker (1912). Macdonald, 1951. 10s. 6d.*
A popular novel of the theatre.

The Four Winds of Love. *Chatto (1937–1940). 8 vols. 7s. 6d. each.*
A distinguished series of conversational novels, now issued as *The Winds of Love*: East, South, West and North, 2 vols. each.

Guy and Pauline. *Secker (1915).*
  New edition, Macdonald, 1952. 10s. 6d.
A charming, graceful and humorous study in youthful love.

Poor Relations. *Secker (1919). Macdonald, 1949. 6s.*
High comedy and satire from the pen of a master.

Sinister Street. *2 vols. Secker (1913, 1914).*
  New edition in one volume, Macdonald, 1949. 10s. 6d.
Likely to become a classic period piece. Here is the author's own generation of youth at Oxford, turning from that city to the ruined ones of France in the war to end war of 1914–1918.

Vestal Fire. (*1927.*) *Chatto, 1951. 7s. 6d.*
A sophisticated comedy: the scene, an Italian island; the characters, a French count and the foreign colony there.

McNEILE, H. C. ('Sapper') (1888–1937)

Sapper's Four Rounds of Bull-Dog Drummond with Carl Petersen.
  Hodder (1951). 18s.
Comprising *Bull-Dog Drummond*; *The Black Gang*; *The Third Round* and *The Final Count*.

MADARIAGA, Salvador de

The Heart of Jade. *Collins (1944).*
The story of Spain at the time of the discovery of America, and of the conquest of Mexico, told in fictional form by the distinguished historian.

MAIR, JOHN (1914–1942)
Never Come Back. *Gollancz (1941).*

The young airman-author unhappily did not come back himself to receive the high praise due to him for one of the best thrillers of recent years. It is in the same class as *Payment Deferred* and *Malice Aforethought*, although quite different in theme.

MANNING, FREDERIC (1887–1935)
Her Privates We. *Peter Davies (1930).*

First published in a limited edition, with some passages revised for the general edition, under the pseudonym of Private 19022. The talented Australian writer wrote in this classic of the first World War of 1914–1918 of a platoon and company on the Somme: 'my concern is with the anonymous troops'.

MARCH, WILLIAM
Company K. *Gollancz (1933).*

Another powerful novel of the 1914 war, this time by an American writer.

MARQUAND, JOHN P.
H. M. Pulham, Esq. *Hale (1941), 1947. 4s. 6d.*
Wickford Point. *Hale (1939).*

Popular and well-written novels by one of the best American novelists of to-day.

MARSH, NGAIO
Death at the Bar. *Collins (1939), 1949. 5s.*

A cleverly told detective story by a New Zealand writer who has been able to keep up a very high standard with all her succeeding 'Crime Club' records.

Surfeit of Lampreys. *Collins (1941), 1951. 6s.*

MARSHALL, BRUCE
Father Malachy's Miracle. *Constable (1931), 1950. 8s. 6d.*

MASEFIELD, JOHN
Bird of Dawning. *Heinemann (1933), 1946. 6s.*
Dead Ned; or, The Autobiography of a Corpse.
    Heinemann (1938), 1950. 8s. 6d.
Live and Kicking Ned: a sequel. *Heinemann (1939).*
The Lost Endeavour. *Nelson (1910). 4s. 6d.*
The Midnight Folk. *Heinemann (1927), 1949. 8s. 6d.*
Sard Harker. *Heinemann (1924). 6s.*
Odtaa. *Heinemann (1926). 6s.*

But seven of many fine stories of adventure unequalled in contemporary literature. Told with the skill of the careful craftsman, the knowledge of an old sailor, and the style of a poet alive to the magic of words, they are read with enjoyment by both young and old. Sometimes, as in *Bird of*

Dawning, a sailor's yarn; sometimes, as in *The Midnight Folk*, a tale of fantasy and the wonder of youth; yet others, as the last two listed, are tales of intense suspense, excitement and thrills.

MASEFIELD, Lewis Crommelin (1910–1942)

The Passion Left Behind. *Faber (1947). 8s. 6d.*

The first, and alas, owing to the last war, the only novel by a young writer with much to say and potential talent needing only time to develop it. Introduction and memoir by John Masefield.

MASON, A. E. W. (1865–1948)

At the Villa Rose. *Hodder (1910). 6s.*
The Broken Road. *Murray (1907). 6s.*

A romance of India, much admired for its faithful interpretation of local colour and character.

Clementina. *Methuen (1901).*

The heroine is the young princess who was singled out to marry the Old Pretender. A fine historical novel from the pen of this prolific writer.

The Four Feathers. *Murray (1902). 6s.*

A great fictional success for fifty years with all ages and types of readers.

The House of the Arrow. *Hodder (1924). 2s.*
Inspector Renaud Investigates. *Hodder (1931). 17s. 6d.*

An omnibus of three of the best detective stories of the century. They are *At the Villa Rose*, *The House of the Arrow* and *The Prisoner in the Opal*, Hodder (1929), 2s. separately.

MAUGHAM, Robin

The Servant. *Falcon Press (1948). 5s.*

A long-short story of depravity and corruption told with great power and skill.

MAUGHAM, W. Somerset

Cakes and Ale. *Heinemann (1930), 1949. 8s. 6d.*
Liza of Lambeth. *Heinemann (1897), 1951. 8s. 6d.*

The young writer who was afterwards to be famous for his stories of men and women of sophistication and society here told his first tale, which was inspired by his personal knowledge of the lives of the poor in South London. Much has succeeded it and conditions have changed, but it still reads well and is one of his best books.

The Moon and Sixpence. *Heinemann (1919), 1949. 10s. 6d.*
Narrow Corner. *Heinemann (1934), 1951. 8s. 6d.*
Of Human Bondage. *Heinemann (1915), 1950. 15s.*

His masterpiece. Generally considered to have an autobiographical background.

Up at the Villa. *Heinemann (1941).*

A short novel of passion.

MAYOR, F. M.
The Rector's Daughter. *Hogarth Press (1935).*

MEYNELL, Esther
English Spinster: a portrait. *Chapman & Hall (1939).*
The life story of Mary Russell Mitford, author of *Our Village*, told in fictional form.

The Little Chronicle of Magdalena Bach. *Chatto (1925).*
Chapman & Hall, 1940. 6s.

MEYNELL, Laurence
Bluefeather. *Harrap (1928). Guild Books, 1952. 1s. 6d.*
The Bright Face of Danger. *Collins (1949), 1950. 4s. 6d.*
The Creaking Chair. *Collins (1941), 1950. 2s.*
The Man No-one Knew. *Collins (1951).*
Four excellent stories of mystery, adventure and detection. There is a sequel to the first, *Odds on Bluefeather*, being further adventures of Mr George Berkley, Harrap (1934).

MILLAR, George
My Past Was an Evil River. *Heinemann (1947).*
A story of action and a study in character. It concerns a Nazi refugee after the defeat of Germany. The author's first books recount his personal experiences and extraordinary adventures during the war, the first being *Marquis*, Heinemann (1945), 10s. 6d., and the sequel *Horned Pigeon*, Heinemann (1946), 10s. 6d.

MILLIN, Sarah Gertrude
God's Stepchildren. *Constable (1924), 1951. 12s.*
On the colour problems in South Africa. The new edition has a preface.

King of the Bastards. *Heinemann (1950), 1952. 6s.*
Highly praised by the late Field Marshal Smuts, who said it is 'a picture of South African thought such has never been painted before'. The time is the end of the eighteenth century and the beginning of the nineteenth. It has for its theme the history of the origins of a very small community of coloured and half-breed people in South Africa, who are descendants of the Buys family in the Northern Transvaal. Conraad Buys was a white man with a harem of native women.

MILNE, A. A.
The Red House Mystery. *Methuen (1921), 1949. 6s.*
A 'classic' among the detective novels of the century.

MITCHELL, Mary
A Warning to Wantons. *Heinemann (1934). Methuen, 1949. 7s. 6d.*

MITCHISON, NAOMI

Cloud Cuckoo Land. *Cape (1925).*

A novel of Sparta.

The Conquered. *Cape (1923).*

A novel of the Roman conquest of Gaul.

MORGAN, CHARLES

The Fountain. *Macmillan (1932). 8s. 6d.*
Sparkenbroke. *Macmillan (1936). 10s. 6d.*
The Voyage. *Macmillan (1940). 10s. 6d.*

Three of a distinguished list of novels which have not only been amongst the most popular of our time but have also gained for their author the respect of the literary world of both England and France. They are notable for their insistence on the spiritual side of man's nature in circumstances of the modern world which have made many lose their faith or adopt a negative attitude to this saving grace.

MORLEY, CHRISTOPHER

The Haunted Bookshop. *Faber (1920), 1951. 10s. 6d.*

A famous bookish, romantic mystery, written by a bookman for bookmen—and others.

MOTTRAM, R. H.

The Spanish Farm Trilogy, 1914–1918. *Chatto (1927), 1952. 12s. 6d.*

Outstanding novels drawn from the Great War of 1914–1918 which continue to impress readers by their integrity and fidelity. They are: *The Spanish Farm* (1924), *6s.* which won the Hawthornden Prize; *Sixty-Four, Ninety-Four* (1925); and *The Crime at Vanderlynden's* (1926).

MYERS, ELIZABETH (1913–1947)

A Well Full of Leaves. *Chapman & Hall (1943), 1950. 8s. 6d.*

NATHAN, ROBERT

The Barly Fields. *Constable (1939).*

A collection of five novels with an introduction by S. V. Benét. Delicate fantasy and sentiment, sometimes approaching the sentimental, are their characteristics. The 523 pages comprise: *The Fiddler in Barly* (1926); *The Wood-Cutter's House* (1927); *The Bishop's Wife* (1928); *The Orchid* (1931); and *There Is Another Heaven* (1929).

NEWBY, P. H.

A Journey to the Interior. *Cape (1945). 9s. 6d.*

A work of unusual wit and individuality which achieved a striking success and was regarded as a novel from a newcomer to fiction who would be able to sustain his gifts. The scene is a town near the Red Sea where a group of people of various countries intermingle and emotionally react on each other.

O'BRIEN, KATE

That Lady (Esa Señora). *Heinemann (1946), 1948. 4s. 6d.*

'Not a historical novel. It is an invention arising from reflection on the curious external story of Ana de Mendoza and Philip of Spain.' The scene is Madrid and Pastrana and the period 1576 to 1592.

Without My Cloak. *Heinemann (1931), 1950. 7s. 6d.*

A distinguished novel which was awarded both the Hawthornden and the James Tait Black Memorial Prizes.

O'FLAHERTY, LIAM

The Assassin. *Cape (1928).*
The Informer. *Cape (1925), 1949. 8s. 6d.*

Compelling stories of Southern Ireland before the settlement.

O'HARA, JOHN

Appointment in Samarra. *Faber (1935). 8s. 6d.*

One of the best American novels of its decade.

OLDMEADOW, ERNEST JAMES (1867–1949)

Antonio. *Richards (1909).*

An historical novel on the suppression of the monasteries in Portugal in 1834, by the author of a once much-admired but now forgotten trilogy, *Coggin*, Richards (1920).

'OLIVIA'

Olivia. *Hogarth Press (1949). 7s. 6d.*

A tenderly written study in youth, published pseudonymously and acclaimed immediately as a small masterpiece.

OLIVIER, EDITH (1879–1948)

The Love Child. *(1927.) Richards Press, 1951. 7s. 6d.*

The new edition has an introduction by Lord David Cecil, who says it is 'a masterpiece of its kind'. A short novel of exquisite fantasy, it is embellished by woodcuts by Rex Whistler.

The Triumphant Footman. *Secker (1930).*

The most popular novel by a fine countrywoman, in which her gifts of high comedy and fantasy were skilfully engaged.

OLLIVANT, ALFRED (1874–1927)

The Gentleman, a romance of the sea. *Allen & Unwin (1908), 1943.*

A tale of the days of Nelson just before Trafalgar. There is a plot to prevent him from taking command at that crucial time.

Owd Bob, the Grey Dog of Kennuir. *Heinemann (1898), 1949. 8s. 6d.*

The best and certainly the most popular dog story of our time. It looks like taking its place as a minor classic with *Black Beauty*.

OMAN, CAROLA

Crouchback. *Hodder (1929). 7s. 6d.*

A sympathetic and highly praised historical novel in which the character of Richard III is portrayed in a more favourable light than is usual.

Over the Water. *Hodder (1935). 7s. 6d.*

On the 'Forty-Five rebellion.

ONIONS, OLIVER

The Story of Ragged Robyn. *Michael Joseph (1945). 8s. 6d.*

The adventures and dreams of a young stone-mason's apprentice living at the end of the seventeenth century. The scene is London and Yorkshire. Its popular success drew the attention of a new generation of readers to the high qualities of a novelist who had been writing for upwards of forty years. His masterpiece is

Whom God Hath Sundered. *Secker & Warburg (1926), 1948. 15s.*

—a trilogy comprising *In Accordance With the Evidence* (1912); *The Debit Account* (1913); and *The Story of Louie* (1913). It is the story of a murder told from two angles, the last section being the subjective view of the affair as seen by one character.

ORCZY, BARONESS (1865–1947)

The Scarlet Pimpernel: four complete novels. *Hodder (1950). 18s.*

The Scarlet Pimpernel (1905); *I Will Repay* (1906); *Eldorado* (1913); and *Sir Percy Hits Back* (1927). These are the perennial favourites in a long series, and are usually available separately. Forgotten, but prized as a collector's item, is the original series of detective stories by the same author in which for probably the first time problems in crime are solved by conversation and deduction, the detective being immobile: *The Old Man in the Corner*, Greening (1909).

O'RIORDAN, CONAL (1874–1948)

Adam of Dublin *(1920).* **Adam and Caroline** *(1921).* **In London** *(1922).* **Married Life** *(1924).* **Soldier Born** *(1927).* **Soldier of Waterloo** *(1928).*

A series of historical novels of Irish and English military life in the first quarter of the nineteenth century. They were respected and well-praised but never achieved much popularity. If they had, more would have followed. They were published by Collins and are well worth revival.

ORWELL, GEORGE (1903–1949)

Animal Farm. *Secker & Warburg (1945). 6s.*

A fable, and an amusing, keen piece of satire. Revolting against the farmer, the animals run their farm themselves on the most approved and up-to-date ideological methods, inspired, no doubt, by the antics of certain well-known experimenters in government in this century. It is agreed, however, that although all animals are equal, 'some are more equal than others'. Alas, the modern Swift cannot exaggerate. Truth outdistances the wildest jests of both Low and the best satiric novelists of our time.

Coming Up for Air. *Gollancz (1939), 1950. Secker & Warburg. 10s. 6d.*
1984. *Secker & Warburg (1949). 12s. 6d.*

With *Brave New World* and *Ape and Essence*, *1984* must take its place as amongst the most horrifying novels of fantasy nearly coming true ever written. Totalitarianism pursued to its extremes; text-book rationalism for humans worked out like a theorem in algebra. The death of a society of human beings for the sake of the machine. See, however, E. M. Forster's terrifying fable *The Machine Stops*, in his collected stories, for a ray of hope.

PARKER, ERIC

Playing Fields. *(1922.) Carrol & Nicholson, 1950. 12s. 6d.*

A novel of Eton, beloved by old Etonians and admired by many other readers.

PATON, ALAN

Cry, the Beloved Country. *Cape (1948). 9s. 6d.*

One of the most moving novels of the last few years which found a wide public both here and in America. 'A story of comfort in desolation', and the South African native in his world as it has been made for him. Dramatized by Maxwell Anderson as *Lost in the Stars*, Cape & Lane (1951), 6s.

PHILLPOTTS, EDEN

The Mother. *(1908.) Ward Lock, 1951. 5s.*
Widecombe Fair. *(1913.) Eyre & Spottiswoode, 1947. 6s.*

Two of the best of over twenty novels of Dartmoor and Devonshire country life written by a competent craftsman whose output for well over half a century has been prolific. A well-printed uniform edition was published 1927 by Macmillan, at 10s. 6d. each volume. Others of quality in this series are *The Forest, The Secret Woman, The Thief of Virtue*. Some were made into plays, published by Duckworth.

PLOMER, WILLIAM

Sado. *Chatto (1931). 6s.*

Valued for the authentic insight it gives into things Japanese.

POSTGATE, RAYMOND

Verdict of Twelve. *Michael Joseph (1940), 1947. 8s. 6d.*

A detective story of unusual skill, much admired by collectors of outstanding crime stories.

POWELL, ANTHONY

Afternoon Men. *Duckworth (1931).*
New edition, Heinemann, 1952. 12s. 6d.

From a View to a Death. *Duckworth (1933).*
New edition, Lehmann, 1948. 3s. 6d.

POWYS, T. F.

Mr Weston's Good Wine. *Chatto & Windus (1928). 6s.*

The best of a large number of country novels, this being an allegory written in prose of distinction. Many consider it the best of its kind written in this century.

PREEDY, GEORGE

General Crack. *Lane (1928).*
The Rocklitz. *Lane (1930). 7s. 6d.*

Having made several reputations as a novelist under several pen-names, the author of the minor classic *The Viper of Milan*, in these historical novels made yet another under a new pseudonym, which was not revealed until their popularity was well established on their own considerable merits.

PRICHARD, KATHERINE SUSANNAH

The Roaring Nineties. *Cape (1946). 10s. 6d.*
Golden Miles. *Cape (1948), 1951. 5s.*
Winged Seeds. *Cape (1950). 12s. 6d.*

A trilogy, being the story of Sally Gough and Dinny Quin against a background of Australian gold fields. The last of the three continues the story from about 1936 when there was much depression, up to 1946.

PRIESTLEY, J. B.

Angel Pavement. *Heinemann (1930), 1950. 8s. 6d.*
The Good Companions. *Heinemann (1929), 1950. 8s. 6d.*
They Walk in the City. *Heinemann (1936), 1951. 8s. 6d.*
Wonder Hero. *Heinemann (1933), 1951. 8s. 6d.*

Four popular novels in a new uniform edition. They display the high qualities and variety of talent of this genial writer who has so much of Wells's gift of humour and liking for the ordinary men and women of industry and the town. The last is a particularly high-spirited comedy on the extravagances of modern publicity and advertising.

PROKOSCH, FREDERIC

The Asiatics. *Faber (1935), 1949. 10s. 6d.*

Highly praised by Thomas Mann, this novel by an American poet, tells in the first person singular of a young adventurer in Asia. With the charm and something of the wit of Byron's Don Juan he traverses most of the countries of the East in search of personalities, excitement, love and pleasure, in a picaresque, fairy-tale atmosphere.

PYM, Barbara

Some Tame Gazelle. *Cape (1950). 9s. 6d.*

A quiet, charming novel of the kind which is so much more difficult to write than the story of excitement and crime. Two middle-aged sisters in a village, a curate, a colonial Bishop, a librarian and his deputy, together with an archdeacon and his wife on holiday, are the characters in a comedy of distinction.

RANSOME, Arthur

Peter Duck. *Cape (1932), 1950. 9s.*

Perhaps the best of a grand series of adventure stories, perhaps the first among equals. Written for young readers they are all just as popular with grown-ups as they are with teen-agers. There are a round dozen of them, and for many, *Swallows and Amazons* (1931) and *We Didn't Mean to Go to Sea* (1937) lead the way. The complete series is published in a uniform edition, charmingly illustrated, by Cape, 9s. each.

RAWLINGS, Marjorie

The Yearling. *Heinemann (1932). Barker, 1952. 6s.*

This may become a modern classic for both young and old, like that other book of the same class, *Black Beauty*.

RAYMOND, Ernest

Once in England. *Cassell (1932).*

An immensely popular trilogy of English family life: *A Family That Was* (1929); *The Jesting Army* (1930); and *Mary Leith* (1932).

Tell England. *Cassell (1922), 1953. 7s. 6d.*

One of the most popular novels to come from the European War of 1914–1918. 'A study in a generation': schooldays; war. The campaign is the epic of Gallipoli and Dardanelles.

We the Accused. *Cassell (1935), 1950. 7s. 6d.*

RAYMOND, Walter (1852–1931)

A Book of Crafts and Characters. *(1907.) New edition. Dent, 1933. 5s.*
Two Men o' Mendip. *(1899.) New edition. Dent, 1933. 5s.*

A tale of the lead miners of the Mendip Hills in the beginning of the nineteenth century. For a delightful essay on the literary work and the character of this Somerset author see Richard Church's *A Window on the Hill*, Hale, 1951. 15s.

READ, Sir Herbert

The Green Child. *(1935.) Eyre & Spottiswoode, 1947. 6s.*

RHODE, John

The Murders in Praed Street. *Bles (1928).*

Not only a good mystery and criminal hunt but also a notable story for its authentic 'Paddington' atmosphere.

RICHARDSON, Dorothy

Pilgrimage. *4 vols. Dent (1938). 8s. 6d. each.*
  Boxed edition, 30s. the set.

This edition collected the twelve separate volumes which have had the respect and admiration of all readers and literary critics interested in originality and experiment. Here in 1915 English readers were first able to appreciate the subtleties and pleasures of the interior monologue and the stream of consciousness. Afterwards a larger public responded to both devices and others, in the novels of James Joyce and Proust in translation. The complete series is:

  Vol. 1: *Pointed Roofs* (1915); *Backwater* (1916); *Honeycomb* (1917).
  Vol. 2: *The Tunnel* (1919); *Interim* (1919).
  Vol. 3: *Deadlock* (1921); *Revolving Lights* (1923); *The Trap* (1925).
  Vol. 4: *Oberland* (1927); *Dawn's Left Hand* (1931); *Clear Horizon* (1935); *Dimple Hill* (1938).

These were all published separately by Duckworth at 8s. 6d. each. The story of Miriam which they tell will be enjoyed by a new generation which is now finding unusual pleasure in *Remembrance of Things Past*.

ROBERTS, Cecil

The Pilgrim Cottage Omnibus. *Hodder (1938), 1950. 15s.*
  Pilgrim Cottage; *The Guests Arrive*; *Volcano*. All frequently available separately at 6s. each.

ROBERTS, Elizabeth Madox

The Time of Man. *Cape (1926).*
A finely-written novel of the Kentucky hill dwellers.

ROBERTS, Kenneth

Arundel. *Lane (1930), 1936. 5s.*
A chronicle of the Province of Maine and the secret expedition against Quebec.

Northwest Passage. *Collins (1937). 6s.*
Rabble in Arms. *Collins (1933).*

ROBERTSON, E. Arnot

Four Frightened People. *Cape (1931).*
Ordinary Families. *Cape (1933), 1950. 5s.*

ROGERS, Samuel

Dusk at the Grove. *Hurst & Blackett (1934).*

ROYDE-SMITH, Naomi

The Delicate Situation. *Gollancz (1931).*
The Tortoiseshell Cat. *Constable (1925).*

NOVELS

SABATINI, Rafael (1875–1950)

Bardelys the Magnificent. *Nelson (1906), 1947. 3s.*
Captain Blood. *Hutchinson (1922), 1948. 6s.*
Scaramouche. *Hutchinson (1921), 1949. 6s.*
The Sea Hawk. *Nelson (1915), 1948. 3s.*

Historical novels written in an exciting, full-blooded style, with simple characterization, colour, romance and swiftly moving incidents. They, and many others by the same author, achieved great and lasting popularity.

SACKVILLE-WEST, Edward

Simpson: a life. *Heinemann (1931).*
  New edition, Weidenfeld & Nicolson, 1951. 12s. 6d.

The moving story of a Nanny, whose life consists largely of looking after other people's children.

The Sun in Capricorn. *Heinemann (1934).*

A 'topical' novel of its decade. Finely written; a study in political violence, decadence and frustration. By reason of its quality and the course of events, a timeless novel, too.

SACKVILLE-WEST, V.

All Passion Spent. *Hogarth Press (1931). Chatto, 1950. 6s.*
The Edwardians. *Hogarth Press (1930). Chatto, 1952. 7s. 6d.*

SADLEIR, Michael

Fanny by Gaslight. *Constable (1940), 1950. 8s. 6d.*

The author believes in a good plot, strong characterization and atmosphere. Here he gave all in such good measure that both in book and subsequent film he drew an enormous public from all classes of readers.

SANSOM, William

The Body. *Hogarth Press (1949). 9s. 6d.*

Distinctive study in jealousy. It achieved considerable renown and was agreed to be amongst the best novels of its year.

SANTAYANA, George (1863–1952)

The Last Puritan. *Constable (1925).*

A long novel in the form of a memoir of a quality not often met with in contemporary fiction. Slow-moving, subtle and intellectual; with the excitement which comes from contact with the philosophical, highly civilized mind of a distinguished thinker.

SASSOON, Siegfried

The Complete Memoirs of George Sherston. *Faber (1937). 15s.*

Separately they are *Memoirs of a Fox-Hunting Man* (1928), 1942, 6s.; *Memoirs of an Infantry Officer* (1930), 1944, 7s. 6d.; and *Sherston's Progress* (1936), 1944, 6s. Many readers regard them as autobiography but the author's intention was to offer the trilogy as fiction. Childhood in the English countryside of farm, gentle-folk, hounds, horses and the meet; the shattering of trench warfare in Flanders in 1914–1918; recovery and intellectual development in a wrecked world.

SAYERS, DOROTHY

Busman's Honeymoon. *Gollancz* (*1937*). *5s.*
Murder Must Advertise. *Gollancz* (*1933*). *5s.*
The Nine Tailors. *Gollancz* (*1934*). *4s. 6d.*

But three of a rewarding number of excellent detective novels: fun with Lord Peter Wimsey of the apt quotations, and his ingenious solutions of many a dark crime. The last is particularly clever in conception.

SEYMOUR, BEATRICE KEAN

The Chronicles of Sally. *Heinemann* (*1940*).

An omnibus of 1448 pages, being a trilogy also published separately: *Maids and Mistresses*, Heinemann (1932), 1950, 10s. 6d.; *Interlude for Sally*, Heinemann (1934); and *Summer of Life*, Heinemann (1936).

SHARP, MARGERY

Four Gardens. *Collins* (*1935*), *1950. 7s. 6d.*

The quiet life of Caroline Smith from youth, through marriage and prosperity, the war and family troubles, to her widowhood and life in a London flat.

SHAW, G. BERNARD (1856–1950)

Cashel Byron's Profession. *Constable* (*1882*), *1951. 7s. 6d.*
Immaturity. *Constable* (*1930*), *1951. 7s. 6d.*
The Irrational Knot. *Constable* (*1880*), *1951. 7s. 6d.*
Love Among the Artists. *Constable* (*1881*), *1951. 7s. 6d.*
An Unsocial Socialist. *Constable* (*1883*), *1951. 7s. 6d.*

Interesting only to skim through on the look-out for early signs of the satiric genius awaiting its dramatic opportunity to flower. Certainly 'novels of my nonage', but even so passages here and there would have to find a place in 'the essential G.B.S.'. *Immaturity* was written in 1879, and the preface has some interesting autobiographical details.

SHEEHAN, PATRICK AUGUSTINE (1852–1913)

The Graves at Kilmorna. *Longmans* (*1915*), *1950. 10s. 6d.*

A grim, realistic story of the Fenian Rising of 1867. The new edition has an introduction by J. B. Morton. The other outstanding novel by this half-forgotten writer was *The Queen's Fillet* (Longmans, 1911), a well-told story of the French Revolution.

SHEPPARD, ALFRED TRESIDDER (1871–1947)

Brave Earth. *Cape* (*1925*).
Here Comes an Old Sailor. *Hodder* (*1927*).
Running Horse Inn. *Hodder* (*1906*).

The best of a number of well-written historical or period novels of action.

NOVELS

SHUTE, Nevil
The Chequer Board. *Heinemann (1947), 1950. 7s. 6d.*
Most Secret. *Heinemann (1945), 1951. 7s. 6d.*
A Town Like Alice. *Heinemann (1950). 10s. 6d.*

Three distinguished novels by a writer with a narrative gift linked with an instinct for a good plot, serious themes, and strong characterization. The last named was one of the great fictional successes of its year with all classes of readers. A uniform collected edition of the novels is in progress at 7s. 6d. each volume.

SIDGWICK, Ethel
The Bells of Shoreditch. *Sidgwick & Jackson (1928).*

Other notable novels, mainly social comedies written with grace and style, were *Laura*, Sidgwick & Jackson (1924); *Promise* (1910) and *Succession* (1913).

SIMPSON, Helen (1897–1940)
Boomerang. *Heinemann (1932).*

Australian life and history illustrated in a story of three episodes: mid-century; the 1870's, and the turn of the century. Sir John Marriott said 'it certainly makes a real contribution to an understanding of Australia, social and political'.

SINCLAIR, May (1865–19   )
Mary Olivier: a life. *(1919.) New edition, Lehmann, 1949. 3s. 6d.*

SINCLAIR, Upton
The Jungle. *Werner Laurie (1906), 1949. 10s. 6d.*

The first novel which gave the author a world-wide audience. Its theme is the stockyards of Chicago and the evil practices which went on there at the beginning of the century.

Oil. *Werner Laurie (1927), 1947. 10s. 6d.*

A representative novel of this sociological writer who has no equals in modern literature in his work of exposing social and commercial evils of our time through the medium of the novel. His latest work has taken the form of a record of our times from the American point of view from 1913 to yesterday conceived on a vast, Balzacian scale. The series centres round the adventures of Lanny Budd and commences with *World's End* (1913–1919), Werner Laurie, 1940, 15s. Others in chronological order, all published by Werner Laurie, are: *Between Two Worlds* (1919–1929), 1941, 15s.; *Dragon's Teeth* (1929–1934), 1942, 15s.; *Wide is the Gate* (1934–1937), 1944, 15s.; *Presidential Agent* (1937–1938), 1945, 15s.; *Dragon Harvest* (1938–1940), 1946, 15s.; *World to Win* (1940–1942), 1947, 15s.; *Presidential Mission* (1942–1943), 1948, 15s.; *One Clear Call* (1943–1944), 1949, 15s.; and *O Shepherd, Speak* (1944–1946), 1950, 15s. Cheaper editions of some of these volumes were available in 1952 at 10s. 6d. each.

SITWELL, Edith
I Live Under a Black Sun.
Gollancz (1937). New edition, Lehmann, 1948. 3s. 6d.
Jonathan Swift, Stella and Vanessa.

SITWELL, Sir Osbert
Before the Bombardment. *Duckworth (1926). 8s. 6d.*
The Man Who Lost Himself. *Duckworth (1946).*
Miracle on Sinai. *Duckworth (1933). 8s. 6d.*

SMITH, Emma
The Far Cry. *MacGibbon & Kee (1949). 9s. 6d.*
Awarded the James Tait Black Prize.

SMITH, Pauline
The Beadle. *Cape (1926).*
The Little Karoo. *Cape (1925), 1950. 4s. 6d.*
Poignant, delicate stories of South Africa.

SNAITH, J. C. (1876–1936)
Broke of Covenden. *Long (1904).*
William Jordan, Junior. *Long (1908).*
Two good novels by a half-forgotten writer with a long list to his credit,
some historical, some, like these two, studies in character and environment.

SNOW, C. P.
Strangers and Brothers. *Faber (1940). Macmillan, 1951. 8s. 6d.*
The Light and the Dark. *Faber (1947). Macmillan, 1951. 8s. 6d.*
Time of Hope. *Faber (1949). Macmillan, 1951. 8s. 6d.*
The Masters. *Macmillan (1951). 12s. 6d.*
Four of a projected series of eleven novels unfolding the character and
life of Lewis Eliot. The third is regarded as a key volume; all may be read
as separate novels.

SOMERVILLE, E. Œ. (1861–1950) and Martin Ross (1865–1915)
The Irish R.M. and His Experiences. *Faber (1928). 9s. 6d.*
A collection of 34 of the short stories, with a preface. *Some Experiences
of an Irish R.M.* was first published 1899; *Further Experiences* followed
in 1908. Throughout the century the country humour and charm of these
stories of character and incident have gained and kept for their inseparable
authors a constant circle of readers. The two are available in one volume in
Everyman's Library, Dent, 1944, 5s.
The Real Charlotte.
(1894) New edition, O.U.P. 1948. 7s. (World's Classics.)

SPENSER, James
The Five Mutineers. *(1935.) New edition, Lehmann, 1949. 3s. 6d.*
An authentic modern picaresque story by 'Limey'.

SPRING, HOWARD

Fame is the Spur. *Collins (1940), 1949. 10s. 6d.*
My Son, My Son. *Collins (1938), 1950. 7s. 6d.*
When first published was entitled *O Absolom!*

Shabby Tiger. *Collins (1934), 1949. 5s.*
Rachel Rosing. *Collins (1935), 1949. 5s.*
These two should be read as a pair.

STAPLEDON, OLAF

Last and First Men. *Methuen (1931).*
Last Men in London. *Methuen (1932).*
The Star Maker. *Methuen (1937).*
Powerful, imaginative fantasies.

STEAD, CHRISTINA

The Beauties and the Furies. *Peter Davies (1936).*

STEEL, FLORA ANNIE (1847–1929)

On the Face of the Waters. *Heinemann (1896).*

A novel of the Indian Mutiny, notable for its accuracy. Sir John Marriott thought well of the work and wrote of it in high terms: it 'might indeed be described as an indispensable authority'.

STEEN, MARGUERITE

Matador. *Gollancz (1934). New edition, Falcon Press, 1950. 10s. 6d.*
The One-Eyed Moon. *(1935.) New edition, Falcon Press, 1950. 10s. 6d.*
The Tavern. *(1935.) New edition, Falcon Press, 1950. 10s. 6d.*
Three novels in sequence, known as *The Spanish Trilogy*.

The Sun is My Undoing. *Collins (1941), 1950. 12s. 6d.*
A long chronicle of a family with its roots in the port of Bristol.

STEINBECK, JOHN

Grapes of Wrath. *Heinemann (1939), 1949. 10s. 6d.*

A powerful social novel on the plight of poverty-stricken American families in search of work and money in the orange-growing districts of California.

Of Mice and Men. *Heinemann (1937).*

A long-short story of tragic import. It is reprinted in a *Steinbeck Omnibus*, Heinemann, 1951, 12s. 6d. This volume contains extracts from the major novel, some short stories, and *The Red Pony* complete for the first time in this country in its four parts.

STEPHENS, JAMES (1882–1950)

The Charwoman's Daughter. *Macmillan (1912).*
The Crock of Gold. *Macmillan (1912). 3s. 6d.*
The Demi-Gods. *Macmillan (1914).*
Here Are Ladies. *Macmillan (1913).*

In *The Crock of Gold* this gifted Irish poet gave us a modern classic. Half fantasy, half fairy tale, and written in a unique style with a poet's sense of phrase, wit and rhythm.

STERN, G. B.
The Rakonitz Chronicles. *Chapman & Hall (1932).*

A trilogy: *The Tents of Israel* (1924); *The Deputy Was King* (1926); and *Mosaic* (1930).

STEWART, GEORGE R.
Earth Abides. *Gollancz (1950). 12s. 6d.*

A work of imagination in which life in America is overwhelmed almost completely by plague. The few survivors start all over again. In the final chapters the author's style takes on a Biblical dignity. The whole work has something of H. G. Wells's realism and power.

STOKER, BRAM (1847–1912)
Dracula. *(1897.) New edition, Rider, 1950. 6s.*
Foulsham, 1951. 1s. 6d.

This horrific thriller seems to have established itself as a minor classic of its type. A successor, *The Lair of the White Worm* (1911), Foulsham, 1951, 1s. 6d., may also be recommended to those who enjoy this form of literature of which Mary Shelley's *Frankenstein* is the classic example.

STONE, IRVING
Lust for Life. *Lane (1935). 7s. 6d.*
A novel on the life of Vincent Van Gogh.

STRACHEY, JULIA
Cheerful Weather for the Wedding. *Hogarth (1932).*
New edition, Lehmann, 1950. 3s. 6d.

STREET, A. G.
A Crook in the Furrow. *Faber (1940), 1951. 9s. 6d.*

A countryman's day off with crime and detection, this ingenious and amusing novel is in a class of its own.

The Gentleman of the Party. *Faber (1936), 1950. 6s.*

STRONG, L. A. G.
Corporal Tune. *Gollancz (1934). Methuen, 1946. 6s.*
The Director. *Methuen (1944).*

The impact of Python Films of Hollywood on a coastal village in County Kildare. Paul Deakin is the Director, and his scale of values is severely upset by tragedy, a young poet, and Father McCubberty.

The Garden. *Gollancz (1931). New edition, Methuen, 1948. 6s.*

STUART, FRANCIS
Redemption. *Gollancz (1949). 4s. 6d.*

SWINNERTON, FRANK
The Harvest Comedy. *Hutchinson (1937), 1951. 8s. 6d.*
Thought by many readers to be the best of a gifted writer's long list.
Nocturne.
> *Secker (1917). New edition, O.U.P. 1937. (World's Classics) and Hutchinson, 1950. 1s. 6d.*

A masterpiece with a formal beauty rarely found in modern English fiction. The pocket edition has a new introduction.

TATE, ALLEN
The Fathers. *Eyre & Spottiswoode (1939).*

THIRKELL, ANGELA
August Folly. *Hamish Hamilton (1936), 1949. 6s.*
The Brandons. *Hamish Hamilton (1939), 1950. 6s.*
Growing Up. *Hamish Hamilton (1944), 1951. 6s.*

Three in a uniform edition of the many pleasant novels of English family life.

THOMAS, ALAN
The Death of Laurence Vining. *Benn (1928), 1951. 6s.*
A mystery novel by the Editor of *The Listener* which is already a collector's item.

THOMAS, DYLAN
Portrait of the Artist as a Young Dog.
> *Dent (1940). Guild Books, 1948. 1s. 6d.*

Robust, Welsh realism, probably semi-autobiographical, written with a poet's gift of words.

THORNDIKE, RUSSELL
Doctor Syn on the High Seas. *Rich & Cowan (1936), 1951. 6s.*
The first of a famous and very popular series of adventure stories in which a young Oxford scholar of mid-eighteenth century pursues an errant wife and her lover from Dymchurch in Kent to the Americas, and in doing so turns himself from parson to pirate. There are six sequels.

THORNE, ANTHONY
Delay in the Sun. *(1935.) New edition, Lehmann, 1949. 3s. 6d.*

TOLKIEN, J. R. R.
The Hobbit; or, There and Back Again. *Allen & Unwin (1937). 8s. 6d.*
A rare treat: one of those fantastic stories written for children; treasured by adults. A tale of elves told with Carollian nonsense.

TOMLINSON, H. M.

All Our Yesterdays. *Heinemann (1930).*

Among the six greatest novels which came out of the European War of 1914–1918.

Gallions Reach. *Heinemann (1927). Hart-Davis, 1950. 7s. 6d.*

A great novel of sea adventure written by one of the best prose writers of our time.

TOYNBEE, PHILIP

Tea With Mrs Goodman. *Chatto, 1947. 7s. 6d. (Horizon Books.)*

A study in character told in an oblique symbolic style which is said to reflect in modern terms the eternal quest for the Holy Grail.

TRESSELL, ROBERT (18?–1911). Pseudonym of ROBERT DOONAN

The Ragged Trousered Philanthropist. *Richards (1914), 1949. 7s. 6d.*

The author was a house-painter: hence his choice of pseudonym. His posthumous and only novel has become a classic of working-class life of the Edwardian era, and to date well over 120,000 copies have been sold.

TRILLING, LIONEL

The Middle of the Journey. *Secker & Warburg, 1948. 12s. 6d.*

A novel of great distinction by an American critic whose reputation grows with each new book.

ULLMAN, ALLAN and FLETCHER, L.

Sorry, Wrong Number. *Gollancz (1948). 7s. 6d.*

From the film script by Lucille Fletcher. An unusually thrilling story of a crime. It has the brevity and suspense of the best stories of its kind. May be strongly recommended for a train journey.

VACHELL, H. ANNESLEY

The Hill. *Murray (1905), 1948. 6s.*

A novel of youth at Harrow Public School.

Quinneys. *Murray (1914), 1948. 6s.*

A delightful story centred round the character of an antique dealer. Continued in a book of short stories *Quinney's For Quality* (Ward, Lock, 1938).

VAN DINE, S. S. (1888–1939)

The Benson Murder Case. *Benn (1926), 1951. 6s.*
The Greene Murder Case. *Benn (1928), 1950. 6s.*

But two of many immensely popular detective novels by this pseudonymous author who in real life was Willard Huntington Wright.

VINES, SHERARD

Green to Amber. *Cape (1940).*

High comedy and satire in the manner of Aldous Huxley and in parts quite as good.

VOYNICH, E. L.

The Gadfly. *Heinemann (1897).*

A once popular novel of great dramatic power on the Italy of 1830 to 1848, by an author who has written very little. In fact it was not until 1946 that in *Put Off Thy Shoes* (Heinemann), attention was again drawn to her talent.

WADDELL, HELEN

Peter Abelard. *Constable (1933), 1949. 10s.*

The author is a scholar whose work on medieval learning enabled her to offer not only a novel of absorbing interest but a brilliant reconstruction of the life and times of Abelard and Heloïse.

WALLACE, EDGAR (1875–1932)

Bosambo of the River. *Ward Lock (1914), 1950. 5s.*

One of the five 'Sanders of the River' books. They are all competently written novels of adventure and humour. The scene is a remote part of uncivilized Africa.

The Four Just Men. *Hodder (1905), 1950. 5s.*

The most famous of all the extremely skilful stories of crime and excitement by a prolific author with a world audience.

WALLING, R. A. J. (1869–1949)

The Coroner Doubts. *Hodder (1938).*
A Corpse Without a Clue. *Hodder (1945).*

Two of a number of distinctive detective stories by a West country author with a sense of style and craftsmanship.

WALMSLEY, LEO

Three Fevers. *Cape (1932). New edition, Collins, 1948. 7s. 6d.*

WALSH, MAURICE

The Key Above the Door. *Chambers (1926), 1950. 6s.*
The Small Dark Man. *Chambers (1929), 1950. 6s.*
While Rivers Run. *Chambers (1928), 1950. 6s.*

Three exciting adventure stories which have enjoyed immense popularity.

WARNER, REX

The Aerodrome. *Lane (1941). 7s. 6d.*
The Professor. *Lane (1939). 7s. 6d.*

A strange story of a classical scholar with a passionate belief in democracy. As Chancellor he becomes the tool of Fascists, who have to kill him in the end.

The Wild-Goose Chase. *Lane (1937). 7s. 6d.*
Why Was I Killed? *Lane (1943). 7s. 6d.*
The story is told in the form of a dialogue between the dead unknown
warrior and the passer-by.

WARNER, Sylvia Townsend
Lolly Willowes. *Chatto (1926). 6s.*
Mr Fortune's Maggot. *Chatto (1927). Penguin Books, 1950. 1s. 6d.*
Delicate fantasies of unusual charm.

WARREN, Robert Penn
Nightrider. *Eyre & Spottiswoode (1938).*

WAUGH, Evelyn
Black Mischief. *Chapman & Hall (1932), 1948. 7s. 6d.*
Brideshead Revisited. *Chapman & Hall (1945), 1949. 8s. 6d.*
Although the compiler thinks this one of the best novels written during
the war years it must be admitted that to some critics it was the author's
worst.

Decline and Fall. *Chapman & Hall (1928), 1947. 7s. 6d.*
A Handful of Dust. *Chapman & Hall (1934), 1948. 7s. 6d.*
There is even in this most serious and beautifully written book much
of the wit and humour which are the author's characteristic contributions
to current literature. The fusion of the two elements makes it one of the
most important of modern novels, comparable with Aldous Huxley at his
best.

The Loved One. *Chapman & Hall (1948). 7s. 6d.*
A little masterpiece of satire on the current practice of American
'morticians'.

Scott-King's Modern Europe. *Chapman & Hall (1947). 5s.*
Another brief satire, this time on certain attitudes and antics adopted by
totalitarian officials.

Vile Bodies. *Chapman & Hall (1930), 1950. 7s. 6d.*
Perhaps the most famous satirical novel of its decade. It deserves to
become a permanent 'period' piece.

WEBSTER, Elizabeth Charlotte (*d.* 1934)
Ceremony of Innocence. *Cape (1950). 9s. 6d.*
A remarkable novel of gentle fun poked tastefully at subjects usually
left alone by the satirist. Certainly an outstanding novel of originality.

WELCH, Denton (1917–1948)
A Voice Through a Cloud. *Lehmann (1950). 10s. 6d.*
A heart-rending pathos comes from these pages. The novel shows the
young writer to have had talent to a high degree. Probably semi-autobiographical in conception.

WEST, REBECCA
The Thinking Reed. *Hutchinson (1936), 1948. 10s. 6d.*
A long, serious novel. The title is from Pascal.

WESTERBY, ROBERT
Wide Boys Never Work. *(1937.) New edition, Lehmann, 1948. 3s. 6d.*
A thriller of English spivs.

WHITE, ANTONIA
Frost In May. *(1934.) Eyre & Spottiswoode, 1948. 6s.*
A sensitive study of girlhood and the impact of religious feelings of some depth on a young mind. In her introduction to the new edition Elizabeth Bowen pays tribute to its quality, and says it has acquired 'further meaning with the passage of time'.

WHITE, T. H.
The Elephant and the Kangaroo. *Cape (1948). 8s. 6d.*
A satirical fantasy.

The Ill-Made Knight. *Collins (1941).*
A delightful and original comedy.

The Sword in the Stone. *Collins (1938), 1950. 6s.*
A modern classic which may take its place with those few books which are read with as great enjoyment by children as by adults. It is high comedy and fun on the theme of magician Merlin and the legendary times of King Arthur and his knights.

WILDER, THORNTON
The Bridge of San Luis Rey. *Longmans (1927). 6s.*
A best-seller, and a very distinguished piece of work with an original device connecting the lives of the characters.

WILLIAMSON, HENRY
The Flax of Dream. *Faber.*
A series of four distinguished novels:
The Beautiful Years (1921), 1929. 6s.
Dandelion Days (1922), 1932. 5s.
The Dream of Fair Women (1924), 1933. 8s. 6d.
The Pathway (1928), 1947. 8s. 6d.

Salar the Salmon. *Faber (1935), 1944. 6s.*
Illustrated edition, 1948. 10s. 6d.

Tarka the Otter. *Putnam (1927), 1949. 8s. 6d. School edition, 4s.*
Two famous nature stories, the latter the best of its kind in modern literature. It was awarded the Hawthornden Prize.

WILSON, Harry Leon (1867–1939)
Ruggles of Red Gap. *Lane (1917).*

An amusing comedy of an English butler in America. It made a good film.

WILSON, Romer (1891–1930)
The Death of Society. *Collins (1921).*

A strange, haunting novel showing considerable talent and well worth remembering.

WODEHOUSE, P. G.
Blandings Castle. *Jenkins (1935), 1950. 5s.*
Right Ho, Jeeves. *Jenkins (1934), 1950. 5s.*
Very Good, Jeeves. *Jenkins (1930), 1950. 5s.*
The Week-End Wodehouse. *Jenkins (1939), 1951. 12s. 6d.*

An excellent selection of choice episodes from some of the novels and a few short stories, with an introductory essay in appreciation by Hilaire Belloc.

A personal choice from the many droll volumes. For the complete list see the publisher's catalogue.

WOLFE, Thomas (1900–1938)
Look Homeward, Angel. *Heinemann (1929).*
Of Time and the River. *Heinemann (1935).*
The Web and the Rock. *Heinemann (1939), 1947, in Great Britain.*
You Can't Go Home Again. *Heinemann (1940), 1947, in Great Britain.*

Written with almost overwhelming power and realism, full to the brim with a wild, exulting sense of the tragedy of life. There is something of the strange quality of Joyce in the conception of the novels. A volume of selections from them (720 pp.) was published by Heinemann, 1952. 12s. 6d.

WREN, P. C. (1885–1941)
Beau Geste. *Murray (1924), 1950. 7s. 6d.*
Beau Ideal. *Murray (1928), 1950. 7s. 6d.*
Beau Sabreur. *Murray (1926), 1950. 7s. 6d.*

A famous and ever-popular trilogy of impossibly romantic adventure in Morocco, Algeria and the Sahara.

WYLIE, Elinor (1885–1928)
Mr Hodge and Mr Hazard. *Heinemann (1928).*
The Venetian Glass Nephew. *Heinemann (1925).*

These two graceful and charming novels were once available in one volume with two others: *Jennifer Lorn*, Grant Richards, and *The Orphan Angel*, Secker (1934). The second is a fantastic romance of the days of Casanova in Venice; the first a comedy in the Peacockian vein.

111

YATES, DORNFORD

And Berry Came Too. *Ward Lock* (*1936*), *1950. 6s.*
Berry and Co. *Ward Lock* (*1921*), *1950. 6s.*
The Brother of Daphne. *Ward Lock* (*1920*), *1950. 6s.*

Three of a series of eight 'Berry' books; light-hearted, impossible, gay. Written in a remarkably skilful style.

Storm Music. *Ward Lock* (*1934*), *1950. 6s.*

A very good thriller indeed. Altogether there are thirty novels in the Dornford Yates list which have delighted scores of thousands of readers for years. Ideal train-journey books.

YOUNG, E. H. (1880–1949)

The Curate's Wife. *Cape* (*1934*), *1950. 7s. 6d.*
Miss Mole. *Cape* (*1930*), *1950. 5s.*

Awarded the James Tait Black Prize.

The Vicar's Daughter. *Cape* (*1928*), *1950. 5s.*
William. *Cape* (*1925*), *1950. 5s.*

A quiet, authentic talent was hers, in the sound tradition of Jane Austen, Fanny Burney and Trollope. Her last showed no falling off; *Chatterton Square*, Cape, 1947, 9s. 6d.

YOUNG, FRANCIS BRETT

The Black Diamond. *Heinemann* (*1921*), *1950. 10s. 6d.*
My Brother Jonathan. *Heinemann* (*1928*), *1950. 10s. 6d.*
Portrait of Clare. *Heinemann* (*1927*), *1950. 12s. 6d.*
The Young Physician. *Heinemann* (*1919*), *1950. 12s. 6d.*

Four popular novels in a uniform *Severn* edition of this author's many works which have excited the admiration of a great public as well as that of literary critics.

For details of other twentieth-century authors see also in *An English Library* under Stacy Aumonier, Maurice Baring, James Barrie, Arnold Bennett, Stella Benson, J. D. Beresford, Ernest Bramah, John Buchan, Donn Byrne, G. K. Chesterton, Joseph Conrad, E. M. Delafield, Conan Doyle, Ronald Firbank, F. Scott Fitzgerald, F. M. Ford, John Galsworthy, R. M. Gilchrist, R. B. Cunninghame Graham, Kenneth Grahame, Rider Haggard, Radclyffe Hall, W. F. Harvey, O. Henry, Maurice Hewlett, Richard Hillary, Winifred Holtby, Anthony Hope, Stephen Hudson, W. H. Hudson, W. W. Jacobs, Henry James, James Joyce, Rudyard Kipling, D. H. Lawrence, W. J. Locke, Jack London, E. V. Lucas, A. G. Macdonell, Katherine Mansfield, W. B. Maxwell, Leonard Merrick, C. E. Montague, George Moore, H. H. Munro, L. H. Myers, Barry Pain, Marmaduke Pickthall, Sir Arthur Quiller-Couch, Forrest Reid, H. H. Richardson, A. D. Sedgwick, M. P. Shiel, May Sinclair, Edward Thompson, W. J. Turner, Hugh Walpole, Mary Webb, H. G. Wells, Edith Wharton, Charles Williams, Virginia Woolf.

SOCIAL AND POLITICAL HISTORY

'Make scholars more literate and writers more scholarly' pleads a distinguished American publisher. There is indeed no greater need in the world
of modern literature and no section where it is of more importance than
in this one. Hence the pleasure of realizing the good fortune of readers of
English in being presented with so many great and good books, written by
specialists and scholars yet with such charm and liveliness of style that
they reach an enormous public, and even at times become best-sellers.
Trevelyan, Bryant, Rowse, Wedgwood, Hammond, Coulton, Fay: these
are but a few of scores of authors whose historical writings are honoured and
respected for their scholarship and at the same time are read by educated
people in all walks of life.

Then too, in this history section, we have an abundance of brilliantly
written monographs presented in a form brief enough to allow of rapid
reading, yet full enough to communicate the author's knowledge accurately
and without distortion. In the first book to be mentioned and in D. C.
Somervell's abridgement of Toynbee's great work we have two masterly
compressions; in Winston Churchill's record of the years he helped to
make great and inspiring we have history written on the grand scale of
Clarendon and in the style of a modern master.

ADAMS, HENRY (1838–1919)

The Formative Years. *Condensed and edited by* HERBERT AGAR.
   2 vols. Collins, 1948. 42s.

The original work in nine volumes dealt exhaustively with the admini-
strations of Jefferson and Madison, 1801–1817. This era saw the final
shaping of America during the Napoleonic period and the 1812 war with
Great Britain. First published 1889–1890, the classic and monumental
piece of historical research and writing is one of the masterpieces of
American scholarship. The abridgement does for it what Somervell's
abridgement does for Toynbee's *A Study of History*.

ADAMS, JAMES TRUSLOW

The Epic of America. *Routledge (1933, 1939), 1950. 8s. 6d.*

ADDISON, WILLIAM

The English Country Parson. *Dent (1947). 16s.*

An entertaining byway of social history.

AGAR, HERBERT

A Time for Greatness. *Eyre & Spottiswoode (1943).*

An American analyses the causes of twentieth-century chaos, and
indicates with powerful and persuasive argument the path the nations
must travel if we are to have an era of constructive peace.

ALLEN, C. KEMP
Law in the Making. *O.U.P. (1927). 5th edition, 1951. 35s.*

ANTHONY, KATHERINE
Catherine the Great. *Cape (1926). 4s. 6d.*

ARNOLD, SIR THOMAS and GUILLAUME, A. (Editors)
The Legacy of Islam. *O.U.P. (1931). 21s.*

ASHLEY, SIR WILLIAM and ALLEN, G. C.
The Economic Organization of England: an outline history.
Longmans (1930). 3rd edition, 1949. 10s. 6d.

ASHTON, T. S.
The Industrial Revolution, *1760–1830.*
O.U.P. (1948). 6s. (Home University Library.)

BAILEY, CYRIL (Editor)
The Legacy of Rome. *O.U.P. (1923). 18s.*

BARKER, SIR ERNEST
Political Thought in England, 1848–1914. *O.U.P. (1915).*
2nd revised edition, 1947. 6s. (Home University Library.)
One of a series of four. See under Davidson, Gooch, and Laski for others.

BARKER, SIR ERNEST (Editor)
The Character of England. *O.U.P. (1947). 42s.*
A survey by a number of historical and literary writers designed to reveal the nature of the people of England traditionally, at their work, at play, and in the shaping of a Commonwealth.

BASKERVILLE, GEOFFREY
English Monks and the Suppression of the Monasteries.
Cape (1937), 1950. 18s.

BAYNES, NORMAN H. and MOSS, H. ST L. B.
Byzantium: an introduction to East Roman Civilization.
O.U.P. (1948). 25s.

BEARD, CHARLES AUSTIN (1874–1948) and BEARD, M. R.
The Rise of American Civilization. *Cape (1927), 1950. 30s.*

BELL, CLIVE
Civilization. *Chatto & Windus (1928). Penguin Books, 1938. 1s. 6d.*

BELLOC, HILAIRE

The French Revolution. *O.U.P. (2nd edition, 1911). 6s.*
(Home University Library.)
How the Reformation Happened. *Cape (1928), 1950. 10s. 6d.*
Marie Antoinette. *Methuen (1910), 1951. 25s.*

BENNETT, H. S.

Life on the English Manor, *1150–1400. C.U.P. (1937). 25s.*

BENNS, F. LEE

Europe Since 1914. *Bell (revised edition, 1947).*

BEVAN, E. R. and **SINGER**, CHARLES (Editors)
The Legacy of Israel. *O.U.P. (1927). 21s.*

BLUNDEN, EDMUND

Undertones of War. *(1928.) Lane, 1950. 5s.*
   One of the most distinguished books to come from the War of 1914–1918.
A personal experience expressed so finely that it conveyed with classic
permanence the impact of the war on a whole generation of sensitive,
intellectual youth. See also Kenneth Hopkins's *Selection of Poetry and
Prose by Edmund Blunden*, Hart Davis, 1950, 15s. for selections from this
work.

BOWERS, C. G.

Jefferson and Hamilton. *New York, Houghton, 1925.*
Jefferson in Power. *New York, Houghton, 1936.*
   Two important works considered by American writers to be indispensable for the understanding of the growth and character of the American
political genius. The first is the story of 'the struggle for democracy in
America', and its sequel of the political and social forces engaged in
'the death struggle of the Federalists'.

BOWLE, JOHN

The Unity of European History. *Cape (1948). 18s.*
   A political and cultural survey.

BRADBY, E. D.

A Short History of the French Revolution, 1789–1795.
   O.U.P. (1926). 8s. 6d.

BRINTON, CRANE

The Anatomy of Revolution. *Cape (1938). Revised edition 1953. 35s.*
   A witty study of four revolutions: the Cromwellian; the American; the
first French Revolution; and the Russian Revolution of 1917. It does not
perhaps go deep enough into causes to satisfy the scholar but it is entertaining and provocative.

BROWN, P. HUME

A Short History of Scotland. *Oliver & Boyd (1908).*
New edition revised by H. W. MEIKLE. *1951. 12s. 6d.*

The standard work is in three volumes: *A History of Scotland,* by
P. Hume Brown, C.U.P., 21*s.* each volume; library edition, 40*s.* each.
In the latter the final volume is 'from the Revolution of 1689 to the year
1910', whereas the ordinary edition is limited to 1689–1843. The revised
shorter work has 200 illustrations, portraits and tables.

BRYANT, ARTHUR

English Saga: 1840–1940. *Collins (1940), 1943. 12s. 6d.*
King Charles II. *Longmans (1931), 1936. 18s. and 8s. 6d.*
The Years of Endurance, 1793–1802. *Collins (1942), 1950. 15s.*
Years of Victory, 1802–1812. *Collins (1944), 1950. 15s.*
The Age of Elegance, 1812–1832. *Collins (1950). 15s.*

Next to Trevelyan's *Social History* these historical narratives and interpretations of the character of the English people in times of peril and trial
are the most widely read books of their kind in modern times. Com-
manding the respect of specialists and scholars, the author has succeeded
in making history as popular as fiction.

BURKE, THOMAS (1886–1946)

The English Townsman. *Batsford (1945), 1947. 12s. 6d.*
The Streets of London. *Batsford (1940), 1949. 12s. 6d.*
Travel in England. *Batsford (1943), 1946. 12s. 6d.*

Light, entertaining byways in English social history, local lore and
topography. All are well illustrated and make agreeable introductions
to their subjects.

BURKITT, M. C.

The Old Stone Age. *C.U.P. (1933), 1949. 15s.*
Our Early Ancestors. *C.U.P. (1926), 1929. 15s.*
Prehistory. *C.U.P. (1925).*

BURLINGHAME, ROGER

Engines of Democracy. *New York, Scribner (1940). 42s. 6d. (approx.).*

The author thinks that national unity in his country has been achieved
by the inventive genius of Americans. This is the background to the vivid
story he tells of the telephone and telegraph, radio, the typewriter,
industrial machines, the cinematograph, quick printing, the teleprinter,
etc., and the social effects of their introduction.

BUTTERFIELD, HERBERT

George III, Lord North and the People, 1779–1780. *Bell (1949). 30s.*

The history of the year of crisis, when Britain's most inept government
brought the country to the brink of disaster with North America, the
colonies, France, Spain and Ireland.

CAREY, G. V. and H. S. SCOTT
An Outline History of the Great War, 1914–1918.
C.U.P. (*1928*).

CARLETON, PATRICK
Buried Empires. *Edward Arnold* (*1939*), *1950. 12s. 6d.*
The story of the earliest civilizations of the Middle East: Iraq, Iran, and the Indus Valley.

CARR, E. H.
Studies in Revolution. *Macmillan* (*1950*). *9s. 6d.*
Contributions to *The Times Literary Supplement* gathered together with a Third Programme talk, by the distinguished historian whose *Twenty Years' Crisis, 1919–1939*, Macmillan (1946), 12s. 6d., is the best introduction to the study of international relations between the wars.

CARRINGTON, C. E.
The British Overseas. *C.U.P.* (*1950*). *50s.*
A masterly survey of 1092 pages, with illustrations and maps. The best one-volume history available.

CHAPMAN, F. SPENCER
The Jungle is Neutral. *Chatto* (*1948*), *1951. 18s.*
A notable piece of writing by a well-known explorer, telling of the campaign in Malaya during the second world war, and particularly of the author's extraordinary adventures with Chinese guerrillas fighting the Japanese.

CHAPMAN, GUY (Editor)
Vain Glory. *Cassell* (*1937*), *1950. 8s. 6d.*
A miscellany of the First World War, 1914–1918 'written by those who fought in it, on each side, and on all fronts', embodying personal experiences, reflections and memories of anguished disillusionment. Introduction by the editor.

CHARLESWORTH, M. P. (1895–1951)
The Roman Empire. *O.U.P.* (*1951*). *6s.* (*Home University Library.*)
A companion book to Fowler's *Rome*, which see below.

CHILDE, V. G.
The Dawn of European Civilization.
Routledge & Kegan Paul (*1939*). *Third revised edition, 1948, 28s.*

CHRIMES, S. B.
English Constitutional History.
O.U.P. (*1948*). *6s.* (*Home University Library.*)

CHURCHILL, WINSTON SPENCER

The World Crisis, 1911–1918. *4 vols. Macmillan (1923–1929.)*
The Aftermath: a sequel. *Macmillan (1929).*

Originally published by Macmillan dealing respectively with 1911–1914; 1915; 1916–1918. A brilliant record of the First World War by the participant who was destined to become the chief architect of victory in the Second. An abridged and revised version in one volume, with an additional chapter on the 'Battle of the Marne', was published in 1931 by Butterworth.

The Eastern Front. *Macmillan (1931).*

The tailpiece to the main narrative.

The Second World War. *Cassell (1948)—In progress. 30s. each volume.*
, Vol. 1: *The Gathering Storm (1948).*
Vol. 2: *Their Finest Hour (1949).*
Vol. 3: *The Grand Alliance (1950).*
Vol. 4: *The Hinge of Fate (1951).*
Vol. 5: *Closing the Ring (1952).*

The War Speeches, *1938–1945. Edited by Charles Eade.*
Definitive edition, 3 vols. Cassell (1951). 18s. each.

Collecting the separate volumes: *Step By Step, 1936–1939 (1939)*; *Into Battle (1941)*; *The Unrelenting Struggle (1942)*; *Onwards to Victory (1944)*; *The Dawn of Liberation (1945)*; *Secret Session Speeches (1946)*; *Victory (1946)*. The great speeches in the definitive edition are royal octavo in size ($6\frac{1}{4} \times 10$). Printed on parchment paper they have a format worthy of their high quality as indispensable source-books for historians and as works of classic literature.

The Sinews of Peace. *Cassell (1948). 16s.*

CLAPHAM, SIR J. H. (1873–1946)

Concise Economic History of England. *C.U.P. (1949). 21s.*

The principal work is in three volumes: *The Early Railway Age, 1820–1850*; *Free Trade and Steel, 1850–1886*; *Machines and National Rivalries, 1887–1914*, with *An Epilogue, 1914–1929.* Published by C.U.P., 45s. each. One of the greatest histories written in the twentieth century.

CLARK, GRAHAME

Archaeology and Society. *Methuen (1939).*
Second revised edition, 1947, 10s. 6d.
Prehistoric England. *Batsford (1940). Fourth edition, 1948. 12s. 6d.*

Popular in approach, but authoritative and scholarly. Well illustrated.

CLARK, G. N.

The Wealth of England, 1496–1760.
O.U.P. (1946). 6s. (Home University Library.)

COLE, G. D. H. and POSTGATE, RAYMOND
The Common People. *Methuen (1938). 4th edition, 1949. 12s. 6d.*

COLSON, F. H.
The Week. *C.U.P. (1926). 10s. 6d.*
On the origin and significance of the division of our year into seven-day periods.

COULTON, GEORGE GORDON (1858–1947). (Editor)
Life in the Middle Ages: Cambridge Anthologies.
    4 vols. C.U.P. (1928–1930).
    Vol. 1: *Religion, Folklore and Superstition. 12s. 6d.*
    Vol. 2: *Chronicles, Science and Art. 8s. 6d.*
    Vol. 3: *Men and Manners. 8s. 6d.*
    Vol. 4: *Monks, Friars and Nuns. 16s.*
For details of Coulton's own historical works, see *An English Library.*

COWELL, F. R.
Cicero and the Roman Republic. *Pitman (1948). 20s.*

CRANAGE, D. H. S.
The Home of the Monk. *C.U.P. (1934).*
An allied theme is examined in the same author's *Cathedrals and How They Were Built,* C.U.P. (1948), 1951, 12s. 6d.

CRESTON, DORMER
In Search of Two Characters. *Macmillan (1945).*
Napoleon and his son are the main characters, with some picturesque but neglected aspects of the First Empire as the background. A similar method is used in the same author's *The Regent and His Daughter,* Eyre & Spottiswoode (1934), 1947, 16s., which is a study of Charlotte, daughter of George IV and Caroline.

CRUMP, C. G. and JACOB, E. F. (Editors)
The Legacy of the Middle Ages. *O.U.P. (1926). 21s.*

CUMMINGS, E. E.
The Enormous Room. *Cape (1928).*
An early prose work by the American poet, drawn from his dreadful experience in a prison camp during the first World War. The horrors of the Second War were here foreshadowed. Preface by Robert Graves.

DAVIDSON, W. L.
Political Thought in England: the Utilitarians from Bentham to J. S. Mill.
    O.U.P. (1915). 6s. (Home University Library.)
One of a series of four. *See also under* Barker, Gooch and Laski for the others.

DE CHAIR, SOMERSET
The Golden Carpet. *Faber (1944), 1950. 7s. 6d.*

The two parts of this narrative of the British expedition in 1941 which saved Iraq from the Germans, and of the subsequent campaign in Syria, were first published separately in limited editions, as *The Golden Carpet*, and *The Silver Crescent*, Golden Cockerel Press, 1943.

DERRY, T. K. and JARMAN, T. L.
The European World, 1870–1945. *Bell (1950). 20s.*

For the general reader as well as the student, with suggestions at the end of each chapter for further reading.

DICKINSON, G. LOWES (1862–1932)
Revolution and Reaction in Modern France, 1789–1871.
Allen & Unwin (1892), 1927.

For other books by this author, see *An English Library*.

DILLON, MYLES
The Cycles of the Kings. *O.U.P. (1946). 10s. 6d.*

An important collection of the royal tales of Ancient Ireland.

EVANS, A. J.
The Escaping Club. *Lane (1921).*

Escaping from prison camps in wartime has now become an established sport whenever war breaks out. This is a famous story of escapes during 1916 to 1918.

FAY, C. R.
Life and Labour in the Nineteenth Century.
C.U.P. (2nd edition, 1933). 10s. 6d.

Not only an important book for students of social history but also an absorbing one for the general reader who may regard it as a necessary background to the study of English fiction, particularly the novels of Mrs Gaskell, Kingsley and Dickens.

FEDDEN, ROBIN
Syria. *Hale (1946). 21s.*
'An historical appreciation.'

FEILING, KEITH
England Under the Tudors and Stuarts.
O.U.P. (1927). 6s. (Home University Library.)

The History of the Tory Party, 1640–1714. *O.U.P.* (*1924*), *1950. 21s.*
A standard book followed in 1938 by *The Second Tory Party, 1714–1832*, Macmillan, 21*s.*

FELLOWS, ARNOLD
The Wayfarer's Companion. *O.U.P.* (*1937*), *1946. 15s.*
An illustrated survey of England's history in her buildings and countryside.

FERGUSSON, BERNARD
Beyond the Chindwin. *Collins* (*1945*), *1951. 6s.*
The Wild Green Earth. *Collins* (*1946*). *10s. 6d.*
The first book deals with the amazing exploits of No. 5 Column of Wingate's expedition into Burma, 1943, and both in the high quality of the style and in content was considered one of the best books of the war. The second is a record of the later expedition, when the author was a brigadier.

FOWLER, W. WARDE
The City State of the Greeks and Romans. *Macmillan* (*1893*), *1952. 8s. 6d.*
A standard book for students; the best short study for general readers.
Rome. *O.U.P.* (*1911*).
Revised second edition by M. P. CHARLESWORTH, *1947, 6s.* (*Home University Library*.)
Social Life at Rome in the Age of Cicero. *Macmillan* (*1908*).

FOX, SIR CYRIL
The Personality of Britain: its influence on inhabitant and invader in prehistoric and early historic times. *National Museum of Wales* (*1932*). *Revised 4th edition, 1943. 7s. 6d.*
Regarded by scholars as the foundation of all work on the influence of environment on early man and his cultures in Britain.

FULFORD, ROGER
George the Fourth. *Duckworth* (*1935*). *Revised edition, 1949. 15s.*

GARRATT, G. T. (Editor)
The Legacy of India. *Introduction by the* MARQUESS OF ZETLAND. *O.U.P.* (*1937*). *18s.*

GELDART, W. M.
Elements of English Law. *O.U.P.* (*1911*).
Revised 5th edition by SIR WILLIAM HOLDSWORTH *and* H. G. HANBURY, *1948. 6s.* (*Home University Library*.)
Probably the best brief study available for the general reader.

GIBSON, GUY (1918–1944)

Enemy Coast Ahead. *Michael Joseph (1946), 1951. 7s. 6d.*

Wing-Commander Gibson, V.C. led the great attack on the Ruhr dams May 1943. His book is among the first dozen of 1939–1946 war books written by combatants themselves.

GIEDION, SIGFRIED

Space, Time and Architecture.
O.U.P. (1941). Revised edition, 1949. 50s.

Mechanization Takes Command. *O.U.P. (1948). 75s.*

The first book is the substance of the Charles Eliot Norton lectures for 1938–1939, on the growth of a new tradition, and is one of the most remarkable books of the century both for professional architects and for the public. The second book continues the theme. Both show in text and in 821 outstanding illustrations how mechanization has influenced architecture, painting, and design, and hence, life and feeling.

GLANVILLE, S. R. K. (Editor)

The Legacy of Egypt. *O.U.P. (1942). 18s.*

A well-illustrated collection of scholarly contributions to the archaeology and history of ancient Egypt.

GOOCH, G. P.

Frederick the Great. *Longmans (1947). 21s.*

The best modern English study.

A History of Our Time, 1885–1914. *O.U.P. (1911).*
2nd edition, 1946. 6s. (Home University Library.)
Political Thought in England from Bacon to Halifax.
O.U.P. (1914). 6s. (Home University Library.)

One of a series. For the others *see under* Barker, Davidson, Laski.

GORER, GEOFFREY

The Americans. *Cresset Press (1948). 12s. 6d.*

A study in national character written with wit but no malice; with penetration and insight, but no smugness.

GRAHAM, STEPHEN

Peter the Great. *Benn (1929), 1950. 16s.*

A knowledge of the policy of Peter is essential for those who want to understand the development of Russia and the aims and motives behind her foreign policy whether under crowned or uncrowned rulers.

GRANT, A. J. (1862–1948)

A History of Europe, 1494–1610. *Methuen (1931). 8th edition, 1951. 25s.*

GRANT, A. J. and TEMPERLEY, HAROLD
Europe in the Nineteenth and Twentieth Centuries, 1789–1950.
Longmans (1926). 6th edition, revised and edited by LILLIAN M. PENSON
(1950). 25s.

GRAVES, ROBERT and HODGE, ALAN
The Long Week-end. *Faber (1940), 1950. 16s.*
A social history of Great Britain, 1918–1939, presented by comment, quotation and record.

GRETTON, R. H.
Modern History of the English People, 1880–1922.
Secker & Warburg (1930).
In a volume of 1185 pages the author provides one of the most readable surveys of the period.

GRINNELL-MILNE, DUNCAN (Editor)
An Escaper's Log. *Lane (1926).*
True stories of escapes from German prison camps during the War of 1914–1918.

GROSE-HODGE, HUMFREY
Roman Panorama. *C.U.P. (1944). 15s.*
In this 'background to Latin', written with learning lightly penned, the author impresses on the reader the permanent value to the modern world of the best in Roman civilization. The picture of daily life in Rome and its Empire is so well done that those who start the book with little or no interest in the subject soon find they have to extend their reading to other studies and to primary sources.

HACKETT, FRANCIS
Henry the Eighth. *Cape (1929), 1950. 15s.*
One of the most widely-read books of its kind and respected by historians as well as general readers.

HADDON, A. C.
A History of Anthropology. *Watts (1910), 1934. 2s. 6d.*
Wanderings of Peoples. *C.U.P. (1911). 6s.*
A brief but scholarly study of the early movements of European tribes and communities, and hence a necessary preface to the study of modern history.

HAMILTON, HENRY
History of the Homeland. *Allen & Unwin (1947). 18s.*

HAMMOND, J. L. (1872–1949) and HAMMOND, BARBARA

The Age of the Chartists, 1832–1854. *Longmans (1930).*

'A study in discontent.'

The Rise of Modern Industry. *Methuen (1925).*
   8th revised and enlarged edition, 1951. 18s.

The Village Labourer, 1760–1832. *Longmans (1911).*

The Town Labourer, 1760–1832: the new civilization. *Longmans (1917).*

The Skilled Labourer, 1760–1832. *Longmans (1919).*

The three 'Labourer' books form a notable trilogy, being a study in the government of England before the Reform Bill. A major and enduring work widely read by both student and general reader.

HARDY, J. L.

I Escape. *Lane (1927.)*

Another narrative of a remarkable escape from a German prison camp during the War of 1914–1918, with an introduction by Sir A. CONAN DOYLE.

HARRISON, G. B.

The Elizabethan Journals. *Routledge (1933).*

A Jacobean Journal of the years 1603–1606. *Routledge (1941). 18s.*

The first is a record of the things most talked of during the years 1591–1603, and the second, following the same ingenious method, continues the story. Gathered from original sources, diaries, state papers, tracts, etc., the compilation fills in the gaps left by formal histories, and illuminates the general narrative of history.

HARRISON, JANE ELLEN (1850–1928)

Ancient Art and Ritual. *O.U.P. (1913). 6s. (Home University Library.)*

HARRISON, M. C. C. and CARTWRIGHT, H. A.

Within Four Walls. *Edward Arnold (1930), 1949. 10s. 6d. and 4s. 6d.*

A further record of a remarkable escape from a German prison camp in the War of 1914–1918.

HART, LIDDELL

' **T. E. Lawrence': in Arabia and after.** *Cape (1935), 1950. 12s. 6d.*

HARTLEY, DOROTHY (Editor)

The Old Book. *Allen & Unwin (1930). 32s. 6d.*

A medieval anthology of prose and poetry, edited and illuminated, and with an introduction by George Saintsbury. The editor has cast her net wide and has gathered in odd and deeply interesting scraps from many sources including even old cook books. 'Parsley and onion and mince them into vinegar and pepper and salt and eat him so.' 'If anybody does not feel the charm of that', said Saintsbury, '"and eat him so", he has no sense of the beauty of the arrangement of words.'

HASLUCK, E. L.
Foreign Affairs, 1919–1937. *C.U.P.* (*1938*). *12s. 6d.*
A brief study of the all-important years when so much went wrong and so little right.

HATTERSLEY, A. F.
A Short History of Western Civilization. *C.U.P.* (*1927*).

HAWKES, JACQUETTA
A Land. *Cresset Press* (*1951*). *21s.*
An important and distinguished book which only a poet could have written. Its personal, almost autobiographical, style enhances its value as an attempt to portray the growth of England from age-old rocks to its present shape.

HAWKES, JACQUETTA and CHRISTOPHER
Prehistoric Britain. *Chatto* (*1947*). *16s.*
An expansion of a Penguin Book published in 1944, containing a unique feature: 'a practical archaeological guide to Britain'; the regions and sites; descriptions; and how to reach them.

HEMINGFORD, LORD
What Parliament Is and Does. *C.U.P.* (*1947*). *10s. 6d.*
Written for the layman and for students requiring an introduction to the standard books on Parliament.

HENNELL, THOMAS (1903–1945)
Change on the Farm. *C.U.P.* (*1934*).
The Countryman at Work. *Architectural Press* (*1947*). *12s. 6d.*
Written and illustrated by Hennell, published posthumously, with a memoir by H. J. MASSINGHAM. A good writer, a fine draughtsman and a true countryman, his love of old crafts, from the making of a farmer's cart to the thatching of a cottage, enabled him to write books about English life and people which will always remain amongst the best of their kind, alongside classics such as *The Wheelwright's Shop* by George Sturt and *Hodge and His Masters*, by Jefferies.

HODGKIN, R. H.
A History of the Anglo-Saxons, A.D. 360–900.
2 vols. O.U.P. (*1935*). *2nd edition, 1939.*
798 pages with such a title sounds forbidding; far from it. This well-illustrated and scholarly book is so finely presented both in style and by the publisher that it has been made as readable as a popular biography.

HOGBEN, LANCELOT
From Cave Painting to Comic Strip. *Max Parrish* (*1949*). *21s.*
The story of 'how man has become a communicating animal'. Illustrated with over 200 coloured and black and white drawings.

HOLDSWORTH, Sir William (1871–1944)
Some Makers of English Law. *C.U.P.* (*1938*).

ILBERT, Sir Courtenay P.
Parliament. *O.U.P.* (*1911*).
  3rd edition with Sir Cecil Carr, *1948. 6s.* (*Home University Library.*)
Its history, constitution and practice. The new edition contains a glossary of parliamentary terms.

INNES, Arthur D.
England Under the Tudors, 1485–1603. *Methuen* (*1905*).
  13th edition revised by J. M. Henderson. *1951. 21s.*

JEKYLL, Gertrude (1843–1932) and JONES, Sydney R.
Old English Household Life. *Batsford* (*1925*), *1945. 12s. 6d.*
The life of farm and cottage. A footnote to all the books on English social history, concentrating on the farms and cottages and the crafts of the yeoman and peasant stock of England.

JENKS, Edward
The Book of English Law. *Murray* (*1928*). *4th edition, 1936. 12s. 6d.*
A description of the framework and principles of the whole of English law as at the end of 1935 for the educated layman and the student.

A Short History of English Law from the earliest times to the end of 1938.
  Methuen. 6th edition, 1949. 21s.

JENNINGS, W. Ivor
The British Constitution. *C.U.P.* (*1947*), *1950. 15s.*
A survey of 'actuality' rather than an historical record.

Cabinet Government. *C.U.P.* (*1936*). *2nd revised edition, 1951. 37s. 6d.*
Parliament. *C.U.P.* (*1939*). *37s. 6d.*
The best modern survey of its kind; detailed enough for the parliamentarian, civil servant and historian; within the grasp of the general reader whose time and specific interest in the subject is limited. Complementary to *Cabinet Government.*

JONES, E. H.
The Road to En-Dor. *Lane* (*1919*).
A true story of the War of 1914–1918, being an account of how two prisoners of war at Yozgad in Turkey won their way to freedom.

KING-HALL, Stephen
Our Own Times; 1913–1934. *2 vols. Faber* (*1935*).
  Revised and enlarged edition, 1941. 21s.
'A political and economic survey.'

KIRKPATRICK, F. A.

The Spanish Conquistadores. *Black (1934), 1946. 25s.*

The story of Spanish discovery and conquest in America told with scholarship and brilliance.

KITTO, H. D. F.

The Greeks. *Penguin Books (1951). 6s.*

LAMB, HAROLD

The Crusades: flame of Islam. *Eyre & Spottiswoode (1931).*
The Crusades: iron men and saints. *Eyre & Spottiswoode (1944).*
Ghenghis Khan: Emperor of all men. *Eyre & Spottiswoode (1933).*

LASKI, HAROLD J. (1893–1950)

The Danger of Being a Gentleman, and other essays.
Allen & Unwin (1939).
A Grammar of Politics. *Allen & Unwin (1925), 1938. 18s.*
Liberty and the Modern State. *Allen & Unwin (1930).*
New edition, 1948. 8s. 6d.
Political Thought in England: from Locke to Bentham.
O.U.P. (1920). 6s. (Home University Library.)

For the companion volumes in this series *see under* Barker, Gooch, and Davidson.

Reflections on the Revolution of Our Time. *Allen & Unwin (1943). 15s.*

The Russian Revolution, Fascism, Democracy, and current trends in government examined from the viewpoint of a left-wing political philosopher.

The Rise of European Liberalism. *Allen & Unwin (1936). 7s. 6d.*

An essay in interpretation.

LATHAM, RONALD

In Quest of Civilization. *Jarrolds (1946), 1950. 10s. 6d.*

'A very remarkable book.' E. E. Kellett in *Time and Tide.*

LEIGHTON, ISABEL (Editor)

The Aspirin Age, 1919–1941. *Lane (1950). 16s.*

Twenty-two brilliant journalists contribute to this symposium which recalls with excitement and the vividness of high-powered journalism the dramas behind the headlines of the period, from the Versailles 'Peace' Treaty making to Pearl Harbour, including some horrific American episodes such as *The Man On the Ledge* and the strange case of Aimée MacPherson.

LEWIS, ROY and MAUDE, ANGUS

The English Middle Classes. *Phoenix House (1949). 15s.*

A history and a social commentary of outstanding interest and importance.

LIPS, Julius E.
The Origin of Things. *Harrap (1949). 21s.*
A cultural history of man.

LIPSON, Ephraim
The Growth of English Society. *Black (1949), 1952. 25s.*
A short economic history in which the emphasis is on the life and development of the worker.

LIVINGSTONE, Sir R. W.
The Greek Genius and its Meaning to Us.
   O.U.P. 2nd edition, 1915. 10s.
Greek Ideals and Modern Life. *O.U.P. (1935). 8s. 6d.*

LIVINGSTONE, Sir R. W. (Editor)
The Legacy of Greece. *O.U.P. (1921). 18s.*
The Mission of Greece. *O.U.P. (1928). 12s. 6d.*
The Pageant of Greece. *O.U.P. (1923). 12s. 6d.*

LLOYD, Sir John Edward (1861–1947)
The History of Wales: from the earliest times to the Edwardian conquest.
   Longmans (1911). New edition, 1939. 42s.
The standard work.

MACKINDER, Sir Halford John (1861–1947)
Britain and the British Seas. *O.U.P. (1902).*
   2nd revised edition, 1907; 1950. 17s. 6d.
An important work and an essential book for students of history, linking geography with history; environment and climate with national character and destiny.

MACLEAN, Fitzroy
Eastern Approaches. *Cape (1949). 15s.*
One of the major books of the 1939 war, being personal experiences in the U.S.S.R., in the Western Desert, and later with Tito in Jugoslavia during the critical year.

MADARIAGA, Salvador de
The Rise of the Spanish American Empire. *Hollis & Carter (1947). 21s.*
The Fall of the Spanish American Empire. *Hollis & Carter (1947). 21s.*

MARGARY, Ivan D.
Roman Ways in the Weald. *Phoenix House (1948). 25s.*

MARTIN, B. Kingsley
The Triumph of Lord Palmerston. *Allen & Unwin (1924), 1926. 10s. 6d.*
A study of public opinion in the England before the Crimean War.

MITCHELL, JAMES LESLIE (1901–1935)
The Conquest of the Maya. *Jarrolds (1934).*

The author wrote his well-known trilogy of Scottish life under the pseudonym of L. G. Gibbon; this piece of research was published under his real name, with an introduction by Sir G. Elliott Smith. It is a standard work to which the adjective 'great' has been applied.

MITCHELL, R. J. and LEYS, M. D. R.
A History of the English People. *Longmans (1950). 42s.*

An unusual and noteworthy book of informal history; in its 612 pages, with illustrations drawn from contemporary sources, it records the history of the people in their homes, at work and at play, washing, shopping, talking. The authors have used old letters and diaries, news sheets and bills, and similar records, to obtain facts often overlooked in formal histories. Here we can learn how our ancestors shaved and accompany them on the first bargain sales to be held in the shops of London.

MOORE, E. W. (1906–1953)
The Roman Commonwealth. *Hodder (1942). 15s.*

MOOREHEAD, ALAN
African Trilogy. *Hamish Hamilton (1944).*
Eclipse. *Hamish Hamilton (1945). 12s. 6d.*

The best account by a journalist on the spot throughout the African and European campaigns of 1941 to 1945. The second book tells of the foothold gained in Europe and the subsequent triumphant surge over the Rhine.

MORISON, S. E. and COMMAGER, H. S.
The Growth of the American Republic.
2 vols. O.U.P. 4th edition, 1951, 70s.

1670 pages, with 44 maps; has been described as the best short general history of the United States. Vol. 1 deals with the period from A.D. 1000 to 1865; Vol. 2 with 1865 to 1942.

MURRAY, MARGARET A.
The Splendour that was Egypt. *Sidgwick & Jackson (1949). 35s.*

NAMIER, L. B.
1848: the Revolution of the Intellectuals. *O.U.P. (1946). 10s. 6d.*
The Raleigh Lecture on History, 1944.

NEALE, J. E.
The Elizabethan House of Commons. *Cape (1949). 18s.*
Queen Elizabeth. *Cape (1934), 1950. 15s.*

Just as the first is more than a parliamentary history, so is the second more than a biography. The first is complementary to the other and is a study of personalities and procedure.

NICOLSON, HAROLD

The Congress of Vienna. *Constable (1946), 1949. 18s.*
'A study in Allied unity, 1812–1922.'

Diplomacy. *O.U.P. (1939), 1950. 6s. (Home University Library.)*

NOTESTEIN, WALLACE

English Folk. *Cape (1943).*

OGG, DAVID

England in the Reign of Charles II. *2 vols. O.U.P. (1934).*
The most important and only reliable guide to the whole period.

Europe in the Seventeenth Century. *Black (1925).*
5th revised edition, 1948. 21s.
Louis XIV. *O.U.P. (1933). 6s. (Home University Library.)*

ORWELL, GEORGE (1903–1949)

Homage to Catalonia. *Secker & Warburg (1938), 1951. 10s. 6d.*
A combatant's account of the Civil War in Spain. Orwell fought against
Franco as a British volunteer. His vivid book is of permanent value.

OXFORD HISTORY OF ENGLAND. *14 vols. O.U.P. 25s. each.*
In progress. General Editor, G. N. CLARK.

> COLLINGWOOD, R. G. and MYRES, J. N. L. *Roman Britain and the English Settlements.* 2nd edition, 1937.
> STENTON, Sir FRANK. *Anglo-Saxon England.* 2nd edition, 1947.
> POOLE, A. LANE. *From Domesday Book to Magna Charta, 1087–1216* (1951).
> MACKIE, J. D. *The Earlier Tudors, 1485–1558 (1952).*
> BLACK, J. B. *The Reign of Elizabeth, 1558–1603* (1936).
> DAVIES, GODFREY. *The Early Stuarts, 1603–1660* (1937).
> CLARK, G. N. *The Later Stuarts, 1660–1714* (1934).
> WILLIAMS, BASIL. *The Whig Supremacy, 1714–1760* (1939).
> WOODWARD, E. L. *The Age of Reform, 1815–1870* (1938).
> ENSOR, R. C. K. *England, 1870–1914* (1936).

Each volume is an independent book, but when completed the series
will be a continuous history from the Roman occupation to the twentieth
century. The four volumes to come are: *The Thirteenth Century,* by
SIR MAURICE POWICKE; *The Fourteenth Century,* by G. BARRACLOUGH;
The Fifteenth Century, by E. F. JACOB; and *The Reign of George III,*
by RICHARD PARES.

PARES, SIR BERNARD

A History of Russia. *Cape (1937). Revised edition, 1947. 30s.*
One of the best and most authoritative books on the subject, by an
historian who has spent many years in Russia. His *Fall of the Russian
Monarchy,* Cape (1939), 18s. was praised for its objectivity and freedom
from bias.

PARKINSON, C. NORTHCOTE (Editor)

The Trade Winds. *Allen & Unwin (1948). 21s.*

An unusually interesting study of a subject often referred to, but seldom given detailed attention. Although subtitled 'A Study of British Overseas Trade during the French Wars, 1793–1815', and a collective work, it is a deeply interesting volume for all who like the byways of history.

PARRY, E. JONES

The Spanish Marriages, 1841–1846. *Macmillan (1936).*

A study of the influence of dynastic ambition upon foreign policy.

PATERSON, SIR ALEXANDER (1884–1947)

Across the Bridges. *Edward Arnold (1911).*

A classic study of life and social conditions in Edwardian Bermondsey (the South London riverside) by a famous prison reformer to whom the Borstal system is due. His writings on prison reform and allied subjects including penal administration, have been collected as *Paterson on Prisons,* edited by S. K. RUCK, Muller, 1951, 15s.

PAUL, ELLIOT

A Narrow Street. *Cresset Press (1942), 1951. 12s. 6d.*

A young American journalist chose to live with humble Parisians in a narrow street before 1939, rather than in the good class hotel his newspaper would have paid for. Hence this moving, poignant book, with its unforgettable pages of humour and pathos, is one of the best ever written on the people of Paris. Paul watched the Germans march in, and saw his closest friends suffer.

PEAKE, HAROLD and FLEURE, H. J.

The Corridors of Time. *9 vols. O.U.P. 10s. 6d. each.*

>   Vol. 1: *Apes and Men* (1927).
>   Vol. 2: *Hunters and Artists* (1927).
>   Vol. 3: *Peasants and Potters* (1927).
>   Vol. 4: *Priests and Kings* (1927).
>   Vol. 5: *The Steppe and the Sown* (1928).
>   Vol. 6: *The Way of the Sea* (1929).
>   Vol. 7: *Merchant Venturers in Bronze* (1931).
>   Vol. 8: *The Horse and the Sword* (1933).
>   Vol. 9: *The Law and the Prophets* (1936).

A simply written and well illustrated series of books designed to tell the story of man's evolution from the beginnings to the age of iron and the coming of the classical age in the Mediterranean.

PETRIE, SIR CHARLES

The Jacobite Movement: the first phase, 1688–1716.
>   *Eyre & Spottiswoode (1949). 15s.*
The Jacobite Movement: the last phase, 1716–1807.
>   *Eyre & Spottiswoode (1950). 15s.*

PICKTHORN, KENNETH
Early Tudor Government. *2 vols. C.U.P. (1934).*
  Vol. 1: *Henry VII. 25s.*
  Vol. 2: *Henry VIII. 50s.*

PIGGOTT, STUART
British Prehistory. *O.U.P. (1949). 6s. (Home University Library.)*

POLLARD, ALBERT FREDERICK (1869–1948)
The Evolution of Parliament. *Longmans (1920).*
  4th edition, 1938.
Factors in American History. *C.U.P. (1924). 15s.*
Factors in Modern History. *Constable (1907).*
  3rd edition, 1932, 1949. 8s. 6d.
Henry VIII. *Longmans (1902). Revised edition, 1913; 1951. 18s.*
A History of England. *O.U.P. (1912). 6s. (Home University Library.)*
  A study in political evolution 55 B.C. to A.D. 1911.
Thomas Cranmer and the English Reformation. *Putnam (1904).*
  New edition, 1926.
Wolsey. *Longmans (1929), 1953. 25s.*
  As will be seen, the best work of this distinguished historian was con-
cerned with the growth of the English Parliament and with the govern-
ment of the Tudors. The first book is likely to remain a standard work on
Parliament although it is itself an indication of the research still required
on the subject.

POWER, RHODA
How It Happened: myths and folk-tales. *C.U.P. (1930).*

POWICKE, SIR F. MAURICE
Medieval England, 1066–1485. *O.U.P. (1931). 6s.*
  (Home University Library.)
Ways of Medieval Life and Thought. *Odhams (1950). 12s. 6d.*
  The greatest English authority on the Middle Ages here addresses himself
in fourteen essays to a general public and not, as in his greatest work,
King Henry III and the Lord Edward, 2 vols, O.U.P. (1947), 50s., mainly
to an academic one.

PRESCOTT, H. F. M.
Mary Tudor. *Eyre & Spottiswoode (1940). Revised edition 1953. 30s.*
  Awarded the James Tait Black Historical Prize.

PRESTAGE, EDGAR
The Portuguese Pioneers. *Black (1933), 1950. 18s.*

PREVITÉ-ORTON, C. W. (1877–1947)

The Shorter Cambridge Medieval History.
2 vols. *C.U.P.* (*1952*). *55s.*

The essence of a great collective work of scholarship in eight volumes is presented here by one of the original editors, with 300 illustrations. It is well described as 'almost an encyclopaedia of the European Middle Ages'. See also in *An English Library*.

RAWLINSON, H. G.

India. *Cresset Press. Revised edition* (*1947*), *1952. 42s.*

Probably the best one volume modern history of India.

READ, CONYERS

Mr Secretary Walsingham, and the Foreign Policy of Queen Elizabeth.
3 vols. *O.U.P.* (*1925*). *84s.*

Although learned and detailed, this important book is an absorbing study for all readers with the leisure to give to it.

REDDAWAY, W. F. (1872–1949)

Frederick the Great and the Rise of Prussia. *Putnam* (*1935*).
Revised edition, 1948. 15s.
A History of Europe, 1610–1715. *Methuen* (*1948*). *25s.*
A History of Europe, 1715–1814. *Methuen* (*1936*).
3rd edition, 1951. 25s.

REINHARD, JOHN R.

Medieval Pageant. *Dent* (*1939*), *1950. 16s.*

'Hundreds of tales from a thousand years' in 672 pages.

REITZ, DENEYS

Commando. *Faber* (*1929*), *1953. 8s. 6d.*

A Boer journal of the Boer War, with a preface by the late J. C. Smuts.

Trekking On. *Faber* (*1933*), *1944. 7s. 6d.*

A continuation.

RENIER, G. J.

The English, Are They Human? *Williams & Norgate* (*1931*). *9s. 6d.*

Witty but kindly; shrewd and salutary. Criticism, with a dash of appreciation, from a tolerant Dutchman who knows us and our language well.

REYNOLDS, E. E.

Ourselves and the Community. *C.U.P.* (*1932*).
3rd edition, 1950. 6s. 6d.

Intended for the young voter, this best of all brief books on citizenship deserves to be widely read. Chapters XI–XXI deal with the Constitution, Parliament and the Law.

ROBERTSON, Sir Charles Grant
Chatham and the British Empire.
English Universities Press (1946). 6s. (Teach Yourself History Series.)

ROSE, Walter
Good Neighbours. *C.U.P. (1942). 15s.*
The Village Carpenter. *C.U.P. (1937). 15s.*

Two books on the countryman's England to be strongly recommended to those who like the works of Jefferies, George Sturt, and Thomas Hennell. They are recollections of an English village and its people.

ROWSE, A. L.
The England of Elizabeth: the structure of society. *Macmillan (1950). 25s.*
The Spirit of English History. *Cape (1943), 1950. 7s. 6d.*
Tudor Cornwall: portrait of a society. *Cape (1941), 1950. 21s.*
The Use of History. *English Universities Press (1946), 1951. 6s.*

The introductory volume to the series *Teach Yourself History*, by the general editor.

RUNCIMAN, Steven
A History of the Crusades. *2 vols. C.U.P. (1951, 1952). 30s. 42s.*

One of the successes of 1951, the first volume of this major work of scholarship and research dealt with the founding of the Kingdom of Jerusalem and the First Crusade; the second continues the history from 1100 to 1157 and deals with the kingdom and the Frankish East. The *History* is to be completed in a third volume.

SALUSBURY, G. T.
Street Life in Medieval England. *(1939.)*
Pen-in-Hand-Books, 1948. 8s. 6d.

SALZMAN, L. E.
English Life in the Middle Ages. *O.U.P. (1926). 15s.*

SAYLES, G. O.
The Medieval Foundations of England. *Methuen (1948).*
Revised edition, 1950, 18s.

A scholarly work much respected by students.

SELLEY, W. T.
England in the Eighteenth Century. *Black (1934).*
2nd edition, 1949. 12s. 6d.

SHAKESPEARE'S ENGLAND: an account of the life and manners of his age.
2 vols. O.U.P. (1916), 1926. 63s.

A collective work of 1192 pages, with many illustrations, useful to the student as a background to formal studies, absorbing to all readers of history and Shakespeare.

SIMPSON, F. A.
The Rise of Louis Napoleon. *Longmans (1909)*, *1950. 25s.*
Louis Napoleon and the Recovery of France, 1848–1856.
   Longmans (1923). 3rd edition, 1951. 30s.
   The best books on the subject, finely written and authoritative, presenting the theme and the main characters in an absorbing manner not always achieved in standard works of this kind.

SITWELL, EDITH
Fanfare for Elizabeth. *Macmillan (1946). 12s. 6d.*

SITWELL, SACHEVERELL
The Gothick North. *Duckworth (1929–1930).*
   3 vols. New edition, Lehmann, 1950. 15s.
   A highly individual study of medieval life and art in Northern Europe. The first edition in three volumes, and the new one, with illustrations, recreate the medieval scene with the skill of a novelist and the insight of a poet.

SMELLIE, K. B.
A History of Local Government. *Allen & Unwin (1946). 9s. 6d.*
   An essential background book for readers of history, especially for the England of the nineteenth century.

SMITH, SIR GRAFTON ELLIOT (1871–1937)
Human History. *Cape (1934).*
In the Beginning: the origin of civilization. *Watts (1932), 1950. 2s. 6d.*

SMITH, HERBERT MAYNARD (1869–1949)
Henry VIII and the Reformation. *Macmillan (1948).*
Pre-Reformation England. *Macmillan (1938).*

SOMERVELL, D. C.
British Politics Since 1900. *Dakers (1950). 15s.*
English Thought in the Nineteenth Century. *Methuen (1928), 1950. 9s.*
Modern Britain, 1870–1939. *Methuen (1941), 1951. 11s. 6d.*
Modern Europe, 1871–1939. *Methuen (1940), 1947. 6s.*

SPEARS, E. L.
Prelude to Victory. *Cape (1939), 1950. 18s.*
   Brigadier-General Spears's account of the last twelve months of the fighting in the 1914–1918 War has not been bettered. It is introduced with commendation by Winston Churchill.

STEED, WICKHAM
The Hapsburg Monarchy. *Constable (1913).*
   The best monograph on the dynasty, its years of power, decline and fall.

STUART, DOROTHY MARGARET
The Mother of Victoria: a period piece. *Macmillan (1942). 15s.*

Noteworthy for its research into the affairs of Sir John Conroy, the Comptroller, and for the detailed attention given to the formative years of 1830 to 1837.

TAWNEY, R. H.
The Acquisitive Society. *Bell (1920), 1921. 6s.*

A famous little book which examines the basis of existing society and pleads persuasively for the encouragement of new motives in industry.

Religion and the Rise of Capitalism. *Murray (1923), 1948. 10s. 6d.*

The Holland Memorial Lectures, 1922. A remarkable historical study, with a preface by Bishop Gore.

Social History and Literature. *C.U.P. for N.B.L. (1950). 2s. 6d.*

TAYLOR, A. J. P.
The Habsburg Monarchy. *Hamish Hamilton (1941).*
Revised and enlarged edition, 1949. 15s.

A useful up-to-date survey and summary.

TAYLOR, G. R. STIRLING
A Modern History of England, 1485–1932. *Cape (1932).*

An individual interpretation. The same author's study of *Oliver Cromwell*, Cape (1928), is a most persuasive essay in depreciation.

TEMPERLEY, GLADYS
Henry VII. *Constable (1914).*

TEMPERLEY, HAROLD
The Foreign Policy of Canning, 1822–1827. *Bell (1925).*

An important work on England, the 'Neo-Holy Alliance' and the New World, expanded from the author's contribution on this subject to the second volume of the *Cambridge History of British Foreign Policy.*

THOMAS, BERTRAM
The Arabs. *Eyre & Spottiswoode (1937).*

A popular account of Arab civilization from pre-Islamic times up to the revival of Islam after 1918.

THOMPSON, J. M.
The French Revolution. *Blackwell (1943), 1951. 37s. 6d.*

Is considered to be the modern standard work for both students and general readers. Admirably planned, with a list of 'The Fifty Best Books on the Revolution' and a French glossary.

THOMSON, GEORGE

Studies in Ancient Greek Society. *Lawrence & Wishart (1949). 42s.*

Learned and scholarly, with highly individual interpretations of the records and of what may be surmised of society in the early Aegean. Its reception was controversial but it was considered by some to be comparable almost to *The Golden Bough.*

THOMSON, GLADYS SCOTT

Life in a Noble Household, 1641–1700. *Cape (1937), 1950. 18s.*

Preface by G. M. Trevelyan. By using the account books belonging to the Bedford household at Woburn the author has been able to present an authentic picture of daily life which is almost as fully recorded as that of the Verney household through the *Verney Papers.*

THONEMANN, H. E.

Tell the White Man. *Collins (1950).*

The life story of Buludja, an aboriginal lubra (girl) of the Mungari tribe in Australia, taken down, translated and adapted by the Managing Partner of a station on Roper River, Northern Territory. This deeply interesting and sometimes poignant story of Australian life from the early 1890's to 1940, and 'the white man's war with another tribe' deserves to be widely read.

TILLYARD, E. M. W.

The Elizabethan World Picture. *Chatto (1943). 8s. 6d.*

On the influence of medieval philosophy on Elizabethan writers. In some respects it is supplementary to the same author's study of *Shakespeare's History Plays*, Chatto, 1944, 18s.

TOYNBEE, ARNOLD J.

Civilization on Trial. *O.U.P. (1948). 12s. 6d.*

An important book for to-day, discussing the problems before every government and all men and women whose thoughts are allowed reasonably free expression.

A Study of History. *Vols 1–3, 2nd edition, 1935, 75s.*
Vols 3–6, 1939, 84s. O.U.P.

A gigantic work of research and interpretation in 3548 pages. The major work of our time of which Sir Maurice Powicke said in the *Manchester Guardian* that 'no such survey of history, sustained for so long on a high level of reflection, has ever been written'. For those who have insufficient leisure or capacity to assimilate such a long work there is the masterly *Abridgement of Volumes I to VI*, by D. C. SOMERVELL, O.U.P. (1946), 25s. This compresses the main work into 632 pages, and will no doubt be followed by another volume abridging the completion of the study when that is published.

TREND, J. B.
The Civilization of Spain.
 O.U.P. (1944). 6s. (Home University Library.)

TREVELYAN, G. M.
English Social History. *Longmans (1944), 1946. 25s.*

A masterpiece of modern historical writing, being a survey of six centuries of English life from Chaucer to Victoria.

Illustrated English Social History. *4 vols.*
 Longmans, 1949–1952. 25s. each volume.

 Vol. 1: *Chaucer's England and the Early Tudors.*
 Vol. 2: *The Age of Shakespeare and the Stuart Period.*
 Vol. 3: *The Eighteenth Century.*
 Vol. 4: *The Nineteenth Century.*

This is a special edition of the one-volume work, with many illustrations and portraits selected and annotated by RUTH C. WRIGHT.

England Under Queen Anne.
 3 vols. Longmans (1930–1934). 17s. 6d. each.

 Vol. 1: *Blenheim* (1930). Vol. 2: *Ramillies and the Union with Scotland* (1932). Vol. 3: *The Peace and the Protestant Succession* (1934).

British History in the Nineteenth Century, and after, 1782–1919.
 Longmans (1922), 1937. 25s.
England in the Age of Wycliffe. *Longmans (1899), 1909. 15s.*
 Revised in 1904 and again in 1909.
England Under the Stuarts. *Methuen (1904).*
 Revised edition, 1949. 21s.
The English Revolution, 1688–1689.
 O.U.P. (1938). 6s. (Home University Library.)
Garibaldi. *Longmans (1933).*

A great trilogy, more historical than biographical, published in a one-volume edition and also in three separate volumes: *Garibaldi's Defence of the Roman Republic, 1848–1849*, Longmans (1907), 1949; *Garibaldi and the Thousand, May, 1860*, Longmans (1909), 1948; *Garibaldi and the Making of Italy, May–November, 1860*, Longmans (1911), 1948. 17s. 6d. each.

The History of England. *Longmans (1926), 1945. 25s.*
History and the Reader. *C.U.P. for the N.B.L., 1945. 2s.*

TREVOR-ROPER, H. R.
The Last Days of Hitler. *Macmillan (1947), 1950. 15s.*

A young historian was given the absorbing task of sifting the evidence for and against the truth of the report of Hitler's last weeks in the Berlin bunker and of his suicide. The story makes fascinating reading and will remain one of the most interesting books of the war.

TURBERVILLE, A. S. (Editor)
Johnson's England. *2 vols. O.U.P. (1933). 63s.*

A collective work of scholarship, well illustrated and presenting a comprehensive account of the life and manners of the age of Dr Johnson.

TURNER, E. S.
Roads to Ruin. *Michael Joseph (1950). 12s. 6d.*

A salutary book, being twelve studies in the opposition to social reforms during the nineteenth century. From the distance of a few decades human stupidity seems fantastic, incredible and boundless.

TURNER, F. C.
James II. *Eyre & Spottiswoode (1948). 25s.*

It is thought that this will become the standard book on the subject.

TYLOR, Sir Edward B. (1832–1917)
Anthropology. *2 vols. Watts (1881), 1930. 2s. 6d. each. (The Thinker's Library.)*

An introduction to the study of man and civilization.

URE, P. N.
Justinian and His Age. *Penguin Books (1951). 1s. 6d. (paper covers); 6s. (bound).*

VINOGRADOFF, Sir Paul (1854–1925)
Common-sense in Law. *(1913.) Revised edition by* H. G. Hanbury. *O.U.P. (1946). 6s. (Home University Library.)*
The Growth of the Manor. *Allen & Unwin (1904), 1911. 18s.*

WADDELL, Helen
The Wandering Scholars. *Constable (1932), 1949. 10s.*

A study of medieval learning and the dawn of the renaissance.

WALBANK, F. Alan (Editor)
The English Scene. *Batsford (1941). Revised edition, 1947. 7s. 6d.*

A picture of England in history and landscape, relic and ritual, by a selection of passages from famous writers. Sir John Squire implies in his preface that it is likely to become a permanent anthology in praise of England.

WALDMAN, Milton
Elizabeth and Leicester. *Collins (1944), 1950. 6s.*

WALKER, Eric A.
The British Empire: its structure and spirit. *O.U.P. (1943), 1950. 14s.*

WALSH, James Joseph

Thirteenth, Greatest of Centuries.
   New York, McMullen. 6th edition, 1920. $3.50.

WEBSTER, Sir Charles

British Diplomacy, 1813–1815. *Bell (1921). 12s. 6d.*

On the foreign policy of England and its makers told in select documents dealing with the reconstruction of Europe.

The Congress of Vienna. *Bell (1919), 1934. 10s. 6d.*

Supplements the above and deals with the critical year of 1814–1815.

The Foreign Policy of Castlereagh, 1812–1815. *Bell (1931). 30s.*
The Foreign Policy of Castlereagh, 1815–1822. *Bell (1934). 27s. 6d.*

The standard work, and one of the classic historical works of the twentieth century. The first volume deals with Britain and the reconstruction of Europe, the second with Britain and the European Alliances.

The Foreign Policy of Palmerston, 1830–1841. *2 vols. Bell (1951). 63s.*

Continuing his monumental work on this all-important period the author here treats of the Liberal Movement in Britain and Europe, and of Palmerston's genius in formulating an enduring and farseeing policy on the Eastern Question, which in our time once again rears its head with Russian policy following traditional lines but with enormously increased power as a world force.

WEDGWOOD, C. V.

The Thirty Years' War. *Cape (1938), 1950. 15s.*

A major work and the best on the subject written in this century, uniting scholarly research with a skill in presenting the unhappy record which is rewarding to both students and general readers of history.

William the Silent. *Cape (1944), 1950. 18s.*

The best modern monograph on William of Orange, 1533 to 1584. Awarded the James Tait Black Memorial Prize for 1944.

WEST, Rebecca

The Meaning of Treason. *Macmillan (1949).*
   Enlarged edition, 1951. 21s.

One of the most brilliant books of its kind to emerge from the tragedies of 1939–1946. It is a skilled journalist's report and comment on the characters and trials of the men who were tried for treason as a result of their activities during the World War. The revised and enlarged edition includes two additional chapters on the trials of Dr Emil Fuchs and Dr Alan Nunn May.

WILKINS, Vaughan

Endless Prelude. *Routledge (1937).*

Compiled from contemporary memoirs, papers and letters, and ancient chronicles, it is presented as a survey 'telling in part the history of the English-speaking peoples'.

WILLIAMS, CHARLES (1886–1945)
James I. *Barker (1934), 1951. 10s. 6d.*

WILLIAMSON, JAMES A.

The Age of Drake. *A. & C. Black (1938). Third revised edition 1953. 25s.*
Acknowledged as the best book on Tudor naval history.

The Evolution of England. *O.U.P. (1931).*
Revised edition, 1944. 18s.

This masterly commentary on the facts is quite unequalled as a deeply interesting and brilliantly written record of the growth of the English spirit and the Englishman's character. No better book can be recommended to those who wish to understand why we are what we are and the secret of our greatness and pride.

The Ocean in English History. *O.U.P. (1941). 18s.*

The Ford Lectures, 1939–1940. Allied to it is the same author's *Maritime Enterprise, 1485–1558.* O.U.P. (1913), 18s.

A Short History of British Expansion. *2 vols. Macmillan.*

Vol. 1: *The Old Colonial Empire* (1930), 3rd edition, 1945, 20s. Vol. 2: *The Modern Empire and Commonwealth* (1930), 3rd edition, 1943, 18s. Regarded as the best survey, but according to some authorities equalled by C. E. Carrington's *The British Overseas*, which see under the author above.

WINGFIELD-STRATFORD, ESMÉ

The History of British Civilization. *Routledge (1928), 1930. 30s.*

In the one volume edition this enormous work totals 1352 pages and is a reference book for the student as well as an excellent summary in detail for the general reader.

WOODWARD, E. L.

A History of England. *Methuen (1947), 1951. 7s. 6d.*
A masterpiece of compression for a series of Home Study Books.

WOOLLEY, SIR LEONARD

Ur of the Chaldees. *Benn (1929), 1950. 10s. 6d.*

The best and most popular brief account of the archaeological record of the earliest civilization. Reprinted in Penguin Books series 1938, 1s. 6d., it again achieved the popularity of a best-seller.

YOUNG, G. M.

Charles I and Cromwell. *(1935.)*
New edition, Hart Davis, 1950. 7s. 6d.
The new edition has an introduction.

Early Victorian England, 1830–1865. *2 vols. O.U.P. (1934). 50s.*

A collective work of surpassing interest, in 1006 pages, with 138 plates illustrating the various sections. The volumes are both edited by G. M.

YOUNG, whose famous last chapter has been extended by him to cover the whole of Queen Victoria's reign to 1901 and is published separately as

Victorian England: the portrait of an age. *O.U.P.* *(1936)*, *1953*. *18s*.

ZIMMERN, ALFRED

The Greek Commonwealth. *O.U.P. 5th edition (1931).* *18s.*

Has scarcely been bettered as a brilliant introduction to the politics and economics of Athens and its civilization in the fifth century B.C.

Other twentieth-century historians will be found in *An English Library* under J. F. Baddeley, W. G. Bell, J. H. Breasted, Z. N. Brooke, J. B. Bury, J. F. Chance, R. G. Collingwood, G. G. Coulton, C. R. M. F. Cruttwell, H. W. C. Davis, G. Lowes Dickinson, C. H. Firth, H. A. L. Fisher, Tenney Frank, T. R. Glover, Philip Guedalla, A. C. Haddon, C. H. Haskins, F. J. C. Hearnshaw, D. G. Hogarth, Mark Hovell, A. B. Keith, Bolton King, T. E. Lawrence, Richard Lodge, R. R. Marett, J. A. R. Marriott, F. S. Marvin, Ramsay Muir, F. S. Oliver, Charles Oman, W. Flinders Petrie, Eileen Power, C. W. Previté-Orton, J. H. Rose, G. Elliot Smith, Preserved Smith, J. A. Spender, J. C. Stobart, P. M. Sykes, H. W. V. Temperley, Edward Thompson, C. S. Terry, A. A. Tilley, A. S. Turberville, A. W. Ward.

PHILOSOPHY AND RELIGION

It has been said that thinking is the solving of problems, but Goethe reminds us that every solution of a problem brings a new one before our minds. Hence, no doubt, the reason for the difficulty of most of the books in this section. Yet many profound thinkers have had the gift of lucidity in the exposition of abstruse ideas, and some few have been able to reach a large public with their books. We of this century have, for example, Bertrand Russell, one of the wittiest of philosophers, and probably the greatest teacher of tolerance and the good life of the contemporary world. His gift of a clear style, free from ambiguity, yet never distorting his argument by over-simplification, has commanded the attention of a world audience. In Santayana we had a highly civilized mind which gave us one of the few systems of philosophy to be presented in English since Spencer's; in Whitehead a profound yet approachable thinker of the first order whose work has influenced others to a remarkable degree; in G. E. Moore a teacher whose impact on a whole generation of intellectuals is still felt directly and indirectly.

The late Susan Stebbing, brilliantly logical in her approach to modern thought, exercised a salutary influence on the ordinary reader; Caudwell and Hulme were young thinkers who were sadly snatched away from their work by war's wastage, but who nevertheless managed to produce books of vital importance. In Gilbert Ryle we have a brilliant newcomer whose greatest influence is still to be felt, but who has already impressed a relatively wide circle of thinkers.

Readers may be reminded of A. D. Ritchie's excellent introduction to a limited theme in his *British Philosophers*, published by Longmans, 2s., some of whose comments are quoted in the notes.

ALEXANDER, SAMUEL (1854–1938)

Space, Time and Deity. *Macmillan (1920)*
> *Vision Press. 2 vols. 1950. 80s.*

The Gifford Lectures, 1916–1918. A sustained examination of the concepts of mental space-time.

AYER, A. J.

Language, Truth and Logic. *Gollancz (1936). Revised, 1946. 10s. 6d.*

A notable and influential summary of logical positivism, a hotly debated modern view of certain aspects of philosophy and human behaviour. *See also under* Joad.

BARKER, ERNEST

The Values of Life. *Blackie (1939).*

'Essays on the circles and centres of duty.'

BARNES, E. W.

The Rise of Christianity. *Longmans (1947). 18s.*

So great was the controversy aroused by this individual interpretation of the development of the Christian religion that it became the most widely-read work of non-fiction for many months after its first publication.

BELLAMY, H. S.

The Atlantis Myth. *Faber (1948). 10s. 6d.*

BOWMAN, ARCHIBALD ALLEN (1883–1936)

A Sacramental Universe.
  Princeton Univ. Press; Great Britain, O.U.P. (1939). 32s. 6d.

A study in the metaphysics of experience. A. D. Ritchie says of it: 'one of the really fertile philosophical efforts of our day'.

BRIFFAULT, ROBERT (1876–1948)

The Mothers. *3 vols. Allen & Unwin (1927).*

In his interpretation of the early history of human culture the author evolved a matriarchal theory of social evolution.

BROWN, JOHN

The History of the English Bible. *C.U.P. (1912). 6s.*
  (*Cambridge Manuals.*)

BUTLER, E. M.

The Myth of the Magus. *C.U.P. (1948). 30s.*
Ritual Magic. *C.U.P. (1949). 30s.*
The Fortunes of Faust. *C.U.P. (1952). 30s.*

A trilogy showing how the legend of the sixteenth-century Faust was traditionally related to the prehistoric rite of the god-priest-king. The last part discusses the meaning of Faust in literature.

CAUDWELL, CHRISTOPHER (1907–1937)

Illusion and Reality. *Macmillan (1937).*
  Lawrence & Wishart, 1946. 21s.

Studies in a Dying Culture. *Lane (1938). 9s. 6d.*
Further Studies in a Dying Culture. *Lane (1949). 9s. 6d.*

The first book is a philosophical study of the sources of the poetic instinct. The last has a preface by Edgell Rickword, and with its companion, presents a number of essays in philosophy, psychology, bourgeois aesthetics and allied themes, all of which had for the author a political significance.

CHAPMAN, GUY

Culture and Survival. *Cape (1940). 8s. 6d.*

At the time of its publication it did indeed seem that our culture could scarcely survive. The struggle still continues and a reading of this book helps to clarify the mind amidst modern confusions.

COHEN, M. R.
A Preface to Logic. *Routledge (1946). 8s. 6d.*

CRAWSHAY-WILLIAMS, RUPERT
The Comforts of Unreason. *Routledge (1947). 12s. 6d.*
A study of the motives behind irrational thought in journalists, writers and the general public.

CROCKFORD PREFACES. *O.U.P. (1947). 12s. 6d.*
For the first time a collection was here made of some of the famous annual prefaces to Crockford's *Clerical Directory*, in which problems, achievements and controversies as they affected, or were affected by, the Church of England, were discussed by our leading Churchmen.

CURTIS, LIONEL
Civitas Dei. (The Commonwealth of God.) *3 vols. Macmillan (1934, 1937). One-volume edition, 1938. Second revised edition, Allen & Unwin, 1951. 30s.*
A philosophical interpretation of history from the appearance of man to the United Nations. Where has human society come from? Where is it going? Where ought it to go?

DARWIN, F. D. S.
The English Medieval Recluse. *S.P.C.K. (1944). 6s.*
'A byway of English religious life.'

DAWSON, CHRISTOPHER
Religion and Culture. *Sheed & Ward (1948). 10s. 6d.*
Religion and the Rise of Western Culture. *Sheed & Ward (1950). 15s.*
The Gifford Lectures for 1947, 1948 and 1949.

DEWEY, JOHN (1859–1952)
Experience and Nature. *Allen & Unwin (1925).*
The Quest for Certainty. *Allen & Unwin (1930).*
The Gifford Lectures for 1929. For a detailed collective examination of the characteristic writings of this distinguished thinker refer to the volume in The Library of Living Philosophers Series, edited by P. A. SCHILPP, C.U.P. (1943). New edition, 1951. 50s.

DIBDIN, SIR LEWIS TONNA (1852–1938)
Establishment in England. *Church Book Room (1932). 7s. 6d.*
A collection of essays containing much out of the way information on the relations of Church and State.

DIXON, W. MACNEILE
The Human Situation. *Edward Arnold (1937). 12s. 6d.*
The Gifford Lectures for 1935. A volume of outstanding importance, wisdom and high thinking. 'A superbly written book.' A. D. Ritchie.

DODD, C. H.
The Bible To-Day. *C.U.P. (1946). 10s.*

DUNNE, J. W. (1875–1949)
An Experiment With Time. *Faber (1927), 1939. 10s. 6d.*
The Serial Universe in Nature. *Faber (1934), 1940. 12s. 6d.*
An original theory of premonition and foreknowledge developed with extraordinarily convincing arguments based on the author's personal experience.

DURANT, WILL
The Story of Philosophy. *Benn (1926), 1947. 21s.*
Expanded from lectures. It is one of the most popular books of its kind and has been translated into every major language.

EDDINGTON, SIR ARTHUR (1882–1944)
The Nature of the Physical World. *C.U.P. (1928). 15s.*
A masterly presentation of the modern physicist's view of cosmology, and one of the most widely-read books of its time.

EDMAN, IRWIN
Philosopher's Holiday. *Constable (1939).*

EVANS, JOAN
Taste and Temperament. *Cape (1939), 1951. 10s. 6d.*
'A brief study of psychological types in their relation to the visual arts.' Sub-title.

FAWCETT, DOUGLAS
Oberland Dialogues. *Macmillan (1939). 12s. 6d.*
On the soul of man.

The Zermatt Dialogues. *Macmillan (1931). 12s. 6d.*
'Outlines of a philosophy of mysticism.' Both books are notable contributions to the author's philosophy of imaginism, or the idealistic interpretation of the fundamental realities of the universe.

GLOVER, EDWARD
War, Sadism and Pacifism. *Allen & Unwin (1933), 1947. 9s. 6d.*
Essays on group psychology and war.

GLOVER, T. R. (1869–1943)
The Springs of Hellas. *C.U.P. (1946). 12s. 6d.*
On classical life and literature.

GRAVES, ROBERT

The White Goddess. *Faber (1948). Revised and enlarged edition, 1952. 35s.*

A 'Golden Bough' of the poetic art, in which one of the major poets of our time explores the primitive sources of the poetic myth. A difficult book, but rewarding to readers of poetry and to anthropologists.

HAWTON, HECTOR

Philosophy for Pleasure. *Watts (1949). 10s. 6d.*

An excellent introduction, with a glossary of terms, a table of dates and an index. Introduction by A. E. HEATH.

HULME, T. E. (1883–1917)

Speculations. *Routledge (1924), 1936. 15s.*

A seminal work. His death in the First World War deprived our time of a luminous and civilized mind. These essays in humanism and the philosophy of art are edited by Sir HERBERT READ, with a foreword, and a frontispiece by JACOB EPSTEIN.

HUMPHREYS, CHRISTMAS

Buddhism. *Penguin Books (1951). 6s.*

HUXLEY, ALDOUS

The Perennial Philosophy. *Chatto (1946). 15s.*

A synthetical presentation of the mystic philosophy of the great European and Eastern mystics by quotation and interpretative comment.

JEANS, SIR JAMES (1877–1946)

The Mysterious Universe. *C.U.P. (1933). 6s.*
Physics and Philosophy. *C.U.P. (1942). 12s. 6d.*
The Stars in Their Courses. *C.U.P. (1931). 10s. 6d.*
The Universe Around Us. *C.U.P. (1929). 15s.*

The author's gift of lucid presentation of his ideas concerning the universe and his ability to convey to non-mathematical readers some fundamental concepts of modern physicists gave him an enormous public. He and Eddington succeeded in interesting the ordinary reader in cosmology as no other scientists had ever been able to do before.

JOAD, C. E. M. (1891–1953)

Critique of Logical Positivism. *Gollancz (1950). 10s. 6d.*
See also Ayer's book.
Guide to Modern Thought. *Faber (1933). 8s. 6d.*
Guide to Philosophy. *Gollancz (1936). 8s. 6d.*
Guide to the Philosophy of Morals and Politics.
Gollancz (1936). 10s. 6d.
Introduction to Modern Philosophy. *O.U.P. (1923). 5s.*

KENYON, Sir Frederick (1863–1952)

Our Bible and the Ancient MSS. *Eyre & Spottiswoode (1895).*
Revised, 1939. 18s.

A standard book on the text of the Holy Scriptures and how we got them, with illustrations and facsimiles of papyri and MSS., and of the early printed versions.

LE BON, Gustave

The Crowd. *(1896.) Revised 1903. Benn, 1947. 8s. 6d.*

A study of the popular mind. It came prophetically at the turn of the century, when the popular press developed to its full strength, and when films and radio were not far distant to add weight to its argument.

LEVY, G. R.

The Gate of Horn. *Faber (1948). 42s.*

A study of the religious conceptions of the Stone Age and their influence on European thought.

LEWIS, C. S.

Mere Christianity. *Bles (1952). 8s. 6d.*

A revised and amplified edition of three books also available separately, 2s. 6d. each: *Broadcast Talks (1942); Christian Behaviour (1943); and Beyond Personality (1944).*

The Screwtape Letters. *Bles (1942). 5s.*

LIPPMANN, Walter

The Good Society. *Allen & Unwin (1937).*
A Preface to Morals. *Allen & Unwin (1929). 10s.*
Public Opinion. *Allen & Unwin (1922), 1950. 32s.*

LIVINGSTONE, Sir R. W.

Some Thoughts on University Education. *C.U.P. for N.B.L. (1948). 2s. 6d.*

MACKINNON, James

A History of Modern Liberty. *3 vols. Longmans (1906–1908). 18s. each.*
Vol. 1: *Introduction; Origins; The Middle Ages.*
Vol. 2: *The Age of the Reformation.*
Vol. 3: *The Struggle With the Stuarts, 1603–1647.*

MacMURRAY, John

Reason and Emotion. *Faber (1935). 8s. 6d.*

MALINOWSKI, Bronislaw

Magic, Science, and Religion; and other essays.
Selected with an Introduction by Robert Redfield. *Allen & Unwin (1949). 27s. 6d.*

MANSON, T. W.
The Teaching of Jesus. *C.U.P. (2nd edition, 1935). 18s.*

MATHEW, DAVID
Catholicism in England. *Eyre & Spottiswoode (1935), 1949. 15s.*
A notable historical study of Catholic life during four centuries, brought up to recent times in the last revised edition, including a character sketch of Cardinal Hinsley.

MOORE, G. E.
Ethics. *O.U.P. (1912). 6s. (Home University Library.)*
Principia Ethica. *C.U.P. (1903). 21s.*
One of the most influential books of the century. On its first appearance its insistence on private virtue and the good life exercised a profound and lasting influence on the brilliant group of young men and women who were later, with Maynard Keynes, Clive Bell and Virginia Woolf, to be the centre of the intellectual life of London in the 'twenties. There is an examination of and critical introduction to the most important and characteristic philosophical writings of this distinguished thinker in The Library of Living Philosophers Series, C.U.P. (1943), 50s.

MORAN, LORD
The Anatomy of Courage. *Constable (1945), 1949. 4s.*
A thoughtful examination of what is meant when a man or woman is said to be a brave person. Bravery on the battlefield is often spectacular and is displayed by those who are surprised when they are told about it afterwards; there are other kinds of bravery and these too are examined ethically and psychologically.

MURRAY, GILBERT
Five Stages of Greek Religion.
Watts (1913; revised edition, 1925), 1950. 2s. 6d.
Greek Studies. *O.U.P. (1946). 15s.*
Stoic, Christian and Humanist. *Watts (1940), 1950. 6s.*

NEEDHAM, JOSEPH
Time, the Refreshing River: essays and addresses, 1932–1942.
Allen & Unwin (1943). 16s.

OGDEN, C. K. and RICHARDS, I. A.
The Meaning of Meaning. *Routledge (1923), 1949. 25s.*
An influential work on semantics, being 'a study of the influence of language upon thought and of the science of symbolism'.

ROBERTS, HARRY and HORDER, LORD
The Philosophy of Jesus. *Dent (1945). 5s.*

ROBINSON, James Harvey
The Mind in the Making. *Preface by* H. G. Wells. *Cape (1923).*
New edition, Watts, 1946. 2s. 6d.

RUSSELL, Bertrand
Authority and the Individual. *Allen & Unwin (1949). 6s.*
The Conquest of Happiness. *Allen & Unwin (1930). 8s. 6d.*
A History of Western Philosophy. *Allen & Unwin (1946). 21s.*
'From Bacon and Descartes to James.' Sub-title.

Human Knowledge: its Scope and Limits. *Allen & Unwin (1948). 21s.*
In Praise of Idleness, and other essays. *Allen & Unwin (1935). 8s. 6d.*
On Education, especially in early childhood.
Allen & Unwin (1926). 7s. 6d.
An Outline of Philosophy. *Allen & Unwin (1927). 15s.*
Philosophy and Politics. *C.U.P. (1947). 2s. 6d.*
Published for the National Book League, being the text of the Fourth Annual Lecture held in London, 1946.

Religion and Science. *O.U.P. (1935). 6s.*
A volume in the Home University Library.

Sceptical Essays. *Allen & Unwin (1928). 8s. 6d.*
Some of Bertrand Russell's philosophical and mathematical works are beyond the comprehension of the ordinary reader, but those listed above convey in lucid and witty prose most of his ideas on life and the universe. One of the greatest public educators of our time, his tolerance and intellectual courage have contributed much to the cause of the good life. Readers may be directed also to the standard examination of his philosophy in the Bertrand Russell volume in the Library of Living Philosophers Series, edited by P. A. Schilpp, C.U.P. (1944), 50s. This critical introduction to his thought contains an autobiographical essay, and a reply by Russell to some criticisms.

RYLE, Gilbert
The Concept of Mind. *Hutchinson (1949). 12s. 6d.*

SACKVILLE-WEST, V.
The Eagle and the Dove. *Michael Joseph (1943). 10s. 6d.*
St Teresa of Avila and St Thérèse of Lisieux: 'a study in contrasts'.

SAMUEL, Viscount
Creative Man, and other addresses. *Cresset Press (1949). 9s. 6d.*
On democracy, its failings and future; science and philosophy; the criminal: is society to blame; the decline and revival of religion. A notable book by a statesman and liberal philosopher whose many years in the public service has enriched English life.

Leisure in a Democracy. *C.U.P.* (*1949*). *2s.*

Published for the National Book League, being the text of the Sixth Annual Lecture held in London, 1948.

Practical Ethics. *O.U.P.* (*1935*). *6s.*

A volume in the Home University Library.

SANTAYANA, GEORGE (1863–1952)

Dialogues in Limbo. *Constable* (*1925*).

The Life of Reason; or, The Phases of Human Progress.
   5 vols. Constable (*1923*).

   Vol. 1: *Introduction; Reason in Common Sense.* Vol. 2: *Reason in Society.* Vol. 3: *Reason in Religion.* Vol. 4: *Reason in Art.* Vol. 5: *Reason in Science.*

Soliloquies in England; and Later Soliloquies. *Constable* (*1922*).

Next to his novel, which *see under* Fiction, these soliloquies inspired by his sojourn in England during the tragic years of 1914–1918, are the best introduction for the general reader to the trend of thought and essential wisdom of this civilizing philosopher. For a critical and appreciative introduction and study see the Santayana volume in the Library of Living Philosophers Series, edited by P. A. Schilpp, C.U.P. (1943), 50s. As with others in this standard series, there is an autobiographical sketch, together with the philosopher's answer to some of his critics.

SAWYER, W. W.

Mathematician's Delight. *Penguin Books* (*1943*). *1s. 6d.*

SCHRODINGER, ERWIN

What is Life? *C.U.P.* (*1944*). *10s. 6d.*

SELWYN, EDWARD GORDON

A Short History of Christian Thought.
   Revised edition, Bles (*1949*). *5s.*

Of the author's edition of the Greek text of the *First Epistle of St Peter*, with introduction, notes and essays, Macmillan (1946), 25s., Charles Morgan wrote 'It is among the very few quiet, selfless, and truly great books of our time.'

SHERRINGTON, SIR CHARLES

Man on His Nature. *C.U.P.* (*1940*). *Revised edition, 1951. 30s.*

SINCLAIR, W. A.

Introduction to Philosophy. *O.U.P.* (*1944*). *6s.*

An excellent, brief study for the beginner in the problems and function of metaphysical and non-mathematical philosophy.

SORLEY, W. R. (1855–1953)

A History of English Philosophy. *C.U.P.* (*1920*). *25s.*

Considered to be the best one-volume history of British contributions to philosophical thought up to about 1900. There is an English translation of a German standard work by Rudolf Metz, *A Hundred Years of British Philosophy*, Allen & Unwin (1938), 30*s*.

The Moral Life and Moral Worth.
C.U.P. (*1911*), *1930. 6s.* (*Cambridge Manuals.*)

STEBBING, L. SUSAN (1885–1943)

Ideals and Illusions. *Watts* (*1941*), *1948. 3s. 6d.*

A constructive thinker and alert logician, Susan Stebbing was not afraid to tackle Jeans and other eminent leaders of thought in their searchings after the truth about cosmology.

A Modern Elementary Logic. *Methuen* (*1943*), *1949. 8s. 6d.*

Suitable for first-year university students. A larger work for more advanced students and readers is *A Modern Introduction to Logic*, Methuen (1930), 6th edition, 1950, 18*s. 6d. See also* her monograph *Logic in Practice*, Methuen, 4*s. 6d.*

Thinking to Some Purpose. *Penguin Books* (*1939*). *1s. 6d.*

In the same series will be found a cheap edition of her *Philosophy and the Physicists*, originally published by Methuen.

STOUT, G. F. (1860–1944)
Mind and Matter. *C.U.P.* (*1931*).

TAYLOR, A. E.
Socrates. *Peter Davies* (*1932*), *1951. 6s.*

VEBLEN, THORNSTEIN (1857–1929)
The Theory of the Leisure Class.
Allen & Unwin (*1899*), *1925. 12s. 6d.*

A strange American thinker and economic teacher whose influence has been deeply felt in left-wing circles for half a century.

WHITEHEAD, A. N. (1861–1947)
Essays in Science and Philosophy. *Rider* (*1948*). *15s.*

For a brief introduction to the mathematician's way of thinking see the volume in the Home University Library, *An Introduction to Mathematics*. O.U.P. (1911), 1948, 6*s*.

Process and Reality; an essay in cosmology. *C.U.P.* (*1928*).
New edition, Vision Press, 1950. 40s.
Adventures of Ideas. *C.U.P.* (*1934*), *1938. 9s.*
Science and the Modern World. *C.U.P.* (*1925*). *6s.*

A philosophical trilogy and one of the greatest works of its kind published in the century. The first were the Gifford Lectures for 1927–1928;

the last the Lowell Lectures. Difficult in argument, yet expressed in compelling prose which will carry the general reader through much of it with interest and concentration. Subtle in reasoning, with flashes of illuminating parallels from literary criticism. For example, to prove or make clear a philosophical argument we are given passages from Plato's *Timaeus*, from Milton, or from Newton's *Scholium*, and even the hymn *Abide With Me*.

Nature and Life. *C.U.P.* (*1934*). *5s.* (*Cambridge Miscellany.*)

See also the Whitehead volume in the standard series The Library of Living Philosophers, edited by P. A. Schilpp, C.U.P. (1944), 1951, 50s. This is similar to the arrangement of the other volumes mentioned above under Dewey, Moore, Russell and Santayana.

WILLEY, BASIL

The Seventeenth Century Background. *Chatto & Windus* (*1934*). *18s.*

A mingling of literary criticism, history and philosophy, being a study of the characteristic thought of the century in relation to religion and poetry.

The Eighteenth Century Background. *Chatto & Windus* (*1940*). *18s.*

On the idea of nature as developed in the characteristic thought of the century.

Nineteenth Century Studies. *Chatto & Windus* (*1949*). *18s.*

The last of the distinguished trilogy, ranging in this volume from Coleridge to Matthew Arnold.

WOOD, H. G.

Christianity and Civilization. *C.U.P.* (*1942*). *3s. 6d.*

A brief discussion in Current Problems Series.

Details of books by other twentieth-century philosophers and writers on religious themes will be found in *An English Library* under the following: Samuel Alexander, E. R. Bevan, Bernard Bosanquet, F. H. Bradley, J. B. Bury, R. G. Collingwood, G. G. Coulton, A. E. Crawley, G. Lowes Dickinson, Sir James Frazer, Charles Gore, T. H. Green, William James, H. W. B. Joseph, J. Maynard Keynes, R. R. Marett, P. E. More, C. Lloyd Morgan, J. K. Mozley, J. H. Muirhead, J. W. Oman, Leighton Pullan, Hastings Rashdall, Carveth Read, H. W. Robinson, F. C. S. Schiller, J. L. Stocks, B. H. Streeter, William Temple, and E. A. Westermarck.

POETRY AND POETIC DRAMA

The poet has to make his own audience; the reader of poetry to find his own poets. That is why it will always be difficult for poets to get into print, and having achieved this, to make and keep an understanding circle of readers. The poet is denied the publicity sometimes at the service of the novelist, for poetry cannot be filmed. He is denied the interest of publishers who confine their activities to books with commercial possibilities, for poetry seldom makes money. Hence the necessity for patronage in one or other of its modern forms.

But the reader must help, for, as the Professor of Poetry at the University of Oxford (C. Day Lewis) said in his Inaugural Lecture (O.U.P., 1951, 2s.), 'Yes, the only way to knowledge about poetry is through love of poetry'.

The list that follows is intended to help. Nearly one hundred poets are brought together to this quiet meeting place. Probably the catalogue and bibliography page is the only place where so many modern poets could meet in the peace of amity, for no reader is so scornful and harsh in his criticism as poets are of the work of some of their contemporaries. Settle's mayfly numbers pleased but for one day, but the poet who flung his deadly dart at their badness was so great and skilful that through him they have a kind of immortality.

If poetry is what we think it is, then there are no minor poets. There are writers of poetry and there are versifiers. In the collected works of the great poets will usually be found examples of both verse and poetry. Both forms have their interest and value for us, and both can be read with enjoyment. But they are different, as different as a photograph and an oil painting or a drawing. Certain poems, a particular group of words set in their unique, permanent mould by the poet, stand out alive for us on the printed page. Then we know we have found poetry for ourselves. And that particular group of vital words is just as likely to be found in the pages of a book of our own time as it is in those books which are handed to us as the acknowledged great; just as likely to be waiting for us in a book we have rejected a year or two ago as in one we constantly read.

The discovery of poetry is one of the most vital and significant mental activities mankind is capable of; the communication of the discovery to others one of the most pleasant.

ALDINGTON, RICHARD
Complete Poems. *Wingate* (*1949*). *16s.*

ANDERSON, JOHN REDWOOD (1883–1942)
The Curlew Cries. *O.U.P.* (*1940*), *1950. 6s.*
The Human Dawn. *O.U.P.* (*1934*), *1950. 5s.*
The Tower To Heaven: a play. *O.U.P.* (*1936*).
Transvaluations. *O.U.P.* (*1932*), *1950. 6s.*

ARMSTRONG, Martin
Collected Poems. *Secker & Warburg (1931). 7s. 6d.*

AUDEN, W. H.
Collected Shorter Poems. *Faber (1950). 15s.*

Self-chosen and arranged, including all that has been published except *New Year Letter*, Faber, 1941, 10s. 6d.; *For the Time Being*, Faber, 1945, 8s. 6d.; *The Age of Anxiety*, Faber, 1948, 8s. 6d.; and the plays. The last are entered below, having been written in collaboration with Christopher Isherwood, partly in prose, partly in verse.

Some Poems: a selection. *Faber (1940), 1950. 3s. 6d.*
(*Sesame Books.*)

AUDEN, W. H. and ISHERWOOD, Christopher
The Ascent of F6. *Faber (1937). 7s. 6d.*
The Dog Beneath the Skin; or, Where is Francis?
Faber (1935). 10s. 6d.
On the Frontier: a melodrama. *Faber (1938). 6s.*

BARKER, George
Eros in Dogma. *Faber (1944). 6s.*
News of the World. *Faber (1950). 8s. 6d.*

BELLOC, Hilaire
Sonnets and Verse: collected poems. *Duckworth (1895), 1949. 10s. 6d.*
Stories, Essays and Poems. *Dent (1938), 1950. 5s.*
(*Everyman's Library.*)

BETJEMAN, John
Selected Poems. *Edited by* John Sparrow. *Murray (1948). 8s. 6d.*

BLUNDEN, Edmund
A Selection of Poetry and Prose. *Made by* Kenneth Hopkins.
Hart Davis (1950). 15s.

Poems, 1914–1930; and *Poems, 1930–1940*, were published in 1935 and 1941 respectively by Cobden Sanderson and Macmillan, 10s. 6d. each.

BOTTOMLEY, Gordon (1874–1948)
Grauch; and, Britain's Daughter. *Constable (1921), 1950. 7s. 6d.*

Awarded the Femina Vie Heureuse Prize. The first play is conceived as a prelude to Shakespeare's *Macbeth*.

King Lear's Wife. *Constable (1920). New edition, 1922.*

A prelude to Shakespeare's play, first published in 1915 and then included in the 1920 volume with *The Crier by Night* (1900), *The Riding to Lithend* (1907), *Midsummer Eve* (1901), and *Laodice and Danae* (1906).

Lyric Plays. *Constable (1932). 5s.*

Six pieces written to bring poetry back to the stage, and in continuation of the experiments 'in theatric method' contained in the volume *Scenes and Plays* issued in 1929.

Poems of Thirty Years. *Constable (1925).*

Poems and Plays. *Selected and with an introduction by* CLAUDE COLLEER ABBOTT.
　Lane (1953). 30s.

Contains ten plays and ninety pages of poetry.

BOTTRALL, RONALD
Selected Poems. *Poetry, London (1946). 4s. 6d.*

BULLETT, GERALD
Poems. *C.U.P. (1949). 7s. 6d.*

A choice made from *Poems in Pencil* and *Winter Solstice*; *Poems in Pencil* is published by Dent (1937), 1950. 5s.

CAMERON, NORMAN (1905–1953)
The Winter House, and other poems. *Dent (1935). 3s.*

Other poems in *Work in Hand*, with Robert Graves and Alan Hodge, Hogarth Press (1942).

CAMPBELL, ROY
Collected Poems. *Lane (1949). 15s.*
Sons of the Mistral: selected poems.
　Faber (1941). 3s. 6d. (Sesame Books.)

CHURCH, RICHARD
Collected Poems. *Dent (1948). 15s.*
Selected Lyrical Poems. *Staples Press (1951). 8s. 6d.*

CLARKE, AUSTIN
Collected Poems. *Introduction by* PADRAIC COLUM.
　Allen & Unwin (1933). 7s. 6d.

COLUM, PADRAIC
Poems. *Macmillan (1932).*

COMFORT, ALEX
A Wreath for the Living. *Routledge (1942). 2s. 6d.*

CUMMINGS, E. E.
One Times One. *Chatto (1947). 8s. 6d. (Horizon Books.)*

DANE, CLEMENCE
Will Shakespeare: an invention.
　Heinemann (1921). New edition, with an introduction by BASIL DEAN, *1951. 4s.*

DE LA MARE, Walter

Collected Poems. *Faber (1940), 1942. 15s.*

Contains all the poems in two volumes previously published by Constable, and later reprinted by Faber, with the exception of the poems written for children, for which *see below*. The separate volumes *Peacock Pie: a book of rhymes*, 1941, 7s. 6d. and 8s. 6d., *The Listeners, and other poems*, 1942, 5s., and *The Veil* are now published by Faber.

Collected Rhymes and Verses. *Faber (1944). 12s. 6d.*

Poems written for children, gathered together from the separate volumes.

Inward Companion, and other poems. *Faber (1950). 8s. 6d.*
Stories, Essays and Poems. *Dent (1938), 1950. 5s. (Everyman's Library.)*
Time Passes, and other poems. *Faber (1942). 2s. 6d. (Sesame Books.)*

DICKINSON, Patric

Stone in the Midst. *Methuen (1949). 7s. 6d.*
Theseus and the Minotaur, and poems. *Cape (1946).*

DOUGLAS, Keith (1920–1942)

Collected Poems. *Edited by* John Waller *and* G. S. Fraser.
  Editions Poetry, London, 1951. 12s. 6d.

DUGGAN, Eileen

Poems. *Allen & Unwin (1937).*

With an introduction by Walter de la Mare in praise of this New Zealand poet.

DUNCAN, Ronald

The Mongrel, and other poems. *Faber (1950). 8s. 6d.*
Stratton: a play. *Faber (1950). 9s. 6d.*
This Way to the Tomb: a masque and anti-masque. *Faber (1946). 8s. 6d.*

DURRELL, Lawrence

On Seeming to Presume. *Faber (1948). 8s. 6d.*

DYMENT, Clifford

Poems, 1935–1948. *Dent (1950). 7s. 6d.*

A selection from earlier volumes, together with new work.

EBERHART, Richard

Selected Poems. *Chatto & Windus (1951). 6s.*

A gathering from *A Bravery of Earth*, Cape (1930); *Reading the Spirit*, Chatto & Windus (1936); *Song and Idea*, Chatto (1940); and *Burr Oaks*, Chatto (1947), 6s. An American poet of distinction.

ELIOT, T. S.

The Cocktail Party: a comedy. *Faber (1950). 10s. 6d.*
Collected Poems, 1909–1935. *Faber (1936). 10s. 6d.*
The Family Reunion: a play. *Faber (1939). 8s. 6d.*
Four Quartets. *Faber (1944). 6s.*

The four long poems in the poet's later style: *Burnt Norton* (1936), *East Coker* (1940), *The Dry Salvages* (1941), *Little Gidding* (1942). These were all originally published separately. As the theme presents difficulties, a most useful commentary and explanation of the allusions in the whole work may be recommended: *Four Quartets Rehearsed*, by Raymond Preston. Sheed & Ward (1946). 5s.

Murder in the Cathedral: a play. *Faber (1935), 1937. 6s.*

The celebrated play on Thomas à Becket, which after Bottomley's pioneer work probably did more to bring back verse to the stage than any other modern play.

The Waste Land, and other poems: a selection.
Faber (1940). 3s. 6d. (Sesame Books.)

The title poem is the poet's best known work, and its first publication by the Hogarth Press in 1922, after its appearance in the magazine *The Criterion*, marks an epoch in modern English poetry.

EMPSON, William

The Gathering Storm. *Faber (1940).*
Poems. *Chatto & Windus (1935).*

FROST, Robert

Complete Poems. *Cape (1951). 18s.*

The collected work of the greatest living American poet. A previous collection was published in 1943.

FRY, Christopher

The Lady's Not For Burning: a comedy. *O.U.P. (1949). 6s.*
A Phoenix Too Frequent: a comedy. *(1946.) O.U.P. (1949). 6s.*
A Sleep of Prisoners: a play. *O.U.P. (1951). 6s.*
Venus Observed: a comedy. *Oxford U.P. (1950). 7s. 6d.*

FULLER, Roy

Epitaphs and Occasions. *Lehmann (1949). 6s.*
The Middle of a War. *Hogarth Press (1942). 3s. 6d.*

GAWSWORTH, John

Collected Poems. *Sidgwick & Jackson (1949). 10s. 6d.*

GEORGE, Daniel
To-morrow Will be Different. *Cape (1932), 1950. 5s.*
A unique poem in free verse which may be re-read at intervals with undiminished pleasure. Allusive (a 'ragbag' of apt quotations), ribald, realistic, witty, robustly humorous; yet with the authentic strain of the jester's seriousness apparent on every page.

GIBBON, Monk
This Insubstantial Pageant. *Phoenix House (1951). 10s. 6d.*
Contains as well as new work, a selection of earlier poems.

GIBSON, Wilfrid Wilson
Collected Poems, 1905–1925. *Macmillan (1926).*
Solway Ford, and other poems. *Faber (1945). 2s. 6d. (Sesame Books.)*

GRAHAM, W. S.
The White Threshold. *Faber (1949). 8s. 6d.*

GRAVES, Robert
Collected Poems. *Cassell (1938), 1948. 12s. 6d.*
Poems, 1938–1945. *Cassell (1945), 1950. 5s.*
These poems are included in the above volume.
No More Ghosts: selected poems. *Faber (1941). 2s. 6d. (Sesame Books.)*

HARDS, Terence and others.
Poems. *Longmans (Dorchester) (1952). 6s.*
Poems by Terence Hards, Rex Taylor and Martin Seymour-Smith.

HASSALL, Christopher
The Slow Night, and other poems, 1940–1948.
Barker (1949). 7s. 6d.

HEATH-STUBBS, John
The Swarming of the Bees. *Eyre & Spottiswoode (1950). 7s. 6d.*
Poems written 1945–1947.

HIGGINS, F. R. (1896–1932)
The Gap of Brightness. *Macmillan (1940). 3s. 6d.*

HODGE, Alan and others
Work in Hand. *Hogarth Press (1942). 2s. 6d.*
Poems by Robert Graves, Alan Hodge and Norman Cameron.

IREMONGER, Valentin
Reservations. *Macmillan (1950). 6s.*

KEYES, SIDNEY (1922–1943)
Collected Poems. *Routledge (1945). 10s. 6d.*
With a memoir and notes.

LEE, LAURIE
The Bloom of Candles. *Lehmann (1947). 3s. 6d.*
The Sun My Monument. *Hogarth Press (1944).*
The Voyage of Magellan: a play written for broadcasting.
Lehmann (1948). 10s. 6d.

LEWIS, ALUN (1915–1944)
Ha! Ha! Among the Trumpets. *Allen & Unwin (1945). 5s.*

LEWIS, CECIL DAY
Collected Poems, 1929–1936. *Hogarth Press (1936), 1949. 10s. 6d.*
Contains *Transitional Poem* (1929); *From Feathers to Iron* (1931); *The Magnetic Mountain* (1933). The gap between this collection and the next group may be filled by *Overtures to Death*, Cape (1938), 1951, 5s.; and *Word Over All*, Cape (1943), 1951, 3s. 6d.
Poems, 1943–1947. *Cape (1948), 1951. 6s.*

LYON, LILIAN BOWES (1895–1948)
Collected Poems. *Cape (1948). 8s. 6d.*
Work distinguished by its grace and tenderness, and by the poet's spontaneous freshness of approach to age-old themes. Introduction by C. Day Lewis.

M'DIARMID, HUGH
A Drunk Man Looks at the Thistle. *Blackwood (1926).*
A Kist of Whistles. *Glasgow, Maclellan (1947). 6s.*
To Circumjack Cenrastus; or, The Curly Snake.
Blackwood (1930). 8s. 6d.
Written in Scottish dialect.

MACNEICE, LOUIS
Christopher Columbus: a play written for broadcasting.
Faber (1944). 8s. 6d.
Collected Poems, 1925–1948. *Faber (1949). 15s.*
Selected Poems. *Faber (1940). 3s. 6d. (Sesame Books.)*

MADGE, CHARLES
The Disappearing Castle. *Faber (1937). 6s.*
The Father Found. *Faber (1941). 6s.*

MASEFIELD, John

Collected Poems. *Heinemann (1923). Revised edition entitled* **Poems.**
Heinemann (1948). 21s.

A King's Daughter: a tragedy. *Heinemann (1923), 1950. 6s.*

Philip the King, and other poems. *Heinemann (1914), 1950. 6s.*

Reynard the Fox; or, Ghost Heath Run; with selected sonnets and lyrics.
Heinemann (1919), 1950. 3s. 6d.

Selected Poems. *Heinemann (1950). 10s. 6d.*

'The best I have been able to do.' And amongst the best of any work
written in the century. Apart from the many fine lyrics and ballads which
have attracted thousands of readers in the English-speaking world, there
are the incomparable narrative poems, of which the masterpiece, *Reynard
the Fox*, with its heart-warming colour, beauty and vigour, must always
be accorded a special place of honour.

The Tragedy of Pompey the Great. *Sidgwick & Jackson (1910).*
Revised edition, 1914, 3s. 6d. (paper covers).

A play with lyrics.

Tristan and Isolt: a play in verse. *Heinemann (1927), 1950. 6s.*

MEW, Charlotte (1869–1928)

The Farmer's Bride. *Poetry Bookshop (1916).*
New edition with eleven additional poems, 1921. Available, 1948, from
Duckworth, 5s.

The Rambling Sailor. *Poetry Bookshop (1929), 1948. Duckworth. 5s.*

MILLAY, Edna St Vincent (1892–1950)

Poems. *Secker & Warburg (1923).*

A sequence of 52 sonnets, *Fatal Interview*, was published in 1931 by
Hamish Hamilton, and *The Buck in the Snow, and other poems*, by
Harper (London) in 1928.

MOORE, Marianne

Collected Poems. *Faber (1951). 12s. 6d.*

MUIR, Edwin

The Labyrinth. *Faber (1949). 8s. 6d.*

The Narrow Place. *Faber (1943). 6s.*

Variations on a Time Theme. *Dent (1934), 1950. 3s.*

The Voyage, and other poems. *Faber (1946). 6s.*

NICHOLSON, Norman

Five Rivers. *Faber (1944). 6s.*

The Old Man of the Mountains: a play. *Faber (1946). 8s. 6d.*

Prophesy To The Wind. *Faber (1950). 8s. 6d.*

A remarkable play of a probable future in a desolate North land, when
all the world is one huge 'bombed site'.

Rock Face. *Faber (1946), 1950. 7s. 6d.*

PALMER, Herbert

Collected Poems, 1918–1931. *Dent (1933), 1951. 10s. 6d.*
The Old Knight. *Dent (1949). 7s. 6d.*
Season and Festival. *Faber (1943). (Sesame Books.)*

A selection from the author's published work from 1918.

PEAKE, Mervyn

The Glassblowers. *Eyre & Spottiswoode (1950). 7s. 6d.*

Inspired by the artist's work during the war when he placed on pictorial record many aspects of life in England 1939–1945, and in particular the strange, glowing fantasy of the glass-blower's works.

PITTER, Ruth

The Bridge: poems 1939–1944. *Cresset Press (1945).*
Urania. *Cresset Press (1951). 10s. 6d.*

The author's own selection of the best of her work from three earlier volumes: *A Trophy of Arms, The Spirit Watches,* and *The Bridge* (1945).

POUND, Ezra

The Pisan Cantos. *Faber (1949). 12s. 6d.*
Selected Poems. *Edited with introduction, by* T. S. Eliot.
    Faber (1940). New edition, 1949. 12s. 6d.

PUDNEY, John

Selected Poems. *Lane (1946). 3s. 6d.*

RAINE, Kathleen

The Pythoness. *Hamish Hamilton (1949). 6s.*
Stone and Flower. *Poetry, London (1943). 6s.*

RANSOM, John Crowe

Selected Poems. *Eyre & Spottiswoode (1948). 9s.*

An aloof, difficult poet whose work commands respect both in America, his own country, and in Great Britain.

READ, Sir Herbert

Collected Poems. *Faber (1946). 8s. 6d.*
Thirty-five Poems. *Faber (1940). 2s. 6d. (Sesame Books.)*

REED, Henry

A Map of Verona. *Cape (1946). 3s. 6d.*

REEVES, James

The Imprisoned Sea, and other poems. *Poetry, London (1949). 5s.*
The Natural Need. *Seizin Press (1934).*

Two volumes of mature work the latter now out of print and scarce.

The Password, and other Poems. *Heinemann (1952). 10s. 6d.*
The Wandering Moon. *Heinemann (1950). 6s.*
Poems written primarily for young people, with illustrations by Evadne Rowan.

RICKWARD, EDGELL
Collected Poems. *Lane (1947). 7s. 6d.*

RIDING, LAURA
Collected Poems. *Cassell (1938), 1948. 15s.*

RIDLER, ANNE
Henry Bey, and other plays. *Faber (1950). 10s. 6d.*
The Nine Bright Shiners. *Faber (1943).*
The Shadow Factory: a Nativity play. *Faber (1946). 6s.*

ROBERTS, LYNETTE
Gods With Stainless Ears. *Faber (1950). 7s. 6d.*
Poems. *Faber (1944). 6s.*

ROBERTS, MICHAEL (1902–1948)
Poems. *Cape (1936), 1951. 5s.*

SACKVILLE-WEST, EDWARD
The Rescue. *Secker & Warburg (1945). 8s. 6d.*
A play from the *Odyssey*, written for broadcasting. The text has illustrations by HENRY MOORE.

SACKVILLE-WEST, V.
Collected Poems. Vol. I. *Hogarth Press (1933). 10s. 6d.*
The Land. *Heinemann (1928), 1950. 6s.*
One of the best long poems in modern poetry, taking the reader through the four seasons with distinguished literary craftsmanship and a country-woman's accurate knowledge of farming and the life of the fields.

SANTAYANA, GEORGE
Poems. *Constable (1923).*

SASSOON, SIEGFRIED
Collected Poems. *Faber (1947). 10s. 6d.*
Poems: newly selected, 1916–1935.
    Faber (1940). 3s. 6d. (Sesame Books.)

SAYERS, DOROTHY L.
Four Sacred Plays. *Gollancz (1948). 4s. 6d.*
The Devil to Pay, The Just Vengeance, He That should Come, The Zeal of Thy House.

SHANKS, Edward
Poems, 1912–1932. *Macmillan (1933). 10s. 6d.*

SITWELL, Edith
The Canticle of the Rose: selected poems, 1920–1947.
Macmillan (1949). 15s.
Façade, and other poems, 1920–1935. *Duckworth (1950). 8s. 6d.*
Introductory essay by Jack Lindsay.

Poems New and Old. *Faber (1940). 3s. 6d. (Sesame Books.)*
The Song of the Cold. *Macmillan (1945). 7s. 6d.*
Poems from *Green Song*; *Street Songs*; together with three new ones.

SITWELL, Sir Osbert
The Collected Satires and Poems. *Duckworth (1931).*
The limited edition at 63*s.* is the only edition available until the new one is ready.

Selected Poems Old and New. *Duckworth (1943). 7s. 6d.*

SITWELL, Sacheverell
Collected Poems. *Duckworth (1940).*
The Cyder Feast, and other poems. *Duckworth (1927). 7s. 6d.*
Selected Poems. *Duckworth (1948). 8s. 6d.*
With a preface by Sir Osbert Sitwell.

SNAITH, Stanley
Fieldfaring. *Nelson (1935).*
Green Legacy. *Cape (1937).*
The Inn of Night. *Dent (1947). 6s.*

SPENCER, Bernard
Aegean Islands. *Poetry, London (Nicholson & Watson) (1947). 6s.*

SPENDER, Stephen
Poems of Dedication. *Faber (1947). 6s.*
Ruins and Visions. *Faber (1942). 7s. 6d.*
Selected Poems. *Faber (1940). 3s. 6d. (Sesame Books.)*
Trial of a Judge: a tragic statement in five acts.
Faber (1935), 1938. 7s. 6d.

SQUIRE, Sir John Collings
Collected Parodies. *Heinemann (1921).*
Selected Poems. *Moxon (1948). 8s. 6d.*

STEPHENS, James (1882–1950)
Collected Poems. *Macmillan (1926).*

TATE, ALLEN
Poems, 1920–1945. *Eyre & Spottiswoode (1948). 10s. 6d.*

THOMAS, DYLAN
Collected Poems. *Dent (1952). 12s. 6d.*
Deaths and Entrances. *Dent (1946), 1949. 5s.*
The Map of Love: stories and poems. *Dent (1938).*
Twenty-five Poems. *Dent (1937).*

TILLER, TERENCE
The Inward Animal. *Hogarth Press (1944), 1950. 2s.*
Unarm, Eros. *Hogarth Press (1948), 1950. 2s.*

TODD, RUTHVEN
The Planet in My Hand. *Grey Walls Press (1947). 6s.*

TREECE, HENRY
The Haunted Garden. *Faber (1947). 7s. 6d.*
Invitation and Warning. *Faber (1942). 6s.*

TREVELYAN, R. C. (1872–1950)
Collected Works. *2 vols. Longmans (1939).*
Vol. 1: Poems; Vol. 2: Plays. Vol. 2 in print, 1950, 15s. The poet is one of the most distinguished translators of Greek and Latin poetry, and has translated Leopardi's work with success.

WALEY, ARTHUR
Chinese Poems. *Allen & Unwin (1946). 8s. 6d.*
Translations selected from four books by the gifted Sinologist, who has also rendered into English the strange *Nō Plays of Japan*, Allen & Unwin, 1921, 18s.

WATKINS, VERNON
The Ballad of the Mari Lwyd, and other poems. *Faber (1947). 7s. 6d.*
The Lady with the Unicorn. *Faber (1948). 8s. 6d.*

WELLESLEY, DOROTHY
Poems of Ten Years, 1924–1934. *Macmillan (1934).*
Selected Poems. *Williams & Norgate (1949). 10s. 6d.*

WHISTLER, LAURENCE
The World's Room: collected poems. *Heinemann (1949). 15s.*
With decorations by Rex Whistler.

YATES, PETER

The Assassin: a play. *Chatto (1945). 6s.*

On the murderer of Abraham Lincoln, John Wilkes Booth.

The Burning Mask: a play. *Chatto (1948). 6s.*
The Motionless Dancer. *Chatto (1943). 5s.*

YOUNG, ANDREW

Collected Poems. *Illustrated. Cape (1950). 10s. 6d.*

A gathering from a number of smaller books which offer the best nature poetry of our time. The former collection of 1936 is superseded by the later volume, which includes the play *Nicodemus*, with incidental music by IMOGEN HOLST, formerly separately published, Cape, 1937.

MODERN POETRY—ANTHOLOGIES
ARRANGED UNDER EDITORS

CALDWELL, THOMAS
The Golden Book of Modern English Poetry, 1870–1930.
Additions arranged by PHILIP HENDERSON *for enlarged edition. Dent (1935), 1950. 5s. (Everyman's Library.)*

CHURCH, RICHARD and BOZMAN, M. M.
Poems of Our Time. *Dent (1945), 1950. 5s. (Everyman's Library.)*

THE ENGLISH ASSOCIATION
The Modern Muse: Poems of To-day, British and American.
O.U.P. (1934), 1949. 6s.
Poems of To-day. *3 vols (1915–1937).*
Vols. 1 and 2: Sidgwick & Jackson (1915, 1922), 1950. Separately 5s. each; together in one volume 10s. 6d.
Vol. 3: Macmillan (1937), 1950, 4s., (School edition, 2s. 6d.).
Vol. 4: Macmillan (1951), 7s. 6d.
Primarily compiled for use in Secondary Schools, but widely used by all beginners.

GREACEN, ROBERT and IREMONGER, VALENTIN
Contemporary Irish Poetry. *Faber (1949). 8s. 6d.*

GRIGSON, GEOFFREY
Poetry of the Present: an anthology of the 'thirties and after.
Phoenix House (1949), 1951, 6s.
'None of the poets here was born before 1904.' There are thirty-five of them. The editor's preface ends on a note of despondency. 'There are never so many good poets, alas, as there seem to be.'

JONES, PHYLLIS
Modern Verse, 1900–1940. *O.U.P. (1940). 5s. (World's Classics.)*

LEWIS, CECIL DAY and STRONG, L. A. G.
A New Anthology of Modern Verse, 1920–1940.
Methuen (1941), 1950. 6s. (School edition, 3s. 6d.)

LINDSAY, MAURICE
Modern Scottish Poetry: an anthology of the Scottish Renaissance, 1920–1945. *Faber (1946). 6s.*

LYND, ROBERT
An Anthology of Modern Poetry. *Nelson (1939), 1950. 5s.*

MATTHIESSEN, F. O.
The Oxford Book of American Verse. *With an introduction by the editor.*
O.U.P. (1950). 36s.

A large collection of 511 poems written from Colonial times to the
present day. But more than half of the 1132 pages are devoted to work
written in the twentieth century. In all, fifty-one poets are represented.

METHUEN, SIR ALGERNON
An Anthology of Modern Verse. *Methuen (1921), 1950. 7s. 6d. (and with*
notes, 3s. 6d.).

The poems included here are mainly of the Georgians and all were
written by 1920.

MONRO, HAROLD
Twentieth Century Poetry.
Chatto & Windus (1929), 1933. 6s. (Phoenix Library.)

NICHOLS, ROBERT
An Anthology of War Poetry, 1914–1918. *Nicholson & Watson (1943).*

OXFORD POETRY. *Blackwell.*
(Annually) from 4s. each volume.

PESCHMANN, HERMANN
The Voice of Poetry, 1930–1950. *Evans (1951). 8s. 6d.*

POEMS IN PAMPHLET SERIES. *Hand & Flower Press. 1950—in*
progress. 1s. each.

A well-printed series offering work by new poets; each volume is about
thirty pages in length, paginated continuously from the first so that
eventually a full-sized volume may be bound.

RHYS, KEIDRYCH
Modern Welsh Poetry. *Faber (1944). 6s.*

RIDLER, ANNE
A Little Book of Modern Verse. *Introduction by* T. S. ELIOT.
Faber (1942). 5s.

ROBERTS, MICHAEL
The Faber Book of Modern Verse. *Faber (1936), 1951. 12s. 6d.*

The revised edition is prepared by ANNE RIDLER in conformity with the
original editor's wishes.

SERGEANT, HOWARD
An Anthology of Contemporary Northern Poetry.
Harrap (1947). 8s. 6d.

SITWELL, EDITH

The American Genius. *Lehmann (1951). 12s. 6d.*

There is a long introduction by the compiler, critical and appreciative; then follow poems by twenty-six writers, most of whom are late nineteenth and present century poets.

SQUIRE, SIR JOHN COLLINGS

Selections from Modern Poets. *Secker & Warburg. Complete edition (1st and 2nd series) published in one volume (1927). New edition in three volumes, 1948, 4s. 6d. each*

WOLLMAN, MAURICE

Modern Poetry, 1922–1934. *Macmillan (1935), 1951. 4s.*
Poems of the War Years. *Macmillan (1948). 12s. 6d. and 5s.*

A selection from the work of 100 authors writing from 1939 to 1946. The cheaper edition is in the *Scholar's Library* series, and has notes and brief biographies.

Poems of Twenty Years, 1918–1938.
Macmillan (1938). 7s. 6d. (Scholar's Library edition, 5s.)

YEATS, W. B.

The Oxford Book of Modern Verse, 1892–1935.
O.U.P. (1936), 1950. 18s.

A selection which strongly represents the distinguished editor's personal taste. It was received with controversy.

Details of volumes of poetry by twentieth-century poets no longer living will be found under the following names in *An English Library*: Lascelles Abercrombie, Maurice Baring, Stephen Vincent Benet, Robert Binyon, Robert Bridges, Rupert Brooke, G. K. Chesterton, Hart Crane, W. H. Davies, C. M. Doughty, Lord Alfred Douglas, Ernest Dowson, John Drinkwater, J. Elroy Flecker, Michael Field, John Freeman, Gerald Gould, Ivor Gurney, Thomas Hardy, Maurice Hewlett, A. E. Housman, Sidney Keyes, D. H. Lawrence, Vachell Lindsay, Alice Meynell, Harold Monro, T. Sturge Moore, Robert Nichols, Wilfred Owen, Isaac Rosenberg, G. W. Russell, C. H. Sorley, J. B. Tabb, Edward Thomas, Edward Thompson, W. J. Turner, Sir William Watson, Charles Williams, and W. B. Yeats.

PROSE DRAMA

Plays reflect so faithfully current modes of speech and thought that few are readable as literary entertainment a decade or so after their stage success. It will be remembered that this section in *An English Library* is the smallest in the book, but that may be because in addition to changes in fashion, prose drama in England between the age of the great Carolines and that of Wilde had very little of importance to say for itself. But from Robertson's *Caste* (1867) to the death of Bernard Shaw (1950) it will be conceded that the English stage experienced a renaissance of European importance. Largely owing to the genius of Pinero, Wilde, Shaw, Granville-Barker, Coward, O'Casey, Priestley and Rattigan, dramatic writers found the stage as lively and intellectual a focus for their ideas as did their great predecessors. Hence the establishment of a modern habit of publishing plays for reading as soon as they have been produced, and sometimes before. In the United States there rapidly developed a native drama as individual and vigorous as here.

In the 'twenties and 'thirties those who enjoy reading plays were well catered for by the annual appearance of collections of the best plays of each year or group of years. These excellent volumes, published principally by Gollancz, may still be bought at secondhand bookshops. A few publishers initiated series of modern plays in book form. Of these Benn's *Contemporary Dramatists* was the principal. Such ventures are now being resumed, for in 1950 the dramatic critic J. C. Trewin started a new series with a selection of the best plays of 1949 and the Gollancz series will start once more in 1953.

The specialists in this kind of literature are Samuel French, whose lists include nearly every notable play of the century in acting editions. Attention may here be drawn to this firm's admirable *Guide to Selecting Plays*, 1951 edition, 2s. 6d., and to the most comprehensive bibliography of the subject, and bibliography of the theatre, *The Player's Library*—being the catalogue of the vast collection in the library of the British Drama League, published 1950, Faber, 30s.; first supplement, 1952, 8s. 6d.

In the selection listed below an attempt has been made to give particulars of noteworthy British and American plays of the last fifty years which may be read with pleasure whether one has seen them on the stage or not including the collected plays of the major modern dramatists from Shaw to Priestley, O'Neill, Bridie, Coward, O'Casey, Milne and Housman.

ACKERLEY, J. R.

The Prisoners of War. *Chatto (1925).*

A remarkably fine study in the psychology of a group of men who have to endure each other's company in a Swiss internment prison during the 1914–1918 war. The author wrote a first-class travel book which will be found in its section.

ACKLAND, Rodney
After October. *Gollancz (1936).*
Strange Orchestra. *Gollancz (1932).*

ARCHER, William (1856–1924)
The Green Goddess. *New York (1921). Heinemann (1923).*

ARMSTRONG, Anthony
Ten Minute Alibi. *Gollancz (1933).*

BAGNOLD, Enid
Two Plays. *Heinemann (1951). 7s. 6d.*
Contains *Lottie Dundass* (1944) and *Poor Judas.*

BAKER, Elizabeth
Chains. *Sidgwick & Jackson (1921). 3s. 6d.*

BALDERSTON, John L. and SQUIRE, Sir John
Berkeley Square. *Longmans (1929).*
A play constructed from Henry James's unfinished novel, *The Sense of the Past.*

BANCROFT, George Pleydell
The Ware Case. *Methuen (1927). 4s.*

BATES, H. E.
The Day of Glory. *Michael Joseph (1945).*

BAX, Clifford
Socrates. *Gollancz (1930).*
Valiant Ladies: three plays. *Gollancz (1931).*
Contains *The Venetian; The Rose without a Thorn; The Immortal Lady.*

BERKELEY, Reginald (1890–1935)
The Lady With a Lamp. *Gollancz (1929). 5s.*

BESIER, Rudolf (1878–1942)
The Barretts of Wimpole Street. *Gollancz (1930). 4s. 6d. (paper).*
Lady Patricia. *Fisher Unwin (1923). Benn.*

BRIDIE, James (1888–1951)
Colonel Witherspoon, and other plays. *Constable (1934), 1950. 10s.*
John Knox, and other plays. *Constable (1949). 10s.*
John Knox; Dr Angelus; It Depends What You Mean; The Forrigan Reel.
A Sleeping Clergyman, and other plays. *Constable (1934), 1950. 12s. 6d.*
A Sleeping Clergyman; The Amazed Evangelist; Jonah and the Whale; Tobias and the Angel; The Anatomist.
Moral Plays. *Constable (1936), 1950. 10s.*

COLLIS, Maurice
White of Mergen. *Faber (1945). 8s. 6d.*
A dramatic presentation of the life of Samuel White, the seventeenth-century Englishman whose adventures in tropical Asia are recorded in a biography by the same author, *Siamese White*, Faber (1936), 1951. 15s.

CONNELLY, Marc
The Green Pastures. *Gollancz (1930).*
A remarkable negro play in which the Deity is translated literally as a kindly, very busy Lawd, with a roll-top desk, ready to help as much as human beings will allow him to.

COWARD, Noel
Play Parade. *3 vols. In progress. Heinemann (1949). 12s. 6d. each.*
Vol. 1: *Design for Living*; *Cavalcade*; *Bitter Sweet*; *The Vortex*; *Post-Mortem*; *Hay Fever*. 1949.
Vol. 2: *This Year of Grace*; *Words and Music*; *Operetta*; *Conversation Piece*; *Easy Virtue*; *Fallen Angels*. 1950.
Vol. 3: *The Queen Was In the Parlour*; '*I'll Leave It to You*'; *The Young Idea*; *Sirocco*; *The Rat Trap*; '*This Was a Man*'; *Home Chat*. 1950.

DANE, Clemence
A Bill of Divorcement. *Heinemann (1921).*

DAVIOT, Gordon
Richard of Bordeaux. *Gollancz (1933).*

DAVISON, John
The Shadows of Strife. *Dent (1930).*
Introduction by Sir Barry Jackson.

DUKES, Ashley
The Man With a Load of Mischief. *Benn (1924), 1948. 2s.*

EGAN, Michael
The Dominant Sex. *Deane (1935). 3s. 6d.*

ERVINE, St John
The First Mrs Frazer. *Allen & Unwin (1929). 4s. 6d.*
Jane Clegg. *Sidgwick & Jackson (1911). 3s. 6d.*
John Ferguson. *Allen & Unwin (1914), 1919. 4s. 6d.*

GEORGE, Ernest
Down Our Street. *Gollancz (1929), 1948. 5s.*
The early edition was entitled *Belle*.

GINSBURY, Norman
The First Gentleman. *Hammond, Hammond (1947). 8s. 6d.*

GREEN, PAUL
In Abraham's Bosom. *Allen & Unwin (1926), 1929. 5s. and 3s. 6d.*
Awarded the Pulitzer Prize.

Out of the South: collected plays. *Allen & Unwin (1939). 12s. 6d.*
'The life of a people in dramatic form.'

HAMILTON, PATRICK
Gas Light. *Constable (1939), 1949. 3s. (paper covers).*
A Victorian thriller which has had many revivals on the radio.
Rope. *Constable (1929), 1949. 3s. (paper covers).*
Certainly one of the best thrillers of the century.

HART, MOSS and KAUFMAN, GEORGE
The Man Who Came to Dinner. *(1939.)*
    English Theatre Guild edition, 1945. 4s.
One of the best American comedies of recent years.
Once in a Lifetime. *Gollancz (1930).*

HARWOOD, H. M.
The Grain of Mustard Seed. *Benn (1920), 1948. 2s.*

HELLMAN, LILLIAN
The Little Foxes. *Hamish Hamilton (1939).*
The Watch On the Rhine. *English Theatre Guild edition (1946). 4s.*

HODGE, MERTON
The Wind and the Rain. *Gollancz (1934).*

HOME, W. D.
Now Barabbas. *Longmans (1947). 6s.*

HOUSMAN, LAURENCE
The Death of Socrates. *Sidgwick & Jackson (1925).*
A dramatic scene founded upon two of Plato's dialogues, the *Crito* and
the *Phaedo*.
Little Plays of St Francis.
    *3 vols. Sidgwick & Jackson (1922 and 1931), 1950. 7s. 6d. each, and
    separately in paper covers at 1s. each.*
A dramatic cycle from the Life and Legend of St Francis of Assisi, with
scene designs by the author.
Victoria Regina: a dramatic biography. *Cape (1934), 1950. 10s. 6d.*
Happy and Glorious. *Cape (1945), 1950. 7s. 6d.*
Two omnibus volumes of the many Victorian plays, side-scenes from the
life of Queen Victoria.

HUXLEY, ALDOUS
Verses and a Comedy. *Chatto & Windus (1931), 1946. 7s. 6d.*
Contains early poems, *Leda, The Cicadas* and the play *The World of Light.*

JOHNSTON, DENIS
The Moon in the Yellow River. *Cape (1934), 1949. 6s.*

LEVY, BENN W.
Springtime for Henry: a farce. *Secker & Warburg (1932).*

LONSDALE, FREDERIC
Canaries Sometimes Sing. *Methuen (1929). 4s.*
The Last of Mrs Cheyney. *Collins (1925).*
On Approval. *Collins (1927).*

MACKENZIE, RONALD (1903–1932)
The Maitlands. *Gollancz (1934).*
Musical Chairs. *Gollancz (1932).*
A display of talent in the Tchehov manner.

MALLESON, MILES and BROOKS, H.
Six Men of Dorset. *Gollancz (1934), 1951. 6s.*

MASEFIELD, JOHN
The Tragedy of Nan, and other plays. *(1909.) Heinemann (1926).*

MAUGHAM, W. SOMERSET
Collected Plays. *3 vols. Heinemann (1952). 15s. each.*
The new collection takes the place of a set of six volumes published 1931–1934. It comprises eighteen plays chosen by the author from his total output of thirty.

MAYOR, BEATRICE
The Pleasure Garden. *Sidgwick & Jackson (1925).*

MILNE, A. A.
First Plays. *Chatto & Unwin (1917), 1928. 7s. 6d.*
The Boy Comes Home; Belinda; Wurzel Flummery; The Lucky One; The Red Feathers.
Second Plays. *Chatto & Windus (1921), 1928. 7s. 6d.*
Mr Pim Passes By; The Romantic Age; Make Believe; The Camberley Triangle; The Stepmother.
Three Plays. *Chatto & Windus (1923). 7s. 6d.*
The Great Broxopp; The Dover Road; The Truth About Blayds.
Four Plays. *Chatto & Windus (1926), 1929. 7s. 6d.*
Michael and Mary; To Have the Honour; The Perfect Alibi; Portrait of a Gentleman in Slippers.

MORGAN, CHARLES
The Flashing Stream. *Macmillan (1938), 1948. 12s. 6d.*
With an essay on 'Singleness of Mind', and a foreword.

MURRAY, T. C.
Autumn Fire. *Allen & Unwin (1925), 1952. 5s.*

O'CASEY, SEAN
Collected Plays. *Macmillan. 4 vols. (1949–1951). 12s. 6d. each.*
Vol. 1: *Juno and the Paycock; The Shadow of a Gunman; The Plough and the Stars; The End of the Beginning; A Pound On Demand.*
Vol. 2: *The Silver Tassie; The Star Turns Red; Within the Gates.*
Vol. 3: *Red Roses For Me; The Purple Dust; The Hall of Healing.*
Vol. 4: *Oak Leaves and Lavender; Cock-a-Doodle Dandy; Time to Go; Bedtime Story.*

ODETS, CLIFFORD
Golden Boy. *Gollancz (1938). 5s.*
Three Plays. *Gollancz (1936).*
Awake and Sing ; Waiting for Lefty; Till the Day I Die.

O'NEILL, EUGENE
The Emperor Jones, The Straw, *and* **Diff'rent.** *Three plays.*
Cape (1922). Uniform edition, 1953. 10s. 6d.
The Hairy Ape, Anna Christie, *and* **The First Man.** *Three plays.*
Cape (1923), 1950. 8s. 6d.
The Iceman Cometh. *Cape (1947), 1950. 8s. 6d.*
Mourning Becomes Electra. *Cape (1932), 1950. 8s. 6d.*
A great trilogy and one of the outstanding contributions to the stage of the century. A modern treatment of the ancient theme of the Aeschylean trilogy, sometimes called *The House of Atreus.*
The Moon of the Caribbees, and six other plays of the sea.
Cape (1923), 1951. 8s. 6d.
Strange Interlude. *Cape (1928). Uniform edition, 1953. 10s. 6d.*
Another great play of considerable length, with a variation of the old-fashioned device of earlier dramatists known as the aside.
The plays of this greatest of all American playwrights are published in three handsome volumes, New York, Random House. This set does not include the last play, *The Iceman Cometh.*

PHILLPOTTS, EDEN and ADELAIDE EDEN
Devonshire Plays. *Duckworth (1927).*
Devonshire Cream (1925); *The Farmer's Wife* (1917); and (with ADELAIDE EDEN PHILLPOTTS) *Yellow Sands* (1926).

PRIESTLEY, J. B.

Plays. *3 vols. Heinemann (1948–1950). 16s. each.*

Vol. 1: *Dangerous Corner*; *Eden End*; *Time and the Conways*; *I Have Been Here Before*; *Johnson Over Jordan*; *Music at Night*; *The Linden Tree* (1948).

Vol. 2: *Laburnum Grove*; *Bees on the Boat Deck*; *When We Are Married*; *Goodnight, Children*; *The Golden Fleece*; *How Are They At Home*; *Ever Since Paradise* (1949).

Vol. 3: *Summer Day's Dream*; *Cornelius*; *People At Sea*; *Desert Highway*; *An Inspector Calls*; *Home Is To-Morrow* (1950).

RATTIGAN, TERENCE

Adventure Story. *Hamish Hamilton (1950).*
Flare Path. *Hamish Hamilton (1943).*
French Without Tears. *Hamish Hamilton (1937).*
Playbill; The Browning Version; *and* **Harlequinade.**
    Hamish Hamilton (1949). 4s. 6d. (boards).
The Winslow Boy. *Hamish Hamilton (1946).*

Three of the above have been reprinted to make one volume in *Pan Books, 1950. 2s.*

RICE, ELMER

Plays: *The Adding Machine* (1922); *Street Scene* (1929); *See Naples and Die* (1933); *Counsellor At Law* (1931).

Formerly published in one volume, Gollancz, 1933.

ROBINSON, LENNOX

Plays. *Macmillan (1928).*

The Round Table (1922); *Crabbed Youth and Age* (1922); *Portrait* (1925); *The White Blackbird* (1925); *The Big House* (1926); *Give a Dog* (1928); *The White-Headed Boy.* Putnam (1920).

SAROYAN, WILLIAM

The Time of Your Life, and two other plays. *Faber (1942). 8s. 6d.*

The others are *Love's Old Sweet Song*, and *My Heart's In the Highlands*.

SHAIRP, MORDAUNT (1887–1939)

The Crime At Blossoms. *Allen & Unwin (1932). 4s. 6d.*
The Green Bay Tree. *Allen & Unwin (1933).*

SHAW, G. BERNARD (1856–1950)

Plays. *Standard edition. 16 vols.*
    Constable *(1931–1932; 1947; 1951), 1951. 12s. 6d. each.*
    Androcles and the Lion; *Overruled*; *Pygmalion* (1916).
    Back to Methuselah; *a metabiological pentateuch* (1921).
    Buoyant Billions; *Far-fetched Fables*; *and Shakes versus Shav* (1951).

176

The Doctor's Dilemma; *Getting Married*; *The Shewing-up of Blanco Posnet* (1911).

Geneva; *Cymbeline Refinished*; *Good King Charles* (1947).

Heartbreak House; *Great Catherine*; *O'Flaherty, V.C.*; *The Inca of Perusalem*; *Augustus Does His Bit*; *Annajanska* (1919).

John Bull's Other Island; *How He Lied to Her Husband*; *Major Barbara* (1907).

Man and Superman; *a comedy and a philosophy* (1903).

Misalliance; *The Dark Lady of the Sonnets*; *Fanny's First Play* (1914).

Plays Pleasant; *Arms and the Man*; *Candida*; *The Man of Destiny*; *You Never Can Tell* (1898).

Plays Unpleasant: Widowers' Houses; *The Philanderer*; *Mrs Warren's Profession* (1898).

Saint Joan; and *The Apple Cart* (1924, 1929).

The Simpleton of the Unexpected Isles; *The Six of Calais*; *The Millionairess* (1936).

Three Plays for Puritans: The Devil's Disciple; *Caesar and Cleopatra*; *Captain Brassbound's Conversion* (1900).

Too True To Be Good; *Village Wooing*; *On the Rocks* (1934).

Translations and Tomfooleries (1926).

In addition to this standard edition there is a special edition of *Back To Methuselah* in the World's Classics Series, O.U.P., 1945, 5s., with a postscript and some textual revision.

SHERRIFF, R. C.

Badger's Green. *Gollancz* (*1930*).
Journey's End. *Gollancz* (*1929*).

Included in *Modern Plays*, Dent (1937), 5s. (*Everyman's Library*.).

SHERWOOD, ROBERT

Idiot's Delight. *Heinemann* (*1938*).
Reunion In Vienna. *Scribner's* (*1932*). *3s. 6d.* (*paper*).

SHIELS, GEORGE

Three Plays: Professor Tim; Paul Twyning; The New Gossoon.
 Macmillan (*1945*). *8s. 6d.*

These plays were all first produced at the Abbey Theatre, Dublin.

STRODE, W. CHETHAM

The Guinea Pig. *Low* (*1946*). *6s.*

THURBER, JAMES and NUGENT, ELLIOTT

The Male Animal. *Hamish Hamilton* (*1950*). *8s. 6d.*
First published in New York, 1940.

VAN DRUTEN, JOHN

London Wall. *Gollancz* (*1931*).
Young Woodley. *Gollancz* (*1928*).

VANE, Sutton (1888–1913)
Outward Bound. *Chatto & Windus (1924).*

WILLIAMS, Emlyn
The Corn Is Green. *Heinemann (1939), 1950. 6s.*
Night Must Fall. *Gollancz (1935).*

WINTER, Keith
The Rats of Norway. *Heinemann (1933).*

WOOLF, Leonard
The Hotel. *Hogarth Press (1939), 1950. 5s.*

PROSE DRAMA—COLLECTIONS

ARRANGED UNDER EDITORS

HAWTREY, ANTHONY (Editor)

Embassy Successes. *3 vols. 1946–1949. Low. 8s. 6d. each.*

Collections of plays first produced by the Editor at his Embassy Theatre in London.

Vol. 1: *Worm's Eye View*, by R. F. DELDERFIELD; *Zoo in Silesia*, by RICHARD POLLOCK; *Father Malachy's Miracle*, by BRIAN DOHERTY, from the novel by BRUCE MARSHALL.

Vol. 2: *National Velvet*, by ENID BAGNOLD; *No Room at the Inn*, by JOAN TEMPLE; *Skipper Next to God*, by JAN DE HARTOG.

Vol. 3: *Peace Comes to Peckham*, by R. F. DELDERFIELD; *Let My People Go*, by IAN HAY; *Away From it All*, by VAL GIELGUD.

MARRIOTT, J. W. (Editor)

The Best One-Act Plays of 1948–1949. *Harrap (1950). 9s. 6d.*

One of a series.

Modern Plays. *Dent (1937), 1950. 5s. (Everyman's Library.)*

Milestones, by EDWARD KNOBLOCK and ARNOLD BENNETT; *Journey's End*, by R. C. SHERRIFF; *Hay Fever*, by NOEL COWARD; *The Dover Road*, by A. A. MILNE; *For Services Rendered*, by W. SOMERSET MAUGHAM.

TREWIN, J. C. (Editor)

Plays of the Year. *In progress 1949–*
  Paul Elek. Vols. 1–3, 15s. each; vol. 4, 18s.

Vol. 1: 1948–1949: *Cockpit*, by BRIDGET BOLAND; *Family Portrait*, by LENORE COFFEE and W. JOYCE COWAN; *The Happiest Days of Your Life*, by JOHN DIGHTON; *The Miser*, adapted from Molière's play by MILES MALLESON; *The Paragon*, by ROLAND and MICHAEL PERTWEE; *Don't Listen Ladies*, adapted from Sacha Guitry's play, by STEPHEN POWYS and GUY BOLTON.

Vol. 2: 1949: *Ann Veronica*, adapted from H. G. Wells's novel, by RONALD GOW; *Dark of the Moon*, by HOWARD RICHARDSON and WILLIAM BERNEY; *Black Chiffon*, by LESLEY STORM; *The Late Edwina Black*, by WILLIAM DINNER and WILLIAM MORUM; *The King of Friday's Men*, by MICHAEL MOLLOY; *Before the Party*, adapted from W. Somerset Maugham's story, by RODNEY ACKLAND.

Vol. 3: 1949–1950: *The Holly and the Ivy*, by WYNYARD BROWNE; *Top of the Ladder*, by TYRONE GUTHRIE; *Tartuffe*, adapted from Molière's play, by MILES MALLESON; *Castle in the Air*, by ALAN MELVILLE; *Young Wives' Tale*, by RONALD JEANS; *Bonaventure*, by CHARLOTTE HASTINGS.

Vol. 4: 1950: *Seagulls Over Sorrento*, by HUGH HASTINGS; *His Excellency*, by DOROTHY and CAMPBELL CHRISTIE; *Background*, by W. CHETHAM

STRODE; *To Dorothy, A Son*, by ROGER MACDOUGALL; *The Thistle and the Rose*, by WILLIAM D. HOME.

For the later volumes to date see the complete list in the current edition of the publisher's catalogue.

Details of published plays by other dramatists of the twentieth century no longer living will be found in *An English Library* under the following names: Sir James Barrie, Arnold Bennett, Rudolf Besier, Harold Chapin, G. K. Chesterton, John Drinkwater, J. Elroy Flecker, John Galsworthy, H. Granville-Barker, Lady Gregory, St John Hankin, W. Stanley Houghton, Henry Arthur Jones, Allan Monkhouse, J. M. Synge, and W. J. Turner.

TRAVEL AND EXPLORATION

Modern literature is unusually rich in works of travel of the first order. Since Kinglake wrote his delightful *Eothen* in 1844 genius for travel has often again been united with the gift of language. The list could, therefore, have been double its present length and still some hundreds of good books would have been omitted. Nevertheless, brief as it comparatively is, the section not only records many of the famous books but draws attention to some which may be entirely unknown to the younger generations of readers and have probably been forgotten by older readers simply because of the abundance of good books available or because many have been allowed to go out of print.

It is a pleasure to find still available after forty years of quiet popularity such a delightful book as Abraham's *Surgeon's Log*; and leaping over the years to come upon a book with as much individual flavour as Jim Corbett's *Man-Eaters of Kumaon*. For reprints of some grand old favourites of fifty years ago and more we must be grateful to such series as the *Mariner's Library*, which has given us not only modern adventurous voyages but semi-classics such as E. F. Knight's record of *The Falcon* cruising in the Baltic and the story of the venturesome Captain Voss traversing the globe in a converted Indian dug-out canoe.

Of a different order are Robert Gibbing's inimitable four books, with their easy, racy humour, genial, talkative Irish style and beautiful illustrations. Indeed there is as much diversity here as there is in the Essays section, and one can flit from Cherry-Garrard's *Worst Journey* to the charming and witty Evelyn Eaton; from Fraser Darling's Island Farm to the strange study of *The Muria*.

ABRAHAM, J. JOHNSTON
The Surgeon's Log. *Chapman & Hall (1911), 1950. 9s. 6d.*

These impressions of the Far East have been reprinted thirty times since the first edition. The book is one that goes on being recommended. Seldom advertised, its merit is such that one reader speaks of it to another and so it goes on. And well it deserves to go on with both young and old.

ACKERLEY, J. R.
Hindoo Holiday. *Chatto (1932), 1952. 8s. 6d.*

This Indian journal has an individual quality of humour, characterization, and observation which will probably keep it alive for decades in much the same way as the book above.

AYSCOUGH, FLORENCE
Travels of a Chinese Poet. *2 vols. Cape (1934), 1950. 21s. each.*

Of Tu Fu, Guest of Rivers and Lakes, A.D. 712–770, illustrated by Lucille

Douglass. The author's distinctive gift for interpreting things and people of China has been offered to readers in other books, of which *A Chinese Mirror*, Cape (1925) and *Chinese Women: yesterday and to-day*, Cape, (1938) are the best.

BAKER, R. ST BARBE
Africa Drums. (*1942*.)
New revised edition, G. RONALD, *1951*. *12s. 6d.*

An introduction by Bronislaw Malinowski pays tribute to the importance and interest of the book. It is indeed an absorbing record of most extraordinary experiences of a 'Man of the Trees', who became the friend and adviser of native tribes in British East Africa.

BATES, H. E.
The Country Heart. *Michael Joseph* (*1949*). *12s. 6d.*

A revision in one volume of two earlier works: *O! More Than Happy Countryman* (1943) and *The Heart of the Country* (1942), both first published by Country Life, in well-illustrated editions.

BEEBE, WILLIAM
Half-Mile Down. *Lane* (*1935*).

A fascinating record of strange life unseen except by those who can explore the depths of the sea in Dr Beebe's bathysphere.

BELLOC, HILAIRE
The Cruise of the 'Nona'. *Constable* (*1925*). *7s. 6d.*
The Four Men. *Nelson* (*1912*). *5s.*

Perhaps the most treasured of all the author's open-air books. The county is Sussex, celebrated in song and prose by the same author.

The Old Road. *Constable* (*1904*), (*1952*). *8s. 6d.*

A mixture of archaeology, history and description concerning the ancient way from Winchester to Canterbury.

On Sailing the Sea. *Hart-Davis* (*1951*). *10s. 6d.* (*Mariner's Library.*)

A choice gathering of Belloc's most characteristic writings on the theme. The selection has been made from many of his books, some of which are now out of print.

Prose and Verse. *Selected by* W. N. ROUGHEAD.
Hart-Davis (*1951*). *15s.*

An anthology attempting to show this versatile writer in his most characteristic styles. The selection is drawn from some fifteen different books, ranging from historical biographies to humorous verse for children.

BONE, JAMES
The London Perambulator. *Cape* (*1925*), *1950*. *10s. 6d.*

Finely illustrated by the author's brother, Muirhead Bone, this pleasantly informal saunter through some of the highways and byways of London has established itself as a modern classic.

BRADLEY, KENNETH

Diary of a District Officer. *Harrap (1943). 5s.*

Tribal life in Northern Rhodesia, where the author was a D.O. for fifteen years.

BREWSTER, RALPH H.

The 6000 Beards of Athos. *(1935.)*
  New edition, Hogarth Press, 1949.

Preface by Dame Ethel Smyth. The author was a mystic himself and his description of the monks and their strange life in the monastery at Athos is of great interest.

BROWN, IVOR

The Heart of England. *Batsford (1935). Revised, 1951. 12s. 6d.*

A homely introduction to the character of the British people, and to our wayward, lovable institutions. Preface by J. B. PRIESTLEY.

CABLE, MILDRED and FRENCH, FRANCESCA

The Gobi Desert. *Hodder (1943). 25s.*
Through Jade Gate and Central Asia. *Constable (1927).*
  New edition, Hodder (1937), 1950. 4s. 6d.

An account of journeys in Kansu, Turkestan, and the Gobi Desert.

CAMPBELL, REGINALD

Teak-Wallah: personal experiences. *Hodder (1935).*
  Abridged edition, University of London Press, 1951. 5s.

A travel-autobiography. The author served for many years as a Forest Assistant in Northern Siam—hence his title.

CHAPMAN, F. SPENCER

Memoirs of a Mountaineer. *Chatto & Windus (1951). 16s.*

A new composite edition in one volume made from two earlier works: *Helvellyn to Himalaya* (1940), and *Lhasa: the Holy City* (1938). Both have been out of print for some years. The first recounts the author's great feat in ascending to the peak of Chomolhari with a single porter only.

CHERRY-GARRARD, APSLEY

The Worst Journey in the World. *Chatto (1922), 1951. 10s. 6d.*

A modern classic, being a personal record of the author's experiences when he accompanied Scott on his British Antarctic Expedition, 1910–1913.

CLEMENTS, REX

A Gipsy of the Horn. *(1924.) New edition, Hart-Davis, 1951. 9s. 6d. (Mariner's Library.)*

A narrative of a voyage round the world in a windjammer, *The Arethusa*, at the beginning of the century. The author joined her as an apprentice.

CLUNN, H. P.

The Face of London. (*1932.*) *Phoenix House, new edition, 1952. 30s.*

A well-illustrated survey and record of a century's changes and developments in the whole immense area of central and greater London. The most comprehesive book in one volume of its kind, by a Londoner who has spent a long life walking and driving over every part of his town. The new edition incorporates changes due to the 1939 war.

COHEN-PORTHEIM, Paul

The Spirit of London. *Batsford* (*1935*), *1950. 12s. 6d.*

The accident of alphabetization brings this foreigner's view of London and its people next to the factual and historical record above. The author was a true cosmopolitan and planned to translate his own work into French and German, but died before he was able to. His most individual view of London has been brought up-to-date and slightly revised by RAYMOND MORTIMER, who adds a preface.

CONWAY, Sir W. Martin (1856–1937)

The Alps From End to End. *Constable* (*1895*).

A classic survey by a great climber.

CORBETT, Jim

Man-Eaters of Kumaon. *O.U.P.* (*1944*). *10s. 6d.*

In the Indian village where the author lived tigers were killers, and in his extraordinary book he tells how he discovered the reason and tracked them down. A thrilling, unusual book written in a simple but compelling style.

The Man-Eating Leopard of Rudraprayag. *O.U.P.* (*1948*). *8s. 6d.*

It reads like a boy's adventure story, and with its predecessor, takes a place amongst the great books of travel.

CROFT, Andrew

Polar Exploration. *A. & C. Black* (*1948*). *15s.*

A well-documented record suitable for young readers as well as adults.

DARLING, F. Fraser

Island Farm. *Bell* (*1943*). *15s.*
Island Years. *Bell* (*1940*). *15s.*

The lure of island life was stronger in war-time than ever before, and the story of the author's sojourn for many years on Tanera Mor, one of the Summer Islands, was read with envy when the books first came out. But like his work for the crofters who were farming under great difficulties, his two volumes have a permanent value, as literature, and as records of wild life, the habits of seals and of the island birds.

DAVID-NEEL, Alexandra

Tibetan Journey. *Lane* (*1936*).

DOUGLAS, NORMAN (1868–1952)

Fountains in the Sand. *Secker & Warburg (1923).*
Old Calabria. *Secker & Warburg (1928).*

Delicate, allusive, urbane and civilized, these two characteristic books by the author of *South Wind* have a literary quality which puts them in a class of their own in modern travel literature.

DU BATY, RAYMOND RALLIER

Fifteen Thousand Miles in a Ketch. *Nelson (1912), 1948. 4s.*

The record of an amazing voyage from Boulogne in 1907 to Melbourne 1909.

DUGUID, JULIAN

Green Hell. *Cape (1931). 3s. 6d.*

A record of travel and strange adventure in the forests and jungle of Central Bolivia.

EATON, EVELYN

Every Month Was May. *Gollancz (1950).*

For the compiler this was one of the best books of its year. Autobiographical sketches with illustrations in the text, written with a gaiety and charm not often found in modern writing. Every month was May in Paris and France for the author because where there was wit and emotion she responded immediately. The sequel *The North Star is Nearer*, Gollancz (1951), could scarcely maintain the same standard.

ELWIN, VERRIER

The Muria and Their Ghotal. *O.U.P. (1947). 42s.*

An important and deeply interesting anthropological study of a tribe in Central India where adolescents are trained in a Ghotal, or communal home, in order that they may experience fully the social and erotic enjoyments of life in their primitive community, hitherto protected from the strange contradictions of modern civilization as known in other parts of India.

EVANS, H. MUIR

Sting-fish and Seafarer. *Faber (1943).*

The unique researches of a surgeon-naturalist in the habits of poisonous and dangerous fish which seafarers have learnt to fear mainly through tradition and on hitherto unsubstantiated evidence.

FELLOWS, ARNOLD

The Wayfarer's Companion. *O.U.P. (1937), 1946. 15s.*

Intended as a sort of guide book for the intelligent traveller, this well-illustrated account of some aspects of England's history in buildings and countryside has a range of interest over many subjects.

FERMOR, PATRICK LEIGH

The Traveller's Tree. *Murray (1950). 21s.*

Journeys through the Caribbean Islands, illustrated. Awarded the Heinemann Foundation Prize for 1950.

FIRBANK, THOMAS

I Bought a Mountain. *Harrap (1940), 1950. 8s. 6d.*
Sheep farming in North Wales.

FLEMING, PETER

Travels in Tartary. *Cape (1948).*

Two books in one volume: *One's Company*, Cape (1934), 1950, 4s. 6d., and *News From Tartary*, Cape, 1936, the first being the narrative of a journey from Peking to Kashmir, and the second of a journey to China. The latter was reprinted separately, Cape, 1951, 12s. 6d.

Brazilian Adventure. *Cape (1933). 12s. 6d.*

The illustrated account of the author's travels and adventures in the forests and almost unknown parts of Brazil in search of the missing explorer, Colonel Fawcett, known now to have been killed.

FORTESCUE, SIR JOHN (1859–1933)

The Story of a Red Deer. *Macmillan (1897), 1950. 5s.*

GALLOP, RODNEY (1901–1948)

Book of the Basques. *Macmillan (1930).*
Mexican Mosaic. *Faber (1939).*
Portugal: a book of folk-ways. *C.U.P. (1936).*

GIBBINGS, ROBERT

Coming Down the Wye. *Dent (1942), 1949. 16s.*
Lovely is the Lee. *Dent (1944), 1950. 16s.*
Continued in *Sweet Cork of Thee*, Dent, 1951, 16s.

Sweet Thames Run Softly. *Dent (1940), 1949. 16s.*

Four of the most delightful travel books of the century, written in prose as persuasive as the personality of the author, and illustrated with beautiful examples of his own wood-engravings. The first is of the upper reaches of Welsh Wye from Plynlimon, the second of a pleasant jaunt in County Cork and the islands off the coast, the third of country and river flowing to the capital.

GORER, GEOFFREY

Africa Dances. *Faber (1935). New edition, Lehmann, 1949. 15s.*

An outstanding book of travel, and of interpretation of the West African negro.

GRAHAM, ANGUS

The Golden Grindstone. *Chatto (1935).*
Abridged edition, by DENYS THOMPSON *for young people. Heinemann, 1951. 4s.*

The record of an adventurous journey to the Yukon gold-fields from 1897 onwards made by George M. Mitchell of Toronto and narrated to the author.

GRAHAM, STEPHEN

The Gentle Art of Tramping. *Nelson (1927). 3s. 6d.*

GREENE, GRAHAM

Journey Without Maps. *Heinemann (1936), 1950. 8s. 6d.*
A journey through Liberia described.

HALLIBURTON, RICHARD (1900–1939)

The Flying Carpet. *Bles (1933). 10s. 6d.*
A lightly-written, amusing record of a flight round the world.
Glorious Adventure. *Bles (1936). 10s. 6d.*
New Worlds to Conquer. *Bles (1930). 10s. 6d.*

Although no more than good journalism these books provide diverting reading and have a value as records of an observer of many countries and peoples between the wars.

HARRISON, PAUL W.

Doctor in Arabia. *Hale (1943).*

Dr Harrison thought Arabia 'presented the whole range of disease and distress and wickedness', so he decided to practise there. He performed major operations for a shilling or two, or for nothing, treated 125 patients daily in a hospital run on a total annual budget of £350. Not satisfied even then, he treated Bedouins in the desert from his automobile dispensary. The literature of modern Arabian travel is large, but there is no other book like this one.

HARTLEY, DOROTHY

The Countryman's England. *Batsford (1935).*
Revised edition, 1943. 12s. 6d.

The author surveys the countryside through the people who live in, by, and for it, casting a craftsman's eye on the old country industries. Preface by A. G. STREET. For a beautiful book devoted entirely to the crafts of the English countryside, the same author's *Made in England*, Methuen (1939), 16s., with many illustrations, is to be strongly recommended.

HASTINGS, A. C. G.

Nigerian Days. *Cape (1930).*
Introduction by R. B. CUNNINGHAME GRAHAM.

HIVES, FRANK
Justice in the Jungle. *Lane (1932).*
An earlier volume written with GASCOIGNE LUMLEY was *Ju-Ju and Justice in Nigeria*, Lane (1930).

HOGG, GARRY
And Far Away. *Phoenix House (1946). 12s. 6d.*
The Road Before Me. *Phoenix House (1948). 15s.*
One of the most knowledgeable walkers of his time, the author has a gift for writing informally about country and people met, and usually carries a good camera with him.

HOWARD, SIDNEY
Thames to Tahiti. *Bell (1933).*
New edition, Hart-Davis, 1951, 9s. 6d. (Mariner's Library.)
In 1930 the *Pacific Moon*, a 38-foot cutter, sailed on her long voyage, with the author and a friend as sole crew. Neither knew the art of navigation.

HUXLEY, ALDOUS
Beyond the Mexique Bay. *Chatto (1934), 1950. 8s. 6d.*
Jesting Pilate. *Chatto (1926), 1948. 8s. 6d.*

IRVING, R. L. G.
The Alps. *Batsford (1937). Revised edition, 1947. 15s.*
The mountains of the five countries of the Alps described and photographed.
Ten Great Mountains. *Dent (1940), 1950. 12s. 6d.*

JARVIS, C. S.
Three Deserts. *Murray (1936), 1947. 8s. 6d.*

JONES, SYDNEY R.
English Village Homes. *Batsford (1936), 1947. 12s. 6d.*
On craftsmanship and village life, with some fine illustrations.

KINGDON-WARD, F.
Burma's Icy Mountains. *Cape (1949). 15s.*
The story of two expeditions, 1937–1939 into mountains 20,000 ft. high.
From China to Hkamti Long. *Edward Arnold (1924).*
A plant-hunting journey across mountains between China and Burma.
Modern Exploration. *Cape (1945), 1950. 6s.*
The Romance of Plant Hunting. *Edward Arnold (1924).*

KITCHEN, FRED

Brother to the Ox. *Dent (1940), 1950. 10s. 6d.*
Life On the Land. *Dent (1941), 1950. 12s. 6d.*

Two remarkable books of agricultural life and work by a true son of the soil. Simply yet finely written, the first, mainly autobiographical, illustrated with photographs and the second, January to December on the farm, with wood engavings by FRANK ORMROD. They are amongst the most authentic records of their kind in modern literature.

KNIGHT, EDWARD FREDERICK (1852–1925)

'The Falcon' on the Baltic. *(1888.) New edition, Hart-Davis, 1951, 9s. 6d.*

A welcome addition to the *Mariner's Library* of an old favourite of happy-go-lucky former days.

LEIGH, MARGARET MARY

Highland Homespun. *Bell (1936), 1950. 7s. 6d.*

The late H. J. Massingham said of this that it is 'one of the best farming books written in our century'.

LEIGHTON, CLARE

Four Hedges. *Gollancz (1935).*

Written and with 88 wood-engravings by a countrywoman who follows the twelve months from April to March in pleasant informal talk about plants, flowers and gardens.

LEWIS, EILUNED

In Country Places. *Country Life (1951). 10s. 6d.*

LLOYD, CHRISTOPHER

Pacific Horizons. *Allen & Unwin (1946). 10s. 6d.*

On the exploration of the Pacific before Captain Cook.

LOCKLEY, R. M.

Dream Island Days. *Witherby (1943). 10s. 6d.*
Island Farmers. *Witherby (1946). 10s. 6d.*
The Way to an Island. *Dent (1941), 1947. 10s. 6d.*

In part the autobiography of a young man who succeeded in simplifying life and found happiness in the lonely way of the island farmer. Skokholm, off the Pembrokeshire coast, fulfilled the dreams of his youth. For the full story see also the earlier book, *I Know An Island*, Harrap (1938), 1948. *8s. 6d.*

LUNN, ARNOLD

Mountains of Memory. *Hollis & Carter (1948). 15s.*
The Mountains of Youth. *Eyre & Spottiswoode (1925), 1949. 10s. 6d.*

A classic of mountain literature. Lord Conway thought it among the best books ever written. Climbing, sport on the slopes, conversation on hotel verandas. All recounted with a wit as dry as the wine he has enjoyed with so many other climbers.

McMULLEN, R. T. (1830–1891)
Down Channel. (*1869.*) *2nd enlarged edition, 1893.*
New edition, Hart-Davis, 1949, 9s. 6d. (*Mariner's Library.*)

A famous old book of the sea much loved by yachtsmen and those who like the ways of small craft on lonely voyages. The reprint is introduced by DIXON KEMP, and has an interesting biographical foreword by ARTHUR RANSOME. None of the voyages was outside the home waters.

MASSINGHAM, H. J.
Chiltern Country. *Batsford* (*1940*), *1949. 12s. 6d.*

With photographs and drawings by THOMAS HENNELL, himself a countryman and craftsman.

Cotswold Country. *Batsford* (*1937*), *1950. 12s. 6d.*
English Downland. *Batsford* (*1936*), *1949. 12s. 6d.*

On the limestone belt from Lincolnshire to the Severn.

MONCKTON, C. A. W.
Some Experiences of a New Guinea Resident Magistrate.
2 vols. Lane (*1920*). *4s. 6d. each.*

MULHAUSER, GEORGE H. P. (1870?–1923)
The Cruise of the 'Amaryllis'. (*1924.*)
New edition, Hart-Davis, 1950, 9s. 6d. (*Mariner's Library.*)

MUSPRATT, ERIC (1900–1949)
Fire of Youth. *Duckworth* (*1948*), *1951. 12s. 6d.*

Forty-five years of wandering by a roamer who made a great success with his first book:

My South Sea Island. *Duckworth* (*1931*).
Wild Oats. *Duckworth* (*1932*).

The sequel was *The Journey Home*, Duckworth (1933).

NESBITT, L. M.
Desert and Forest. *Cape* (*1934*).

The exploration of Abyssinian Danakil.

Desolate Marshes. *Cape* (*1934*).

An engineering survey of Orinoco Llanos.

NOEL, J. B. L.
Through Tibet to Everest. *Edward Arnold* (*1927*), *1950. 4s. 6d.*

ORTZEN, LEN
Rue de Paris. *Cassell* (*1939*).

The author found he could live in Paris on a small income happily, well-fed and with good companions from the mean streets. His personal record of Paris life is nearer the heart of the matter than many more pretentious books and in some ways conveys more of the essence of characteristic French civilization before the war than any other book except ELLIOT PAUL's *A Narrow Street*, Cresset Press (1942), 12s. 6d.

PAKINGTON, HUMPHREY

English Villages and Hamlets. *Batsford (1934).*
4th revised edition, 1945; 1949, 12s. 6d.

Illustrated with drawings by SYDNEY R. JONES and with many pleasant photographs, with an introduction by G. M. YOUNG on the historical basis of the English village. In brief, this notable book is an architect's survey of beauty and history in small places.

PARKER, ERIC

The Countryman's Week-end Book. *Seeley Service (1946). 12s. 6d.*

One of a series of miscellanies; this particular book is designed to interest, inform and divert the farmer, the gardener, the sportsman, the animal lover and the amateur naturalist.

PATTERSON, J. H.

In the Grip of the Nyika. *Macmillan (1909).*
The Man-Eaters of Tsavo. *Macmillan (1907). 7s. 6d.*

Adventures in British East Africa. The first-named is a continuation and the two together form an interesting story of exploration and adventure in the wilderness, or 'nyika', from Nairobi, at the time of the building of the Uganda Railway, 1898.

PHILBY, H. ST J. B.

The Empty Quarter. *Constable (1948). 21s.*

A descriptive record of travel in the great South Desert of Arabia, known as Rub' Al Khali.

Sheba's Daughters. *Methuen (1939).*

Travel in Southern Arabia, with a map and rock pictures in the text.

PIDGEON, HARRY

Around the World Single-Handed. *(1933.)*
New edition, Hart-Davis, 1950, 9s. 6d. (The Mariner's Library.)

In a home-built boat, a 34-foot yawl, called *The Islander*.

PONTING, HERBERT G.

The Great White South; or, With Scott in the Antarctic.
Duckworth (1921), 1950, 15s.

The classic story of Scott in the Antarctic, 1910–1913, by one of the explorer's companions who was the official photographer. There are 175 of his photographs of outstanding interest and much material on the nature life of the region round the South Pole, particularly of the Weddell Seals. Preface by LADY SCOTT.

POPE-HENNESSY, James
West Indian Summer: a retrospect. *Batsford (1943).*

An evocation of Caribbean life as seen by nine travellers from sixteenth to nineteenth century, finely illustrated with reproductions from old woodcuts, engravings and lithographs.

PRIESTLEY, J. B.
English Journey. *Heinemann (1934), 1951. 10s. 6d.*

The new edition has an introduction. The book may live as a permanent record of the people and life of England during the years of the great industrial depression.

RANSOME, Arthur
Racundra's First Cruise. *Cape (1927). New edition, 1948. 10s. 6d.*
Illustrated from 35 photographs by the author.

REBELL, Fred
Escape to the Sea. *Murray (1939), 1950. 10s. 6d.*

A born wanderer, who found rules and regulations irksome, and passports something to be bought, the author fled from North Europe and found himself happily navigating an open boat for 9000 miles across the Pacific. This is the log of the incredible voyage which lasted one year and one week. Introduction by Richard Hughes.

RICHARDSON, A. E.
The Old Inns of England. *Batsford (1935), 1952. 12s. 6d.*

There are many jovial, sentimental books on English inns. This one is by a distinguished architect who is equipped by his professional knowledge to deal with his subject with an artist's eye for fine craftsmanship and style, as well as historically and socially. Many beautiful plates, and a preface by Sir Edwin Lutyens, help to make this an agreeable volume for both traveller and architect.

ROBINSON, William Albert
Deep Water and Shoal. *Cape (1932). Hart-Davis, 1949, 9s. 6d.*
30,000 miles in a thirty-foot sailing boat.

Voyage to Galapagos. *Cape (1936).*

RUTTLEDGE, Hugh
Everest, 1933. *Hodder (1934), 1950. 4s. 6d.*
Everest, the Unfinished Adventure. *Hodder (1937). 25s.*

SACKVILLE-WEST, V.
Knole and the Sackvilles. *Heinemann (1922).*
   New edition, Lindsay Drummond (now Benn), 1948. 12s. 6d.

The story and description of the great family and their country house and estate at Knole, Kent.

Passenger to Teheran. *Hogarth (1926).*

SHACKLETON, Sir Ernest (1874–1922)

South. *Heinemann (1919), 1951. 7s. 6d.*

One of the great and permanent books of Antarctic exploration, being the record of the author's last expedition, 1914–1917, with many illustrations.

SITWELL, Edith

Bath. *Faber (1932). Revised edition, 1948, 12s. 6d.*

The story of the beautiful city of the south-west, once a centre of social life and gaiety.

SITWELL, Sir Osbert

Winters of Content, and other discursions on Mediterranean art and travel. *Duckworth (1950). 21s.*

A new edition, with illustrations, of notable books first published separately: *Winters of Content* (1932), *Discursions* (1925) and some short stories from the volume *Dumb Animal.*

SMITH, David

No Rain in Those Clouds. *Dent (1943), 1951. 10s. 6d.*

A farmer's book, illustrated with line drawings and photographs of the Essex country scene.

SMITH, Emma

Maiden's Trip. *Putnam (1949).*

New edition. MacGibbon & Kee, 1950. 8s. 6d.

Amusing account of war-time life on a barge, navigating as a volunteer with friends, the canals of England. Awarded the John Llewellyn Rhys Memorial Prize.

SMYTHE, F. S. (1900–1949)

The Adventures of a Mountaineer. *Dent (1940), 1950. 10s. 6d.*
Kamet Conquered. *Hodder (1932), 1948. 20s.*
The Kangchenjunga Adventure. *Gollancz (1930).*
The Mountain Scene. *A. & C. Black (1937).*

Four books of permanent value by the greatest mountaineer-photographer of his time. Mountains for F. S. Smythe were one of the main reasons for living, and in fact, helped him to keep himself alive. All of his books are enhanced in value by the superb illustrations from his own photographs. Of his many books on the Alps and other mountain regions, the last one listed above is chosen for its quite outstanding beauty and because it deals with the modest hills of Britain, as well as the great peaks of the European ranges, and the mightier ones still of Everest, Kamet and Kangchenjunga.

STARK, FREYA

East is West. *Murray (1945). 12s. 6d.*

This amazing traveller, whose understanding of the East and particularly of the Arab world, did so much to keep the Arabs friendlily disposed to Great Britain from 1939 to 1945, here tells of her war-time travels to Aden and Yemen, and of her successful combat with Italian propaganda. Here, too, are some beautiful illustrations.

The Southern Gates of Arabia. *Murray (1936), 1948. 6s.*

A journey in the Hadhramant.

The Valleys of the Assassins, and other Persian travels.
Murray (1934), 1948. 6s.

A Winter in Arabia. *Murray (1940), 1948. 8s. 6d.*

A record of travel and adventure, illustrated with some beautiful photographs.

STARKIE, WALTER

Raggle-Taggle. *Murray (1933), 1948. 9s. 6d.*

High-spirited adventures with a fiddle in Hungary and Rumania.

Spanish Raggle-Taggle. *Murray (1934).*

More adventures with a fiddle, this time in Barbary, Andalusia, and La Mancha, North Spain.

SUTCLIFFE, HALLIWELL (1870–1932)

The Striding Dales. *Warne (1929), 1950. 7s. 6d.*

An illustrated book describing the people and scenery of part of Yorkshire.

TAMBS, ERLING

The Cruise of the 'Teddy'. *(1933.)*
New edition, Hart-Davis, 1949, 9s. 6d. (The Mariner's Library.)

ARTHUR RANSOME introduces this book about the *Teddy* and her crew, 'altogether unlike all other books of the kind'. A long voyage with a honeymoon wife. It ended with a family and alas, the total loss of the grand old boat.

THOMAS, BERTRAM

Arabia Felix. *Cape (1932).*

With an introduction by T. E. SHAW, that is T. E. LAWRENCE.

THOMAS, SIR WILLIAM BEACH

The Way of a Countryman. *Michael Joseph (1944).*

The experiences of a fine journalist and naturalist.

TILMAN, H. W.

The Ascent of Nanda Devi. *C.U.P.* (*1937*).

With thirty-five plates and two maps. Foreword by Dr T. G. LONGSTAFF. One of the permanent books of mountain exploration.

Mount Everest, 1938. *C.U.P.* (*1948*), *1950. 21s.*
Two Mountains and a River. *C.U.P.* (*1949*), *1950. 25s.*
When Men and Mountains Meet. *C.U.P.* (*1946*), *1950. 21s.*

TOMLINSON, H. M.

London River. *Cassell* (*1921*).
New illustrated edition in crown quarto, with revisions, and another book **Tidemarks** (*1934*), *1951. 25s.*
The Sea and the Jungle. *Duckworth* (*1912*), *1949. 7s. 6d.*

Personal experiences in a voyage to South America, and through the Amazon forests. Written in some of the best prose of the century.

TSCHIFFELY, A. F.

Tschiffely's Ride. *Heinemann* (*1933*). *Hodder, 1947. 10s. 6d.*

10,000 miles in the saddle, through the Americas from Argentina to Washington. The greatest ride of the century, to prove that a certain underestimated breed of Patagonian pony could endure the rigours of such a journey as well as the rider. The two horses, Mancho and Gato, have a book all to themselves, as well they deserve one: *The Tale of Two Horses*, of which a new illustrated edition was published in 1944, Hodder, *9s. 6d.*

ULLMAN, J. R.

High Conquest. *Gollancz* (*1942*). *16s.*
The story of mountaineering.

VALE, EDMUND

How to Look at Old Buildings. *Batsford* (*1940*), *1946. 6s.*
See For Yourself. *Dent* (*1933*), *1949. 7s. 6d.*

Both well illustrated, with photos, plans and sketches. 'Field books for sightseers.'

The Seas and Shores of England. *Batsford* (*1936*), *1950. 12s. 6d.*

With a preface by Sir ARTHUR QUILLER-COUCH. England and its coast seen from an unusual viewpoint: from the sea instead of the land.

VESEY-FITZGERALD, BRIAN

Gypsies of Britain. *Chapman & Hall* (*1944*).

An introduction to their history. It is considered to be the best book of its kind.

VILLIERS, A. J.

Falmouth For Orders. *Bles (1929), 1950. 10s. 6d.*

The story of the last clipper ship race around Cape Horn.

The Voyage of the 'Parma'. *Bles (1933), 1934. 18s.*

On the great grain race of 1932.

VOSS, JOHN CLAUS (1854–1922)

Venturesome Voyages. *(1913.)*
  New edition, Hart-Davis, 1949. 9s. 6d. (Mariner's Library.)

The new edition has a preface by RICHARD HUGHES, who points out that Captain Voss's achievement in circumnavigating the earth in a small canoe was in some respects more amazing than Captain Slocum's celebrated voyage.

WARREN, C. HENRY

A Cotswold Year. *(1936.) Bles. 7s. 6d.*
England is a Village. *Eyre & Spottiswoode (1940), 1950. 5s.*

The true life of a village just before the war, told mainly in easy-going conversations. A lovable and distinguished book made beautiful to look at by the illustrations done by 'B.B.'

WATKINS-PITCHFORD, D. J. ('B.B.')

The Idle Countryman. *Illustrated by the author.*
  Eyre & Spottiswoode (1944). 10s. 6d.

WEST, REBECCA

Black Lamb and Grey Falcon. *2 vols. Macmillan (1942). 42s.*

This 'record of a journey through Yugoslavia in 1937' made publishing history, for although it is a long, serious work, and indeed one of the most important travel books of the century, it immediately attracted a large number of readers. For many years the demand outran the supply, limited as that was by war-time restrictions.

WILKINSON, WALTER

Vagabonds and Puppets. *Bles (1930). 7s. 6d.*

One of many charming books recording the author's wanderings with his puppet show.

WILLIAMS, J. H.

Elephant Bill. *Hart-Davis (1950). 21s.*

After twenty years experience in the Burmese jungle the author found himself adviser on elephants to the 14th Army. One of the great books of the war, it is also a permanent contribution to the literature of travel, adventure and the care of elephants.

WOOD, THOMAS (1892–1950)

Cobbers. *O.U.P.* (*1934*). 1953. 18s.

A personal record of a journey from Suffolk to Australia, Tasmania, and some of the reefs and islands on the Coral Sea, from 1930 to 1932. The author was a music master at Tonbridge School, Kent.

Cobbers Campaigning: the Empire at War. *Cape* (*1940*).

With its companion above, will probably become a modern classic.

WRAY, J. W.

South Sea Vagabonds. *Jenkins* (*1939*). Revised edition, 1953. 12s. 6d.

Having built a small boat out of driftwood, the young adventurer sets out to cruise around the South Pacific and enjoy himself.

YOUNG, GEOFFREY WINTHROP

On High Hills. *Methuen* (*1927*), 1947. 18s.

A great mountaineer, a fine prose writer, and a poet of the mountains here gives us his best general book of memories of the Alps, and in praise of 'the treasure of heights'. 'Only a hill, earth set a little higher Above the face of earth: a larger view of little fields and roads.' So he writes in his book of poems. Many of the ascents were new ones first made by the author.

Books of travel by other twentieth-century authors, no longer living, will be found in *An English Library* under Henry Adams, Maurice Baring, Sir Charles Bell, Gertrude Bell, Stella Benson, A. G. Bradley, Edward G. Browne, C. G. Bruce, Robert Byron, Edmund Candler, R. G. Collingwood, Joseph Conrad, C. M. Doughty, Havelock Ellis, Ford Madox Ford, R. W. F. Gann, R. B. Cunninghame Graham, Sir Wilfred Grenfell, Aubrey Herbert, W. H. Hudson, Sir Reginald Johnston, Rudyard Kipling, A. B. Lubbock, C. E. Montague, Lisle March Phillipps, Llewelyn Powys, C. H. Prodgers, Walter Runciman, Robert Falcon Scott, Captain Joshua Slocum, Sir Aurel Stein, Sir Percy Sykes, Arthur Symons, Edward Thomas, Sir Frederick Treves, and Sir Francis Younghusband.

LIST OF PUBLISHERS

W. H. ALLEN   43 Essex Street, W.C. 2

ALLEN & UNWIN   40 Museum Street, W.C. 1

EDWARD ARNOLD & CO.   41 Maddox Street, W. 1

ARTHUR BARKER   30 Museum Street, W.C. 1

JAMES BARRIE, Publishers   3 and 4 Clement's Inn, W.C. 2

B. T. BATSFORD   4 Fitzhardinge Street, W. 1

G. BELL & SONS   6 Portugal Street, W.C. 2

ERNEST BENN   Bouverie House, 154 Fleet Street, E.C. 4

A. & C. BLACK   4, 5, and 6 Soho Square, W. 1

BLACKIE & SON   17 Stanhope Street, Glasgow, C. 4, *and* 16 William IV
    Street, W.C. 2

BASIL BLACKWELL   49 Broad Street, Oxford

W. BLACKWOOD & SONS   45 George Street, Edinburgh, *and* 1 Bateman's
    Buildings, Soho Square, W. 1

GEOFFREY BLES   52 Doughty Street, W.C. 1

BODLEY HEAD   *See* John Lane

BRITISH COUNCIL, THE   *See* Longmans

BURNS OATES & WASHBOURNE   28 Ashley Place, S.W. 1

THORNTON BUTTERWORTH   *See* Eyre & Spottiswoode

CAMBRIDGE UNIVERSITY PRESS   Bentley House, 200 Euston Road, N.W. 1

JONATHAN CAPE   30 Bedford Square, W.C. 1

CARROLL & NICHOLSON   Tudor House, Princeton Street, W.C. 1

CASSELL & CO   37–38 St Andrew's Hill, Queen Victoria Street, E.C. 4

W. & R. CHAMBERS   11 Thistle Street, Edinburgh 2, *and* 6 Dean Street, W. 1

CHAPMAN & HALL   37–39 Essex Street, W.C. 2

CHATTO & WINDUS   40–42 William IV Street, W.C. 2

CHURCH BOOK ROOM PRESS   7 Wine Office Court, Fleet Street, E.C. 4

CLARENDON PRESS   *See* Oxford University Press

WILLIAM COLLINS, SONS & CO.   14 St James's Place, S.W. 1

CONSTABLE & CO.   10 and 12 Orange Street, W.C. 2

COUNTRY LIFE   2–10 Tavistock Street, W.C. 2

CRESSET PRESS   11 Fitzroy Square, W. 1

GEOFFREY CUMBERLEGE   *See* Oxford University Press

PETER DAVIES   38 Bedford Square, W.C. 1

H. F. W. DEANE & SONS   31 Museum Street, W.C. 1

J. M. DENT & SONS   Aldine House, 10–13 Bedford Street, W.C. 2

DENNIS DOBSON   12 Park Place, St James's Street, S.W. 1

LINDSAY DRUMMOND   *See* Benn

GERALD DUCKWORTH & CO.   3 Henrietta Street, W.C. 2

ELEK BOOKS   14 Great James Street, W.C. 1

ENGLISH THEATRE GUILD   75 Berwick Street, W. 1
ENGLISH UNIVERSITIES PRESS   St Paul's House, Warwick Square, E.C. 4
EYRE & SPOTTISWOODE (Publishers)   15 Bedford Street, W.C. 2
FABER & FABER   24 Russell Square, W.C. 1
FALCON PRESS (London)   6–7 Crown Passage, Pall Mall, S.W. 1
FORE PUBLICATIONS   28–29 Southampton Street, W.C. 2
W. FOULSHAM & CO.   20–21 Red Lion Court, Fleet Street, E.C. 4
SAMUEL FRENCH   26 Southampton Street, W.C. 2
VICTOR GOLLANCZ   14 Henrietta Street, W.C. 2
GRAYSON & GRAYSON   16 Maddox Street, W. 1
GREY WALLS PRESS   6–7 Crown Passage, Pall Mall, S.W. 1
ROBERT HALE   63 Old Brompton Road, S.W. 7
HAMISH HAMILTON   90 Great Russell Street, W.C. 1
HAMMOND, HAMMOND & CO.   87 Gower Street, W.C. 1
HAND & FLOWER PRESS   Symnells, Aldington, nr Ashford, Kent
GEORGE HARRAP & CO.   182 High Holborn, W.C. 1
RUPERT HART-DAVIS   36 Soho Square, W. 1
WILLIAM HEINEMANN   99 Great Russell Street, W.C. 1
HER MAJESTY'S STATIONERY OFFICE   Atlantic House, Holborn Viaduct,
   E.C. 1
HODDER & STOUGHTON   St Paul's House, Warwick Square, E.C. 4
HOGARTH PRESS   40–42 William IV Street, W.C. 2
HOLLIS & CARTER   25 Ashley Place, S.W. 1
HOME & VAN THAL   36 Great Russell Street, W.C. 1
HURST & BLACKETT   See Hutchinson
HUTCHINSON & CO. (Publishers)   Hutchinson House, Stratford Place, W. 1
JARROLDS (Publishers)   London   See Hutchinson
HERBERT JENKINS   3 Duke of York Street, St James's, S.W. 1
MICHAEL JOSEPH   26 Bloomsbury Street, W.C. 1
JOHN LANE, THE BODLEY HEAD   28–30 Little Russell Street, W.C. 1
T. WERNER LAURIE   1 Doughty Street, W.C. 1
LAWRENCE & WISHART   81 Chancery Lane, W.C. 2
JOHN LEHMANN   25 Gilbert Street, W. 1
JOHN LONG   See Hutchinson
LONGMANS (Dorchester)   The Friary Press, 4 Cornhill, Dorchester, Dorset
LONGMANS, GREEN & CO.   6 and 7 Clifford Street, W. 1
SAMPSON LOW, MARSTON & CO.   25 Gilbert Street, Oxford Street, W. 1
MACDONALD & CO. (Publishers)   16 Maddox Street, W. 1
MACGIBBON & KEE   30 St Anne's Terrace, N.W. 8
MACMILLAN & CO.   St Martin's Street, W.C. 2
METHUEN & CO.   36 Essex Street, W.C. 2
MILLS & BOON   50 Grafton Way, Fitzroy Square, W. 1
FREDERICK MULLER   24A–26A Earls Court Gardens, S.W. 5

JOHN MURRAY (Publishers) 50 Albemarle Street, W. 1

MUSEUM PRESS 63 Old Brompton Road, S.W. 7

EVELEIGH NASH & GRAYSON *See* Grayson & Grayson

THOMAS NELSON & SONS Parkside Works, Dalkeith Road, Edinburgh, *and* 3 Henrietta Street, W.C. 2

IVOR NICHOLSON & WATSON 32–33 Gosfield Street, W. 1

OLIVER & BOYD Tweeddale Court, High Street, Edinburgh, *and* 98 Great Russell Street, W.C. 1

OXFORD UNIVERSITY PRESS Amen House, Warwick Square, E.C. 4

PAN BOOKS 8 Headfort Place, S.W. 1

MAX PARRISH & CO. Adprint House, Rathbone Place, W. 1

PEN-IN-HAND PUBLISHING CO. *See* Tower Bridge Publications

PENGUIN BOOKS Harmondsworth, Middlesex

PHOENIX HOUSE 38 William IV Street, W.C. 2

SIR ISAAC PITMAN & SONS 39–41 Parker Street, Kingsway, W.C. 2

PUTNAM & CO. 42 Great Russell Street, W.C. 1

MAX REINHARDT 66 Chandos Place, W.C. 2

RICH & COWAN *See* Hutchinson

RICHARDS PRESS 8 Charles II Street, S.W. 1

RIDER & CO. *See* Hutchinson

GEORGE RONALD Wheatley, Oxford

ROUTLEDGE & KEGAN PAUL 68–74 Carter Lane, E.C. 4

CHARLES SCRIBNER'S SONS 23 Bedford Square, W.C. 1

MARTIN SECKER & WARBURG 7 John Street, Bloomsbury, W.C. 1

SEELEY SERVICE & CO. 196 Shaftsbury Avenue, W.C. 2

SHEED & WARD 110–111 Fleet Street, E.C. 4

SIDGWICK & JACKSON 44 Museum Street, W.C. 1

S.P.C.K. (SOCIETY FOR PROMOTING CHRISTIAN KNOWLEDGE) Northumberland Avenue, W.C. 2

STAPLES PRESS Mandeville Place, W. 1

STUDIO 66 Chandos Place, W.C. 2

TOWER BRIDGE PUBLICATIONS 10 Benfleet Road, Hadleigh, Essex

UNICORN PRESS *See* Richards Press

T. FISHER UNWIN *See* Benn

VISION PRESS Callard House, 74A Regent Street, W. 1

WARD, LOCK & CO. 6 Chancery Lane, W.C. 2

FREDERICK WARNE & CO. 1–4 Bedford Court, Bedford Street, Strand, W.C. 2

C. A. WATTS & CO. 5–6 Johnson's Court, E.C. 4

GEORGE WEIDENFELD & NICOLSON 7 Cork Street, W. 1

WILLIAMS & NORGATE 36 Great Russell Street, W.C. 1

ALLAN WINGATE (Publishers) 12 Beauchamp Place, S.W. 3

H. F. & G. WITHERBY 5 Warwick Court, High Holborn, W.C. 1

INDEX OF AUTHORS AND EDITORS

Where authors are referred to in a note the page number is followed by 'n.'

Abbott, Edwin A., 29
Abraham, J. J., 181
Ackerley, J. R., 170, 181
Ackland, Rodney, 171, 179 n.
Adams, Henry, 113
Adams, J. Q., 21
Adams, J. T., 113
Addison, William, 113
Agar, Herbert, 113
Agate, James, 1
Aldington, Richard, 19 n., 29, 50 (ed.), 64, 154
Alexander, Samuel, 143
Allen, Beverley S., 29
Allen, C. K., 114
Allen, G. C. (joint author), *see* Ashley, William
Allen, Hervey, 20
Allen, Walter, 30
Allingham, Margery, 64
Anderson, J. R., 154
Anthony, Katherine, 19 n., 114
Archer, William, 171
Armstrong, Anthony, 171
Armstrong, Martin, 50 (ed.), 53, 155
Arnold, Thomas, 114
Ashford, Daisy, 64
Ashley, William, 114
Ashton, Helen, 64
Ashton, T. S., 114
Auden, W. H., 155
Austin, F. Britten, 65
Ayer, A. J., 143
Ayscough, Florence, 181

B.B., *see* Watkins-Pitchford
Bagnold, Enid, 65, 171, 179 n.
Bailey, Cyril, 114 (ed.)
Bailey, H. C., 65
Baker, Denys Val, 52 (ed.)
Baker, Elizabeth, 171
Baker, R. St Barbe, 182
Balchin, Nigel, 65
Balderston, J. L., 171
Bancroft, G. B., 171
Barfield, Owen, 30
Barker, A. L., 53
Barker, Ernest, 114, 114 (ed.), 143
Barker, George, 65, 155
Barnes, Djuna, 65
Barnes, E. W., 144
Baron, Alexander, 65
Barton, Margaret (joint editor), *see* Sitwell, Osbert

Baskerville, Geoffrey, 114
Bates, H. E., 16, 52 n., 53, 66, 171, 182
Bates, Ralph, 66
Bateson, F. W., 30
Batho, E. C., 26 n.
Baty, R. R. du, *see* Du Baty
Bax, Clifford, 1, 171
Baynes, Norman H., 114
Beachcroft, T. O., 53
Beard, C. A. and M. R., 114
Beebe, William, 182
Beerbohm, Max, 30, 31, 66
Bell, Adrian, 50 (ed.), 66
Bell, Clive, 31, 114
Bell, H. C. F., 20
Bell, Quentin, 31
Bellamy, H. S., 144
Belloc, Hilaire, 20 n., 31, 53, 115, 155, 182
Benedict, Ruth, 31
Bennett, Arnold (joint author), *see* Knoblock, Edward
Bennett, H. S., 115
Bennett, Joan, 16 n
Benns, F. L., 115
Benson, Theodora, 53
Bentley, E. C., 66
Bentley, Eric, 22
Bentley, Phyllis, 66
Berkeley, Anthony, 67
Berkeley, Reginald, 171
Berners, Lord, 1
Berney, William (joint author), *see* Richardson, Howard
Besier, Rudolf, 171
Betjeman, John, 155
Bevan, E. R., 115 (ed.)
Bibesco, Elizabeth, 53
Billany, Dan, 67
Birkett, Norman, 31
Birmingham, George, 67
Birrell, Francis, 17
Black, J. B., *see Oxford History*, 130
Blackwood, Algernon, 54, 67
Blake, George, 67
Blake, Nicholas, 67
Bliss, Trudy, 14 (ed.)
Blixen, Karen, 54
Blunden, Edmund, 17 n., 23, 32, 115, 155
Boden, F. C., 67
Bodkin, Maud, 32
Boland, Bridget, 179 n.
Bon, G. Le, *see* Le Bon
Bone, David W., 54
Bone, James, 182

Bottome, Phyllis, 54, 67
Bottomley, Gordon, 155, 156
Bottrall, Ronald, 156
Bowen, Elizabeth, 32, 54, 68
Bowen, Marjorie, 68
Bowers, C. G., 115
Bowle, John, 115
Bowman, Archibald, 144
Boyd, Martin, 68
Bozman, M. M. (joint ed.), see Church, R.
Bradbrook, M. C., 32
Bradby, E. D., 115
Bradley, Kenneth, 183
Brailsford, H. N., 25
Brewster, Ralph H., 183
Bridge, Ann, 68
Bridie, James, 171
Brier, Royce, 69
Briffault, Robert, 144
Brinton, Crane, 115
Bromfield, Louis, 69
Brooke, Jocelyn, 1, 10 n.
Brooks, H. (joint author), see Malleson,
  Miles
Brooks, Van Wyck, 32
Brophy, John, 69
Broster, D. K., 69
Brown, Hilton, 54 (ed.)
Brown, Ivor, 21, 32, 69, 183
Brown, John, 144
Brown, P. Hume, 116
Browne, Wynward, 179 n.
Bryant, Arthur, 20, 116
Buck, Pearl, 69
Bullett, Gerald, 16, 24 n., 54, 69, 156
Burdett, Osbert, 13
Burke, Thomas, 54, 116
Burkitt, M. C., 116
Burlinghame, Roger, 116
Burnett, I. Compton-, see Compton-Burnett
Burnett, W. R., 70
Butler, E. M., 144
Butterfield, Herbert, 116

Cabell, J. B., 70
Cable, Mildred, 183
Cain, J. M., 70
Calder-Marshall, A., 70
Caldwell, Thomas, 167 (ed.)
Cambridge, Elizabeth, 70
Cameron, Norman, 156. See also Hodge,
  Alan
Campbell, Reginald, 183
Campbell, Roy, 156
Campion, Sarah, 15
Canfield, Dorothy, 70
Cannan, Gilbert, 70
Cardus, Neville, 2, 33
Carey, G. V., 117
Carleton, Patrick, 117
Carr, Cecil (joint author), see Ilbert, Charles
Carr, E. H., 117

Carr, Emily, 2
Carr, John Dickson, 70
Carrington, C. E., 117
Carswell, Catherine, 13, 19
Carter, Reginald, 70
Cartwright, H. A. (joint author), see
  Harrison, M. C. C.
Cary, Joyce, 70, 71
Caudwell, Christopher, 144
Cecil, Algernon, 33
Cecil, Lord David, 15, 17, 19, 27, 33
Chair, S. de, see Somerset de Chair
Chambers, E. K., 15 n., 21
Chandler, Raymond, 71
Chaplin, Sid, 54, 71
Chapman, C. M., 2
Chapman, F. Spencer, 117, 183
Chapman, Guy, 12, 117 (ed.), 144
Chapman, R. W., 12
Charlesworth, M. P., 117, 121
Chase, Stuart, 33
Cherry-Garrard, A., 183
Cheyney, Peter, 52 (ed.)
Child, Harold H., 33
Childe, V. G., 117
Chrimes, S. B., 117
Christie, Agatha, 71
Christie, D. and C,, 179 n.
Church, Richard, 71, 156, 167 (ed.)
Churchill, Winston S., 2, 19, 33, 118
Clapham, J. H., 118
Clark, G. N., 118; see also Oxford History,
  130
Clark, Grahame, 118
Clarke, Austin, 156
Clements, Rex, 183
Clewes, Howard, 71
Cloete, Stuart, 71
Clunn, H. P., 184
Coffee, Lenore, 179 n.
Coghill, Nevill, 14
Cohen, M. R., 145
Cohen-Portheim, Paul, 184
Colbourne, Maurice, 22
Cole, G. D. H., 119
Collier, John, 71
Collingwood, R. G., see Oxford History, 130
Collins, Norman, 71
Collis, J. S., 33, 172
Collis, Maurice, 25
Colson, F. H., 119
Colum, Padraic, 156
Comfort, Alex, 33, 72, 156
Commager, H. S. (joint author), see
  Morison, S. E.
Compton-Burnett, I., 72
Connelly, Marc, 172
Connolly, Cyril, 33, 34, 55 (ed.), 72
Converse, Florence, 72
Conway, W. Martin, 184
Cooper, Duff, 24
Cooper, William, 72

Coppard, A. E., 55
Corbett, Jim, 184
Coulton, G. G., 119 (ed.)
Coupland, Reginald, 19, 25
Cowan, W. J. (joint author), see Coffee, L.
Coward, Noel, 2, 55, 172, 179 n.
Cowell, F. R., 119
Cranage, D. H. S., 119
Crawshay-Williams, R., 145
Creston, Dormer, 13 n., 119
Crockford, 145
Croft, Andrew, 184
Crofts, Freeman Wills, 72
Cronin, A. J., 72
Crump, C. G. (ed.), 119
Cummings, E. E., 119, 156
Curtis, Brian, 34
Curtis, James, 73
Curtis, Lionel, 145

Dane, Clemence, 73, 156, 172
Darling, F. Fraser, 184
Darwin, Bernard, 34
Darwin, F. D. S., 145
David-Neel, A., 184
Davidson, W. L., 119
Davies, Godfrey, see Oxford History, 130
Davies, Rhys, 73
Daviot, Gordon, 172
Davison, John, 172
Dawson, Christopher, 145
De Chair, Somerset, 120
De Hartog, Jan, 179 n.
De la Mare, Walter, 34, 55, 73, 157
De Selincourt, Ernest, 25 n.
De Selincourt, Hugh, 73
Deeping, Warwick, 73
Delderfield, R. F., 179 n.
Dennis, Geoffrey, 34, 73
Dent, E. J., 17
Derry, T. K., 120
Dewey, John, 145
Dibdin, Lewis, T., 145
Dickinson, G. Lowes, 120
Dickinson, Patric, 157
Dighton, John, 179 n.
Dillon, Myles, 120
Dinner, William, 179 n.
Dixon, W. Macneile, 145
Dobrée, Bonamy, 29 n., 34; (joint editor),
  see Read, Herbert (ed.)
Dodd, C. H., 146
Doherty, Brian, 179 n.
Dos Passos, John, 73
Douglas, David, 27
Douglas, Keith, 157
Douglas, Norman, 74, 185
Doyle, Lynn, 55
Drew, Elizabeth, 14, 16 n.
Druten, J. Van, see Van Druten, J.
Du Baty, R. R., 185
Du Maurier, Daphne, 74

Duggan, Eileen, 157
Duguid, Julian, 74, 185
Dukes, Ashley, 172
Duncan, Ronald, 157
Dunne, J. W., 146
Durant, Will, 146
Durrell, Lawrence, 157
Dyment, Clifford, 157

Eaton, Evelyn, 185
Eberhart, Richard, 157
Eddington, Sir Arthur, 146
Edman, Irwin, 146
Edwards, Hugh, 74
Egan, Michael, 172
Eliot, T. S., 35, 158
Elton, Lord, 35
Elwin, Malcolm, 15 n., 19, 35
Elwin, Verrier, 185
Empson, William, 35, 158
English Association, 50 (ed.), 55, 167
Ensor, R. C. K., see Oxford History, 130
Ertz, Susan, 74
Ervine, St John, 172
Evans, A. J., 120
Evans, Bergen, 35
Evans, H. Muir, 185
Evans, Joan, 35, 146

Farjeon, Eleanor, 2, 74
Farjeon, J. J., 74
Farleigh, John, 36
Farnol, Jeffrey, 75
Farrell, James, 75
Faulkner, William, 75
Fausset, Hugh I'Anson, 2, 15, 24 n.
Fawcett, Douglas, 146
Fay, C. R., 120
Fedden, Robin, 120
Feiling, Keith, 27, 120, 121
Fellows, Arnold, 185
Ferguson, Rachel, 75
Fergusson, Bernard, 121
Fermor, Patrick Leigh, 186
Firbank, Thomas, 186
Fitzgerald, B. Vesey-, see Vesey-Fitzgerald,
  B.
Fleming, Peter, 186
Fletcher, Lucille (joint author), see Ullman,
  Allan
Fleure, H. J. (joint author), see Peake, H.
Flower, Newman, 17 n.
Flower, Robin (trans.), see O'Crohan, T.
Forester, C. S., 75, 76
Forster, E. M., 36, 55, 76
Fortescue, John, 186
Fothergill, John, 36
Fowler, W. Warde, 121
Fox, Cyril, 121
Fraser, Ronald, 76
Freeman, H. W., 76
Freeman, R. Austin, 56

French, Francesca (joint author), *see* Cable, Mildred
Frost, Robert, 158
Fry, Christopher, 158
Fulford, Roger, 121
Fuller, Roy, 158

Gallop, Rodney, 186
Gardner, Helen, 16
Gardner, W. H., 17
Garnett, David, 76
Garrard, A. Cherry-, *see* Cherry-Garrard, A.
Garratt, G. T., 121 (ed.)
Garrod, H. W., 26 n., 36
Garstin, Crosbie, 77
Gathorne-Hardy, Robert, 23
Gaunt, William, 36
Gawsworth, John, 158
Geldart, William, 121
George, Daniel, 159
George, Ernest, 172
Gerhardi, William, 24, 77
Gibbings, Robert, 186
Gibbon, Lewis Grassic, 77
Gibbon, Monk, 159
Gibbons, Stella 77
Gibbs, Lewis, 23
Gibbs, Philip, 77
Gibson, Guy, 122
Gibson, W. W., 159
Giedion, Sigfried, 122
Gielgud, Val, 179 n.
Ginsbury, Norman, 172
Glanville, S. R. K., 122 (ed.)
Glover, Edward, 146
Glover, Halcott, 77
Glover, T. R., 146
Godden, Rumer, 77
Gogarty, Oliver St J., 2
Goldring, Douglas, 16
Gollancz, Victor, 50 (ed.)
Gooch, G. P., 122
Gordon, George S., 21
Gorer, Geoffrey, 122, 186
Gow, Ronald, 179 n.
Gowers, Ernest, 36
Graham, Angus, 187
Graham, Stephen, 122, 187
Graham, W. S., 159
Grant, A. J., 122, 123
Graves, Robert, 3, 37, 78, 123, 147, 159
Gray, Cecil, 17
Greacen, Robert (joint editor), 167
Green, F. L., 78
Green, Henry, 78
Green, Julian, 3
Green, Paul, 173
Greene, Graham, 56, 78, 79, 187
Greenwood, Walter, 79
Greig, J. Y. T., 18, 24
Gretton, R. H., 123

Grey, Lloyd E., 20
Grierson, Herbert, 37
Grigson, Geoffrey (167 ed.)
Grinnell-Milne, Duncan, 123 (ed.)
Grose-Hodge, Humfrey, 123
Grove, Victor, 37
Guillaume, A. (joint editor), *see* Arnold, Thomas
Gunn, Neil M., 56, 79
Guthrie, Tyrone, 179 n.

Hackett, Francis, 123
Haddon, A. C., 123
Hall, S. King-, *see* King-Hall, S.
Halliburton, Richard, 187
Hamilton, Lord Frederic, 3
Hamilton, Henry, 123
Hamilton, Patrick, 79, 173
Hammett, Dashiell, 79
Hammond, Barbara and J. L., 21, 124
Hampson, John, 79
Hanbury, H. G. (joint author), *see* Geldart, William
Hanley, James, 56, 80
Hanson, L. and E. M., 13, 14 n.
Harcourt-Smith, Simon, 12
Hards, Terence, 159
Hardy, G. H., 38
Hardy, J. L., 124
Hardy, R. Gathorne-, *see* Gathorne-Hardy, R.
Hare, Cyril, 80
Harland, Henry, 80
Harrison, Frederick, 38
Harrison, G. B., 38, 124
Harrison, Jane E., 3, 124
Harrison, M. C. C., 124
Harrison, Paul W., 187
Hart, Liddell, 124
Hart, Moss, 173
Hart-Davis, Rupert, 33 (ed.)
Hartley, Dorothy, 124 (ed.), 187
Hartley, L. P., 80
Hartog, Jan de, *see* De Hartog
Harwood, H. M., 173
Hasluck, E. L., 125
Hassall, Christopher, 159
Hastings, A. C. G., 187
Hastings, Charlotte, 179 n.
Hastings, Hugh, 179 n.
Hathaway, K. B., 80
Hattersley, A. F., 125
Hawkes, Christopher, 125
Hawkes, Jacquetta, 125
Hawton, Hector, 147
Hawtrey, Anthony, 179 (ed.)
Hay, Ian, 179 n.
Haynes, E. S. P., 38
Healy, Maurice, 38
Heath-Stubbs, John, 38, 159
Hellman, Lillian, 173
Hemingford, Lord, 125

Hemingway, Ernest, 38, 56, 80, 81
Henn, T. R., 26 n.
Hennell, Thomas, 125
Hennessy, Pope-, see Pope-Hennessy
Henriques, Robert, 81
Herbert, A. P., 38, 81
Hewlett, Dorothy, 18
Hichens, Robert, 81
Higgins, F. R., 159
Hine, Reginald L., 39
Hinkley, Laura, 13 n.
Hives, Frank, 188
Hodge, Alan, 159; see also Graves, Robert
Hodge, H. Grose-, see Grose-Hodge, H.
Hodge, Merton, 173
Hodgkin, R. H., 125
Hodson, J. L., 81
Hogben, Lancelot, 125
Hogg, Garry, 188
Holdsworth, William, 126; see also Geldart, William
Holme, Constance, 56, 81
Holmyard, E. J., 27
Home, Michael, 82
Home, W. D., 173, 180
Hone, Joseph, 26
Hopkins, Kenneth, 32 (ed.)
Horder, Lord (joint author), see Roberts, Harry
Horniman, Roy, 82
Houghton, Claude, 82
Hoult, Norah, 82
Housman, Laurence, 82, 173
Howard, Sidney, 188
Howe, P. P., 17 n.
Hughes, M. Vivian, 3
Hughes, Richard, 82
Hull, Richard, 82
Hulme, T. E., 147
Humphreys, Christmas, 147
Hurst, Fannie, 83
Hutchinson, Francis E., 19 n.
Hutchinson, R. C., 83
Huxley, Aldous, 18, 39, 56, 57, 83, 147, 174, 188
Huxley, Julian, 39

Ilbert, Courtenay, 126
Iles, Francis, 83
Innes, A. D., 126
Innes, Michael, 84
Inwards, Richard, 50 (ed.)
Iremonger, Valentin, 159
Iremonger, Valentin (joint editor), see Greacen, Robert
Irving, R. L. G., 188
Irwin, Margaret, 84
Isaacs, J., viii n.
Isherwood, Christopher, 3, 84
Isherwood, Christopher (joint author), see also Auden, W. H.

Jackson, Holbrook, 39, 50 (ed.)
Jacob, E. F. (joint editor), see Crump, C. G.
James, R. A. Scott-, see Scott-James
James, William, 21 n.
Jameson, Storm, 84, 85
Jarman, T. L. (joint author), see Derry, T. K.
Jarvis. C. S., 188
Jeans, Sir James, 147
Jeans, Ronald, 179 n.
Jefferson, Joseph, 4
Jekyll, Gertrude, 126
Jenkins, Elizabeth, 12 n., 19, 85
Jenks, Edward, 126
Jennings, John, 85
Jennings, W. Ivor, 126
Jepson, Edgar, 4
Jepson, Selwyn, 85
Jesse, F. Tennyson, 85
Joad, C. E. M., 4, 23, 147
Johnston, Denis, 174
Johnston, Mary, 85
Jones, E. H., 126
Jones, Jack, 85
Jones, Phyllis, 167 (ed.)
Jones, Sydney R., 188
Jones, Sydney R. (joint author), see also Jekyll, Gertrude

Karsavina, Tamara, 4
Kaufman, George (joint author), see Hart, Moss
Kavan, Anna, 57
Kaye-Smith, Sheila, 12 n., 86
Kellett, E. E., 39
Kendon, Frank, 4
Kennedy, Margaret, 86
Kenyon, Frederick, 148
Kersh, Gerald, 86
Keverne, Richard, 86
Keyes, Sidney, 160
Keynes, Geoffrey, 13 n.
King, Francis, 86
Kingdon-Ward, F., 188
King-Hall, Stephen, 126
Kingsmill, Hugh, 17, 27, 40, 50 (ed.), 86
Kirkpatrick, F. A., 127
Kitchen, Fred, 189
Kitchin, C. H. B., 86
Kitto, H. D. F., 127
Knight, Edward F., 189
Knight, G. Wilson, 21, 22
Knights, L. C., 40
Knoblock, Edward, 179 n.
Knox, Ronald A., 86
Krutch, J. W., 18

Lack, David, 40
Lamb, Harold, 127
Lamborn, E. A. G., 40
Lane, Frank W., 40
Langley, Noel, 86

Lardner, Ring, 57
Lascelles, Mary, 12
Laski, Harold J., 127
Latham, Ronald, 127
Laver, James, 86
Lavin, Mary, 57
Lawson, Jack, 4
Le Bon, Gustave, 148
Leavis, F. R., 40
Lee, Laurie, 160
Lehmann, John, 57 (ed.)
Lehmann, Rosamund, 87
Leigh, Margaret M., 189
Leighton, Clare, 189
Leighton, Isabel, 127 (ed.)
Lejeune, C. A., 41
Leon, Derrick, 21 n.
Leverson, Ada, 87
Levy, Benn W., 174
Levy, G. R., 148
Lewis, Alun, 57, 160
Lewis, C. S., 148
Lewis, Cecil Day, 160; (joint editor), 167
Lewis, Eiluned, 87, 189
Lewis, Roy, 127
Lewis, Sinclair, 87
Lewis, Wyndham, 41, 87
Leys, M. D. R. (joint author), see Mitchell, R. J.
Liddell, Robert, 41
Lindsay, Maurice, 167 (ed.)
Linklater, Eric, 4, 87, 88
Lippmann, Walter, 148
Lips, Julius E., 128
Lipson, Ephraim, 128
Lister, Stephen, 88
Livingstone, Sir R. W., 128, 128 (ed.), 148
Lloyd, Christopher, 189
Lloyd, J. E., 128
Lockitt, C. H., 51 (ed.)
Lockley, R. M., 189
Lonsdale, Frederick, 174
Lovat, Laura, 12
Low, D. M., 16
Lowndes, Mrs Belloc, 5, 88
Lubbock, Percy, 5, 41
Lucas, F. L., 41
Lunn, Arnold, 189
Lynch, Patricia, 5
Lynd, Robert, 41, 167 (ed.)
Lyon, Lilian Bowes, 160

Macaulay, Rose, 51 (ed.), 88
MacCarthy, Desmond, 23, 41
MacCarthy, Mary, 5, 88
McCutcheon, Roger P., 41
M'Diarmid, Hugh, 160
Macdonald, Isobel, 88
MacDougall, Roger, 180 n.
MacGregor, A. A., 5
Machen, Arthur, 5, 57, 89

Mackenzie, Compton, 89
Mackenzie, Ronald, 174
Mackie, J. D., see Oxford History, 130
Mackinder, H. J., 128
Mackinnon, Frank Douglas, 6
Mackinnon, James, 148
Maclaren-Ross, J., 57
McLaverty, Michael, 57
Maclean, Catherine M., 17, 25
Maclean, Fitzroy, 128
MacMillan, Norman, 52 (ed.)
McMullen, R. T., 190
MacMurray, John, 148
Macneice, Louis, 160
McNeile, H. C., 89
Macpherson, H., 27
Madariaga, Salvador de, 89, 128
Madge, Charles, 160
Mair, G. H., 41
Mair, John, 90
Malinowski, Bronislaw, 148
Malleson, Miles, 174, 179 n.
Manhood, H. A., 57
Manning, Frederic, 90
Manson, T. W., 149
March, William, 90
Margary, Ivan D., 128
Marquand, J. P., 90
Marriott, J. W., 179 (ed.)
Marsh, Edward, 6
Marsh, Ngaio, 90
Marshall, A. Calder-, see Calder-Marshall, A.
Marshall, Bruce, 90
Martin, B. Kingsley, 128
Masefield, John, 6, 22, 42, 90, 161, 174
Masefield, Lewis C., 91
Masefield, Muriel, 13
Mason, A. E. W., 91
Massingham, H. J., 6, 42, 190
Mathew, David, 149
Mathew, Theobald, 42
Matthiessen, F. O., 16 n., 18, 168 (ed.)
Maude, Angus (joint author), see Lewis, Roy
Maugham, Robin, 91
Maugham, W. Somerset, 6, 42, 58, 91, 174, 179 n.
Mayor, Beatrice, 174
Mayor, F. M., 92
Melville, Alan, 179 n.
Methuen, Algernon, 168 (ed.)
Metz, Rudolf, 152 n.
Mew, Charlotte, 161
Meynell, Esther, 92
Meynell, Everard, 25
Meynell, Laurence, 92
Meynell, Viola, 58
Millar, George, 92
Millay, Edna St Vincent, 161
Miller, Betty, 13 n.
Millin, Sarah G., 92

Milne, A. A., 42, 92, 174, 179 n.
Milner, D. Grinnell-, see Grinnell-Milner, D.
Mitchell, James L., 129
Mitchell, Mary, 92
Mitchell, R. J., 129
Mitchison, Naomi, 58, 93
Molloy, Michael, 179 n.
Monckton, C. A. W., 190
Monro, Harold, 168 (ed.)
Moore, Doris L., 42
Moore, E. W., 129
Moore, G. E., 149
Moore, John, 42
Moore, Marianne, 161
Moorehead, Alan, 129
Moran, Lord, 149
Mordaunt, Elinor, 58
Morgan, Charles, 42, 93, 175
Morison, S. E., 129
Morley, Christopher, 93
Mortimer, Raymond, 42
Morum, William (joint author), see Dinner, William
Moss, H. St L. B. (joint author), see Baynes, N. H.
Mottram, R. H., 93
Muhlhauser, George H. P., 190
Muir, Edwin, 43, 161
Munthe, Axel, 6
Murray, Gilbert, 43, 149
Murray, Margaret A., 129
Murray, T. C., 175
Murry, J. Middleton, 7, 18, 19 n., 22, 43
Muspratt, Eric, 190
Myers, Elizabeth, 93
Myres, J. N. L., see Oxford History, 130

Namier, L. B., 129
Nathan, Robert, 93
Neale, J. E., 129
Needham, Joseph, 149
Neel, A. David-, see David-Neel, A.
Nesbitt, L. M., 190
Newby, P. H., 93
Nichols, Robert, 168 (ed.)
Nicholson, Norman, 161
Nicoll, Allardyce, 43
Nicolson, Harold, 13, 14, 15, 24, 43, 130
Noel, J. B. L., 190
Notestein, Wallace, 130
Nowell-Smith, Simon, 18 n.
Nugent, Elliott (joint author), see Thurber, James

O'Brien, Kate, 94
O'Casey, Sean, 7, 175
O'Connor, Frank, 58
O'Crohan, Tomás, 7
Odets, Clifford, 175
O'Donnell, Peadar, 58
O'Faolain, Sean, 43, 58, 94

O'Flaherty, Liam, 58, 94
Ogden, C. K., 149
Ogg, David, 130
O'Hara, John, 94
Oldmeadow, E. J., 94
'Olivia', 94
Olivier, Edith, 44, 94
Ollivant, Alfred, 94
Oman, Carola, 20, 95
Ommanney, F. D., 7
O'Neill, Eugene, 175
Onions, Oliver, 58, 95
Orczy, Baroness, 95
O'Riordan, Conal, 95
Ortzen, Len, 190
Orwell, George, 7, 44, 95, 96, 130
O'Sullivan, Maurice, 7

Pakington, Humphrey, 191
'Palinurus', see Connolly, Cyril
Palmer, Herbert, 162
Pares, Bernard, 130
Parker, Dorothy, 58
Parker, Eric, 96, 191
Parkinson, C. Northcote, 131 (ed.)
Parry, E. Jones, 131
Passos, J. Dos, see Dos Passos
Patch, Blanch, 23
Paterson, Alexander, 131
Paton, Alan, 96
Patterson, J. H., 191
Paul, Elliot, 131
Peake, Harold, 131
Peake, Mervyn, 162
Pearson, Hesketh, 22, 23, 24, 40 n.
Pertwee, Michael and R., 179 n.
Peschmann, Hermann, 168 (ed.)
Petrie, Charles, 14, 131
Philby, H. St J. B., 191
Phillpotts, Eden, 59, 96, 175
Pickthorn, Kenneth, 132
Pidgeon, Harry, 191
Piggott, Stuart, 132
Pitchford, D. J. Watkins-, see Watkins-Pitchford, D. J.
Pitter, Ruth, 162
Plomer, William, 12, 59, 96
Plowman, Max, 13 n.
Pocock, Guy, 29 n.
Pollard, A. F., 132
Pollock, Richard, 179 n.
Ponting, Hubert G., 191
Poole, A. Lane, see Oxford History, 130
Pope-Hennessy, James, 17, 192
Pope-Hennessy, Una, 16
Porter, Katherine A., 59
Portheim, P. Cohen-, see Cohen-Portheim, P.
Postgate, Raymond, 96 (joint author), see also Cole, G. D. H.
Potter, Stephen, 15 n.
Pound, Ezra, 162

Powell, Anthony, 97
Power, Rhoda, 132
Powicke, F. M., 132
Powys, John Cowper, 44
Powys, Stephen, 179 n.
Powys, T. F., 59, 97
Preedy, George, 97
Prescott, H. F. M., 132
Prestage, Edgar, 132
Preston, Raymond, 16 n.
Prévité-Orton, C. W., 133
Prichard, K. S., 97
Priestley, J. B., 44, 97, 176, 192
Pritchett, V. S., 44, 59
Prokosch, Frederic, 97
Pudney, John, 52 (ed.), 162
Pym, Barbara, 98

Queen, Ellery, 59, 59 (ed.)
Quennell, Peter, 13, 14, 21, 27

Raine, Kathleen, 162
Ramsay, A. A. W., 20
Ransom, John Crowe, 162
Ransome, Arthur, 98, 192
Rattigan, Terence, 176
Raven, C. E., 28
Rawlings, Marjorie, 98
Rawlinson, H. G., 133
Raymond, Ernest, 98
Raymond, Walter, 98
Read, Conyers, 133
Read, Herbert, 8, 15 n., 25, 44, 45, 51 (ed.), 98, 162
Rebell, Fred, 192
Reddaway, W. F., 133
Reed, Henry, 162
Reeves, David, 45
Reeves, James, 162, 163
Reid, Forrest, 45
Reinhard, John R., 133
Reitz, Deneys, 133
Renier, G. J., 133
Reynolds, E. E., 133
Rhode, John, 98
Rhys, Keidrych, 168 (ed.)
Rice, Elmer, 176
Richards, I. A. (joint author), see Ogden, C. K.
Richardson, A. E., 192
Richardson, Dorothy, 99
Richardson, Howard, 179 n.
Rickert, Edith, 14 n.
Rickward, Edgell, 163
Riding, Laura, 163
Ridler, Anne, 52 (ed.), 163, 168
Ritchie, A. D., 143 n.
Roberts, Cecil, 99
Roberts, Elizabeth M., 99
Roberts, Harry, 149
Roberts, Kenneth, 99
Roberts, Lynette, 163

Roberts, Michael, 45, 163, 168 (ed.
Roberts, S. C., 18 n.
Robertson, C. Grant, 12, 134
Robertson, E. Arnot, 99
Robertson, W. Graham, 8
Robinson, J. H., 150
Robinson, Lennox, 176
Robinson, W. A., 192
Rogers, Samuel, 99
Roper, H. R. Trevor-, see Trevor-Roper, H. R.
Rose, Walter, 134
Ross, J. Maclaren-, see Maclaren-Ross, J.
Roughead, W. N., 31 (ed.)
Rowse, A. L., 8, 17, 134
Royde-Smith, Naomi, 99
Runciman, Steven, 134
Runyon, Damon, 60
Russell, Bertrand, 45, 150
Russell, Leonard, 45 (ed.)
Ruttledge, Hugh, 192
Rylands, G. W. R., 46
Ryle, Gilbert, 150

Sabatini, Rafael, 100
Sackville-West, Edward, 15, 100, 163
Sackville-West, V., 18, 100, 150, 163, 192
Sadleir, Michael, 16, 25, 100
Salusbury, G. T., 134
Salzman, L. E., 134
Samuel, Viscount, 150, 151
Sansom, William, 100
Santayana, George, 8, 46, 100, 151, 163
'Sapper', see McNeile, H. C.
Saroyan, William, 60, 176
Sassoon, Siegfried, 8, 100, 163
Saurat, Denis, 19 n.
Savage, Derek S., 46
Sawyer, W. W., 151
Sayers, Dorothy L., 60, 60 (ed.), 101, 163
Sayles, G. O., 134
Schilpp, P. A., 145 n. (ed.), 149, 150, 151, 153
Schrodinger, Erwin, 151
Scott, H. S. (joint author), see Carey, G. V.
Scott-James, R. A., 46
Seaver, George, 25
Selincourt, Hugh de, see De Selincourt, H.
Selley, W. T., 134
Selwyn, E. Gordon, 151
Sergeant, Howard, 168 (ed.)
Seymour, Beatrice Kean, 101
Seymour-Smith, Martin (joint author), see Hards, Terence
Shackleton, Sir Ernest, 193
Shairp, Mordaunt, 176
Shanks, Edward, 164
Sharp, Margery, 101
Shaw, G. Bernard, 8, 46, 60, 101, 176, 177
Sheehan, P. A., 101
Sheppard, A. T., 101

Sherriff, R. V. C., 177, 179 n.
Sherrington, Charles, 151
Sherwood, Robert, 177
Shiels, George, 177
Shute, Nevil, 102
Sidgwick, Ethel, 102
Simmons, E. J., 25
Simpson, F. A., 135
Simpson, Helen, 102
Sinclair, May, 102
Sinclair, Robert, 46
Sinclair, Upton, 102
Sinclair, W. A., 151
Singer, Charles (joint author), see Bevan, E. R.
Sitwell, Constance 47
Sitwell, Edith, 20, 28, 47, 103, 135, 164, 169 (ed.), 193
Sitwell, Osbert, 8, 9, 47, 60, 103, 164, 193
Sitwell, Sacheverell, 9, 47, 135, 164
Smellie, K. B., 135
Smith, Cecil Woodham-, see Woodham-Smith, C.
Smith, David, 193
Smith, Emma, 103, 193
Smith, G. Elliot, 135
Smith, H. M., 135
Smith, J. C. (joint author), see Grierson, H.
Smith, Martin Seymour-, see Seymour-Smith, M.
Smith, Pauline, 103
Smith, Sheila Kaye-, see Kaye-Smith, S.
Smith, Simon Harcourt-, see Harcourt-Smith, S.
Smith, Simon Nowell-, see Nowell-Smith, S.
Smythe, F. S., 193
Snaith, J. C., 103
Snaith, Stanley, 164
Snow, C. P., 103
Somervell, D. C., 135; see also Toynbee, A. J.
Somerville, E. O. E., 103
Sorley, W. R., 152
Spears, E. L., 135
Spencer, Bernard, 164
Spencer, Theodore, 22
Spender, Stephen, 47, 60, 164
Spenser, James, 103
Spring, Howard, 9, 104
Spurgeon, C. F. E., 22
Squire, J. C., 9, 164, 169 (ed.); (joint author), see Balderston, J. L.
Stapledon, Olaf, 104
Stark, Freya, 9, 194
Starkie, Enid, 20
Starkie, Walter, 194
Stead, Christina, 104
Stebbing, L. Susan, 152
Steed, Wickham, 135
Steel, F. Annie, 104
Steen, Marguerite, 104

Stein, Gertrude, 9
Steinbeck, John, 104
Stenton, Frank, see Oxford History, 130
Stephens, James, 104, 164
Stern, G. B., 12 n., 105
Stevenson, J. A. R., 47
Stevenson, R. A. M., 47
Stewart, G. R., 105
Stoker, Bram, 105
Stone, Irving, 105
Storm, Lesley, 179 n.
Stout, G. F., 152
Strachey, John, 47
Strachey, Julia, 105
Stratford, E. Wingfield-, see Wingfield-Stratford, E.
Street, A. G., 47, 105
Strode, W. Chetham, 177, 179 n.
Strong, L. A. G., 47, 61, 105
(joint ed.), see Lewis, C. Day
Stuart, Dorothy M., 136
Stuart, Francis, 106
Stubbs, J. Heath-, see Heath-Stubbs, J.
Sutcliffe, Halliwell, 194
Swinnerton, Frank, 48, 106
Swinton, Ernest, 61
Sykes, Christopher, 28
Symons, Julian, 14

Tambs, Erling, 194
Tate, Allen, 106, 165
Tawney, R. H., 136
Taylor, A. E., 152
Taylor, A. J. P., 136
Taylor, G. R. Stirling, 15 n., 136
Taylor, Rex (joint author), see Hards, Terence
Temperley, Gladys, 136
Temperley, Harold, 136 (joint author), see also Grant, A. J.
Temple, Joan, 179 n.
Tennyson, Charles, 24 n.
Thirkell, Angela, 9, 106
Thomas, Alan, 106
Thomas, Bertram, 136, 194
Thomas, Dylan, 106, 165
Thomas, Helen, 25
Thomas, William Beach, 48, 194
Thompson, Flora, 10
Thompson, J. M., 20, 21, 136
Thomson, George, 137
Thomson, Gladys Scott, 28, 137
Thonemann, H. E., 137
Thorndike, Russell, 106
Thorne, Anthony, 106
Thurber, James, 48, 177
Tiller, Terence, 165
Tillyard, E. M. W., 19, 22, 48, 137
Tilman, H. W., 195
Todd, Ruthven, 48, 165
Tolkien, J. R. R., 106
Tomlinson, H. M., 107, 195

Toynbee, Arnold J., 137
Toynbee, Philip, 107
Treece, Henry, 165
Trend, J. B., 138
Treneer, Anne, 10
Tressell, Robert, 107
Trevelyan, G. M., 17, 48, 138
Trevelyan, R. C., 165
Trevor-Roper, H. R., 138
Trewin, J. C. 179 (ed.)
Trilling, Lionel, 12, 16, 107
Tschiffely, A. F., 195
Turberville, A. S., 139 (ed.)
Turner, E. S., 48, 139
Turner, F. C., 139
Tylor, E. B., 139

Ullman, Allan, 107
Ullman, J. R., 195
Ure, P. N., 139
Uttley, Alison, 10

Vachell, H. A., 107
Vale, Edmund, 195
Van Dine, S. S., 107
Van Druten, John, 177
Vane, Sutton, 178
Veblen, Thorstein, 152
Vernede, Robert E., 61
Vesey-Fitzgerald, Brian, 195
Vickers, Roy, 61
Villiers, A. J., 196
Vines, Sherard, 49, 108
Vinogradoff, Paul, 139
Voss, John C., 196
Voynich, E. L., 108
Vulliamy, C. E., 18 n.

Waddell, Helen, 108, 139
Walbank, F. Alan, 139 (ed.)
Waldman, Milton, 139
Waley, Arthur, 165
Walker, Eric A., 139
Wallace, Edgar, 108
Walling, R. A. J., 108
Walmsley, Leo, 108
Walsh, James J., 140
Walsh, Maurice, 108
Ward, A. C., 23, 29 n.
Ward, F. Kingdon-, see Kingdon-Ward, F.
Ward, Maisie, 15
Warner, Rex, 108, 109
Warner, Sylvia T., 61, 109
Warren, C. Henry, 196
Warren, Robert Penn, 109
Watkins, Vernon, 165
Watkins-Pitchford, D. J., 196
Watts, Stephen, 61
Waugh, Evelyn, 14, 109
Webling, A. F., 10
Webster, Charles, 140
Webster, Elizabeth C., 109

Wedgwood, C. V., 15, 20, 24, 140
Weekley, Ernest, 49
Welch, Denton, 10, 61, 109
Wellesley, Dorothy, 165
Welty, Eudora, 61
West, E. and V. Sackville-, see Sackville-West
West, Rebecca, 49, 61, 110, 140, 196
Westerby, Robert, 110
Whistler, Laurence, 165
Whitaker, Malachi, 62
White, Antonia, 110
White, T. H., 110
Whitehead, A. N., 152, 153
Whitehouse, J. H., 21 n.
Wilder, Thornton, 110
Wilkins, Vaughan, 140
Wilkinson, Walter, 196
Willey, Basil, 153
Williams, Basil, see Oxford History, 130
Williams, Charles, 21 n., 141
Williams, Emlyn, 178
Williams, J. H., 196
Williams, R. Crawshay-, see Crawshay-Williams, R.
Williamson, Henry, 110
Williamson, J. A., 141
Wilson, Angus, 62
Wilson, Edmund, 49
Wilson, Harry Leon, 111
Wilson, J. Dover, 22
Wilson, Mona, 13, 23
Wilson, Richard A., 49
Wilson, Romer, 111
Wingfield-Stratford, Esmé, 141
Winter, Keith, 178
Withers, Percy, 49
Wodehouse, P. G., 111
Wolfe, Thomas, 111
Wollman, Maurice, 169 (ed.)
Wood, H. G., 153
Wood, Thomas, 197
Woodham-Smith, Cecil, 20
Woodward, E. L., 141, and see also Oxford History, 130
Woolf, Leonard, 178
Woolley, Leonard, 141
Wray, J. W., 197
Wren, P. C., 111
Wyatt, Woodrow, 52 n.
Wylie, Elinor, 111

Yates, Dornford, 112
Yates, Peter, 166
Yeats, W. B., 169 (ed.)
Young, Andrew, 49, 166
Young, E. H., 112
Young, Francis Brett, 112
Young, G. M., 16 n., 141, 142
Young, G. Winthrop, 197

Zimmern, Alfred, 142

INDEX OF TITLES

Titles taking the form of 'Life of...', 'Biography of...' are not included here as the arrangement of the Biography section under subjects enables readers to turn direct to that section for reference. Similarly, formal titles such as 'Collected Essays', 'Collected Poems', 'Poetical Works', 'Poems', 'Short Stories', 'Plays', and the like are also excluded, as readers are able to refer direct to the Author Index or to the relevant section. As in the Author Index, books referred to in notes have been included, page numbers for these being followed by 'n'.

ABC of Plain Words (GOWERS), 37 n.
Abinger Harvest (FORSTER), 36
About Kingsmill (PEARSON), 40 n.
About Levy (CALDER-MARSHALL), 70
Acquisitive Society, The (TAWNEY), 136
Across the Bridges (PATERSON), 131
Adam and Caroline [series] (O'RIORDAN), 95
Adding Machine, The (RICE), 176
Adonais (HEWLETT), 18 n.
Adventure Story (RATTIGAN), 176
Adventures of a Mountaineer (SMYTHE), 193
Adventures of Ellery Queen (QUEEN), 59 n.
Adventures of Ideas (WHITEHEAD), 152
Adventures of Sylvia Scarlett (MACKENZIE), 89
Adventures of the Black Girl (SHAW), 60
Ægean Islands (SPENCER), 164
Aerodrome, The (WARNER), 108
Aesthetic Adventure (GAUNT), 36
Africa Dances (GORER), 186
Africa Drums (BAKER), 182
Africa Trilogy (MOOREHEAD), 129
After Many A Summer (HUXLEY), 83
After October (ACKLAND), 171
After Puritanism (KINGSMILL), 40
Aftermath (CHURCHILL), 118
Afternoon Men (POWELL), 97
Age of Anxiety (AUDEN), 155 n.
Age of Drake (WILLIAMSON), 141
Age of Elegance (BRYANT), 116
Age of Reform (WOODWARD), 130
Age of the Chartists (HAMMOND), 124
Air that Kills, An (KING), 86
Ali the Lion (PLOMER), 12
All Men Are Enemies (ALDINGTON), 64
All Night At Mr Stanyhurst's (EDWARDS), 74
All Our Yesterdays (TOMLINSON) 107
All Passion Spent (SACKVILLE-WEST) 100
All Summer In a Day (SITWELL) 9
All This and That (RUNYON) 60
Along the Road (HUXLEY), 39
Alps, The (IRVING), 188
Alps From End to End, The (CONWAY), 184
Amateur Gentleman (FARNOL), 75
Amazed Evangelist (BRIDIE), 171 n.
Ambush of Young Days (UTTLEY), 10

American Genius, The (SITWELL), 169
Americans, The (GORER), 122
Anatomist, The (BRIDIE), 171 n
Anatomy of Courage (MORAN), 149
Anatomy of Revolution (BRINTON), 115
Ancient Art and Ritual (HARRISON), 124
And Another Thing (SPRING), 9 n.
And Berry Came Too (YATES), 112
And Even Now (BEERBOHM), 30
And Far Away (HOGG), 188
Androcles and the Lion (SHAW), 176 n.
Andromeda in Wimpole Street (CRESTON), 13 n.
Angel Pavement (PRIESTLEY), 97
Anglo-Saxon England (STENTON), 130
Animal Farm (ORWELL), 95
Ann Vickers (LEWIS), 87
Anna Christie (O'NEILL), 175
Annajanska (SHAW), 177 n.
Annals of Innocence and Experience (READ), 8
Anthology of Contemporary Northern Poetry (SERGEANT), 168
Anthology of Modern Poetry (LYND), 167
Anthology of Modern Verse (METHUEN), 168
Anthology of War Poetry (NICHOLS), 168
Anthropology (TYLOR), 139
Antic Hay (HUXLEY), 83
Antonio (OLDMEADOW), 94
Ants (HUXLEY), 39 n.
Ape and Essence (HUXLEY), 83
Apes and Men (PEAKE), 131
Apple-Cart, The (SHAW), 177 n.
Appointment in Samarra (O'HARA), 94
Arabia Felix (THOMAS), 194
Arabs, The (THOMAS), 136
Archaeology and Society (CLARK), 118
Archetypal Patterns in Poetry (BODKIN), 32
Arms and the Man (SHAW), 177 n.
Around the World Single-Handed (PIDGEON), 191
Art (BELL), 31
Art Now (READ), 44
Art o f the Essayist (LOCKITT), 51
Art of Velasquez (STEVENSON), 47
Arundel (ROBERTS), 99
As I Was Going Down Sackville Street (GOGARTY), 2

As It Was (THOMAS), 25
Ascent of F 6 (AUDEN), 155
Ascent of Nanda Devi (TILMAN), 195
Ashenden (MAUGHAM), 58
Asiatics, The (PROKOSCH), 97
Asking For Trouble (BEACHCROFT), 53 n.
Aspects of Modern Poetry (SITWELL), 47
Aspects of the Novel (FORSTER), 36
Aspirin Age, The (LEIGHTON), 127
Assassin, The (YATES), 166
Assassin, The (O'FLAHERTY), 94
Assessment of Twentieth Century Literature (ISAACS), viii n.
Asylum Piece (KAVAN), 57
At Sea (CALDER-MARSHALL), 70
At the Villa Rose (MASON), 91
Atlantis Myth, The (BELLAMY), 144
Audrey (JOHNSTON), 85
August Folly (THIRKELL), 106
Augustus Does His Bit (SHAW), 177 n.
Authority and the Individual (RUSSELL), 150
Autobiography of Alice B. Toklas (STEIN), 9
Autumn Fire (MURRAY), 175
Awake and Sing (ODETS), 175 n.
Axel's Castle (WILSON), 49

Babbitt (LEWIS), 87
Back to Methuselah (SHAW), 176 n.
Backwater (RICHARDSON), 99 n.
Badger's Green (SHERRIFF), 177
Ballad and the Source (LEHMANN), 87
Ballad of the Mari Lwyd (WATKINS), 165
Ballygullion (DOYLE), 55
Bardelys the Magnificent (SABATINI), 100
Barly Fields, The (NATHAN), 93
Barretts of Wimpole Street (BESIER), 171
Bath (SITWELL), 193
Beadle, The (Smith), 103
Beany-Eye (GARNETT), 76
Beast Must Die, The (BLAKE), 67
Beau Geste [series] (WREN), 111
Beauties and the Furies, The (STEAD), 104
Beautiful Years (WILLIAMSON), 110 n.
Bedtime Story (O'CASEY), 175 n.
Bees on the Boat Deck (PRIESTLEY), 176 n.
Before the Bombardment (SITWELL), 103
Before the Fact (ILES), 84 n.
Behold This Dreamer (DE LA MARE), 34
Belinda (MILNE), 174 n.
Bella Donna (HICHENS), 81 n.
Bells of Shoreditch (SIDGWICK), 102
Benson Murder Case (VAN DINE), 107
Bent Twig, The (CANFIELD), 70
Berkeley Square (BALDERSTON), 171
Berry and Co (YATES), 112
Best Broadcast Stories (BROWN), 54
Best Stories [Faber's series], 52 n.
Between Two Worlds (MURRY), 7
Between Two Worlds (SINCLAIR), 102 n.
Beyond Euphrates (STARK), 9

Beyond the Chindwin (FERGUSON), 121
Beyond the Mexique Bay (HUXLEY), 188
Bible To-Day, The (DODD), 146
Big House, The (ROBINSON), 176 n.
Big Money (DOS PASSOS), 73 n.
Big Sleep, The (CHANDLER), 71
Bill of Divorcement (DANE), 172
Bindon Parva (BIRMINGHAM), 67 n.
Bird of Dawning (MASEFIELD), 90
Bird-Watching (HUXLEY), 39
Bishop's Wife, The (NATHAN), 93 n.
Bitter Sweet (COWARD), 172 n.
Black Diamond (YOUNG), 112
Black Dog (COPPARD), 55
Black Gang (MCNEILE), 89 n.
Black Girl, The (SHAW), 60
Black Lamb and Grey Falcon (WEST), 196
Black Mischief (WAUGH), 109
Black Narcissus (GODDEN), 77
Black Sparta (MITCHISON), 58
Black Venus (DAVIES), 73
Blandings Castle (WODEHOUSE), 111
Bloom of Candles (LEE), 160
Bluefeather (MEYNELL), 92
Body, The (SANSOM), 100
Book About Books (HARRISON), 38
Book of Crafts and Characters (RAYMOND), 98
Book of English Law (JENKS), 126
Book of Joad (JOAD), 4
Book of Prose Selections (MASEFIELD), 42
Book of the Basques (GALLOP), 186
Book of Words (BROWN), 32
Bookman's Holiday (JACKSON), 50
Books and Writers (LYND), 41 n.
Boomerang (SIMPSON), 102
Born Under Saturn (MACLEAN), 17
Bosambo of the River (WALLACE), 108
Both Sides of the Blanket (GLOVER), 77
Bottle's Path (POWYS), 59
Boy Comes Home (MILNE), 174 n.
Boy in Blue (BRIER), 69
Boys Will Be Boys (TURNER), 48
Brandons, The (THIRKELL), 106
Brassbounder, The (BONE), 54
Brave and Cruel (WELCH), 61
Brave Earth (Sheppard), 101
Brave New World (HUXLEY), 83
Bravery of Earth (EBERHART), 157 n.
Brazilian Adventure (FLEMING), 186
Breakfast With the Nikolides (GODDEN), 77
Brensham Village (MOORE), 42
Bride, The (IRWIN), 84
Bride Comes to Evensford, The (BATES), 53
Brideshead Revisited (WAUGH), 109
Bridge, The (PITTER), 162
Bridge of San Luis Rey (WILDER), 110
Brief Candles (HUXLEY), 56
Bright Face of Danger (MEYNELL), 92
Brighton Rock (GREENE), 78
Britain and British Seas (MACKINDER), 128
Britain's Daughter (BOTTOMLEY), 155

British Constitution, The (JENNINGS), 126
British Diplomacy (WEBSTER), 140
British Drama (NICOLL), 43
British Empire, The (WALKER), 139
British History in the Nineteenth Century (TREVELYAN), 138
British Overseas (CARRINGTON), 117
British Politics Since 1900 (SOMERVELL), 135
British Prehistory (PIGGOTT), 132
Broad Highway (FARNOL), 75
Broke of Covenden (SNAITH), 103
Broken Road (MASON), 91
Brontës Went to Woolworth's (FERGUSON), 75
Broome Stages (DANE) 73
Brother of Daphne (YATES), 112
Brother to the Ox (KITCHEN), 189
Brothers and Sisters (COMPTON-BURNETT), 72
Brown on Resolution (FORESTER), 75
Browning Version, The (RATTIGAN), 176
Brush Up Your Reading (POCOCK), 29 n.
Buck the Snow, The (MILLAY), 161 n.
Buddhism (HUMPHREYS), 147
Bull-Dog Drummond (McNEILE), 89 n.
Buoyant Billions (SHAW), 176 n.
Buried Empires (CARLETON), 117
Buried Self, The (MACDONALD), 88
Burma's Icy Mountains (KINGDON-WARD), 188
Burning Cactus (SPENDER), 60
Burning Mask, The (YATES), 166
Burnt Norton (ELIOT), 158 n.
Burr Oaks (EBERHART), 157 n.
Busman's Honeymoon (SAYERS), 101
But It Still Goes On (GRAVES), 3 n.
By Order of the Company (JOHNSTON), 85
Byzantium (BAYNES), 114

Cabinet Government (JENNINGS), 126
Caesar and Cleopatra (SHAW), 177 n.
Cage Me a Peacock (LANGLEY), 86
Cakes and Ale (MAUGHAM), 91
Camberley Triangle, The (MILNE), 174 n.
Canaries Sometimes Sing (LONSDALE), 174
Candida (SHAW), 177 n.
Candleford Green (THOMPSON), 10 n.
Canticle of the Rose (SITWELL), 164
Captain Blood (SABATINI), 100
Captain Brasshound's Conversion (SHAW), 177 n.
Captain Hornblower (FORESTER), 75
Captain's Wife, The (LEWIS), 87
Cardinal's Snuff-Box (HARLAND), 80
Carnival (MACKENZIE), 89
Case Book of Ellery Queen (QUEEN), 59
Case Is Altered, The (PLOMER), 59
Cashel Byron's Profession (SHAW), 101
Cask, The (CROFTS), 72
Cat Jumps, The (BOWEN), 54
Cathedrals and How They Were Built (CRANAGE), 119 n.

Catherine the Great (ANTHONY), 114
Catholicism in England (MATHEW), 149
Cavalcade (COWARD), 172 n.
Celestial Omnibus (FORSTER), 55 n.
Ceremony of Innocence (WEBSTER), 109
Chains (BAKER), 171
Change on the Farm (HENNELL), 125
Channel Packet (MORTIMER), 42
Character of England (BARKER), 114
Charles I and Cromwell (YOUNG), 141
Charles Lamb (BLUNDEN), 32
Charlotte's Row (BATES), 66
Charwoman's Daughter (STEPHENS), 104
Chatham and the British Empire (ROBERTSON), 134
Chatterton Square (YOUNG), 112 n.
Chaucer's World (RICKERT), 14
Cheerful Weather for the Wedding (STRACHEY), 105
Chequer Board, The (SHUTE), 102
Cherry Tree (BELL), 66
Chestnuts in Her Lap (LEJEUNE), 41
Child of Queen Victoria (PLOMER), 59 n.
Chiltern Country (MASSINGHAM), 190
Chinese Mirror (AYSCOUGH), 182 n.
Chinese Poems (WALEY), 165
Chinese Women (AYSCOUGH), 182 n.
Chink in the Armour (LOWNDES), 88
Christianity and Civilization (WOOD), 153
Christina (HOUGHTON), 82
Christmas At Cold Comfort Farm (GIBBONS), 77 n.
Christmas Garland (BEERBOHM), 30
Christopher Columbus (MACNEICE), 160
Chronicles of Sally (SEYMOUR), 101
Cicadas, The (HUXLEY), 174 n.
Cicero and the Roman Republic (COWELL), 119
Citadel, The (CRONIN), 72
City of the Soul (HOME), 82
City State of the Greeks and Romans (FOWLER), 121
Civilisation (BELL), 114
Civilisation of Spain (TREND), 138
Civilisation on Trial (TOYNBEE), 137
Civitas Dei (CURTIS), 145
Classical Tradition in Poetry (MURRAY), 43
Claudius the God (GRAVES), 78
Clear Horizon (RICHARDSON), 99 n.
Clementina (MASON), 91
Clio, A Muse (TREVELYAN), 48
Cloak of Monkey Fur (DUGUID), 74
Closing the Ring (CHURCHILL), 118
Cloud Cuckoo Land (MITCHISON), 93
Cloud Howe (GIBBON), 77 n.
Cloudless May (JAMESON), 84
Coat of Many Colours (READ), 44
Cobbers (WOOD), 197
Cobbers Campaigning (WOOD), 197
Cock-a-Doodle-Dandy (O'CASEY), 175 n.
Cocktail Party (ELIOT), 158
Coggin (OLDMEADOW), 94 n.

Cold Comfort Farm (GIBBONS), 77
Collected Essays in Literary Criticism (READ), 44
Collected Ghost Stories (ONIONS), 58
Collected Impressions (BOWEN), 32
Colonel Witherspoon (BRIDIE), 171
Colonel's Daughter (ALDINGTON), 64
Comforts of Unreason (CRAWSHAY-WILLIAMS), 145
Coming Down the Wye (GIBBINGS), 186
Coming Up for Air (ORWELL), 96
Commando (REITZ), 133
Commodore, The (FORESTER), 75 n.
Common Asphodel (GRAVES), 37
Common People, The (COLE), 119
Common-sense in Law (VINOGRADOFF), 139
Commonwealth of God (CURTIS), 145
Company K (MARCH), 90
Complete Memoirs of George Sherston (SASSOON), 100
Concept of Mind (RYLE), 150
Concise Economic History of England (CLAPHAM), 118
Condemned Playground (CONNOLLY), 33
Conference at Cold Comfort Farm (GIBBONS), 77 n.
Confessions of an Innkeeper (FOTHERGILL), 36 n.
Confessions of an Uncommon Attorney (HINE), 39
Confident Years, The (BROOKS), 32
Congress of Vienna (NICOLSON), 130
Congress of Vienna (WEBSTER), 140
Conquered, The (MITCHISON), 93
Conquest of Happiness (RUSSELL), 150
Conquest of the Maya (MITCHELL), 129
Connoisseur, The (DE LA MARE), 55 n.
Constant Nymph (KENNEDY), 86
Contemporary Irish Poetry (GREACEN), 167
Conversation Piece (COWARD), 172 n.
Corduroy (BELL), 66
Corn Is Green, The (WILLIAMS), 178
Cornelius (PRIESTLEY), 176 n.
Cornish Childhood, A (ROWSE), 8
Cornish Years (TRENEER) 10
Coroner Doubts, The (WALLING), 108
Corporal Tune (STRONG), 105
Corpse Without a Clue (WALLING), 108
Corridors of Time [series] (PEAKE), 131
Cotswold Country (MASSINGHAM), 190
Cotswold Year (WARREN), 196
Counsellor-at-Law (RICE), 176
Count Belisarius (GRAVES), 78
Countries of the Mind (MURRY), 43
Country Days (STREET), 47 n.
Country Heart, The (BATES), 182
Country Moods and Tenses (OLIVIER), 44
Countryman at Work (HENNELL), 125
Countryman's Creed (THOMAS), 48
Countryman's England (HARTLEY), 187
Countryman's Week-End Book (PARKER), 191

Cousin Honoré (JAMESON), 84
Crab Apple Jelly (O'CONNOR), 58
Crabbed Age and Youth (ROBINSON), 176 n.
Craft of Fiction, The (LUBBOCK), 41
Creaking Chair, The (MEYNELL), 92
Cream of Thurber, The (THURBER), 48 n.
Creative Craftsman, The (FARLEIGH), 36
Creative Man (SAMUEL), 150
Creatures of Circumstance (MAUGHAM), 58
Cricket Country (BLUNDEN), 32
Cricket Match, The (DE SELINCOURT), 73
Crier by Night, The (BOTTOMLEY), 155 n.
Crime at Blossoms (SHAIRP), 176
Crime at Vanderlynden's (MOTTRAM), 93 n.
Critical Essays (ORWELL), 44
Critical History of English Poetry (GRIERSON), 37
Critique of Logical Positivism (JOAD), 147
Critique of Poetry (ROBERTS), 45
Crock of Gold (STEPHENS), 104
Crockford Prefaces, 145
Crome Yellow (HUXLEY), 83
Crook in the Furrow (STREET), 105
Cross-Currents in Seventeenth-Century Literature (GRIERSON), 37
Crouchback (OMAN), 95
Crowd, The (LE BON), 148
Crown of Life (KNIGHT), 22
Cruise of the Amaryllis (MUHLHAUSER), 190
Cruise of the Nona (BELLOC), 182
Cruise of the 'Teddy' (TAMBS), 194
Crusades, The (LAMB), 127
Cry, the Beloved Country (PATON), 96
Culture and Survival (CHAPMAN), 144
Curate's Wife, The (YOUNG), 112
Curious Traveller, The (MASSINGHAM), 42
Curlew Cries, The (ANDERSON), 154
Curtain of Green (WELTY), 61
Cut and Come Again (BATES), 53
Cycles of the Kings (DILLON), 120
Cyder Feast (SITWELL), 164
Cymbeline Refinished (SHAW), 177 n.

Dandelion Days (WILLIAMSON), 110 n.
Danger of Being a Gentleman (LASKI), 127
Dangerous Corner (PRIESTLEY), 176
Daring Young Man on the Flying Trapeze (SAROYAN), 60 n.
Dark Lady of the Sonnets (SHAW), 177 n.
Dark Mile, The (BROSTER), 69
Darkling Plain, The (HEATH-STUBBS), 38
Darling Tom (STRONG), 61 n.
Daughters and Sons (COMPTON-BURNETT), 72
Dawn of European Civilization (CHILDE), 117
Dawn of Liberation (CHURCHILL), 118 n.
Dawn's Delay, The (KINGSMILL), 86
Dawn's Left Hand (RICHARDSON), 99 n.
Day of Glory, The (BATES), 171
Days Before Yesterday (HAMILTON), 3 n.

Day's End (BATES), 53
Days in the Sun (CARDUS), 33 n.
Day's Play, The (MILNE), 42 n.
Dead Ground (CLEWES), 71
Dead Ned (MASEFIELD), 90
Dead Seagull, The (BARKER), 65
Deadlock (RICHARDSON), 99 n.
Death at the Bar (MARSH), 90
Death at the President's Lodging (INNES), 84
Death in the Afternoon (HEMINGWAY), 38
Death of a Hero (ALDINGTON), 64
Death of His Uncle (KITCHIN), 86
Death of Laurence Vining (THOMAS), 106
Death of My Aunt (KITCHIN), 86
Death of Society (WILSON), 111
Death of Socrates (HOUSMAN), 173
Death of the Heart (BOWEN), 68
Death to the French (FORESTER), 75
Deaths and Entrances (THOMAS), 165
Death-Watch (CARR), 70
Debit Account (ONIONS), 95 n.
Decline and Fall (WAUGH), 109
Deep Water and Shoal (ROBINSON), 192
Defender of the Faith (BOWEN), 68
Delay in the Sun (THORNE), 106
Delicate Situation (ROYDE-SMITH), 99
Demi-Gods (STEPHENS), 104
Demon Lover (BOWEN), 54
Department of Dead Ends (VICKERS), 61
Deputy Was King (STERN), 105 n.
Desert and Forest (NESBITT), 190
Desert Highway (PRIESTLEY), 176 n.
Design For Living (COWARD), 172 n.
Desolate Marches (NESBITT), 190
Destructive Element (SPENDER), 47
Detective Ben (FARJEON), 74
Development of English Biography (NICOLSON), 43
Devil to Pay, The (SAYERS), 163 n.
Devil's Disciple (SHAW), 177 n.
Devonshire Plays (PHILPOTTS), 175
Dew on the Grass (LEWIS), 87
Dialogues in Limbo (SANTAYANA), 151
Diary of a District Officer (BRADLEY), 183
Dickon (BOWEN), 68
Diff'rent (O'NEILL), 175
Dimple Hill (RICHARDSON), 99 n.
Din of a Smithy (STEVENSON), 47
Diplomacy (NICOLSON), 130
Director, The (STRONG), 105
Disappearances of Uncle David (FARJEON) 74
Disappearing Castle (MADGE), 160
Disintegration of a Politician (KINGSMILL), 86
Distant Prospect (BERNERS), 1
Do What You Will (HUXLEY), 39
Dr Angelus (BRIDIE), 171 n.
Doctor in Arabia (HARRISON), 187
Doctor Syn [series] (THORNDIKE), 106
Dr Thorndyke [series] (FREEMAN), 56

Doctors' Delusions (SHAW), 46
Doctor's Dilemma (SHAW), 177 n.
Dog Beneath the Skin (AUDEN), 155
Dominant Sex, The (EGAN), 172
Dover Road, The (MILNE), 174 n.
Down and Out In Paris and London (ORWELL), 7
Down Channel (MCMULLEN), 190
Down Our Street (GEORGE), 172
Down to Earth (COLLIS), 33
Down to the Sea (BLAKE), 67
Dracula (STOKER), 105
Dragon Harvest (SINCLAIR), 102 n.
Dragon's Teeth (SINCLAIR), 102 n.
Drama (MACCARTHY), 41
Dreadful Dragon of Hay Hill (BEERBOHM), 66
Dream Island Days (LOCKLEY), 189
Dream of Fair Women (WILLIAMSON), 110 n.
Drums Under the Windows (O'CASEY), 7
Drunk Man Looks at the Thistle (M'DIARMID), 160
Dry Salvages, The (ELIOT), 158 n.
Dusk at the Grove (ROGERS), 99
Dusty Answer (LEHMANN), 87

Eagle and the Dove (SACKVILLE-WEST), 150
Earlham (LUBBOCK), 5
Early Stuarts, The (DAVIES), 130
Early Tudor Government (PICKTHORN), 132
Early Tudors, The (MACKIE), 130
Early Victorian England (YOUNG), 141
Early Victorian Novelists (CECIL), 33
Earth Abides (STEWART), 105
East Coker (ELIOT), 158 n.
East is West (STARK), 194
Eastern Approaches (MACLEAN), 128
Eastern Front (CHURCHILL), 118
Easy Virtue (COWARD), 172 n.
Eclipse (MOOREHEAD), 129
Economic Organization of England (ASHLEY), 114
Eden End (PRIESTLEY), 176 n.
Education of Uncle Paul (BLACKWOOD), 67
Edwardians, The (SACKVILLE-WEST), 100
Egg Pandervil (BULLETT), 69 n.
Ego [series] (AGATE), 1
1848 (NAMIER), 129
Eighteen Nineties, The (JACKSON), 39 n.
Eighteenth Century Background, The (WILLEY), 153
Eighteenth Century Literature (MCCUTCHEON), 41
Eldorado (ORCZY), 95 n.
Elements of English Law (GELDART), 121
Elements Rage, The (LANE), 40
Elephant and the Kangeroo (WHITE), 110
Elephant Bill (WILLIAMS), 196
Elizabeth and Leicester (WALDMAN), 139
Elizabethan House of Commons (NEALE), 129

Elizabethan Journals (HARRISON), 124
Elizabethan World Picture (TILLYARD), 137
Elmer Gantry (LEWIS), 87
Embassy Successes (HAWTREY), 179
Emperor Jones (O'NEILL), 175
Empty House (BLACKWOOD), 54
Empty Quarter (PHILBY), 191
Encounters (BOWEN), 54
End of the Beginning (O'CASEY), 175 n.
End of the World (DENNIS), 34
End of the World (KINGSMILL), 86
Endless Prelude (WILKINS), 140
Ends and Means (HUXLEY), 39
Enemies of Promise (CONNOLLY), 34
Enemy Coast Ahead (GIBSON), 122
Engines of Democracy (BURLINGHAME), 116
England, 1870–1914 (ENSOR), 130
England in the Age of Wycliffe (TREVELYAN), 138
England in the Eighteenth Century (SELLEY), 134
England in the Reign of Charles II (OGG), 130
England is a Village (WARREN), 196
England of Elizabeth (ROWSE), 134
England Under Queen Anne (TREVELYAN), 138
England Under the Stuarts (TREVELYAN), 138
England Under the Tudors (INNES), 126
England Under the Tudors and Stuarts (FEILING), 120
English, The: Are They Human? (RENIER), 133
English Constitutional History (CHRIMES), 117
English Country Parson (ADDISON), 113
English Downland (MASSINGHAM), 190
English Eccentrics (SITWELL), 28
English Essays of To-Day, 50
English Folk (NOTESTEIN), 130
English Journey (PRIESTLEY), 192
English Language, The (WEEKLEY), 49
English Life in the Middle Ages (SALZMAN), 134
English Literature: Modern (MAIR), 41
English Medieval Recluse (DARWIN), 145
English Middle Classes (LEWIS), 127
English Monks and the Suppression of the Monasteries (BASKERVILLE), 114
English Naturalists (RAVEN), 28
English Poetry (BATESON), 30
English Prose Style (READ), 45
English Revolution, The (TREVELYAN), 138
English Saga (BRYANT), 116
English Scene, The (WALBANK), 139
English Scholars (DOUGLAS), 27
English Social History (TREVELYAN), 138
English Spinster (MEYNELL), 92
English Stories from New Writing (LEHMANN), 57
English Story (WYATT), 52 n.

English Thought in the Nineteenth Century (SOMERVELL), 135
English Townsman, The (BURKE), 116
English Village Homes (JONES), 188
English Villages and Hamlets (PAKINGTON), 191
English Wits, The (RUSSELL), 45
Enormous Room, The (CUMMINGS), 119
Epic of America (ADAMS), 113
Epitaphs and Occasions (FULLER), 158
Eros in Dogma (BARKER), 155
Escape to the Sea (REBELL), 192
Escaper's Log (GRINNELL-MILNE), 123
Escaping Club (EVANS), 120
Essays Ancient and Modern (ELIOT), 35
Essays and Reflections (CHILD), 33
Essays in Science and Philosophy (WHITEHEAD), 152
Essays on Life and Literature (LYND), 41
Essays on Literature and Society (MUIR), 43
Essential Hemingway, The, 56
Essential Neville Cardus, The, 33
Establishment in England (DIBDIN), 145
Eternal Moment (FORSTER), 55 n.
Ethics (MOORE), 149
Euripides and His Age (MURRAY), 43
Europe in the Nineteenth and Twentieth Centuries (GRANT), 123
Europe in the Seventeenth Century (OGG), 130
Europe Since 1914 (BENNS), 115
European World, The (DERRY), 120
Eustace and Hilda (HARTLEY), 80
Ever Since Paradise (PRIESTLEY), 176 n.
Everest, 1933 (RUTTLEDGE), 192
Everest, the Unfinished Adventure (RUTTLEDGE), 192
Every Idle Dream (DARWIN), 34
Every Month Was May (EATON), 185
Evolution of England (WILLIAMSON), 141
Evolution of Parliament (POLLARD), 132
Ex Libris (KELLETT), 39 n.
Experience and Nature (DEWEY), 145
Experiences of a New Guinea Resident (MONCKTON), 190
Experiences of an Irish R.M. (SOMERVILLE and ROSS), 103
Experiment With Time (DUNNE), 146
Explorations (KNIGHTS), 40
Eyeless in Gaza (HUXLEY), 83

Faber Books of Stories [series], 52 n.
Faber Book of Modern Verse (ROBERTS), 168
Façade (SITWELL), 164
Face of London (CLUNN), 184
Factors in American History (POLLARD), 132
Factors in Modern History (POLLARD), 132
Falcon in the Baltic (KNIGHT), 189
Fall, The (KINGSMILL), 86
Fall of Russian Monarchy (PARES), 130 n.
Fall of the Spanish American Empire (MADARIAGA), 128

Fallen Angels (COWARD), 172 n.
Fallow Land (BATES), 66
Falmouth For Orders (VILLIERS), 196
Fame is the Spur (SPRING), 104
Family and a Fortune (COMPTON-BURNETT), 72
Family Background (THOMSON), 28
Family Reunion (ELIOT), 158
Family That Was (RAYMOND), 98 n.
Famous Cases of Dr Thorndyke (FREEMAN), 56
Fanfare for Elizabeth (SITWELL), 135
Fanny by Gaslight (SADLEIR), 100
Fanny's First Play (SHAW), 177 n.
Far Cry, The (SMITH), 103
Far Off Things (MACHEN), 5 n.
Fares Please! (COPPARD), 55 n.
Farewell to Arms, A (HEMINGWAY), 80
Far-Fetched Fables (SHAW), 176 n.
Farmer's Bride (MEW), 161
Farmer's Wife (PHILLPOTTS), 175 n.
Fatal Interview (MILLAY), 161 n.
Father (CAMPION), 15
Father Found, The (MADGE), 160
Father Malachy's Miracle (MARSHALL), 90
Fathers, The (TATE), 106
Fearful Pleasures (COPPARD), 55 n.
Fiddler in Barly (NATHAN), 93 n.
Field of Mustard (COPPARD), 55 n.
Fieldfaring (SNAITH), 164
Fierce and Gentle (MANHOOD), 57 n.
Fiesta (HEMINGWAY), 56 n.
Fifteen Thousand Miles in a Ketch (DU BATY), 185
Fifty Forensic Fables (MATHEW), 42
Fifty Years of English Literature (SCOTT-JAMES), 46
Final Count (McNEILE), 89 n.
Fire of Youth (MUSPRATT), 190
First Childhood (BERNERS), 1
First Epistle of St Peter (SELWYN), 151 n.
First Forty-nine Stories (HEMINGWAY), 56
First Gentleman, The (GINSBURY), 172
First Man, The (O'NEILL), 175
First Mrs Frazer (ERVINE), 172
Five Mutineers (SPENSER), 103
Five Rivers (NICHOLSON), 161
Five Stages in Greek Religion (MURRAY), 149
Flame in Sunlight (SACKVILLE-WEST), 15
Flare Path (RATTIGAN), 176
Flashing Stream, The (MORGAN), 175
Flatland (ABBOTT), 29
Flax of Dream (WILLIAMSON), 110
Flight of the Heron (BROSTER), 69
Flight of Youth (POPE-HENNESSY), 17 n.
Flowering Judas (PORTER), 59
Flowering of New England (BROOKS), 32
Flowers and Elephants (SITWELL), 47
Flowers for the Judge (ALLINGHAM), 64
Flying Carpet (HALLIBURTON), 187
Flying Colours (FORESTER), 75 n.

Flying Draper (FRASER), 76
Follow Thy Fair Sun (MEYNELL), 58
Footsteps at the Lock (KNOX), 86
For Services Rendered (MAUGHAM), 179 n.
For the Time Being (AUDEN), 155 n.
For Whom the Bell Tolls (HEMINGWAY), 80
Foreign Affairs (HASLUCK), 125
Foreign Policy of Canning (TEMPERLEY), 136
Foreign Policy of Castlereagh (WEBSTER), 140
Foreign Policy of Palmerston (WEBSTER), 140
Forest, The (PHILLPOTTS), 96 n.
Form in Modern Poetry (READ), 45
Formative Years, The (ADAMS), 113
Forrigan Reel (BRIDIE), 171 n.
Fortunes of Faust (BUTLER), 144
Forty Centuries Look Down (AUSTIN), 65
Forty-Second Parallel (DOS PASSOS), 73 n.
Fountain, The (MORGAN), 93
Fountains in the Sand (DOUGLAS), 185
Four Countries (PLOMER), 59
Four Feathers, The (MASON), 91
Four Frightened People (ROBERTSON), 99
Four Gardens (SHARP), 101
Four Hedges (LEIGHTON), 189
Four Just Men, The (WALLACE), 108
Four Men (BELLOC), 182
Four Part Setting (BRIDGE), 68
Four Portraits (QUENNELL), 27
Four Quartets (ELIOT), 158
Four Quartets Rehearsed (PRESTON), 158 n.
Four Rounds of Bull-Dog Drummond (McNEILE), 89
Four Sacred Plays (SAYERS), 163
Four Studies in Loyalty (SYKES), 28
Four Winds of Love (MACKENZIE), 89
Frederick the Great (GOOCH), 122
Frederick the Great (REDDAWAY), 133
French Revolution (BELLOC), 115
French Revolution (THOMPSON), 136
French Studies and Reviews (ALDINGTON), 29
French Without Tears (RATTIGAN), 176
Friends and Relations (BOWEN), 68
Friends in Solitude (WITHERS), 49
From a View to Death (POWELL), 97
From Cave Painting to Comic Strip (HOGBEN), 125
From China to Hkamti Long (KINGDON-WARD), 188
From Domesday Book to Magna Charta (POOLE), 130
From Feathers to Iron (LEWIS), 160 n.
From the City, From the Plough (BARON), 65
Frost in April (WHITAKER), 62 n.
Frost in May (WHITE), 110
Furniture (REEVES), 45
Further Studies in a Dying Culture (CAUDWELL), 144

Furthermore (RUNYON), 60 n.
Furys, The (HANLEY), 80
Futility (GERHARDI), 77

Gadfly, The (VOYNICH), 108
Gallion's Reach (TOMLINSON), 107
Game Cock, The (MCLAVERTY), 57
Gap of Brightness (HIGGINS), 159
Garden, The (STRONG), 105
Garden of Allah (HICHENS), 81 n.
Garibaldi (TREVELYAN), 138
Gas Light (HAMILTON), 173
Gate of Horn (LEVY), 148
Gathering Storm (CHURCHILL), 118
Gathering Storm (EMPSON), 158
Gay Galliard, The (IRWIN), 84
General Crack (PREEDY), 97
Geneva (SHAW), 177 n.
Genius Loci (GARROD), 36
Gentle Art of Tramping (GRAHAM), 187
Gentleman, The (OLLIVANT), 94
Gentleman of Stratford (BROPHY), 69
Gentleman of the Party (STREET), 105
George the Fourth (FULFORD), 121
George III, Lord North and the People (BUTTERFIELD), 116
Georgian Literary Scene (SWINNERTON), 48
Getting Married (SHAW), 177 n.
Ghenghis Khan (LAMB), 127
Gipsy of the Horn (CLEMENTS), 183
Give a Dog (ROBINSON), 176 n.
Glass Key, The (HAMMETT), 79 n.
Glassblowers, The (PEAKE), 162
Gleam in the North, The (BROSTER), 69
Glorious Adventure (HALLIBURTON), 187
Goat Wife (MACGREGOR), 5
Gobi Desert (CABLE), 183
God and the King (BOWEN), 68
God's Stepchildren (MILLIN), 92
Gods With Stainless Ears (ROBERTS), 163
Going Abroad (MACAULAY), 88
Golden Book of Modern English Poetry (CALDWELL), 167
Golden Boy (ODETS), 175
Golden Carpet, The (DE CHAIR), 120
Golden Fleece (GRAVES), 78
Golden Fleece (PRIESTLEY), 176 n.
Golden Grindstone (GRAHAM), 187
Golden Miles (PRICHARD), 97
Golf Between Two Wars (DARWIN), 34 n.
Good Companions (PRIESTLEY), 97
Good Days (CARDUS), 33 n.
Good Earth (BUCK), 69
Good King Charles (SHAW), 177 n.
Good Neighbours (ROSE), 134
Good Society, The (LIPPMANN), 148
Goodbye to All That (GRAVES), 3
Goodbye to Berlin (ISHERWOOD), 84
Goodnight Children (PRIESTLEY), 176 n.
Goose Cathedral (BROOKE), 1 n.
Gothick North (SITWELL), 135
Grain of Mustard Seed (HARWOOD), 173

Grain of the Wood (HOME), 82
Grammar of Politics (LASKI), 127
Grand Alliance, The (CHURCHILL), 118
Grapes of Wrath (STEINBECK), 104
Grasshoppers Come, The (GARNETT), 76
Grauch (BOTTOMLEY), 155
Graves of Kilmorna (SHEEHAN), 101
Great Broxopp, The (MILNE), 174 n.
Great Catherine (SHAW), 177 n.
Great God Pan (MACHEN), 89
Great Morning (SITWELL), 9
Great Short Stories of Detection [series] (SAYERS), 60
Great Tradition (LEAVIS), 40
Great White South (PONTING), 191
Greek Commonwealth (ZIMMERN), 142
Greek Genius, The (LIVINGSTONE), 128
Greek Ideals and Modern Life (LIVINGSTONE), 128
Greek Studies (MURRAY), 149
Greeks, The (KITTO), 127
Green Apple Harvest (KAYE-SMITH), 86
Green Bay Tree (SHAIRP), 176
Green Carnation (HICHENS), 81
Green Child (READ), 98
Green Curve Omnibus (SWINTON), 61
Green Goddess (ARCHER), 171
Green Hell (DUGUID), 185
Green Legacy (SNAITH), 164
Green Murder Case (VAN DINE), 107
Green Oranges (DOYLE), 55
Green Pastures (CONNELLY), 172
Green Song (SITWELL), 164 n.
Green to Amber (VINES), 108
Grey Dawn—Red Night (HODSON), 81 n.
Grey Eminence (HUXLEY), 18
Grey Granite (GIBBON), 77 n.
Growing Pains (CARR), 2
Growing Up (THIRKELL), 106
Growth of English Society (LIPSON), 128
Growth of the American Republic (MORISON), 129
Growth of the Manor (VINOGRADOFF), 139
Guests Arrive, The (ROBERTS), 99 n.
Guide to Modern Thought (JOAD), 147
Guide to Philosophy (JOAD), 147
Guide to the Philosophy of Morals and Politics (JOAD), 147
Guinea Pig (STRODE), 177
Gun, The (FORESTER), 75
Gun for Sale (GREENE), 78
Guy and Pauline (MACKENZIE), 89
Gypsies of Britain (VESEY-FITZGERALD), 195

Ha! Ha! Among the Trumpets (LEWIS), 160
Habsburg Monarchy (TAYLOR), 136
Hair Divides, A (HOUGHTON), 82
Hairy Ape, The (O'NEILL), 175
Half an Eye (HANLEY), 56
Half-Mile Down (BEEBE), 182
Hall of Healing (O'CASEY), 175 n.
Hamlet, Revenge! (INNES), 84

Handful of Dust, A (WAUGH), 109
Hangman's Holiday (SAYERS), 60
Hangover Square (HAMILTON), 79
Happy and Glorious (HOUSMAN), 173
Happy Hypocrite, The (BEERBOHM), 66
Happy Return (FORESTER), 75 n.
Hapsburg Monarchy (STEED), 135
Harlequinade (RATTIGAN), 176
Harriet (JENKINS), 85
Harsh Voice, The (WEST), 61
Harvest Comedy (SWINNERTON), 106
Harvest in Poland (DENNIS), 73
Harvest in the North (HODSON), 81
Hatter's Castle (CRONIN), 72 n.
Haunted Bookshop, The (MORLEY), 93
Haunted Garden (TILLER), 165
Haven (BIBESCO), 53
Having the Last Word (BROWN), 32 n.
Hay Fever (COWARD), 172 n.
He and His (CARTER), 70
He That Should Come (SAYERS), 163 n.
Heart of England (BROWN), 183
Heart of Jade (MADARIAGA), 89
Heart of the Country (BATES), 182 n.
Heart of the Matter, The (GREENE), 79
Heartbreak House (SHAW), 177 n.
Heaven Lies About Us (SPRING), 9
Hedge Trimmings (STREET), 47 n.
Helvellyn to Himalaya (CHAPMAN), 183 n.
Henry VII (PICKTHORN), 132
Henry VII (TEMPERLEY), 136
Henry VIII (HACKETT), 123
Henry VIII (PICKTHORN), 132
Henry VIII (POLLARD), 132
Henry VIII and the Reformation (SMITH), 135
Henry Bey (RIDLER), 163
Her Privates We (MANNING), 90
Here Are Ladies (STEPHENS), 104
Here Comes an Old Sailor (SHEPPARD), 101
Here, There and Everywhere (HAMILTON), 3 n.
Herself Surprised (CARY), 70
Hester and Her Family (FREEMAN), 76
Hidden Doors (GUNN), 56 n.
High Conquest (ULLMAN), 195
High Noon (GARSTIN), 77 n.
High Wind in Jamaica (HUGHES), 82
Highland Homespun (LEIGH), 189
Highland River (GUNN), 79
Hill, The (VACHELL), 107
Hill of Dreams (MACHEN), 89
Hindoo Holiday (ACKERLEY), 181
Hinge of Fate (CHURCHILL), 118
His Monkey Wife (COLLIER), 71
History and the Reader (TREVELYAN), 138
History in English Words (BARFIELD), 30
History of Anthropology (HADDON), 123
History of British Civilization (WINGFIELD-STRATFORD), 141
History of Christian Thought (SELWYN), 151
History of England (POLLARD), 132

History of England (TREVELYAN), 138
History of England (WOODWARD), 141
History of English Philosophy (SORLEY), 152
History of Europe (GRANT), 122
History of Europe (REDDAWAY), 133
History of Local Government (SMELLIE), 135
History of Modern Liberty (MACKINNON), 148
History of Our Time (GOOCH), 122
History of Russia (PARES), 130
History of the Anglo-Saxons (HODGKIN), 125
History of the Crusades (RUNCIMAN), 134
History of the English Bible (BROWN), 144
History of the English People (MITCHELL), 129
History of the Homeland (HAMILTON), 123
History of the Tory Party (FEILING), 121
History of Wales (LLOYD), 128
History of Western Philosophy (RUSSELL), 150
H. M. Pulham, Esq. (MARQUAND), 90
Hobbit, The (TOLKIEN), 106
Holiday Round (MILNE), 42 n.
Hollow Sea (HANLEY), 80
Holy Deadlock (HERBERT), 81
Homage to Catalonia (ORWELL), 130
Home Chat (COWARD), 172 n.
Home is To-morrow (PRIESTLEY), 176 n.
Home of the Monk (CRANAGE), 119
Honeycomb (RICHARDSON), 99 n.
Honeysuckle and the Bee (SQUIRE), 9
Horizon Stories (CONNOLLY), 55
Horned Pigeon (MILLAR), 92 n.
Horse and the Sword (PEAKE), 131
Horse's Mouth, The (CARY), 70
Hostages to Fortune (CAMBRIDGE), 70
Hotel, The (BOWEN), 68
Hotel, The (WOOLF), 178
House in Bryanston Square (CECIL), 33
House in Paris (BOWEN), 68 n.
House in the Park (OMMANNEY), 7
House of Shade (HOME), 82
House of the Arrow (MASON), 91
House of Women (BATES), 66
How Are They At Home? (PRIESTLEY), 176 n.
How He Lied To Her Husband (SHAW), 177 n.
How It Happened (POWER), 132
How the Reformation Happened (BELLOC), 115
How to Look at Old Buildings (VALE), 195
Howard's End (FORSTER), 76
Human Boy, The (PHILLPOTTS), 59
Human Dawn (ANDERSON), 154
Human History (SMITH), 135
Human Knowledge (RUSSELL), 150
Human Situation, The (DIXON), 145
Hundred Years of British Philosophy (METZ), 152 n.

Hundred Years of English Literature (VINES), 49
Hunters and Artists (PEAKE), 131
Hunters and the Hunted (SITWELL), 47

I Am Jonathan Scrivener (HOUGHTON), 82
I Bought a Mountain (FIRBANK), 186
I, Claudius (GRAVES), 78
I Escape (HARDY), 124
I Give You My Word (BROWN), 32 n.
I Have Been Here Before (PRIESTLEY), 176 n.
I Knock At the Door (O'CASEY), 7
I Know an Island (LOCKLEY), 189 n.
I Live Under a Black Sun (SITWELL), 103
I Speak of Africa (PLOMER), 59 n.
I, Too, Have Lived in Arcadia (LOWNDES), 5
I Will Maintain (BOWEN), 68
I Will Repay (ORCZY), 95 n.
Iceman Cometh, The (O'NEILL), 175
Ideals and Illusions (STEBBING), 152
Idiot's Delight (SHERWOOD), 177
Idle Countryman (WATKINS-PITCHFORD), 196
I'll Leave it to You (COWARD), 172 n.
Ill-Made Knight (WHITE), 110
Illusion and Reality (CAUDWELL), 144
Immaturity (SHAW), 101
Immortal Lady (BAX), 171 n.
Immortal Sergeant (BROPHY), 69
Imperial Theme (KNIGHT), 22
Imprisoned Sea (REEVES), 162
In a Cumberland Dale (WITHERS), 49
In Abraham's Bosom (GREEN), 173
In Accordance With the Evidence (ONIONS), 95 n.
In Country Places (LEWIS), 189
In Defence of Shelley (READ), 44 n.
In His Own Country (STREET), 47
In London (O'RIORDAN), 95
In Praise of Idleness (RUSSELL), 150
In Quest of Civilization (LATHAM), 127
In Retreat (READ), 8 n.
In Search of Two Characters (CRESTON), 119
In the Beginning (SMITH), 135
In the Grip of the Nyika (PATTERSON), 191
In the Meantime (SPRING), 9 n.
In the Mill (MASEFIELD), 6
Inca of Perusalem, The (SHAW), 177 n.
India (RAWLINSON), 133
Industrial Revolution (ASHTON), 114
Informer, The (O'FLAHERTY), 94
Inishfallen Fare Thee Well (O'CASEY), 7
Inland Far (BAX), 1
Inn of Night (SNAITH), 164
Innkeeper's Diary (FOTHERGILL), 36 n.
Innocence and Experience (BOTTOME), 54
Innocent Eye, The (READ), 8 n.
Innocents (BARKER), 53
Inspector Calls, An (PRIESTLEY), 176 n.

Inspector Hanaud's Investigations (MASON), 91
Insurance Salesman (SAROYAN), 60 n.
Interim (RICHARDSON), 99 n.
Interlude for Sally (SEYMOUR), 101 n.
Into Battle (CHURCHILL), 118 n.
Introduction to Mathematics (WHITEHEAD), 152 n.
Introduction to Modern Philosophy (JOAD), 147
Introduction to Philosophy (SINCLAIR), 151
Intruder in the Dust (FAULKNER), 75
Invective and Abuse (KINGSMILL), 50
Invitation and Warning (TREECE), 165
Inward Animal (TILLER), 165
Inward Companion (DE LA MARE), 157
Irish R.M. and His Experiences (SOMERVILLE and ROSS), 103
Irrational Knot (SHAW), 101
Island Farm (DARLING), 184
Island Farmers (LOCKLEY), 189
Island Years (DARLING), 184
Islanders (O'DONNELL), 58
Islandman, The (O'CROHAN), 7
Israel Rank (HORNIMAN), 82
Israfel (ALLEN), 20
It Depends What You Mean (BRIDIE), 171 n.
It May Never Happen (PRITCHETT), 59

Jack and Jill (WEEKLEY), 49
Jacobean Journal (HARRISON), 124
Jacobite Movement (PETRIE), 131
Jamaica Inn (DU MAURIER), 74
James I (WILLIAMS), 141
James II (TURNER), 139
Jane Clegg (ERVINE), 172
Jefferson and Hamilton (BOWERS), 115
Jefferson in Power (BOWERS), 115
Jennifer Lorn (WYLIE), 111 n.
Jesting Army (RAYMOND), 98 n.
Jesting Pilate (HUXLEY), 188
Jimbo (BLACKWOOD), 67
Joanna Godden (KAYE-SMITH), 86
John Bull's Other Island (SHAW), 177 n.
John Clare (MURRY), 43
John Ferguson (ERVINE), 172
John Knox (BRIDIE), 171
Johnson Over Jordan (PRIESTLEY), 176 n.
Johnson's England (TURBERVILLE), 139
Jonah and the Whale (BRIDIE), 171 n.
Joseph and His Brethren (Freeman), 76
Journey Home, The (MUSPRATT), 190 n.
Journey to the Interior (NEWBY), 93
Journey Without Maps (GREENE), 187
Journey's End (SHERRIFF), 177
Juan in America (LINKLATER), 87
Juan in China (Linklater), 87
Judgement Day (FARRELL), 75 n.
Judgement in Suspense (BULLETT), 69
Ju-Ju and Justice in Nigeria (HIVES), 188 n.

Julian Probert (ERTZ), 74
Jungle, The (SINCLAIR), 102
Jungle is Neutral, The (CHAPMAN), 117
Juno and the Paycock (O'CASEY), 175 n.
Jurgen (CABELL), 70
Jury, The (BULLETT), 69
Just Another Word (BROWN), 32 n.
Just Vengeance (SAYERS), 163 n.
Justice in the Jungle (HIVES), 188
Justinian and His Age (URE), 139

Kamet Conquered (SMYTHE), 193
Kangchenjunga Adventure (SMYTHE), 193
Keats and Shakespeare (MURRY), 18
Key Above the Door (WALSH), 108
King Charles II (BRYANT), 116
King Henry III (POWICKE), 132 n.
King Jesus (GRAVES), 78
King John of Jingalo (HOUSMAN), 82
King Lear's Wife (BOTTOMLEY), 155
King of the Bastards (MILLIN), 92
King's Daughter (MASEFIELD), 161
Kissing the Rod (MEYNELL), 58
Kist of Whistles (M'DIARMID), 160
Klee Wyck (CARR), 2 n.
Knole and the Sackvilles (SACKVILLE-WEST), 192

Laburnum Grove (PRIESTLEY), 176 n.
Labyrinth, The (MUIR), 161
Lacquer Lady (JESSE), 85
Lady in the Lake (CHANDLER), 71
Lady into Fox (GARNETT), 76
Lady Patricia (BESIER), 171
Lady With a Lamp (BERKELEY), 171
Lady With the Unicorn (WELLESLEY), 165
Lady's Not For Burning, The (FRY), 158
Lair of the White Worm (STOKER), 105 n.
Lambs, The (ANTHONY), 19 n.
Lament for a Maker (INNES), 84
Lamp and the Lute (DOBRÉE), 34
Lamp of God (QUEEN), 59 n.
Land, A (HAWKES), 125
Land, The (SACKVILLE-WEST), 163
Language Bar, The (GROVE), 37
Language, Truth and Logic (AYER), 143
Laodice and Danae (BOTTOMLEY), 155 n.
Lark Rise to Candleford (THOMPSON), 10
Last and First Men (STAPLEDON), 104
Last Days of Hitler (TREVOR-ROPER), 138
Last Inspection, The (LEWIS), 57
Last Men in London (STAPLEDON), 104
Last of Mrs Cheyney (LONSDALE), 174
Last Pre-Raphaelite (GOLDRING), 16
Last Puritan (SANTAYANA), 100
Last September, The (BOWEN), 68 n.
Last Sheaf (WELCH), 61 n.
Later Stuarts (CLARK), 130
Laughter in the Next Room (SITWELL), 9
Laura (SIDGWICK), 102 n.
Law and the Prophets (PEAKE), 131
Law in the Making (ALLEN), 114

Lawyer, The (HAYNES), 38
Leaning Tower (PORTER), 59
Leaping Lad (CHAPLIN), 54
Leda (HUXLEY), 174 n.
Left Hand, Right Hand (SITWELL), 8
Left Leg (POWYS), 59
Legacy of Egypt (GLANVILLE), 122
Legacy of Greece (LIVINGSTONE), 128
Legacy of India (GARRATT), 121
Legacy of Islam (ARNOLD), 114
Legacy of Israel (BEVAN), 115
Legacy of Rome (BAILEY), 114
Legacy of the Middle Ages (CRUMP), 119
Legend of the Master (NOWELL-SMITH), 18 n.
Leisure in a Democracy (SAMUEL), 151
Lemon Farm (BOYD), 68
Lhasa (CHAPMAN), 183 n.
Liberty and the Modern State (LASKI), 127
Life and Labour in Nineteenth Century (FAY), 120
Life in a Noble Household (THOMSON), 137
Life in the Middle Ages (COULTON), 119
Life of Reason (SANTAYANA), 100
Life on the English Manor (BENNETT), 115
Life on the Land (KITCHEN), 189
Life Story of the Fish (CURTIS), 34
Light and the Dark (SNOW), 103
Limbo (HUXLEY), 57
Limehouse Nights (BURKE), 54 n.
Limit, The (LEVERSON), 87
Linden Tree (PRIESTLEY), 176 n.
Lion and the Fox (LEWIS), 41
Lion and the Unicorn (ORWELL), 44
Lions and Shadows (ISHERWOOD), 3
Listeners (DE LA MARE), 157 n.
Literary Studies and Reviews (ALDINGTON), 29
Little Book of Modern Verse (RIDLER), 168
Little Caesar (BURNETT), 70
Little Chronicle of Magdalena Bach (MEYNELL), 92
Little Essays (SANTAYANA), 46
Little Foxes, The (HELLMAN), 173
Little Gidding (ELIOT), 158 n.
Little Karoo (SMITH), 103
Little Locksmith (HATHAWAY), 80
Little Mexican (HUXLEY), 56
Little Plays of St Francis (HOUSMAN), 173
Live and Kicking Ned (MASEFIELD), 90
Living (GREEN), 78
Living Novel, The (PRITCHETT), 44
Liza of Lambeth (MAUGHAM), 91
Lodger, The (LOWNDES), 88
Logic in Practice (STEBBING), 152 n.
Lolly Willowes (WARNER), 109
London Book of English Prose (READ), 51
London Child of the Seventies (HUGHES), 3 n.
London Family (HUGHES), 3
London Girl of the Eighties (HUGHES), 3

London Home in the Nineties (HUGHES), 3 n.
London Music in 1888–9 (SHAW), 46
London Perambulator (BONE), 182
London Pride (BOTTOME), 67
London River (TOMLINSON), 195
London Wall (VAN DRUTEN), 177
Lonely Queen (BAILEY), 65
Lonely Tower, The (HENN), 26 n.
Long Ago, The (LAVIN), 57
Long Week-End (GRAVES), 123
Long Will (CONVERSE), 72
Longest Journey (FORSTER), 76
Look at all Those Roses (BOWEN), 54
Look Homeward Angel (WOLFE), 111
Lord Hornblower (FORESTER), 75 n.
Lost Endeavour, The (MASEFIELD), 90
Lottie Dundass (BAGNOLD), 171 n.
Louis XIV (OGG), 130
Louis Napoleon (SIMPSON), 135
Louise and Mr Tudor (GLOVER), 77
Louise in London (GLOVER), 77
Love (DE LA MARE), 34
Love Among the Artists (SHAW), 101
Love Child, The (OLIVIER), 94
Love in Our Time (COLLINS), 71
Love on the Dole (GREENWOOD), 79
Loved One, The (WAUGH), 109
Lovely is the Lee (GIBBINGS), 186
Lovely Ship, The (JAMESON), 85
Love's Old Sweet Song (SAROYAN), 176 n.
Love's Shadow (LEVERSON), 87
Loving (GREEN), 78
Lucky One, The (MILNE), 174 n.
Lummox (HURST), 83
Lust for Life (STONE), 105
Lying Awake (CARSWELL), 13 n.
Lyric Plays (BOTTOMLEY), 156

Made in England (HARTLEY), 187 n.
Magic, Science and Religion (MALINOWSKI), 148
Magnetic Mountain (LEWIS), 160 n.
Magnus Merriman (LINKLATER), 88
Maiden Voyage (WELCH), 10
Maiden's Trip (SMITH), 193
Maids and Mistresses (SEYMOUR), 101 n.
Main Street (LEWIS), 87
Maitlands (MACKENZIE), 174
Major Barbara (SHAW), 177 n.
Major Critical Essays (SHAW), 46
Major Pleasures of Life (ARMSTRONG), 50
Major's Candlesticks (BIRMINGHAM), 67 n.
Make Believe (MILNE), 174 n.
Makers of Astronomy (MACPHERSON), 27
Makers of Chemistry (HOLMYARD), 27
Making of Literature, The (SCOTT-JAMES), 46
Male Animal, The (THURBER), 177
Malice Aforethought (ILES), 83
Maltese Falcon, The (HAMMETT), 79 n.
Man and Superman (SHAW), 177 n.

Man in the Zoo (GARNETT), 76 n.
Man No-one Knew (MEYNELL), 92
Man of Destiny (SHAW), 177 n.
Man on His Nature (SHERRINGTON), 151
Man on My Back (LINKLATER), 4
Man Running (JEPSON), 85
Man Who Came to Dinner (HART and KAUFMANN), 173
Man Who Lost Himself (SITWELL), 103
Man With a Load of Mischief (DUKES), 172
Man Within (GREENE), 79
Man-Eaters of Kumaon (CORBETT), 184
Man-Eaters of Tsavo (PATTERSON), 191
Man-Eating Leopard (CORBETT), 184
Man's Life, A (LAWSON), 4
Manservant and Maidservant (COMPTON-BURNETT), 72 n.
Map of Love (THOMAS), 165
Map of Verona (REED), 162
Maquis (MILLAR), 92 n.
March of the Moderns (GAUNT), 36
Marie Antoinette (BELLOC), 115
Marise (LISTER), 88
Married Life (O'RIORDAN), 95
Martin Arrowsmith (LEWIS), 87
Martin Pippin in the Apple Orchard (FARJEON), 74
Martin Pippin in the Daisy Field (FARJEON), 74 n.
Mary Lee (DENNIS), 73
Mary Leith (RAYMOND), 98 n.
Mary Olivier (SINCLAIR), 102
Mary Tudor (PRESCOTT), 182
Master Sanguine (BROWN), 69
Masters, The (SNOW), 103
Matador (STEEN), 104
Mathematician's Apology (HARDY), 38
Mathematician's Delight (SAWYER), 151
Maxims and Reflections (CHURCHILL), 33
Meaning of Art (READ), 45
Meaning of Meaning (OGDEN and RICHARDS), 149
Meaning of Treason (WEST), 140
Mechanization Takes Command (GIEDION), 122
Medieval England (POWICKE), 132
Medieval Foundations of England (SAYLES), 134
Medieval Pageant (REINHARD), 133
Memoirs of a Fox-Hunting Man (SASSOON), 100 n.
Memoirs of a Midget (DE LA MARE), 73
Memoirs of a Mountaineer (CHAPMAN), 183
Memoirs of an Infantry Officer (SASSOON), 100 n.
Memories of a Victorian (JEPSON), 4
Memories of an Edwardian (JEPSON), 4 n.
Memories of Happy Days (GREEN), 3
Men and Wives (COMPTON-BURNETT), 72
Mendel (CANNAN), 70
Merchant Venturers (PEAKE), 131

Mere Christianity (LEWIS), 148
Merry Wives of Westminster (LOWNDES), 5 n.
Metropolitan Man (SINCLAIR), 46
Mexican Mosaic (GALLOP), 186
Michael and Mary (MILNE), 174 n.
Middle of a War (FULLER), 158
Middle of the Journey (TRILLING), 107
Middle Span (SANTAYANA), 8 n.
Midnight Bell (HAMILTON), 79 n.
Midnight Folk (MASEFIELD), 90
Midsummer Eve (BOTTOMLEY), 155 n.
Midsummer Night Madness (O'FAOLAIN), 58
Milestones (KNOBLOCK and BENNETT), 179
Military Orchid (BROOKE), 1
Milk of Paradise (REID), 45
Millionairess (SHAW), 177 n.
Milton and Wordsworth (GRIERSON), 37
Mind and Matter (STOUT), 152
Mind in the Making (ROBINSON), 150
Mine of Serpents (BROOKE), 1 n.
Mine Own Executioner (BALCHIN), 65
Miner (BODEN), 67
Minor Pleasures of Life (MACAULAY), 51
Miracle on Sinai (SITWELL), 103
Miraculous Birth of Language (WILSON), 49
Misalliance (SHAW), 177 n.
Miss Mole (YOUNG), 112
Mission of Greece (LIVINGSTONE), 128
Mr Fortune's Maggot (WARNER), 109
Mr Hodge and Mr Hazard (WYLIE), 111
Mr Midshipman Hornblower (FORESTER), 75 n.
Mr Norris Changes Trains (ISHERWOOD), 84
Mr Pim Passes By (MILNE), 174 n.
Mr Secretary Walsingham (READ), 133
Mr Weston's Good Wine (POWYS), 97
Mistral Hotel (LISTER), 88
Mrs Warren's Profession (SHAW), 177 n.
Mixture as Before (MAUGHAM), 58
Modern Britain (SOMERVELL), 135
Modern Elementary Logic (STEBBINGS), 152
Modern Europe (SOMERVELL), 135
Modern Exploration (KINGDON-WARD), 188
Modern History of England (TAYLOR), 136
Modern History of the English People (GRETTON), 123
Modern Introduction to Logic (STEBBING), 152 n.
Modern Mind, The (ROBERTS), 45
Modern Muse, The (ENGLISH ASSOCIATION), 167
Modern Plays, 179
Modern Poetry (WOLLMAN), 169
Modern Prelude (FAUSSET), 2
Modern Prose Style (DOBRÉE), 34
Modern Scottish Poetry (LINDSAY), 167
Modern Short Story, The (BATES), 52 n.
Modern Tragedy, A (BENTLEY), 66
Modern Verse (JONES), 167

Modern Welsh Poetry (RHYS), 168
Mongrel, The (DUNCAN), 157
Moon and Sixpence, The (MAUGHAM), 91
Moon in the Yellow River, The (JOHNSTON), 174
Moon of the Caribbees (O'NEILL), 175
Moonlight, The (CARY), 71
Moral Life and Moral Worth (SORLEY), 152
Moral Plays (BRIDIE), 171
More (BEERBOHM), 31
More Than Somewhat (RUNYON), 60 n.
More Women Than Men (COMPTON-BURNETT), 72
Morning Tide (GUNN), 79
Mortal Coils (HUXLEY), 57
Mortal Storm (BOTTOME), 67
Mosaic (STERN), 105 n.
Most Secret (SHUTE), 102
Mother, The (PHILLPOTTS), 96
Mother of Victoria (STUART), 136
Mothers, The (BRIFFAULT), 144
Motionless Dancer (YATES), 166
Mount Everest (TILMAN), 195
Mountain Scene, The (SMYTHE), 193
Mountains of Memory (LUNN), 189
Mountains of Youth (LUNN), 189
Mourning Becomes Electra (O'NEILL), 175
Murder in the Cathedral (ELIOT), 158
Murder Must Advertise (SAYERS), 101
Murder of My Aunt, The (HULL), 82
Murder of Roger Ackroyd, The (CHRISTIE), 71
Murder on the Orient Express (CHRISTIE), 71
Murders in Praed Street, The (RHODE), 98
Muria and their Ghotal (ELWIN), 185
Museum of Cheats (WARNER), 61
Music at Night (HUXLEY), 39
Music at Night (PRIESTLEY), 176 n.
Music in London (SHAW), 46
Musical Chairs (MACKENZIE), 174
My Best Story [series] (FABER'S), 52 n.
My Brother Jonathan (YOUNG), 112
My Heart's in the Highlands (SAROYAN), 176 n.
My Life and Hard Times (THURBER), 48
My Name is Aram (SAROYAN), 86 n.
My Past Was An Evil River (MILLAR), 92
My Son, My Son (SPRING), 104
My South Sea Island (MUSPRATT), 190
My Three Inns (FOTHERGILL), 36
My Uncle Silas (BATES), 53
Mysterious Universe, The (JEANS), 147
Myth of the Magus (BUTLER), 144

Narrow Corner (MAUGHAM), 91
Narrow Place (MUIR), 161
Narrow Street (PAUL), 131
National Velvet (BAGNOLD), 65
Natural History of Nonsense (EVANS), 35
Natural Need (REEVES), 162
Nature and Life (WHITEHEAD), 153

Nature of the Physical World (EDDINGTON), 146

Necessary Evil (HANSON), 14 n.

Nest of Simple Folk (O'FAOLAIN), 58

Never Come Back (MAIR), 90

New Anthology of Modern Verse (LEWIS), 167

New Bearings in English Poetry (LEAVIS), 40

New Chum (MASEFIELD), 6

New England: Indian Summer (BROOKS), 32

New Gossoon (SHIELS), 177

New Worlds to Conquer (HALLIBURTON), 187

New Year Letter (AUDEN), 155 n.

News from Tartary (FLEMING), 186 n.

News of the World (BARKER), 155

Next to Valour (JENNINGS), 85

Nicky Son of Egg (BULLETT), 69 n.

Nicodemus (YOUNG), 166 n.

Nigerian Days (HASTINGS), 187

Night and the City (KERSH), 86

Night Must Fall (WILLIAMS), 178

Night of the Party (BOYD), 68

Night Rider (WARREN), 109

Nightseed (MANHOOD), 57 n.

Nightwood (BARNES), 65

Nine Bright Shiners (RIDLER), 163

Nine Tailors (SAYERS), 101

Nineteen Stories (GREENE), 56

Nineteen Eighty-Four—1984 (ORWELL), 96

Nineteen-Nineteen (DOS PASSOS), 73 n.

Nineteenth Century Childhood (MAC-CARTHY), 5

Nineteenth Century Studies (WILLEY), 153

No Arms, No Armour (HENRIQUES), 81

No Idle Words (BROWN), 32 n.

No Love (GARNETT), 76

No More Ghosts (GRAVES), 159

No Plays (WALEY), 165 n.

No Rain in those Clouds (SMITH), 193

Noble Essences (SITWELL), 9

Nocturne (SWINNERTON), 106

North Cape (OMMANNEY), 7 n.

North Star is Nearer (EATON), 185 n.

Northwest Passage (ROBERTS), 99

Note in Music, A (LEHMANN), 87

Nothing (GREEN), 78

Nothing Like Leather (PRITCHETT), 59 n.

Novel and Our Time, The (COMFORT), 33

Now Barabbas (HOME), 173

Now East, Now West (ERTZ), 74

Number of People, A (MARSH), 6

Nursery in the Nineties (FARJEON), 2

Nymph Errant (LAVER), 86

O! More than Happy Countryman (BATES), 182 n.

O Shepherd Speak! (SINCLAIR), 102 n.

Oak Leaves and Lavender (O'CASEY), 175 n.

Oberland (RICHARDSON), 99 n.

Oberland Dialogues (FAWCETT), 146

Occupation: Writer (GRAVES), 37

Ocean in English History (WILLIAMSON), 141

Odd Man Out (GREEN), 78

Odds on Bluefeather (MEYNELL), 92 n

Odtaa (MASEFIELD), 90

Of Human Bondage (MAUGHAM), 91

Of Mice and Men (STEINBECK), 104

Of Time and the River (WOLFE), 111

O'Flaherty, V.C. (SHAW), 177 n.

Oil (SINCLAIR), 102

Old Book, The (HARTLEY), 124

Old Calabria (DOUGLAS), 185

Old Century and Seven More Years (SASSOON), 8

Old Dominion, The (JOHNSTON), 85

Old English Household Life (JEKYLL), 126

Old Gods Falling (ELWIN), 35

Old Inns of England (RICHARDSON), 192

Old Knight, The (PALMER), 162

Old Man in the Corner (ORCZY), 95 n.

Old Man of the Mountains (NICHOLSON), 161

Old Road, The (BELLOC), 182

Old Stone Age (BURKITT), 116

Olive Field (BATES), 66

Olive Tree (HUXLEY), 39

Oliver Cromwell (TAYLOR), 136 n.

Olivia ('OLIVIA'), 94

On Approval (LONSDALE), 174

On Circuit (MACKINNON), 6

On Education (RUSSELL), 150

On High Hills (YOUNG), 197

On Human Finery (BELL), 31

On Living in a Revolution (HUXLEY), 39

On Prisons (PATERSON), 131 n.

On Sailing the Sea (BELLOC), 182

On Seeming to Presume (DURRELL), 157

On the Edge (DE LA MARE), 55 n.

On the Face of the Waters (STEEL), 104

On the Frontier (AUDEN), 155

On the Margin (HUXLEY), 39

On the Night of the Fire (GREEN), 78

On the Rocks (SHAW), 177 n.

Once a Week (MILNE), 42 n.

Once in a Lifetime (HART and KAUFMAN), 173

Once in England (RAYMOND), 98

One and All (BAKER), 52 n.

One Clear Call (SINCLAIR), 102 n.

One Hundred Years of English Literature (VINES), 49

One Times One (CUMMINGS), 156

One-Eyed Moon (STEEN), 104

One's Company (FLEMING), 186 n.

Onwards to Victory (CHURCHILL), 118 n.

Open Air (BELL), 50

Open the Door (SITWELL), 60

Operetta (COWARD), 172 n.

Orchid, The (NATHAN), 93 n.

Order of Release (JAMES), 21 n.

Ordinary Families (ROBERTSON), 99

Origin of Things (LIPS), 128
Orphan Angel, The (WYLIE), 111 n.
Orphan Island (MACAULAY), 88
Our Bible and the Ancient MSS (KENYON), 148
Our Early Ancestors (BURKITT), 116
Our Own Times (KING-HALL), 126
Our Theatres in the 'Nineties (SHAW), 46
Our Time is Gone (HANLEY), 80
Ourselves and the Community (REYNOLDS), 133
Out of the South (GREEN), 173
Outline History of the Great War (CAREY), 117
Outline of Philosophy (RUSSELL), 150
Outward Bound (SUTTON), 178
Over the Water (OMAN), 95
Over to Candleford (THOMPSON), 10 n.
Overruled (SHAW), 176 n.
Overtures to Death (LEWIS), 160 n.
Owd Bob (OLLIVANT), 94
Owl in the Attic (THURBER), 48
Owl's House (GARSTIN), 77 n.
Oxford Book of American Verse (MATTHIESEN), 168
Oxford Book of Modern Verse (YEATS), 169
Oxford History of England [series], 130
Oxford Poetry, 168

Pacific Horizons (LLOYD), 189
Pageant of Greece (LIVINGSTONE), 128
Pale Horse, The (WATTS), 61
Pandervils, The (BULLETT), 69
Paper Houses (PLOMER), 59 n.
Paradine Case (HICHENS), 81 n.
Parents and Children (COMPTON-BURNETT), 72 n.
Parents Left Alone (BEACHCROFT), 53 n.
Parliament (ILBERT), 126
Parliament (JENNINGS), 126
Passage to India, A (FORSTER), 76
Passenger to Teheran (SACKVILLE-WEST), 192
Passing World (LOWNDES), 5 n.
Passion Left Behind (MASEFIELD), 91
Password, The (REEVES), 163
Pathway, The (WILLIAMSON), 110 n.
Pattern (EVANS), 35
Patterns of Culture (BENEDICT), 31
Paul Twining (SHIELS), 177
Payment Deferred (FORESTER), 75
Peacock Pie (DE LA MARE), 157 n.
Peasants and Potters (PEAKE), 131
Pen Portraits and Reviews (SHAW), 46
Penhales, The (GARSTIN), 77
People at Sea (PRIESTLEY), 176 n.
Perennial Philosophy (HUXLEY), 147
Perfect Alibi (MILNE), 174 n.
Perfect Wagnerite (SHAW), 46 n.
Personal Pleasures (MACAULAY), 51
Personal Principle (SAVAGE), 46

Personal Record (GREEN), 3 n.
Personality of Britain (FOX), 121
Persons and Places (SANTAYANA), 8
Peter Abelard (WADDELL), 108
Peter Duck (RANSOME), 98
Peter the Great (GRAHAM), 122
Peter Warlock (GRAY), 17
Phases of English Poetry (READ), 45
Philanderer (SHAW), 177 n.
Philip the King (MASEFIELD), 161
Philosopher's Holiday (EDMAN), 146
Philosophy and Politics (RUSSELL), 150
Philosophy and the Physicists (STEBBING) 152 n.
Philosophy for Pleasure (HAWTON), 147
Philosophy of Jesus (ROBERTS), 149
Phœnix too Frequent, A (FRY), 158
Physics and Philosophy (JEANS), 147
Pick of To-Day's Short Stories (PUDNEY), 52 n.
Pictures in the Hallway (O'CASEY), 7
Pie in the Sky (CALDER-MARSHALL), 70
Pier and a Band (MACCARTHY), 88
Pilgrim Cottage Omnibus (ROBERTS), 99
Pilgrimage (RICHARDSON), 99
Pisan Cantos (POUND), 162
Place of Little Birds (HOME), 82
Plain Words (GOWERS), 36
Plains of Cement (HAMILTON), 79 n.
Planet in My Hand (TODD), 165
Play Parade (COWARD), 172
Playbill (RATTIGAN), 176
Playing Fields (PARKER), 96
Plays Pleasant and Unpleasant (SHAW), 177 n.
Plays of the Year (TREWIN), 179
Plays Unpleasant (SHAW), 177 n.
Pleasure Garden (MAYOR), 174
Pleasures of Literature (POWYS), 44
Plough and the Stars, The (O'CASEY), 175 n.
Poacher, The (BATES), 66
Pocahontas (GARNETT), 76
Poems in Pamphlet [series], 168
Poems in Pencil (BULLETT), 156 n.
Poems of Dedication (SPENDER), 164
Poems of Our Time (CHURCH), 167
Poems of the War Years (WOLLMAN), 169
Poems of To-Day [series] (ENGLISH ASSOCIATION), 167
Poems of Twenty Years (WOLLMAN), 169
Poetic Diction (BARFIELD), 30
Poetry Direct and Oblique (TILLYARD), 48
Poetry of the Present (GRIGSON), 167
Poets and Storytellers (CECIL), 33
Poet's Pub (LINKLATER), 88
Point Counterpoint (HUXLEY), 83
Pointed Roofs (RICHARDSON), 99 n.
Points of View (ELIOT), 35
Poisoned Chocolates Case (BERKELEY), 67 n.
Poisoned Crown (KINGSMILL), 27
Polar Exploration (CROFT), 184

Political Thought in England [series] (BARKER) 114, (DAVIDSON) 119, (GOOCH) 122, (LASKI) 127
Polyglots, The (GERHARDI), 77
Poor Judas (BAGNOLD), 171 n.
Poor Man's Court of Justice (CHAPMAN), 2
Poor Relations (MACKENZIE), 89
Poor Women (HOULT), 82 n.
Porch, The (CHURCH), 71
Port Allington Stories (VERNÉDE), 61
Portrait (ROBINSON), 176 n.
Portrait of a Genius, But... (ALDINGTON), 19 n.
Portrait of a Gentleman in Slippers (MILNE), 174 n.
Portrait of an Unknown Lady (BROPHY), 69
Portrait of Clare (YOUNG), 112
Portrait of Elmbury (MOORE), 42
Portrait of the Artist as a Young Dog (THOMAS), 106
Portraits (MACCARTHY), 41
Portugal (GALLOP), 186
Portuguese Pioneers (PRESTAGE), 132
Post D (STRACHEY), 47
Post Mortem (COWARD), 172 n.
Postman Always Rings Twice (CAIN), 70
Potterism (MACAULAY), 88
Pound on Demand (O'CASEY), 175 n.
Power House (COMFORT), 72
Practical Ethics (SAMUEL), 151
Preface to Logic (COHEN), 145
Preface to Morals (LIPPMANN), 148
Prehistoric Britain (HAWKES), 125
Prehistoric England (CLARK), 118
Prehistory (BURKITT), 116
Prelude to Victory (SPEARS), 135
Pre-Raphaelite Tragedy (GAUNT), 36
Pre-Reformation England (SMITH), 135
Present Age, The (MUIR), 43
Present Indicative (COWARD), 2
Presidential Agent (SINCLAIR), 102 n.
Presidential Mission (SINCLAIR), 102 n.
Priests and Kings (PEAKE), 131
Prince and Heretic (BOWEN), 68
Principia Ethica (MOORE), 149
Prisoner in Fairyland (BLACKWOOD), 67
Prisoner in the Opal (MASON), 91 n.
Prisoners of War (ACKERLEY), 170
Private Worlds (BOTTOME), 67
Problem of Style (MURRY), 43
Proceed, Sergeant Lamb (GRAVES), 78
Process and Reality (WHITEHEAD), 152
Professor, The (WARNER), 108
Professor Tim (SHIELS), 177
Progress of a Biographer (KINGSMILL), 40
Promise (SIDGWICK), 102 n.
Proper Studies (HUXLEY), 39
Prophesy to the Wind (NICHOLSON), 161
Prospect of Flowers (YOUNG), 49
Proud Servant, The (IRWIN), 84
Public Opinion (LIPPMANN), 148
Purple Dust (O'CASEY), 175 n.

Purple Plain (BATES), 66
Purse of Coppers (O'FAOLAIN), 58
Put Off Thy Shoes (VOYNICH), 108 n.
Pygmalion (SHAW), 176 n.
Pylon (FAULKNER), 75
Pythoness, The (RAINE), 162

Queen Elizabeth (NEALE), 129
Queen Was in the Parlour (COWARD), 172 n.
Queen's Fillett (SHEEHAN), 101 n.
Quest For Certainty (DEWEY), 145
Quinneys (VACHELL), 107
Quinneys for Quality (VACHELL), 107 n.
Quintessence of Ibsenism (SHAW), 46 n.

Rabbit in the Air (GARNETT), 76 n.
Rabble in Arms (ROBERTS), 99
Rachel Rosing (SPRING), 104
Racundra's First Cruise (RANSOME), 192
Ragged-Trousered Philanthropist (TRESSELL), 107
Raggle-Taggle (STARKIE), 194
Rains Came, The (BROMFIELD), 69 n.
Rakonitz Chronicles (STERN), 105
Rambling Sailor (MEW), 161
Rat Trap (COWARD), 172 n.
Rats of Norway (WINTER), 178
Reader Over Your Shoulder (GRAVES), 37
Reading a Novel (ALLEN), 30
Reading of Books (JACKSON), 39
Reading the Spirit (EBERHART), 157 n.
Real Charlotte, The (SOMERVILLE), 103 n.
Reason and Emotion (MACMURRAY), 148
Reason and Romanticism (READ), 44 n.
Rebecca (DU MAURIER), 74
Reconsiderations (KELLETT), 39
Rector's Daughter (MAYOR), 92
Red Feathers (MILNE), 174 n.
Red House Mystery (MILNE), 92
Red Pony (STEINBECK), 104 n.
Red Roses for Me (O'CASEY), 175 n.
Red Saint (DEEPING), 73
Redemption (STUART), 106
Reflections in a Mirror (MORGAN), 42
Reflections on the Revolution of our Time (LASKI), 127
Regent and His Daughter (CRESTON), 119 n.
Regiment of Women (DANE), 73
Reign of Elizabeth (BLACK), 130
Religion and Culture (DAWSON), 145
Religion and Science (RUSSELL), 150
Religion and the Rise of Capitalism (TAWNEY), 136
Religion and the Rise of Western Culture (DAWSON), 145
Religion of Beauty (ALDINGTON), 50
Remembrance (MASSINGHAM), 6
Reminiscences of a Student's Life (HARRISON), 3
Rescue, The (SACKVILLE-WEST), 163
Reservations (IREMONGER), 159

Restoration Comedy (DOBRÉE), 34
Restoration Tragedy (DOBRÉE), 34
Retrospect of Flowers (YOUNG), 49
Return of William Shakespeare (KINGS-MILL), 86
Reunion in Vienna (SHERWOOD), 177
Revaluation (LEAVIS), 41 n.
Revolution and Reaction in Modern France (DICKINSON), 120
Revolving Lights (RICHARDSON), 99 n.
Reynard the Fox (MASEFIELD), 161
Rhetoric and Composition (GRIERSON), 37
Rhondda Roundabout (JONES), 85
Richard of Bordeaux (DAVIOT), 172
Richer Dust (JAMESON), 85
Riding to Lithend (BOTTOMLEY), 155 n.
Right Ho, Jeeves (WODEHOUSE), 111
Rip Van Winkle (JEFFERSON), 4
Ripeness is All (LINKLATER), 88
Rise of American Civilisation (BEARD), 114
Rise of Christianity (BARNES), 144
Rise of European Liberalism (LASKI), 127
Rise of Louis Napoleon (SIMPSON), 135
Rise of Modern Industry (HAMMOND), 124
Rise of the Spanish-American Empire (MADARIAGA), 128
Ritual Magic (BUTLER), 144
Road Before Me, The (HOGG), 188
Road to En-Dor (JONES), 126
Road to Glory (AUSTIN), 65
Roads to Ruin (TURNER), 139
Roaring 90's (PRICHARD), 97
Robin Redbreast (LACK), 40
Rock Face (NICHOLSON), 161
Rock Pool (CONNOLLY), 72
Rocklitz, The (PREEDY), 97
Rogue's Gallery (QUEEN), 59
Roman Britain (COLLINGWOOD), 130
Roman Commonwealth (MOORE), 129
Roman Empire (CHARLESWORTH), 117
Roman Panorama (GROSE-HODGE), 123
Roman Ways in the Weald (MARGARY), 128
Romance of Plant Hunting (KINGDON-WARD), 188
Romance of Words (WEEKLEY), 49
Romantic Age (MILNE), 174 n.
Rome (FOWLER), 121
Room With a View, A (FORSTER), 76
Rope (HAMILTON), 173
Rose and Crown (O'CASEY), 7
Rose Without a Thorn (BAX), 171 n.
Round Table, The (ROBINSON), 176 n.
Round the Corner (CANNAN), 70 n.
Round Up (LARDNER), 57
Royal Flush (IRWIN), 84
Royal Runaway (HOUSMAN), 82
Rudiments of Criticism (LAMBORN), 40
Rue de Paris (ORTZEN), 190
Ruggles of Red Gap (WILSON), 111
Ruins and Visions (SPENDER), 164
Running Horse Inn (SHEPPARD), 101

Runyon on Broadway (RUNYON), 60
Russells in Bloomsbury (THOMSON), 28 n.

Sacramental Universe (BOWMAN), 144
Sacred and Profane Love (SITWELL), 47
Sacred Wood (ELIOT), 35
Sado (PLOMER), 96
Sailor's Return, The (GARNETT), 76
Saint Joan (SHAW), 177 n.
Salar the Salmon (WILLIAMSON), 110
Sanctuary (FAULKNER), 75
Sanity of Art (SHAW), 46 n.
Sard Harker (MASEFIELD), 90
Saturday Match (DE SELINCOURT), 73
Saturday Night at the 'Greyhound' (HAMPSON), 79
Savage Pilgrimage (CARSWELL), 19
Savoy Grill at One (LISTER), 88
Say the Word (BROWN), 32 n.
Scaramouche (SABATINI), 100
Scarlet Pimpernel (ORCZY), 95
Scarlet Tree, The (SITWELL), 8
Scenes and Plays (BOTTOMLEY), 156 n.
Scenes from Provincial Life (COOPER), 72
Sceptical Essays (RUSSELL), 150
School House in the Wind (TRENEER), 10
School of Night (BRADBROOK), 32
Science and the Modern World (WHITE-HEAD), 152
Scotland (BROWN), 116
Scots Quair, A (GIBBON), 77
Scott-King's Modern Europe (WAUGH), 109
Screwtape Letters (LEWIS), 148
Sea and the Jungle (TOMLINSON), 195
Sea Hawk (SABATINI), 100
Seas and Shores of England (VALE), 195
Season and Festival (PALMER), 162
Second Tory Party (FEILING), 121 n.
Second World War (CHURCHILL), 118
Secret Battle (HERBERT), 81
Secret Journey (HANLEY), 80
Secret Session Speeches (CHURCHILL), 118 n.
Secret Woman (PHILLPOTTS), 96 n.
See For Yourself (VALE), 195
See Naples and Die (RICE), 176
Selections from Modern Poets (SQUIRE), 169
Self-Selected Essays (PRIESTLEY), 44
Sense of Glory (READ), 45
Sergeant Lamb of the Ninth (GRAVES), 78
Serial Universe (DUNNE), 146
Servant, The (MAUGHAM), 91
Seven Days in New Crete (GRAVES), 78
Seven Gothic Tales (BLIXEN), 54
Seven Men (BEERBOHM), 30
Seven Types of Ambiguity (EMPSON), 35
Seventeenth Century Background (WILLEY), 153
Shabby Tiger (SPRING), 104
Shadow Factory (RIDLER), 163
Shadow of a Gunman, The (O'CASEY), 175 n.

Shadows of Strife (DAVISON), 172

Shake Hands and Come Out Fighting (STRONG), 47

Shake of the Bag (DOYLE), 55

Shakes Versus Shav (SHAW), 176 n.

Shakespeare, For Books on, *see* Biography Section—Shakespeare, 21–22

Shakespeare's England, 134

Sheba's Daughters (PHILBY), 191

Sherston's Progress (SASSOON), 100 n.

Shining Scabbard (HUTCHINSON), 83

Ship, The (FORESTER), 76

Ship of the Line, A (FORESTER), 75 n.

Shipbuilders (BLAKE), 67

Shooting an Elephant (ORWELL), 44

Shores of Light (WILSON), 49 n.

Short History of British Expansion (WILLIAMSON), 141

Short History of Christian Thought (SELWYN), 151

Short History of English Law (JENKS), 126

Short History of Scotland (BROWN), 116

Short History of the French Revolution (BRADBY), 115

Short History of Western Civilization (HATTERSLEY), 125

Short Stories of To-Day (ENGLISH ASSOCIATION), 55

Short Story, The (O'FAOLAIN), 43

Shorter Cambridge Medieval History (PREVITÉ-ORTON), 133

Shorter Ego (AGATE), 1

Shout, The (GRAVES), 37 n.

Showing-Up of Blanco Posnet (SHAW), 177 n.

Shrimp and the Anemone (HARTLEY), 80

Siamese White (COLLIS), 25

Siege of Pleasure (HAMILTON), 79 n.

Siegfried's Journey (SASSOON), 8 n.

Silver Circus (COPPARD), 55 n.

Silver Crescent (DE CHAIR), 120 n.

Silver Darlings, The (GUNN), 79

Silver Ley (BELL), 66

Silver Tassie, The (O'CASEY), 175 n.

Smpleton, The (SHAW), 177 n.

Simpson (SACKVILLE-WEST), 100

Since Cézanne (BELL), 31

Sinews of Peace (CHURCHILL), 118 n.

Sinister Inn (FARJEON), 74

Sinister Street (MACKENZIE), 89

Sir Percy Hits Back (ORCZY), 95 n.

Sirocco (COWARD), 172 n.

Six Men o' Dorset (MALLESON and BROOKS), 174

Six of Calais, The (SHAW), 177 n.

Six Thousand Beards of Athos (BREWSTER), 183

Sixteen Self Sketches (SHAW), 8

Sixth Heaven (HARTLEY), 80

Sixty-Four, Ninety-Four (MOTTRAM), 93 n.

Sketches in Nineteenth Century Biography (FEILING), 27

Skilled Labourer, The (HAMMOND), 124

Sleep of Prisoners, A (FRY), 158

Sleeping Clergyman (BRIDIE), 171

Slow Night, The (HASSALL), 159

Small Back Room, The (BALCHIN), 65

Small Dark Man, The (WALSH), 108

Small Years, The (KENDON), 4

Smiler With the Knife, The (BLAKE), 67

Sober Truth (SITWELL and BARTON), 47

Social History and Literature (TAWNEY), 136

Social Life at Rome (FOWLER), 121

Socrates (BAX), 171

Socrates (TAYLOR), 152

Soldier Born (O'RIORDAN), 95

Soldier of Waterloo (O'RIORDAN), 95

Soldiers' Pay (FAULKNER), 75

Soliloquies in England (SANTAYANA), 151

Solway Ford (GIBSON), 159

Some Experiences of a New Guinea Resident (MONCKTON), 190

Some Experiences of an Irish R.M. (SOMERVELLE and ROSS), 103 n.

Some Makers of English Law (HOLDSWORTH), 126

Some People (NICOLSON), 43

Some Tame Gazelle (PYM), 98

Some Thoughts on University Education (LIVINGSTONE), 148

Something Beyond (WEBLING), 10

Son of Woman (MURRY), 19 n.

Song and Idea (Eberhart), 157 n.

Song of the Cold (SITWELL), 164

Sons (BUCK), 69

Sons of the Mistral (CAMPBELL), 156

Sorry, Wrong Number (ULLMAN), 107

South (SHACKLETON), 193

South Latitude (OMMANNEY), 7 n.

South Lodge (GOLDRING), 16 n.

South Sea Vagabonds (WRAY), 197

South Wind (DOUGLAS), 74

Southern Gates of Arabia (STARK), 194

Space, Time and Architecture (GIEDION), 122

Space, Time and Deity (ALEXANDER), 143

Spanish Conquistadores (KIRKPATRICK), 127

Spanish Farm Trilogy (MOTTRAM), 93

Spanish Gold (BIRMINGHAM), 67

Spanish Marriages, The (PARRY), 131

Spanish Raggle-Taggle (STARKIE), 194

Spanish Trilogy (STEEN), 104 n.

Sparkenbroke (MORGAN), 93

Speculations (HULME), 147

Spella Ho! (BATES), 66

Spirit of English History (ROWSE), 134

Spirit of London (COHEN-PORTHEIM), 184

Spirit Watches, The (PITTER), 162 n.

Splendid Fairing (HOLME), 81

Splendour that was Egypt (MURRAY), 129

Splendours and Miseries (SITWELL), 47

Springs of Hellas (GLOVER), 146

Springtime for Henry (LEVY), 174
Stamboul Train (GREENE), 79
Star Maker, The (STAPLEDON), 104
Star Quality (COWARD), 55
Star Turns Red (O'CASEY), 175 n.
Stars in Their Courses (JEANS), 147
Stay Me With Flagons (HEALY), 38
Staying With Relations (MACAULAY), 88
Step by Step (CHURCHILL), 118 n.
Stepmother, The (MILNE), 174 n.
Steppe and the Sown (PEAKE), 131
Sting-fish and Seafarer (EVANS), 185
Stoic, Christian and Humanist (MURRAY), 149
Stone and Flower (RAINE), 162
Stone in the Midst (DICKINSON), 157
Storm Music (YATES), 112
Story of a Red-Deer (FORTESCUE), 186
Story of Elizabethan Drama (HARRISON), 38
Story of Ivy (LOWNDES), 88
Story of Louie (ONIONS), 95 n.
Story of Philosophy (DURANT), 146
Story of Ragged Robyn (ONIONS), 95
Story of San Michele (MUNTHE), 6
Storyteller's Childhood (LYNCH), 5
Strange Case of Miss Annie Spragg (BROM-FIELD), 69
Strange Interlude (O'NEILL), 175
Strange Necessity (WEST), 49
Strange Orchestra (ACKLAND), 171
Stranger Prince (IRWIN), 84
Strangers and Brothers (SNOW), 103
Stratton (DUNCAN), 157
Straw, The (O'NEILL), 175
Street Life in Mediaeval England (SALUSBURY), 134
Street of Adventure (GIBBS), 77
Street Scene (RICE), 176
Street Songs (SITWELL), 164 n.
Streets of London (BURKE), 116
Stricken Deer (CECIL), 15
Strictly Personal (MAUGHAM), 6
Striding Dales (SUTCLIFFE), 194
Stronghold, The (CHURCH), 71
Structure of the Novel (MUIR), 43
Studies French and English (LUCAS), 41
Studies in a Dying Culture (CAUDWELL), 144
Studies in Ancient Greek Society (THOMSON), 137
Studies in Revolution (CARR), 117
Studs Lonigan (FARRELL), 75
Study of History (TOYNBEE), 137
Stuff to Give the Troops (MACLAREN-ROSS), 57
Succession (SIDGWICK), 102 n.
Such Darling Dodos (WILSON), 62 n.
Suggestions (KELLETT), 39
Summer Day's Dream (PRIESTLEY), 176 n.
Summer Game (CARDUS), 33 n.
Summer of Life (SEYMOUR), 101 n.
Summing Up (MAUGHAM), 6

Sun and Heir (LISTER), 88
Sun in Capricorn (SACKVILLE-WEST), 100
Sun is My Undoing (STEEN), 104
Sun My Monument, The (LEE), 160
Sunny Side (MILNE), 42 n.
Sunset Song (GIBBON), 77 n.
Surfeit of Lampreys (MARSH), 90
Surgeon's Log (ABRAHAM), 181
Sussex Gorse (KAYE-SMITH), 86
Swallows and Amazons (RANSOME), 98 n.
Swarming of the Bees (HEATH-STUBBS), 159
Sweet Cork of Thee (GIBBINGS), 186 n.
Sweet Thames Run Softly (GIBBINGS), 186
Sword in the Stone (WHITE), 110
Sylvia and Michael (MACKENZIE), 89 n.
Sylvia Scarlett (MACKENZIE), 89 n.
Syria (FEDDEN), 120

Take it Away (RUNYON), 60 n.
Tale of Two Horses (TSCHIFFELY), 195 n.
Tales from Bective Bridge (LAVIN), 57
Tales of Horror and the Supernatural (MACHEN), 57
Tarka the Otter (WILLIAMSON), 110
Tarr (LEWIS), 87
Taste and Temperament (EVANS), 146
Tavern, The (STEEN), 104
T. E. Lawrence (HART), 124
Tea With Mrs Goodman (TOYNBEE), 107
Teaching of Jesus (MANSON), 149
Teak-Wallah (CAMPBELL), 183
Tell England (RAYMOND), 98
Tell the White Man (THONEMANN), 137
Ten Great Mountains (IRVING), 188
Ten Minute Alibi (ARMSTRONG), 171
Tents of Israel (STERN), 105 n.
Teresa (O'FAOLAIN), 58
Terror, The (MACHEN), 57 n.
Testament (HUTCHINSON), 83
Thames to Tahiti (HOWARD), 188
That Lady (O'BRIEN), 94
Theatre Street (KARSAVINA), 4
Their Finest Hour (CHURCHILL), 118
Then We Shall Hear Singing (JAMESON), 85
Theory of the Leisure Class (VEBLEN), 152
There Is Another Heaven (NATHAN), 93 n.
Theseus and the Minotaur (DICKINSON), 157
They Drive By Night (CURTIS), 73
They Walk in the City (PRIESTLEY), 97
Thief of Virtue (PHILLPOTTS), 96 n.
Thin Man, The (HAMMETT), 79
Thin Seam, The (CHAPLIN), 71
Things Near and Far (MACHEN), 5 n.
Thinking Aloud (STREET), 47 n.
Thinking Reed (WEST), 110
Thinking to Some Purpose (STEBBING), 152
Third Round (McNEILE), 89 n.
Thirteenth, Greatest of Centuries (WALSH), 140
Thirty-One Selected Tales (BATES), 53
Thirty Years' War (WEDGWOOD), 140

This Insubstantial Pageant (GIBBON), 159
'This Was a Man' (COWARD), 172 n.
This Way to the Tomb (DUNCAN), 157
This Year of Grace (COWARD), 172 n.
Thomas Cranmer (POLLARD), 132
Those Were the Days (MILNE), 42
Thou Shell of Death (BLAKE), 67
Three Deserts (JARVIS), 188
Three Fevers (WALMSLEY), 108
Three Houses (THIRKELL), 9
Three Imposters (MACHEN), 89
Three Plays for Puritans (SHAW), 177 n.
Through Jade Gate and Central Asia (CABLE and FRENCH), 183
Through Tibet to Everest (NOEL), 190
Tibetan Journey (DAVID-NEEL), 184
Tidemarks (TOMLINSON), 195 n.
Tides in English Taste (ALLEN), 29
Till the Day I Die (O'CASEY), 175 n.
Time and the Conways (PRIESTLEY), 176 n.
Time for Greatness (AGAR), 113
Time, Gentlemen, Time (HOULT), 82
Time Must Have a Stop (HUXLEY), 83
Time of Hope (SNOW), 103
Time of Man (ROBERTS), 99
Time of Your Life (SAROYAN), 176
Time Passes (DE LA MARE), 157
Time, the Refreshing River (NEEDHAM), 149
Time to Go (O'CASEY), 175 n.
Time Was (ROBERTSON), 8
Times of Melville and Whitman (BROOKS), 32
To Be a Pilgrim (CARY), 70
To Circumjack Cenrastus (M'DIARMID), 160
To Have and Have Not (HEMINGWAY), 81
To Have the Honour (MILNE), 174 n.
To Step Aside (COWARD), 55
To the North (BOWEN), 68
Tobias and the Angel (BRIDIE), 171 n.
Tokefield Papers (SWINNERTON), 48
Told By An Idiot (MACAULAY), 88
To-Morrow Will be Different (GEORGE), 159
Too True to be Good (SHAW), 177 n.
Tortoiseshell Cat (ROYDE-SMITH), 99
Towards Fidelity (FAUSSET), 2 n.
Tower to Heaven (ANDERSON), 154
Town Labourer (HAMMOND), 124
Town Like Alice, A (SHUTE), 102
Tracks in the Snow (TODD), 48
Trade Winds (PARKINSON), 131
Tragedy at Law (HARE), 80
Tragedy of Nan (MASEFIELD), 174
Tragedy of Pompey the Great (MASEFIELD), 161
Transitional Poem (LEWIS), 160 n.
Translations and Tomfooleries (SHAW), 177 n.
Transvaluations (ANDERSON), 154
Trap, The (BILLANY), 67
Trap, The (RICHARDSON), 99 n.

Travel in England (BURKE), 116
Travels in Tartary (FLEMING), 186
Travellers, The (STRONG), 61
Traveller's Pack (MORDAUNT), 58
Traveller's Prelude (STARK), 9
Traveller's Tree (FERMOR), 186
Travels of a Chinese Poet (AYSCOUGH), 181
Treatise on the Novel (LIDDELL), 41
Trekking On (REITZ), 133
Trent Intervenes (BENTLEY), 66 n.
Trent's Last Case (BENTLEY), 66
Trent's Own Case (BENTLEY), 66 n.
Trial and Error (BERKELEY), 67
Trial of a Judge (SPENDER), 164
Trimblerigg (HOUSMAN), 82
Triple Fugue (SITWELL), 60
Triple Thinkers (WILSON), 49
Tristan and Isolt (MASEFIELD), 161
Triumph of Lord Palmerston (MARTIN), 128
Triumphant Footman (OLIVIER), 94
Trophy of Arms (PITTER), 162 n.
Truth About Blayds (MILNE), 174 n.
Tschiffely's Ride (TSCHIFFELY), 195
Tudor Cornwall (ROWSE), 134
Tumbling in the Hay (GOGARTY), 2 n.
Tunnel, The (RICHARDSON), 99 n.
Turf-Cutter's Donkey (LYNCH), 5 n.
Turning Wheels (CLOETE), 71
Twentieth Century Literature (WARD), 29 n.
Twentieth Century Poetry (MONRO), 168
Twenty-Four Tales (BULLETT), 54
Twenty Selected Tales (BATES), 53
Twenty Thousand Streets Under the Sky (HAMILTON), 79
Twenty Years A-Growing (O'SULLIVAN), 7
Twenty Years' Crisis (CARR), 117 n.
Two Men o' Mendip (RAYMOND), 98
Two Mountains and a River (TILMAN), 195
Two or Three Graces (HUXLEY), 57
Two Quiet Lives (CECIL), 27
Two Sisters (BATES), 66
Two Villages (ELTON), 35
Tyranny of Words (CHASE), 33

Unarm, Eros (TILLER), 165
Under the Fifth Rib (JOAD), 4 n.
Undertones of War (BLUNDEN), 115
Unforgotten Prisoner (HUTCHINSON), 83
Unity of European History (BOWLE), 115
Universe Around Us, The (JEANS), 147
Unpopular Essays (RUSSELL), 45
Unquiet Grave (CONNOLLY), 34
Unrelenting Struggle, The (CHURCHILL), 118 n.
Unsocial Socialist (SHAW), 101
Up at the Villa (MAUGHAM), 91
Ur of the Chaldees (WOOLLEY), 141
Urania (PITTER), 162
Ursa Major (VULLIAMY), 18 n.
USA (DOS PASSOS), 73
Use and Abuse of Reading (BIRKETT), 31

Use of History (ROWSE), 134
Use of Poetry and Use of Criticism (ELIOT), 35

Vagabonds and Puppets (WILKINSON), 196
Vain Glory (CHAPMAN), 117
Valiant Ladies (BAX), 171
Valleys of the Assassins (STARK), 194
Values of Life (BARKER), 143
Vanished Pomps of Yesterday (HAMILTON), 3 n.
Vanished World of Yesterday (HAMILTON), 3
Variations on a Time Theme (MUIR), 161
Veil, The (DE LA MARE), 157 n.
Venetian, The (BAX), 171 n.
Venetian Glass Nephew (WYLIE), 111
Venturesome Voyages (VOSS), 196
Venus Observed (FRY), 158
Verdict of Twelve (POSTGATE), 96
Verses and a Comedy (HUXLEY), 174
Very Good, Jeeves (WODEHOUSE), 111
Vestal Fire (MACKENZIE), 89
Vicar's Daughter (YOUNG), 112
Victoria Regina (HOUSMAN), 173
Victorian England (YOUNG), 142
Victory (CHURCHILL), 118 n.
Vile Bodies (WAUGH), 109
Village Carpenter (ROSE), 134
Village Labourer (HAMMOND), 124
Village Wooing (SHAW), 177 n.
Viper of Milan (BOWEN), 68
Voice of Poetry (PESCHMANN), 168
Voice Through a Cloud (WELCH), 109
Volcano (ROBERTS), 99 n.
Vortex, The (COWARD), 172 n.
Voyage, The (MORGAN), 93
Voyage, The (MUIR), 161
Voyage Home (JAMESON), 85
Voyage of Magellan (LEE), 160
Voyage of the Parma (VILLIERS), 196
Voyage to Galapagos (ROBINSON), 192
Vulgar Heart (MOORE), 42

Waiting for Lefty (ODETS), 175 n.
Walk in the Wilderness (HANLEY), 56
Wandering Moon (REEVES), 163
Wandering Scholars (WADDELL), 139
Wanderings of Peoples (HADDON), 123
War, Sadism and Pacifism (GLOVER), 146
War Speeches (CHURCHILL), 118
Ware Case, The (BANCROFT), 171
Warning to Wantons (MITCHELL), 92
Waste Land, The (ELIOT), 158
Watch on the Rhine (HELLMAN), 173
Water Gipsies (HERBERT), 81
Waterfront (BROPHY), 69
Way of a Countryman (THOMAS), 194
Way of the Sea (PEAKE), 131
Way to an Island (LOCKLEY), 189
Wayfarer's Companion (FELLOWS), 185
Ways of Mediaeval Life (POWICKE), 132

We Didn't Mean to Go to Sea (RANSOME) 98 n.
We, the Accused (RAYMOND), 98
Weald of Youth (SASSOON), 8 n.
Wealth of England (CLARK), 118
Weather in the Streets (LEHMANN), 87
Weather Lore (INWARDS), 50
Web and the Rock (WOLFE), 111
Week, The (COLSON), 119
Week-end Wodehouse (WODEHOUSE), 111
Well Full of Leaves (MYERS), 93
West Indian Summer (POPE-HENNESSY), 192
West Wind (GARSTIN), 77 n.
What a Word! (HERBERT), 38
What Happens in Hamlet (WILSON), 22
What is Life? (SCHRODINGER), 151
What Parliament Is and Does (HEMINGFORD), 125
Wheat and Chaff (STREET), 47
Wheel of Fire (KNIGHT), 21
When Men and Mountains Meet (TILMAN), 195
When the Bough Breaks (MITCHISON), 58
When We Are Married (PRIESTLEY), 176 n.
Where Angels Fear to Tread (FORSTER), 76
Where Love and Friendship Dwelt (LOWNDES), 5 n.
Whig Supremacy (WILLIAMS), 130
While Rivers Run (WALSH), 108
White Blackbird (ROBINSON), 176 n.
White Goddess, The (GRAVES), 147
White Hour, The (GUNN), 56
White of Mergen (COLLIS), 172
White Threshold (GRAHAM), 159
White-Headed Boy (ROBINSON), 176 n.
Whom God Hath Sundered (ONIONS), 95
Why Didn't They Ask Evans? (CHRISTIE), 71
Why Was I Killed? (WARNER), 109
Wickford Point (MARQUAND), 90
Widdershins (ONIONS), 58 n.
Wide Boys Never Work (WESTERBY), 110
Wide is the Gate (SINCLAIR), 102 n.
Widecombe Fair (PHILLPOTTS), 96
Widowers' Houses (SHAW), 177 n.
Wild-Goose Chase (WARNER), 109
Wild Green Earth, The (FERGUSSON), 121
Wild Oats (MUSPRATT), 190
Will Shakespeare (DANE), 156
William (YOUNG), 112
William and Dorothy (ASHTON), 64
William By the Grace of God (BOWEN), 68
William Cook (KEVERNE), 86
William Jordan, Junior (SNAITH), 103
William the Silent (WEDGWOOD), 140
Wind and the Rain (HODGE), 173
Window on the Hill (CHURCH), 98 n.
Winds of Love (MACKENZIE), 89
Winged Seeds (PRICHARD), 97
Winslow Boy (RATTIGAN), 176
Winter House (CAMERON), 156

INDEX OF TITLES

Winter in Arabia (STARK), 194
Winter Solstice (BULLETT), 156 n.
Winter Song (HANLEY), 80
Winters of Content (SITWELL), 193
Wisdom of the Fields (MASSINGHAM), 42
Wisdom of the Simple (HOLME), 56
Withered Branch (SAVAGE), 46
Within Four Walls (HARRISON), 124
Within the Gates (O'CASEY), 175 n.
Without My Cloak (O'BRIEN), 94
Wolsey (POLLARD), 132
Woman Who Had Imagination (BATES), 53
Wonder Hero (PRIESTLEY), 97
Woodcutter's House (NATHAN), 93 n.
Word in Your Ear, A (BROWN), 32 n.
Word Over All (LEWIS), 160 n.
Words Ancient and Modern (WEEKLEY), 49
Words and Music (COWARD), 172 n.
Words and Poetry (RYLANDS), 46
Work in Hand (HODGE), 159
Works (BEERBOHM), 31
World Crisis, The (CHURCHILL), 118
World of Light (HUXLEY), 174 n.
World of Washington Irving (BROOKS), 32
World to Win (SINCLAIR), 102 n.
World Without End (THOMAS), 25
World's End (SINCLAIR), 102 n.
World's Room (WHISTLER), 165
Worst Journey in the World (CHERRY-
    GARRARD), 183
Wreath for the Living (COMFORT), 156

Writer's Notebook, A (MAUGHAM), 42
Writers on Writing (ALLEN), 30
Wrong Set, The (WILSON), 62
Wurzel Flummery (MILNE), 174 n.

Year in the Country (THOMAS), 48
Year of Grace (GOLLANCZ), 50
Yearling, The (RAWLINGS), 98
Years of Endurance, The (BRYANT), 116
Years of Promise, The (POPE-HENNESSY),
    17 n.
Years of Victory (BRYANT), 116
Yellow Sands (PHILLPOTTS), 175 n.
Yet Again (BEERBOHM), 31
You Can't Go Home Again (WOLFE), 111
You Must Break Out Sometimes (BEACH-
    CROFT), 53 n.
You Never Can Tell (SHAW), 177 n.
Young Ernest (CANNAN), 70 n.
Young Idea, The (COWARD), 172 n.
Young Lonigan (FARRELL), 75 n.
Young Man in a Hurry (BEACHCROFT
    53 n.
Young Melbourne, The (CECIL), 19
Young Physician, The (YOUNG), 112
Young Visiters, The (Ashford), 64
Young Woodley (VAN DRUTEN), 177

Zeal of Thy House (SAYERS), 163 n.
Zermatt Dialogues (FAWCETT), 146
Zuleika Dobson (BEERBOHM), 66